Sir John Pritchard
His Life in Music

Sir John Pritchard
His Life in Music

Helen Conway

ANDRE DEUTSCH

First published in 1993 by
André Deutsch Limited
106 Great Russell Street
London
WC1B 3LJ

ISBN 0 233 98845 9

Cataloguing-in-Publication data for this title
available from the British Library

Printed in Great Britain by
St. Edmundsbury Press
Bury St Edmunds, Suffolk

To Victor, who is always beside me

Contents

vii

List of Illustrations

Acknowledgements

For their courtesy in providing me with personal interviews, I should like to thank the following: Nancy Adler, Richard van Allan, Ande Anderson, Dr Peter Andry, Dr Gordon Atkinson, Dame Janet Baker, Josephine Barstow, Anthony Besch, Thetis Blacker, Luc Bondy, Richard Bradshaw, Peter Brown, Moran Caplat, Joan Carlyle, Sir George Christie, John Claridge, Ileana Cotrubas, John Cox, Hugues Cuenod, Ryland Davies, Bela Dekaney, John Denison, Helga Dernesch, Brian Dickie, John Dobson, Peter Ebert, Matthew Epstein, Sir Geraint Evans, Paul Findlay, Georg Fischer, Rodney Friend, Berthold Goldschmidt, Hilary Griffiths, Nancy Gustafson, Ida Haendel, Bernard Haitink, Iain Hamilton, Professor Dr Michael Hampe, Lord Harewood, Olga Hegedus, Roy Henderson, Claus Henneberg, Hans Werner Henze, John Higgins, Emanuel Hurwitz, Charmian Hughes, Joan Ingpen, Martin Isepp, Keith Jeffery, Peter Jonas, Dame Kiri Te Kanawa, Jan Latham-Koenig, Adèle Enderl Leigh, Elizabeth Lewis, Felicity Lott, Clive Lythgoe, Terry MacInnis, Terry McEwen, Jean Malandaine, Lotfi Mansouri, Karita Mattila, Moira Meighan, Zubin Mehta, Janet Moores, Gerard Mortier, Ann Murray, Paul Myers, Yfrah Neaman, Franz Ohnesorg, Robert Ponsonby, Christopher Raeburn, Tom Redman, Lady Agnes Sekers, Graziella Sciutti, Eric Shaylor, Alan Sievewright, Beverly Sills, Elisabeth Söderström, Dame Joan Sutherland, Wilfred Stiff, Jeffrey Tate, Ellen Thurman, Percy A Timberlake, Sir John Tooley, Yannick Vermeirsch, Peter Wadland, Ian Wallace, Ljuba Welitsch and Howard Wicks.

In addition I am grateful to the following for information and assistance: Hilda Atkin, Paul Campion, Simone Conway, Shura Cherkassky, Jean Fonda Fournier, Barrie Hall, Mair Jones, Daffyd Llewellyn, Michael Ponti, Margaret Price, Roger Pritchard, Dr Anthony R Pugh, Beryl Rich, Professor Derek Sugden and Annette Woolfson.

I AM GRATEFUL TO THE FOLLOWING ORGANISATIONS FOR THEIR CO-OPERATION AND ARCHIVE ASSISTANCE:

Glyndebourne Festival Opera

Sir George Christie
Helen O'Neill — Press and Public Relations/ Editor Programme Book
Joanna Townsend — Assistant to Helen O'Neill
Rosy Runciman — Archivist

San Francisco Opera

Lotfi Mansouri — General Manager
Vivien Baldwin
Sarah Billinghurst
Dr Clifford (Kip) A Cranna Jr

Royal Opera House, Covent Garden

Paul Findlay — Opera Director
Francesca Franchi — Archivist
Terri-Jayne Grey — Opera Company Manager
Helen Anderson — Press Officer
Katherine Wilkinson

Oper der Stadt Köln

Prof. Dr Michael Hampe — Intendant
Dr Franz Peter Kothes
Frau Woessner
Fraulein Kämmerer

Théâtre de la Monnaie/De Munt

Gerard Mortier — Director
Yannick Vermeirsch — Press and Public Relations

Vienna State Opera

Dr Gotthard Böhm — Press Officer

Chicago Lyric Opera

Archive Dept

Houston Opera

Archive Dept

The archive departments of the following:
Phonograph Performance Ltd
EMI Classics
Classics for Pleasure
The Decca Record Company Ltd
Opera Rara
Philips Classics
Castle Communications
Lyrita Recorded Edition
Academy Sound & Vision
British Broadcasting Corporation
London Philharmonic Orchestra
Philharmonia Orchestra
Gramophone Magazine
National Discography Ltd
CBS Records Inc/Sony Music, London

Permissions

Quotations from the Libretto of Benjamin Britten's *Peter Grimes* by Eric Crozier are reproduced by kind permission of Boosey & Hawkes Music Publishers Ltd.

The article 'Rossini: The Stylistic Approach' by Sir John Pritchard from *Glyndebourne – A Celebration* is reproduced by kind permission of Jonathan Cape Ltd.

I am grateful to the Trustees of the Estate of the late Sir Adrian and Lady Boult for permission to publish correspondence.

I should like to thank Lady Barbirolli for permission to publish correspondence from her husband, Sir John Barbirolli.

I am grateful to Sir Oliver Wright and Sir Patrick Reilly for permission to quote from their correspondence with Sir John Pritchard.

Introduction

New York, 1977, Sunday. It was raining. John had invited my husband and me to stay in his rented apartment in the Ansonia. After reading the Sunday newspapers to keep abreast of the arts in Britain, he revealed that he had been asked to write his autobiography. We spent a pleasant half hour throwing titles back and forth, gradually becoming more and more outrageous, before going to a matinée on Broadway. Disliking the cinema because the background music usually imposed and irritated (he liked to cross the Atlantic watching the film in silence, guessing the dialogue), John adored the theatre and would applaud a speech well delivered, like an aria gloriously sung, clapping almost soundlessly. Afterwards for supper at the Algonquin, the Maître d' had reserved the famous 'round table' for us. Continuing to play the titles game, inspired by his surroundings, John smiled, 'How about "Superb is not the word"?'

Through the years we spoke about the intended book, John clarifying his thoughts in various semi-autobiographical articles and interviews. Now, with the full co-operation of his heir, Terence MacInnis, I have had access to his papers, files and archive material. Obviously the format has changed. John intended to write about his colleagues and the people he met. I have interviewed them where necessary and now they, in their turn, speak about him. In his writings John glossed over his childhood and less pleasant moments. I have attempted to present an honest picture, not only focusing on his life but his work and those institutions which often, through him, were at an important time in their development. Consequently I have endeavoured to place his career in its historical context. His influence during his appointments was not merely upon those organisations but his inheritance was in the people he trained and helped, not only

1

assisting them in their musical development but showing them how to enhance their own lives.

Many know John through the television broadcast of the Last Night of the Proms and consequently believe that his time with the BBC Symphony Orchestra was the most important part of his career. This is not so. In the orchestral repertoire and in his own development, the Derby String Orchestra and Royal Liverpool Philharmonic Orchestra established his reputation. The BBC appointment was only a summation, a résumé of all that preceded it. John's greatest achievements took place when he was in the pit of an opera house, his work at Glyndebourne, Cologne and certain work at Covent Garden, San Francisco and Brussels being the basis of that assumption.

There has been a profusion of material from which to select a small part for this book. Reading the later diaries that John intended for use in his autobiography, I was aware that he was writing 'looking over his shoulder'. Self-conscious, written for effect, they do not portray the man as revealed in his earlier confidences and in his letters to his mother.

In excess of five thousand words, in beautiful prose, expressing the hopes and aspirations of a young man, this correspondence reveals the true John. In essence a romantic ('On occasions I have been guilty of enthusing too much about various things I have been doing'), he was to find his ideal in the persona of the great conductor Fritz Busch and on Busch's death, that ideal was to become distilled in the Mozart opera *Idomeneo*. Throughout literature one is aware of the theme of a man on a journey. This book is about one such man whose purpose became the search for the perfect performance of that opera and a determination to bring its beauties to the attention of the music-loving public.

The tragedy of John's life, the reality, is found in another work with which he is associated, Benjamin Britten's *Peter Grimes*. Forced to hide his true feelings during his early years by the constrictions of a narrow society, John was a dreamer whose ambitions and hopes were frustrated frequently. The years of his development finished with the end of his appointment at Liverpool. From that time *he* did not change. The changes that occurred were in the circumstances and surroundings in which he found himself and the change in the attitude of society which gave him the freedom to live his life openly.

Affectionately referred to as 'JP' by male friends and colleagues,

Introduction

I, like other ladies, only thought of him as John and have referred to him as such throughout the text.

During the course of research, I have incurred an enormous debt of gratitude and am fully aware that the many interviews and assistance given reflects the respect and affection which John commanded. Whilst it would seem invidious to single out anyone in particular, I must put on record my thanks to Professor Dr Michael Hampe of Cologne Opera and Gerard Mortier at Théâtre de la Monnaie, who placed their offices and staff at my disposal during my visits. Above all, I am deeply grateful to Paul Findlay and the staff at the Royal Opera House, Covent Garden and Sir George Christie and everyone connected with Glyndebourne Festival Opera, without whose support and belief in me this book could not have been written.

Helen Conway
May 1993

1

Prelude, Overture, Exposition

September 1989. Seeing the conductor arrive, the concierge hurried over. 'Good morning Sir John. I saw you on television. The Last Night of the Proms was wonderful.' Elated, Sir John Pritchard CBE walked into Claridges smiling.

Recognition. At last! Recognition by the British public had always eluded him. In a career spanning nearly fifty years, he was respected and acclaimed abroad and deeply loved by the musicians with whom he worked but his name had never achieved the instant recognition in Britain that others, of arguably lesser ability, received. Fellow professionals are not starry-eyed individuals, yet many use the word 'genius' to describe Sir John Pritchard. This is the remarkable story of a boy who grew up in poverty in London and became an internationally respected artist. His parents had concentrated all their attention from his birth towards a total immersion in music. There was never any question that he would be anything other than a musician.

Today it is customary for a person to boast of their humble origins but Sir John Pritchard felt a need to hide the past. Close friends of many years might spend wonderful hours of conversation with him over a glass of wine or a delightful meal. He was always charming and yet there was a limit beyond which they could not pass. When a journalist tried to probe into his family background, the questions were parried suavely with 'Ah, now you're delving into pre-history.' It was not only a question of personal vanity, wanting to hide his true age and that he had changed his name. There was a very good reason why nostalgia was not part of his personality. He had had a terrible relationship with his father.

Whilst he carried with him the letters he had written to his mother wherever he went, his father's diaries were found in a

5

battered suitcase under the usual debris accumulated in a lifetime at the back of a garage. These diaries are a remarkable find, being the daily chronicle of a young man beginning in 1891, at the age of seventeen, until 1952. With their hopes and aspirations, they are a product of the Victorian era with all its prejudices and class-consciousness, its glories of Empire coupled with his own romantic attitude to life. Named after the Prince of Wales, Albert Edward Pritchard was born in Gravesend, returning there with his wife in the latter years of his life to die and be buried in a family grave surrounded by headstones belonging to the large family from which he came. One of the most beautiful passages in the diaries recounts his joy at walking along the Strand beside the sea and smelling the salty air once again.

The inhabitants of Gravesend, at the mouth of the Thames Estuary in close proximity to Tilbury, earned their living from that great port and its trade. The Doomsday book of 1086 records the existence of ferries between Essex and Kent across the Thames. In parish records of 1799 a Mr Pritchard, curate of nearby Prittlewell, together with several others, was drowned off Gravesend in a ship carrying too much sail. There are records of one Joseph Pritchard, also from Prittlewell, whose son Simon married Sarah and was father of the next Joseph Pritchard, a waterman. This Joseph Pritchard, John's grandfather whom he never knew, having finished his apprenticeship in 1852, left for the Australian gold fields, ferrying miners to the workings and was presented with a nugget from which two rings were made which are still in the possession of the Pritchard family. Becoming a Trinity House North Channel Pilot on his return to England, he lived at 24 East Terrace, Gravesend. His eldest son, also named Joseph, after being apprenticed to his father to become a River Thames pilot, went to sea instead.

His brother, John's father, although generally known as Ted, preferred the formality of Albert. He was apprenticed to a printer, work that he hated as he was incompatible with both authority and his workmates. At the same time he earned money playing the violin at local 'gigs' such as the Clarendon Hotel weekly dance and taught players in the Temperance String Band. A completely self-taught musician, he had bought several instruments through mail order until finally finding his métier with the violin and viola. As the son living at home, he was deeply affected by his father's illness and death from thrombosis, heart disease and dropsy.

Prelude, Overture, Exposition

When Joseph Pritchard died in December 1891, his seventeen-year-old son recorded in his diary that there were thirteen wreaths, that the River Pilots had sent 'a splendid everlasting wreath under a glass case' and that the Trinity Church bell had tolled all day.

Completing his apprenticeship, Albert decided to earn his living from music. Touring the country, taking whatever work was available playing at gigs and with the Rob Roy Company, an itinerant group of musicians in Scotland, he finally found regular work at the Royal County Theatre, Reading. There he met some 'nice' people who invited him 'to tea and a musical afternoon at 203 Caversham Road, Stanley Villas, with, amongst others, Miss Amy Shaylor, the daughter of the house', aged sixteen.

Albert became very friendly with her elder brother Stanley and invited Amy to come to the theatre where he was playing but she was always chaperoned by her mother. Considerably older than Amy, he recorded that he liked walking with her. Mr Shaylor's work, as a launch builder, then took him to London and the Shaylor family moved first to Ealing then later to Chiswick. It was on one of his frequent visits to them, in 1898, that Albert proposed to 'dear Amy'. Marrying five years later in Lowestoft on 29th April 1903, where he was playing in a small orchestra at the Marina Theatre on the pier, on 'the happiest day of my life' they must have looked a strange couple. Amy, young and petite, weighed only 8 stone 5 lbs and Albert Edward, over six foot tall, weighed 17 stone with size 13 boots and a 17 inch collar. With a very conventional gentle common sense, matter of fact 'a spade is a spade' manner, she was the opposite of her husband's highly eccentric, pompous, dictatorial but rather suave, oleaginous manner towards authority.

When their son Eddie was born the following February ('A son born to us'), Albert pronounced that he 'would be our pianist'. Unfortunately, Eddie was a born violinist but his father would have none of that – a pianist he was to be. It was the beginning of a disastrous relationship between father and son and the struggle between them exhausted Amy.

Friction did not only exist at home. Albert argued continually with the theatre managements where he played. He remained as first violin in an orchestra of twelve at the Devonshire Park Theatre in Eastbourne for a year as he enjoyed playing for visiting companies such as the Moody Manners Opera Company in *Il Trovatore*. After several short-lived appointments, finally he was taken on as leader in an orchestra with two violins, cello and piano at King's Hall, Leyton for the 'animated pictures and variety' and after another disagreement with the management, went to the Scala Cinema, Leyton. The family rented a very small terraced house at 17 Cromwell Road in the working-class area in Walthamstow. Here in the living room with its heavy, dark furniture, in the days before television and radio, people would meet to make music and Albert would give lessons to young boys who, disliking his pedantic manner, never remained his pupils for more than a few weeks.

Already in his forties, he applied to be a batman in the First World War but was declared unfit for military service as he was beginning to be troubled by his heart and suffered from eczema and other nervous problems. Amy, after an operation for a tumour at Guy's Hospital, suffering from a thyroid problem and considerable nervous tension from the pressure at home, developed an emaciated look. In the last year of the war, with sugar rationed and long queues for meat and other fresh foods, Albert waited at the Labour Exchange hoping for part-time clerical work during the day. Amy, at the age of thirty-seven, gave birth to a boy, on 5th February 1918.

> DIARY ENTRY: 4.00am. Our second son born, to be named Stanley Frederick [John]. Eddie was mystified as to Amy's illness.

Unhappy with the constant friction between her husband and the fourteen-year-old Eddie, Amy focused her attention on Stanley and, like many a mother, considered her child to be the most beautiful, even entering him for a 'beautiful baby' competition, where he received an honourable mention.

As a little boy Stanley loved going to parties, particularly those in fancy dress. His favourite costume was that of a Red Indian with a feathered headdress. A bright child, he was accepted early at the Maynard Road Infant School. The girl who sat next to him remembers his first day there; a 'podge' who seemed to be 'bursting out of his clothes'.

Shortly after his younger son's fifth birthday, Albert, noticing that Stanley was 'listening intently' to his violin playing during his regular weekly duets with a neighbour, announced that Stanley was going to be the violinist of the family and started to give him his first lessons. John would often relate that he was not allowed to eat lunch until he had practised for half an hour as he would not have been so alert after his meal. Resentment towards the violin built up but in later years John had cause to be grateful for the knowledge gained.

Life at home was not easy for the young child. His father, unable to find work during the day, obsessed by his family medical history and suffering from the same obesity as his father, would walk and walk and walk, in a languid and heavy manner, throughout the day. Rigid in his routine, it was always the same walk, often stopping at a neighbour's house, sitting himself down in the kitchen where he would bore the housewives with his repetitive stories. Despite his limited lifestyle, he was very conceited and would have an irrelevant nickname for everybody. Having always had varicose veins he developed the theory that the worst thing he could do was to play the violin sitting down on a chair for hours with his knees up, that to do so would prove fatal, which led to continual arguments with the cinema management as he insisted on standing while he played. With age, becoming slightly deaf, intonation too became a problem. In his diaries, during courtship and the early days of their marriage, he referred to 'dear Amy', taking long walks together, proudly parading their infant son. Now their relationship was one in which they never seemed to be seen together except when helping at the Church. Even there, Amy avoided his company, preferring not to have direct confrontation with him over every petty matter.

The friction between Eddie, now twenty and his father centred on the young man's outright disobedience regarding girlfriends and the time he came home. Amy, who was seeing the doctor frequently, just could not cope. Finally Eddie left a note on the kitchen table about his 'sweetheart' and when he did not come home early enough, his father decreed, 'Amy – he is bolted out.' Eddie went to live with his Shaylor grandparents who had also rented a house on Cromwell Road. The effect of the arguments in the small house on the young, sensitive brother was quite traumatic but protected by his mother, Stanley learnt how to get his own way without direct confrontation. An uneasy truce between the father and eldest son brought Eddie home again, contributing £1 a week for board and lodging. Shortly afterwards on 3rd October 1931, Albert formally recorded in his dairy: 'Eddie married Winifred Ada Fawkes. The reception was held at the YMCA Hall in Upper Islington with the honeymoon in Torquay.' Afterwards, in the family tradition, they celebrated with music at home. No one was happy with Eddie's choice of bride. Looking at photographs one sees his somewhat weak face, smiling broadly next to a woman whose martinet approach to life makes one think that Eddie had 'jumped out of the frying pan into the fire'. It was a childless marriage.

Eddie's marriage now meant that the father concentrated his attention on the younger child. Despite frequent absences from school, the reaction to events at home, Stanley was first in his class, resulting in a double promotion and found himself sitting next to Percy Timberlake. Throughout their schooling their musical paths were intertwined. Timberlake remembers that the music teacher, Mr W Creuse, was talking about music not always being in unison, that sometimes there were parts to the whole. As an example he chose the two boys to sing the song 'Cherry Ripe'. Stanley took the alto and Percy the treble with great success, much to the teacher's delight.

At the same time, March 1926, Stanley joined Miss Geary's Sunday music class. 'Old Mother Geary' had a brood of daughters, all of whom were music teachers and were involved, in a small way, with Stanley's music-making. Mary Geary went to the Orford Road Baptist Church and would have nothing to do with the Church of England; daughter Elizabeth was Church of England, attending St Stephen's, where she used one of the halls for teaching. Stanley scathingly referred to them as the 'Misses Jeery'. As piano teachers they were not of the same calibre as any of the other musicians who were to influence Stanley later.

Amy, whose instrument was the piano, divined that Stanley's approach to music was going to be with her own instrument. Unknown to Albert, she arranged for her eight-year-old son to go for lessons to the house at 114 Grove Road of Dorothy Parks, the best piano teacher in the area, depriving herself to provide for her son's musical education. The opportunity presented itself when her husband was in hospital for eleven weeks with complications after an operation in the summer of 1926.

John considered that joining the choir at St Stephen's Church in May 1927 was his most important early influence. As a chorister under Mr Charles Mayhew, Stanley sang in church for weddings and played the violin at concerts, winning a book as first prize for his violin playing. Sensing the child's keen interest, Mr Mayhew allowed him to play the organ and always included the young boy in the group he took carol singing, which Stanley enjoyed as he liked the feeling for ensemble. Albert noted proudly in November 1928 that Stanley 'sang alto in quartet at service'. Understanding the pleasure it gave her son, Amy, from a Wesleyan background, was confirmed in the spring into the Church of England by the Bishop of Barking and joined the Parish Council.

Albert always joined the throng watching the Lord Mayor's Show, every Royal Wedding and State Funeral and when a member of the Royal Family died, would edge the diary page in black. At half-term he took the family to the City of London to see the Guildhall and then St Paul's to climb the 368 stairs to the library and whispering gallery for sixpence. Amy took Stanley to Westminster Abbey to hear the choir and then, like any other parent, to Selfridges to see the Christmas displays. During the Christmas holidays she took him to hear oratorio in St Paul's and, at Easter, Handel's *Messiah* at Leyton Chapel.

The mother and younger son were drawing closer together with Stanley's piano playing as their bond. It could not be kept secret for much longer and suddenly Albert mentions it for the first time in his 1928 diary, when his son was playing in a piano and violin competition at Mathers Memorial Church, Brettenham Road, London E.17.

> DIARY ENTRY: His programme: Piano – 'Humoreske' by Rowley. Violin – Miniature Sonata in D by Gurlitt (accompanist Mr Taverner). He received 29 marks out of 40 for the violin and 77 out of a 100 for the piano.

Except for competition marks and prizes Albert Pritchard never mentioned Stanley's piano playing in his diaries.

He was now playing piano solos at St Stephen's Church (such as the 1st movement of Schubert's Sonatina in G minor) and playing string trios at home with Percy Timberlake and his father. Totally in keeping with his unmoving, unsmiling manner, Albert treated these occasions in the front room of 17 Cromwell Road with great seriousness, as if they were professional musicians working together. He would start the session by saying, 'I'll take the tenor' and would announce in a formal, pompous manner what they were going to do. At every mistake he would stop, tap the stand and say, 'No gentlemen – it doesn't go.' Then, 'Back to the commencement, gentlemen, please.' In this somewhat comic

11

situation the two boys would have a whole series of private jokes together, all directed against the old man.

Difficulties with his father were exacerbated by the latter's problem in finding work and lack of occupation. When 'talkies' arrived at the local cinema, Albert Pritchard became unemployed, never to find regular work as a musician again. Except for occasional jobs such as acting as a temporary postman at Christmas and addressing envelopes on a piecemeal basis, he was without any regular income. He wandered the streets, unable even to afford the thruppence for a hot bath at the Municipal Baths, his annual treat. He filled his days with twice weekly visits to the Labour Exchange and a journey every Tuesday to the Musicians' Union, followed by a walk along the Embankment, beside the Thames, listening to a military band. Returning home, he would regale the family with stories he had heard of events and personalities at concerts. One can imagine the young impressionable boy sitting in the kitchen listening to these tales, which had grown in the telling, much as the old man must have listened to the stories of his own seafaring father. Amy found occasional work helping with school dinners but they were dependent on the generosity of her family, friends and Eddie. The diaries for these years provide a tragic picture of the Depression. It was a great relief to them when, a decade later in 1939, Albert was able to draw his old age pension.

In 1928, ten-year-old Stanley sat for a Junior County Scholarship for the Grammar School in Chingford Road and also for the Sir George Monoux Grammar School whose magnificent new building had been opened by the Lord Mayor of London in the previous year. It was a considerable achievement when he was accepted at the latter and followed Percy Timberlake who had gained a scholarship there a year earlier.

Stanley's arrival at the Monoux school in 1929 was the beginning of the second phase in his development. He joined the orchestra immediately, playing with them on Prize Day. Very much a member of what is termed the 'old school', the music master, Mr L C Belchambers, encouraged him. Having studied with Markham Lee at Trinity College, the master was fanatical about Mozart and Stanley received his introduction to the composer's work through him. The boys would joke that 'Old Man Belchambers had built his stool up to a height and it was all Mozart that he sat upon.'

Romantically, John recalled:

I think that almost my first vivid sense of pure Mozartian magic came when as a schoolboy I suddenly heard, during a French lesson, the clarinet theme in the Trio of the 39th Symphony, wafted through open windows from a hall of the school, where a small visiting orchestra was playing to senior boys. The serene tune with its undulating accompaniment was, in a certain odd way, all the more wonderful for being heard on a summer day and at a distance, so that to my sorrow I have *never* recaptured the exact vibrations of that moment: but I feel that the sort of enchantment it produced is not inherently different from our maturer reactions to the marvels of *Idomeneo*. The difference is of degree and not of kind.

Curiously, the next steps in my Mozartian education were not through the symphonies and operas but by way of the piano works and string quartets – an approach which made infinitely clear a cardinal point, that an appearance of technical simplicity on paper cloaked difficulties which only a relentless aiming at perfection would solve. Thus I stumbled my way quite early towards the important principle that anything by Mozart is difficult to rehearse – a judgement I have never later seen reason to doubt, either in opera house or concert hall!

The following March there was a panic when Stanley cut the first finger of his right hand and was rushed to the Connaught Hospital by a master in his car. It was two months before he was able to practise after a confrontation with his father.

DIARY ENTRY: DISAGREED WITH SON STANLEY (NOT READY FOR VIOLIN STUDY).

As an alternative to the hated violin, Stanley compromised, adopting the viola, his father's second instrument. In order to keep his son working with a string instrument, Albert would invite Timberlake and Bert Kenney (cello) to join their ensemble at home when Stanley would always play the viola.

At his first class with the vicar for confirmation (January 1931), he took the prize at the Scripture Union, his father proudly noting that Stanley had made his first public speech. Continuing his studies with Dorothy Parks, Stanley was playing the piano at socials and concert parties which she organised at St Stephen's Church and at the Misses Geary's churches, pieces such as the 1st Movement to Schubert's Sonata in D and the *Shepherd's Dance* by German. A week after his disagreement with his father about playing the violin, he won the piano solo contest at the Leyton Eisteddfod, taking the Bronze Medal for his playing in the other sections, adjudicated by Alec Rowley and the following year in the same competition with the same adjudicator – Alec Rowley.

> DIARY ENTRY:
> *20th January 1932*
> Stanley won first prizes for the following:
> Playing piano
> Accompanying at sight
> Reading at Sight
> Piano Solos.

Finally in February 1935 he won the gold medal for a piano solo and a prize for accompanying at sight. Shortly afterwards, he came third in a piano playing contest at St Brides Institute. Intellectually, as well as musically, that summer he was first in his form at school.

Mr Belchambers ran the school orchestra but Stanley and Percy Timberlake, together with six others, formed their own private orchestra adopting the grandiose title, 'Borough Juvenile Orchestra' because Walthamstow had just received its charter as a municipal borough. They went in for music festival competitions and won a cup at the Leyton Eisteddfod in 1932. This brought them to the notice of Reginald Adler, who was to be the most important influence musically on Stanley during his first twenty years. A fine musician and a good conductor, he was a marvellous teacher of string instruments.

Reg Adler took Stanley and Timberlake into the String Orchestra at the Modern College of Music on the Orford Road, Walthamstow. He encouraged the boys to go to his house on Sunday mornings which necessitated Stanley's resignation from the choir at St Stephen's. At the Adlers' home, with Bert Kenney and Ronald Jennings, they would play the quartets of Haydn, Mozart and Brahms. Working with Reg Adler, Stanley explored a remarkable range of repertoire. In later years when he conducted small orchestras, nearly all the pieces played had been studied under Adler. As a youth he would mock *Hiawatha* but appreciating its popularity with audiences, would programme it later.

The other important influence on Stanley at this stage was Raie Hinde, to whose house at 126 Grove Road, off Cromwell Road, he would go for quartets. Raie Hinde BA was a very competent pianist and her husband a baritone. Vera Kantrovitch, the violinist, who had been a student with her remembered going to the house in Grove Road to play music in the evenings. She found a fourteen-year-old boy struggling to play the viola. 'My friend whispered to me "Don't worry about that, wait till you hear him play the piano." Then we changed instruments and played a trio. He played the piano and it was a dream. We kept in touch through our friend who would tell me about his progress.' Stanley continued to visit Raie Hinde for sonata practice for several years after he left school, meeting Timberlake there after the latter went up to Oxford.

As neither Timberlake nor the Pritchards possessed a radio, Amy took the friends to Eddie's house in Chingford to hear the broadcast of a concert conducted by Sir Landon Ronald. It was the first occasion that Bliss' *A Colour Symphony* was performed and it was an event. On this occasion Timberlake realised that this work, which was entirely new and untempered so far as he was concerned, meant a great deal to Stanley, that he was very much into listening to that kind of music and that, by vocation, he would never be other than a musician.

During the school holidays the two boys would go early in the morning to reserve the wooden seats outside the Queen's Hall to queue for the Henry Wood Promenade Concerts, not knowing until the day itself if they would have the money for the two shillings entry as well as the tuppence bus fare. Just as Timberlake had noticed the effect of Bliss' *A Colour Symphony* on Stanley there was no questioning his breathless excitement the first time he heard Sir Adrian Boult conduct. Amongst pianists he showed the highest regard for Solomon and Louis Kentner but it was Sir Adrian Boult whom he idolised.

During one of their sessions at Reg Adler's when the boys were talking about music and flicking through the pages of a score, Adler told Stanley to look at the score more closely. Stanley said that he had grasped it already. Reg corrected him, 'You mean you *glanced* at it.' 'No,' replied Stanley, 'I *grasped* it.' He had. It prompted Reg to comment, 'You should try conducting.' Whilst one of their group, Godfrey Bramhall, did become a professional conductor, the other boys did not believe this was possible for Stanley. His school friends had often sniggered at his physical appearance; his body was huge but his arms were small and he looked somewhat grotesque. Like his father, he had a heavy

15

attitude – a languor – and was always pompous in his speech but to his peers he appeared to be comically so. As with any sensitive child, he was different from most boys, an oddity. Life at school was not easy but he never appeared shy or abashed, seeming to have a fund of self-assurance.

During Timberlake's vacation from Oxford, Stanley played trios at home with him, Godfrey Bramhall or Kenneth Paton, a violinist who later took up the bass. The old man took them with him to St Martin in the Fields for the Bach Mass in B minor, conducted by Dr Darke. Stanley and Paton became close friends, going on holiday together, not only to Littlestone-on-Sea in Kent but also to Jullouville Le Pins near St Malo in France. In later years, John would stress the importance of travel abroad at an early age, to assimilate as many different cultural experiences as possible and to develop one's artistic personality.

He was very nervous that Timberlake knew his true age and his family background, particularly that his father had never played in a large orchestra or with a well-known conductor. Later, whenever they met, knowing that the other knew the truth as opposed to seemingly autobiographical articles in journals such as the *Radio Times*, John would plead, 'You won't tell anything, will you?' Even though he looked upon his father as a joke, as a romantic John created an image which he presented to the world. He had himself inherited so many of his father's physical characteristics. Six foot six inches tall, with Eddie and his father likewise, the three would seem like giants as they walked together. In later years John was remarked upon for his apparent calm and ability to cope even under the most difficult conditions. He learnt to withdraw from harsh reality, presenting a façade which hid his own private world by immersing himself in music. That he was prone to stress from his vulnerability to the paternal as opposed to maternal influence, probably accounts for his future attitude to managements, transferring them into the ogre that was his father and at the same time retaining his father's working-class perception, 'them and us' or 'he and I' in another form.

The Pritchards were a large family and at every opportunity, as a means of protecting Stanley from the pressure of his father, Amy would take her son to visit his elderly aunt, Ada Pritchard in Gravesend during the half-term holidays, as it was she who assisted the family financially. Amy's brother Stanley and his family lived in Scotland. 'The Scottish branch', as John would refer to them, would come to London every summer during the early thirties as the Pritchards could never afford to travel there. To his younger cousin, Eric Shaylor, the holidays were not necessarily a pleasant time. He had just started playing the piano and although only nine years old, whenever he visited Cromwell Road his uncle wanted him to play the piano constantly. Eric commented: 'I think that the dedication of his father must have helped to produce this marvellous artist. We just thought at the time that he was a slave-driver!' The house in Walthamstow was always filled with the sound of music which, in retrospect, he quite enjoys but at the time he hated. 'I think that the discipline that you have to have to be a musician of standing was from his father but the warmth of his personality was certainly from his mother.' Significantly, he added, 'I never saw his father smile.'

Whilst it was inevitable that Stanley would become a musician, at one time he considered becoming a writer. Fluency and the enjoyment of the play of words and sounds was remarked on early. Never receiving less than an 'A' for English, French and Music at school, his report at the age of twelve was the blueprint for his life: 'He has a distinct bent for linguistic and literary subjects. For his age, he writes an English of exceptional finish, has a wide vocabulary and excellent powers of definition. While these qualities should later stand him in good stead he must at present try to improve his *weak* subjects. Somewhat inconstant in his devotion to *mathematics*.' In his Maths' reports there is a continual pattern of 'C' with a bad report, a subsequent carpeting from his father, followed by a 'B' then a slipping back to 'C' again. '*Conduct*: Occasionally restless and talkative.' Matriculation with honours and three prizes at the final Speech Day were a tribute to his own ability, the devotion of his parents and an exceptional school. The choir at St Stephen's and now his school had refined his accent and given him a polish unobtainable from his background. He showed his gratitude to the Monoux when he arranged for a group of boys to visit Glyndebourne for rehearsals in June 1964.

With money needed at home, he could not continue his music studies. In July, before leaving school, the search began for work. With two other boys he went to Hampton's Furniture Shop where he was offered work at ten shillings a week. Dissatisfied, he tried elsewhere in the hope of a better job. Fortunately, he was recommended by a Mr Allen to the Prudential. After a holiday at his Aunt Ada's in Gravesend, Stanley started work in August (officially commencing in October) at the Prudential offices in Holborn, as a clerk (4th class) for £65 per annum. However, by December he was able to do overtime of one hour daily for eightpence extra. Although he was quite impractical, John kept lists for everything that needed attention; just one glance at his father's diaries reveals the source of this habit. It was this daily keeping of lists rather than mathematics which suited him to book-keeping. In addition, he would earn a shilling by tuning pianos in local church halls.

It was customary during the Depression for a number of seats at concerts to be set aside for the unemployed for sixpence. Often, following a disagreement, Stanley gave his father the money needed to attend. Little did Albert realise that this was his son's way of deflecting attention, of 'buying him off'.

Inheriting a propensity for bronchial problems, which had prevented him from doing gym during his last year at school, he was frequently absent from work. Finally, after a bout of chicken-pox in May 1938, Stanley was admitted to the Connaught Hospital suffering from pleurisy and was hospitalised for a month before being ordered to the seaside for a three month convalescence. The local vicar of St Stephen's gave Amy 12s.6d for the hire of a taxi to Victoria and Eddie took his brother to the Surrey Convalescent Home at Seaford. Together with Eddie and Win, Amy visited him for a couple of weeks, staying in lodgings. She discovered Stanley was enjoying his time with the other twelve male patients, had put on weight and would be able to resume work in October. This illness was later given as the reason why he was not accepted by the army during the war.

When Italy invaded Abyssinia during the period leading up to the Second World War, there was heated debate amongst the British public as to the appropriate method of dealing with aggression. The Pritchard family attended several such discussions at their Church, as to whether 'pacifism should be the true attitude of a Christian'; an attitude that was alien to Albert's patriotism.

With the actual outbreak of war in September 1939, the Prudential moved their headquarters to Torquay but the section to which Stanley belonged was evacuated to Wakefield in Yorkshire where he found lodgings at 4 Westfield Grove. A month after his son had supposedly registered for the army, Albert was shocked to hear that Stanley had registered as a conscientious objector.

Prelude, Overture, Exposition

There was a tremendous row at home but the old man was mollified when the prodigal, returning home for the weekend, 'played a sonata' with him, as well as visiting Raie Hinde for sonata practice. Peace was finally restored after Stanley had his medical examination for the army in Huddersfield in January 1940 and was graded '3', medically unfit for army service.

In September 1940, Amy was away visiting her brother Stanley in Glasgow. With frequent air-raid warnings, Eddie lent his father a camp bed so that he could spend his nights in their neighbour's shelter. Fortunately Albert was in the shelter when a bomb dropped in nearby Grove Road at 4.40am. With two holes in the roof of 17 Cromwell Road, ceilings were damaged, the front door destroyed and many window panes broken. With Eddie's help the house was made habitable again before Amy arrived home.

In November, the lease of their home in Walthamstow came to an end. Notifying the Labour Exchange of a proposed change of address, they said their goodbyes to their friends at the church. With Eddie and Win seeing them off and the ex-mayor sending a cheque to pay their fares, they departed from Paddington Station for 6 Victoria Terrace, Brinscombe near Stroud in Gloucestershire where they looked after Amy's elderly aunt, Edith Pearce, who was able to assist them financially in return. Stanley visited them frequently at weekends.

Stanley hated the name Frederick and like many teenagers had toyed with various alternatives, rather fancying 'Davenport'. Stressing the importance of a person's name there was a time when, in deference to his mother, he wished to be known as Stanley Shaylor Pritchard. Eddie took the name Shaylor Pritchard. To the Prudential he remained Stanley Frederick Pritchard but from this period, dreaming of a career in music, he was generally known as Stanley John Pritchard, later dropping the Stanley. The opening page of his scrapbook is headed with a picture of a pilchard, cut from the wrapping of a tin of that wartime food: 'John Pilchard the famous conductor!'

Continuing with his piano playing and on good terms with his fellow clerks, gravitating to the Wakefield Music Circle, it was the small beginning of his conducting career. The orchestra of twenty string players whose ability, like that of its conductor, was strictly limited, gave their first concert in July 1941 in the Hall of the Wakefield Grammar School. In a programme of works by Purcell, J.S. Bach, Handel, Delius and an early Classic Suite

19

arranged by Anthony Collins, John played a number of piano duos with Erica East in the second half of the concert. Again, at the same venue, he had the opportunity in December 1941 to conduct the choir of the Pontefract High School for girls in the Pastoral Symphony from Bach's *Christmas Oratorio*. The following year, at the Grammar School Carol Concert, he conducted the Old Savilians' String Orchestra, opening with the overture for John Blow's *Venus and Adonis*. The concert, in aid of the Red Cross, raised the then large sum of £10. His services in Wakefield required only for a short period, he was transferred in January 1942 to the Prudential offices in Derby.

In Derby John was appreciated both as a talented pianist (playing excerpts from Gershwin's *Rhapsody in Blue* in March 1943) and as an accompanist. In the Central Hall on 6th October 1943, in aid of the British Red Cross & St John's, Prisoners of War (Derby Branch) he accompanied Arthur Catterall, formerly leader of the BBC Orchestra, whose autograph he had sought as a young boy at the Proms. They played Dohnányi's Sonata for violin and piano, opus 21 and Henry Eccles' Sonata in G minor for violin, cello and piano, with Olga Hegedus. In the second half he accompanied her again, in the Beethoven Sonata in A for cello and piano, opus 69. The recital was very poorly attended as Derby audiences clearly preferred listening to a symphony orchestra.

The Derby Philharmonic Orchestra, of which seventy-five per cent of its sixty or seventy members were amateurs, owed its survival to Mr William Daltrey, who, determined to revive the orchestra, had collected together as many members as were available during the war. As well as coping with the organisation, he had conducted on two previous occasions, not very satisfactorily. A committee was formed 'to remove Mr Daltrey of some of the hard work' and an announcement appeared in the local press on 22nd November 1943: 'Mr John Pritchard, who until then has been principal viola and who is an experienced musician, was asked to become conductor for this season and he has accepted the office.'

John's first concert with the reorganised Derby Philharmonic Orchestra on 29th April in the Central Hall, was well attended. The orchestra was full of enthusiasm, perhaps making up for their lack of proficiency in a programme including three movements

from the Schumann Symphony No 1 in B flat ('The Spring'),
Mozart's *Magic Flute* Overture, Sibelius' *Finlandia* and the Grand
March from *Tannhäuser*, as well as arias sung by Noel Eadie from
La Traviata and items by Purcell and Mozart. The soloist's success
demanded two encores. John's father noted with amazement in
his diary that his son had 'conducted an orchestra of sixty'.

During this 1944 – 45 season there were still restrictions on
travel abroad and it was part of a musician's career to perform
on behalf of charities, such as the Red Cross and War Disabled,
in provincial cities like Derby. It gave John an opportunity
which he would never have had in normal circumstances to
work with artists of calibre. A concert on 14th October 1944
with Léon Goossens as soloist was remarkable for the wide range
of programming. As his accompanist was unavailable, John left
the rostrum accompanying him at sight, much to Goossens'
satisfaction.

Whilst John was praised for his work, the Derby Philharmonic's
standard of playing evoked much criticism. The surprising success
of the evening, from John's point of view, had been Bizet's
L'Arlésienne Suite but the pivot of the programme was the
César Franck Symphony. It had attracted a painfully small
audience. It would surprise today's listener that the César Franck
Symphony, a work which many would regard almost as 'pop'
music, should be regarded as of 'too advanced a nature for the
people of Derby who had not been given the opportunity of
regularly attending orchestral concerts for some time'. Provoking
considerable discussion in the local press, many readers believed
that it was for the radio to introduce new music to the public but
that in their midst they preferred listening to well-loved works,
with an acoustic standard that could not be attained on either their
radios or gramophones.

Replying in a long letter to the *Derby Evening Telegraph* on
25th October 1944, John expressed views on unfamiliar music
that were to remain his philosophy for life. Commenting that he
had a good deal of sympathy with correspondents who were a
trifle uneasy lest unfamiliarity with the works to be played should
mar their appreciation of the concert, many people who heard the
performance of the César Franck Symphony in full for the first
time had assured him that they found no difficulty in enjoying
this beautiful work. He believed that those who mistrusted
a programme including the 'Franck' but were thoroughly at

21

home when listening to Beethoven's 7th Symphony, might be compared with people who, 'after many happy holidays at Llandudno, are unwilling to make the dangerous experiment of a long weekend at Colwyn Bay!' He recognised that whilst standard works of the concert repertoire had a legitimate claim on the main affection of music-lovers and programmes which did not take this into account were not fulfilling their proper function, he would be less than fair to whatever artistic conscience he possessed were he to exclude from the Philharmonic programmes beautiful pieces of music, merely because they were unfamiliar. He concluded: 'I am hopeful that what I have said may remove a possible impression among the musical public of Derby that the Philharmonic's conductor is "riding a hobbyhorse" in search of mere novelty for its own sake.'

However, it was the decision by the Music Club to devote its meeting of 21st July 1943 to a programme of music for a string orchestra that was to have more far-reaching consequences for John. The date had been chosen to enable rehearsals to take place during the summer months when blackout hours were shortest. In a letter of 5th April 1943, the honorary Secretary (later Chairman), Leslie Smart informed members that the 'duty of making the necessary arrangements had been delegated to Mr John Pritchard, who has had considerable experience, to conduct the first rehearsals.' In an Art Gallery concert on 2nd February 1944 with J Yates Greenhalgh (bass) and Eva Metzler (soprano), John introduced a new aspect into his music-making. Her programme with the newly named Derby String Orchestra included the Mozart arias 'Ay, ye who have duly learned' from *The Marriage of Figaro*, 'Hours of Joy' from the *The Magic Flute* and 'When a maiden takes your fancy' from *Il Seraglio*.

Several years older than John, Eva Metzler was an attractive dark-haired lady who had been a singer in Germany. She had had a difficult time coming to Britain, particularly as her mother continued to live in Berlin. Leslie Smart gave the young refugee a room in his house in exchange for assisting his wife Dorothy and a close friendship developed between the two women. Highly knowledgeable about opera and Wagner in particular, Eva had taught John a great deal since the time he first accompanied her at the piano in a concert given by the Derby Home Guard Military Band on 1st November 1942. The obvious rapport in their Art Gallery concert was such that it elicited a warm letter dated 13th February 1944 from Leslie Smart to John. Writing on behalf of his committee, he expressed:

> Congratulations and thanks for the very excellent programme of music which the Derby String Orchestra offered to the Club on February 2nd. The evening was certainly the most successful in the history of the Club. It has already brought us many new members, and the attendance was a record.
>
> My Committee feel that whilst many people contributed to the success of the evening, the chief credit lies with yourself. They feel that you possess great talents in this sphere and that when the time is ripe you should go a long way.

The players felt that they would like to continue working with John giving concerts on a regular basis in the Art Gallery. They even holidayed together and with Leslie Smart went to Crag House, Grasmere in the Lake District, where one evening John accompanied Vera Kantrovitch, Olga Hegedus and Eva Metzler in a concert. Olga Hegedus commented that even at that time John showed a natural authority and was able to get the best from an orchestra with minimum effort.

When Adila Fachiri, the vivacious Hungarian violinist, a great-niece of Joachim, appeared at Derby on 17th February 1945 for the Education Committee in the Art Gallery, Leslie Smart suggested John as her accompanist. Impressed by his accompaniment of Bloch's *Baal Shem*, having only seen the difficult score for the first time just before the concert, she asked him to accompany her in a recital at the Wigmore Hall on 2nd May. His first appearance at the London venue was an exciting moment for John. The reaction to his ability as an accompanist by a soloist of international calibre was to be instrumental in his decision to become a professional musician.

The Derby Philharmonic often worked with the Derby Choral Union. At his first rehearsal with the choir, he told them to 'relax the voice, pay no attention to expression marks, aim at good tone and accuracy of notes' but at the second rehearsal, when they tackled the well-known opening chorus from Mendelssohn's *Elijah*, he took off his jacket, would not allow the singers to sit and worked particularly on their expression. Favourably received, he commented: 'The public is entitled to hear its favourites and to good performances.' Unfortunately the venue for the concerts, the LMS Institute, was unsatisfactory for such large works and for accommodating an audience.

Peace and the Prudential decision to return to its headquarters in Holborn forced John to make a decision. With work as an accompanist, the increasing viability of the Derby String Orchestra, the Derby Philharmonic and now the Derby Choral Union, John realised that he should remain in Derby. He was fortunate that events had combined to take him away from the pressure of his parental background. Informing his mother on 8th July 1945 of his decision to become a professional musician, afraid that his father would not want him to leave a secure job, he wrote on the envelope in pencil, 'To be opened in secret'.

25 Bedford Street, Derby

My dear Mum

I think it would be wrong of me to let any more time go by without telling you of an intention which (perhaps you have guessed) has been in my mind for several months. To come quickly to the point. I think the time will arrive in two or three months for me to give up my work with the Prudential. Needless to say, I haven't reached such a decision without the most terrific thought, and a very deliberate weighing of ways and means.

Briefly, the position is this. As you know, I have been very lucky here in Derby to have such easy working conditions, under a sympathetic chief who has allowed me as much time off as I need for my musical activities. Well, now the time is fast approaching for the Pru. Divisional Centres to return to London and believe me, not only for myself but for all evacuees there is going to be a very difficult time in getting readjusted to the discipline and essential regimentation of Holborn Bars. If I go back to London (where, remember, I have no home to go to) I shall find it absolutely necessary to reduce very much, that which is the breath of life to me, my music. Moreover, I should find myself in the vast London arena, with no conducting appointments and lots of competition I expect for those which do arise.

By comparison, in Derby I have, I really think (without sounding conceited), created a very special position for myself which is quite unchallenged. The new Choral Union appointment carries with it excellent fees, the Derby Philharmonic has guaranteed me fifteen guineas a concert when I become a professional musician and *so has* the Derby String Orchestra. In addition my work as accompanist for the Municipal Concerts will be re-rated at probably five guineas a concert: it has been quite touching while I have been enquiring into the possibilities, to find how many eager friends are anxious to help me, keen, as one of them put it, to help me get to a place 'right at the top of the profession'.

Prelude, Overture, Exposition

What I have in mind to do is this:

1. Spend a good part of my time in Derby to work with:
   a)   the Derby Choral Union
   b)   the Derby String Orchestra
   c)   the Derby Philharmonic
   also a 'cracking' Orchestra for the Derbyshire Education Committee, also the Municipal Concerts, also all the 'odd' engagements which normally come my way as accompanist etc. during the season in Derby.

2. Go to London or any part of the country to accept engagements as Accompanist – in this I am assured of the support of Vera Kantrovitch who would like to work with me on a larger scale and also of Adila Fachiri who wishes me to play for her on every possible occasion. Also I expect to get work through Ibbs & Tillett, the London Concert Agents, whom I am seeing in London this coming Wednesday. You must remember too the large number of famous artists with whom I have played – almost without exception those people have assumed that I *was* a full-time musician and when they learned this was not so, have urged me to take up the profession without delay, as there are so *few* really good accompanists, though there are dozens of *solo* pianists.

Now I do not want you to worry about my future, dear – have faith in my determination and the talents which *you* have helped to give me. As you know, had it not been for our position at home I should have gone from the Monoux on to the Royal Academy or the Royal College of Music, there to train for the musical profession in the orthodox way. As it is, I do not at all regret the years spent with the Prudential: I have kept myself and made my way in the world. It has enabled me to have a fair amount of time for music and has been the means of bringing me to Derby, the first town in which I have really made a first class name as a musician. The choice now is

   a)   whether to go back with the Prudential to London, giving up all my musical work here, keeping music as a hobby and concentrate on earning promotion in a job which now less and less appeals to me and which will eventually become a Government Department, or

   b)   to stay on in Derby, where I am happy in 'cheap' digs, where the cost of living is lower than in London and where I have great influence and literally scores of friends, here to develop all my musical work and attain a really big name in British Music, I hope. I would not make this monumental change in my life if I felt I had only a quite

25

ordinary career as a 'competent' musician ahead of me. But I feel (and I am confirmed by all the opinions of those best qualified to speak) that I can, if I work properly, become a really first-rank conductor and meanwhile I have the useful second string to my bow, piano accompaniment. The more professionals I work with, the more I realise, quite without conceit, that by far the great majority of them have *nothing* that I too do not seem to have.

I have deliberately tried not to be too optimistic in my calculations, so that I am not building up false hopes but the more I think about it, the more sure I am that it is no good shivering on the brink but I must take the plunge now. A further consideration is that the *Regional* broadcasts of the BBC are starting up again and there will be a lot of work going there.

As a final guarantee, my friend Leslie Smart, who constantly urges me not to hesitate, has promised that he will not allow my income to drop below a certain level during the first *two years* of my career as a professional musician. So you need never picture me on the dole! I confidently anticipate getting *sufficient* well-paid engagements (apart altogether from my standing salaried orchestral engagements here) to increase my all-over income quite considerably.

Lastly, I should perhaps even now think twice about this matter if I were married or even intending marriage. As this is *not* so, as a single man I have not the least reason to be cowardly and always clinging to mere security at the expense of happiness in my *true* career. 'He who hesitates is lost.'

I know you will always understand perfectly how I feel and how excited I am at the prospect of giving *all* my time to the beloved art. I'll let you know how things progress! Let me know what you think.

Best love, Yours always
John

P.S. The decision is really forced on me by the Choral Union appointment. With this added to my already full life, I should *without doubt* have had a nervous breakdown this winter!

Leaving the Prudential in September 1945, he had only reached clerk status in the third class (earning £275 pa) – hardly a meteoric rise.

His father noted in his diary:

1st October – Stanley enters the musical profession.

With many qualified people returning to 'civvy street,' John had been understandably nervous about leaving the security of a job. Leslie Smart, who made it financially possible for John to become a professional musician, was a very poor cellist. A timber merchant of 'old Midland stock', not attractive to look at, very tall and with rather bad teeth, which did not worry him, he was an honest, outspoken man. Childless, he and his wife Dorothy treated John and Eva as family. An atheist, with Dorothy non-Conformist, he was rather disgusted, arguing fiercely with John when he determined to become a Roman Catholic in April 1947.

Totally unaware of his religious adherence, never having thought of him as a religious person in an outward sense, many of John's close friends were surprised when his funeral service took place in a Roman Catholic Church. Several reasons for his conversion have been given by those who knew him well, such as the cynical comment that the productions in a Catholic Church are 'very well rehearsed with outstanding sets and beautiful costumes'. During the years after the war there was a certain social cachet in being Catholic and many young people embraced that faith. John wanted to 'belong', to be 'accepted'. Instrumental in his decision was the simple fact that he was happy in his mother's company as opposed to that of his father and it was she who took him to religious ceremonies in spectacular venues such as Westminster Abbey and St Paul's Cathedral. He had worshipped in Wakefield Cathedral, retaining a photograph of the interior amongst his papers. There are notes in his diaries as to times of services, and his attendance in the company of friends, particularly Marie King, a lady whose company he enjoyed.

The influence of St Stephen's Church was not only on his musical development. Winning first prize at the Scripture Union for his confirmation was paralleled by 'A's in the subject at the Sir George Monoux School. Religion helped to satisfy an emotional need. Above all, he needed the Confessional, needed the solace of confiding in someone, of expressing himself in truth, resolving the conflict between his personality and his background.

In 1958 he had wanted to take part in a Catholic Pageant on 10th February at the Royal Albert Hall but as his career developed and he became accepted, his Catholicism changed from a means of public identity to a very deep personal conviction which surfaced when he conducted religious music. He would sometimes slip away to church on his own. Visiting the 'Tosca' church in Rome, there was a moment when he went away and prayed quietly. On holiday in Italy, attending an audience with the Pope, the presence and the atmosphere affected him profoundly. His depth of feeling evinced itself, not just with tolerance but in the respect he showed to others, of whatever religion, thoughtfully endeavouring to assist them in their practice. To them he could confide his feelings.

At this stage in his career, having made the decision to become a professional musician, John had doubts as to his capability to succeed. Although he had not had a formal training in the music colleges, away from the metropolis he was mixing with organisers of concerts who accepted his musicianship. In his nervousness over a proposed appointment at Uttoxeter, a well-known, established Choral Society, he lied. Interviewed prior to a performance of *Messiah* in the Town Hall, Uttoxeter on 7th December 1945, he began by claiming that his father was a violinist with the London Symphony Orchestra. He probably chose this orchestra because the father of one of John's friends played the trombone in that orchestra and occasionally gave John and his father free tickets for their concerts. He then proceeded to assert that he had studied under Tobias Matthay, the well-known professor of piano and Dr Markham Lee, both statements being completely untrue. (Mr Belchambers of the Monoux School had been Markham Lee's pupil.) He then asserted that he 'entered the Royal College of Music in 1934 where I studied the piano, viola and conducting. In 1936 I was appointed conductor of the Chingford (London) Choral Society.' (John had played the piano at a Chingford Choral Concert in December 1934.) However, the article finished with 'Mr Pritchard possesses a brilliant technique both as a conductor and pianist. We are of the opinion that John Pritchard is a young man of whom we shall hear more.'

Absolutely delighted by the performance he gave of *Messiah*, the County Music Organiser considered that the balance of the Choir was 'the best that he had ever heard in the whole of his experience. A very impressive debut.'

Whilst the importance of the Uttoxeter appointment was in the distant future, it was an engagement in Derby by the young violinist, Yfrah Neaman that opened a whole new vista for him.

2

South Africa

Believing that John had a future on a major scale in the world of music, Leslie Smart recommended him to Ibbs & Tillett, the London concert agents, so that when the young violinist Yfrah Neaman was due to play in the Central Hall, Derby on 17th February 1946, his name was suggested as an accompanist. There was an immediate rapport between the two young men.

Yfrah Neaman felt that John was very much the person who 'sensed what you were about to do and was able both to support and guide if necessary and, as might occasionally happen on the platform, when there was always something unexpected, keep up with possible whims. I remember that there was complete and total security with him.'

A few days later, Benjamin Britten and Peter Pears, who had been engaged for recitals in both Kendal and Keswick, cancelled at less than twenty-four hours' notice. Yfrah Neaman recalled: 'I don't remember exactly what happened but there was always a pair of concerts. You did a midday concert in Kendal, a very good society with very good people and a few miles away in Keswick, you did the Music Club recital in the evening. I seem to remember that I was phoned and when asked who I wanted, as we had played together only two or three days before, immediately replied, "Why not John?"' As they had expected Britten and Pears, the societies had sold many tickets and there were a number of people who were very interested.

Yfrah Neaman had studied in Paris with Carl Flesch since the age of nine. With the outbreak of war, on the advice of the British Consul, he took advantage of a ship going to England and whilst working in a war factory, studied with violinist, Max Rostal. When Rostal slipped and fell on the icy platform of a railway station the evening before a concert, Neaman remembers that Emmie Tillett phoned him on the Sunday morning. '"Rostal can't play this afternoon at the Cambridge Theatre with the London Symphony, can you do it?" I had been working very long hours at the factory and had never played before in London with an orchestra. I was young and so I said "yes" and "when was the rehearsal?" And she said, "Now. Put a dark suit in your case and come along immediately."' After this somewhat sensational debut, he was catapulted into public awareness through a photograph of the event on the centre pages in the *Daily Express*. 'That's how concerts, Derby . . . all followed but I still had to make up time in the factory, until in mid '45 or early '46 I was released.'

As a result of their successful collaboration, Ibbs & Tillett began to feel that there was somebody whom they could use. John Tillett who dealt with overseas and so-called more important engagements, asked Yfrah Neaman whether he would consider using John as his accompanist for a South African tour. John did not have anything else of such interest and readily accepted the opportunity to go abroad.

After conducting the City of Birmingham Orchestra on its visit to Derby, at the Central Hall, in a performance of Schubert's Unfinished Symphony (no. 8 in B minor) – he had been handed the baton in a gesture of friendship by George Weldon – John left for London to embark at Tilbury on 28th April 1946 on *MV Dominion Monarch*, a large 27,000 ton ship making her first trip to South Africa since 1939. Having made her maiden voyage to South Africa early in 1939, she was in Australian waters when war broke out and her luxurious cabins and lounges were cleared to accommodate thousands of troops. During the last hectic hours of the allied stand in Singapore she had been in dry dock, her engines partially dismantled for repair. As most of the native labour at the dockyard deserted, it was left to the Chief Engineer to get the engines working and extricate the ship from a position which many regarded as hopeless. Early in 1944, she had ferried a number of German prisoners of war to the United States of America and was still engaged in trooping after the war. Even though they were in civilian clothing, the majority of personnel on board were ex-servicemen. Now en route to South Africa, she was returning Italian prisoners of war to Naples.

For Yfrah Neaman the tour was a great adventure. They were two young men out to have a good time. As he and his partner

30

did not speak about private matters he was unaware that for John there was another dimension. It was not only a question of leaving the austerity and shortages of post-war Britain; John's early years had been dominated by a week by week existence dependent upon the generosity of others. From Derby he sent money regularly to his mother. Now, suddenly, not only was he enjoying the excitement of life on board ship but the opportunity to gorge himself on food such as he had never experienced nor imagined possible. His future obsessive appetite could only have been produced by his childhood deprivation. As his personality developed and refined, it became an epicurean delight. His early diaries have daily commentaries on meals or often, lack of food. His long letters to his mother on this tour expressed his wonderment and almost disbelief at his good fortune. Writing to her on 2nd May:

We sailed, at 11am on the Monday, but it was very misty and one could only just pick out the Gravesend landmarks: but the good old ferries kept passing to and fro as we waited to move! The ship cracked on at a good speed and by the afternoon we were passing the Seven Sisters and by night the lights of Isle of Whyte [*sic*] showed themselves. As I told you the *Dominion Monarch* is a troop ship and so we are subject to the O.C. Troops, a very impressive Lieut. Colonel. First-class passengers are treated as officers for all purposes of dining-rooms, cabins, cigarette and chocolate rations (150 Players per week, costing 5/-), etc. etc. Our routine for the day is somewhat as follows: at 7am the cabin steward brings us tea, then we have until 9am to prepare for '2nd sitting' breakfast. The meals are served in a finely appointed room seating 320, with about ten at each table. The stewards are quick, exceedingly nimble and their only care is to make you as happy as possible, which is not difficult for them as lavish menus are available. For example, at breakfast we have porridge, then fish, then a grill such as egg and bacon, with newly baked rolls, toast, marmalade and coffee or tea. At lunch one has soup, a dish with plentiful cold meat (beef or mutton or tongue) and salad, *then* a grill or roast meat, followed by a sweet and cheese. All the dishes are beautifully cooked and amply varied. There is no official afternoon tea, which has to be 'wangled' with your steward! At night there is a four-course dinner with either two meat dishes, or game or fish and meat, soup, sweet and dessert (fruit). This completes the 'stuffing' for the day and believe me one needs plenty of exercise (6 spans of the promenade deck = 1 mile) to keep in trim on such a diet, to which we have grown unaccustomed in England. Hope it does not make you too envious, as you eke out the butter or corned beef ration at home!

At 10.30 I usually go to the spacious Troops' Recreation Room where I am keeping a friendly eye on arrangements for the ship's concert and amateur talent of *very* various kinds is being welded into some sort of ensemble!

We woke on Thursday morning excited to see land on *both* sides, which meant we were in the Straits of Gibraltar – and sure enough, there was the Rock looming up in the distance. Previously I have thought of the 'gap' between Gib and the African coast as a tiny stretch of water but in fact we passed through almost equidistant from each point of land and it was only possible to pick out with binoculars the main features of Gibraltar, while on the African side it was thrilling to 'sniff' the Arabic atmosphere of the clustered, reddish buildings of Ceuta.

At tea-time I go to the cabin to practise on my dumb piano (which I safely bought in London last week, very cheaply and it is a consolation to have it on the voyage – after all, we *are* going out to work!). There is a German grand, fairly new, in the first-class lounge and a new upright in the Troops' Recreation Room, but needless to say we do not feel like *practising* in these rooms which are nearly always occupied. But all being well we shall do a short Recital to the passengers one evening, Yfrah and I . . .

Tomorrow (Sat) we shall port at Naples, where the hundreds of Italian prisoners of war we are carrying will return to their homeland after five years' absence. You can imagine how voluble they get, clustered in the after-deck, as they get nearer home. Last night they had an open-air concert round the swimming pool – a violinist, an accordionist, a drummer, with a singer. They all listened in rapt silence and it was a wonderful moment, gliding over the Mediterranean, to see all these faces under the ship's floodlights and to hear a real Italian tenor voice floating up in the night.

I do not think we shall be allowed ashore anywhere en route – at least I doubt it, so we shall have to be content to stand at the rail and see everything with our binoculars!

Well, my love, I think that is all I have to tell you for the moment. I think of you *very* often and wish you could share this wonderful experience.

With fondest love, John

Unable to land in Naples on 4th May, they contented themselves with taking photographs of Vesuvius and other sights. They docked at Port Said on 7th May and took the opportunity to go ashore but as the area near the docks was slightly sinister – people trying to sell them diamonds and watches and the Military Police patrolling in groups of four – they lost their courage and quickly returned to the ship. Nevertheless John exercised poetic licence in his next letter to his mother. 'I had a terrific time sneaking ashore with Yfrah, disguised as members of the crew. Port Said is supposed to be a centre of Arab vice and I daresay it is in the darker and smellier byways but we kept to the lighted thoroughfares and this first contact with *the East* was a great experience.'

Overawed by their passage through the Suez Canal, in the seemingly unbearable heat, noting it was 102° in the shade, he expressed a feeling of elation on entering the Indian Ocean: 'It is a deep rich blue in colour and has shortcrested waves in the furrows of which the flying fish disport themselves, "schools" of little white discs about two and a half inches across, which lift themselves up for brief gliding flight and then disappear again beneath the waves.'

Although the young men did some concerts for sailors' charities they were only asked to give one recital using the little boudoir grand. A gala affair, it was very Edwardian with the Captain garlanded in gold and the crew in resplendent white uniforms. They played Dvořák's Sonata in G, the Andante and Finale from Mendelssohn's Concerto in E minor and finally a selection which included Debussy's 'Clair de Lune' and a 'Spanish Dance' by de Falla. John recorded that at the party afterwards they drank too much whisky, beer and iced gin.

The *Dominion Monarch* arrived at Durban with the quarantine flag flying from the masthead. There were thirty cases of chicken-pox on board and a case of smallpox was suspected. Even though many of them had been vaccinated before leaving the United Kingdom, the four hundred passengers all had to be vaccinated before they were permitted to disembark. People started arriving at the docks to greet the ship at first light and by seven o'clock the quayside was crowded with hundreds of enthusiastic welcomers but as the day wore on the crowds gradually dispersed. It was some considerable time, after extra medical help had been brought on board to cope with the innoculation, that people were eventually allowed to disembark.

On the night-time journey by rail from Durban, the two young men were rattled and shaken through the twenty-hour winding ascent to Johannesburg, 6,000 feet above sea level. Tired and somewhat jaded but relieved to arrive the following afternoon, they were greeted by batteries of press cameras and newsmen. Together with radio and press interviews they really felt like celebrities.

Yfrah Neaman recalled that he did not need to 'break the ice with John or that there were things that I would have liked to say but didn't. There were no uncomfortable moments with him. I think that both of us were young and both of us, for the first time, were abroad and so I think that we were slightly, not exactly out of our element but we had to try and find our role. How does a celebrity behave? Travelling abroad we had a certain standard to uphold. Although we were treated as celebrities we were quite new to it.'

Although they included, occasionally, what was considered some adventurous music, they played mostly standard repertoire in their recitals. The ease and sense of relaxation which the climate engendered, the many individuals, not just friendly because it was their job but because they seemed to care, gave them a wonderful feeling of exuberance. Nowadays an artist tends to fly by air from one engagement to another. Then, travel by train, which sometimes took two and a half days from one destination to another, gave them time to think and made them feel that they were really living in the country.

Unconsciously a very fast walker, Yfrah Neaman was aware that:

> [John] took his steps very gently. He did mention that he couldn't be in the forces because he'd had pleurisy in '38 and that ever since then he had to be careful. I should imagine that he understood that people might wonder why a young man in his twenties wasn't serving, so he told people it was because of this and the effect on his heart, that he was rejected from the forces.
>
> I'm very inquisitive and curious and it was nice that he was the same. I know that nowadays all this seems 'vieux jeux' because Africa is no longer such an extraordinary place and thousands of others have been there as well. But in those days, to go and visit a Zulu chief was still fairly unusual. John was always ready for anything like this. On the other hand, he didn't mind how much we rehearsed, how much work we did. I think we gave about five recitals in Johannesburg – one was forever changing programmes and playing different things, interviews, speaking or lunches and it

was very comforting to feel that you could have utter confidence in the person with you, both on the platform and as a general companion. He used to talk about his ultimate dream of becoming a conductor. Then it was a dream because it is not as if a conductor does a little piano playing for fun as an interim occupation. It was very much that he felt that 'I am a pianist but I feel it in me that conducting is what I really want to do'.

At present he was happy to be accepted and treated as a professional accompanist. Writing fully to his mother on 11th June 1946 from Johannesburg, John described their first recital the previous Sunday:

> I'm pleased to tell you it was a lovely success. I think we have made a good impression and people say they like our personalities as well, which is lucky! We played in a fine modern theatre against a most glamorous background of silk floodlit draperies and beautiful flowers. The newspaper critics were kind and about me said 'a pianist whose accompanying has a rare quality of understanding'. 'Neaman is fortunate in his accompanist'. 'Sympathetic and an able soloist, a consistently controlled and delightfully musical performance'. So I think that's not a bad start? Yfrah gets fine notices too.

The welcome in Johannesburg was nothing in comparison to the appreciation and enthusiasm of the audience at the Opera House in Pretoria. Although obviously attention was focused on Neaman, John received equal praise for his rare and unusual talent for accompaniment. Nevertheless reviewers were aware of the subdued modesty in his work.

Writing later from the Queen's Hotel, Sea Point, Cape Town on 1st July, one can feel John's childlike excitement as he described their success to his mother:

> We had nice *warm* audiences at Johannesburg's five concerts but it is a city of very small culture – consider it is only sixty years old, and the people have a hard superficial fast-American-car-cocktail-party-night-club mentality which does not *really* go with violin and piano recitals. Nevertheless we never had a small audience and were quite satisfied with our reception. But when we went to Pretoria – what a difference! The theatre was packed from floor to ceiling, they wouldn't let us go, encore after encore was given, they cheered and stamped, they besieged the Green Room, they threw a large party afterwards for us (recklessly, as we were due to fly at eight the following morning to the Cape but it merely meant we passed one entire night without sleep!). It was a *furore*.

Arriving in Cape Town on 26th June there was so much for the two young men to see and to photograph. In their first recital at City Hall on 27th June, John played two piano solos: Bach's 'Choral Preludes', 'Jesu, Joy of Man's Desiring', transcribed by Myra Hess and 'Jesus Christ the Son of God', transcribed by Rummel. At the second and final recital in Cape Town, the audience demanded three encores; the last a repetition from the first recital of Ibert's 'The Little White Donkey', now a 'must' at all Neaman's appearances. The two young men had received such an ovation at their first concert in Cape Town where the City Hall was full to capacity that they hoped the promotors, African Theatres, would extend their contract. Although John felt it necessary to live in a luxurious manner, spending about £18 – 20 a week as well as buying clothes, every concert above the stipulated number would contribute towards the nest egg he hoped to accumulate from this tour. He continued to his mother:

> We are staying here three miles out of Cape Town, a lovely white hotel in the Dutch style, with the Atlantic at the very *gate*. It is lovely to sit on the verandah in their 'winter' which is like June in England, with the sun shining all day! We are able to take things a trifle easier than in Johannesburg, where we worked extremely hard. And now we are doing all the 'seaside' places, The Cape, Port Elizabeth, Durban. Durban should be very nice as we are there in July which is the 'season' – all the élite, the Governor-General, Smuts, etc. are there.
>
> I have been doing some enjoyable shopping in Cape Town. We haven't time to be measured for suits but yesterday I bought a very nice suit with a wide stripe, ready made (from Simpson's, London!) and a really marvellous fit. When I think of the coupons I am saving! I also have a lovely wristlet watch with a silver 'strap', a Roman lighter, lots of shirts – and socks: don't mention them! I *have* to keep buying socks as holes come in those I wear. I possess a darning outfit but just loathe getting down to the job . . . the most I am prepared to do is sew on a button!
>
> Yesterday I ordered a food parcel to be sent off to you but I doubt that it will reach you in much under six weeks. We are only allowed to send 7lb of food at a time, so I had it made up with marmalade, fruit for puddings and sweets and chocolate. I'll send you another variety soon!

During the train journey from Cape Town to Port Elizabeth there had been an enforced halt at Bonnie Vale, an eleven-hour wait due to an overturned truck. The two young men tried to pass the time sitting in the driver's cabin of the 1894 engine, taking each other's photograph (and from the number of prints of this photograph remaining in his possession, John obviously loved this pose). At last on 6th July, they arrived at Port Elizabeth. Here, at Neaman's second recital, John played the Brahms 'Wiegenlied' (transcribed by Percy Grainger) and the Chopin Waltz in C sharp minor. The enthusiastic audience demanded an encore – Poulenc's 'Pastourel'. Apart from the usual sight-seeing, they had time to meet people and after an agreeable and stimulating evening, became great friends with the family Wallheimer, with John lavishing affection on their Great Dane. It is interesting to see from photographs taken on the beach that other members of the group are wearing bathing clothes but John remains fully dressed, looking self-conscious about his height and the fact that he has obviously put on weight.

Nevertheless he did write to his mother on 25th July saying that he had swum in the sea at Port Elizabeth:

Here in Durban, which is *the* fashionable watering place of the Union, it is high winter season: all the hotels are full and everybody is intent on having a good time. The Governor-General is here and Smuts has just left. Yfrah had a great success with his concertos and our first recital last Tuesday was to a very appreciative audience. Next Tuesday our concert is to be broadcast, then we are giving two studio broadcasts. After that it's not finally decided what we shall do: possibly we go back to Cape Town for more concerts but the final *farewells* to S. Africa have now been fixed!

On (*probably*) Sept 8th we FLY BACK TO ENGLAND. Now if it is by the British Overseas Airways the trip will take about five days but if by the Springbok we get to London in about *forty hours*! I shall want you to come up to London to see me before I go on to Derby, I shall stay at least a night in Town. Who knows, perhaps you could come to the Air Port?! Wouldn't that be exciting . . .

Occasionally we meet people who have just flown out from England and we eagerly ask them how things are. The bread rationing sounds like the final blow – I expect. Dad will notice it and if the quality is poorer you will not enjoy your famous bread and butter. By the way the first parcel I sent included chocolate and I am told this was a mistake as it does not travel well through the tropics: so if it arrives a sticky mess I'm sorry. But the other goods should be alright – *when* they arrive!

Again at Durban, John substituted Brahms and Chopin for the programmed Bach. In Natal, the next stop on their tour, their recitals were broadcast. Here John's solos of Scriabin's Nocturne in F sharp minor and Chopin's Etude in A flat were so well received that he needed to give an encore. Returning to Durban, John heard a rickshaw boy whistle a tune and followed, noting down the melody. From that time on he captivated audiences by playing his own composition, Tune on 4 Variants on a theme by a Bantu native. The final concert at the Curzon Theatre was also broadcast. John hoped that the Municipal Orchestra might invite him to conduct but this did not materialise.

In Pretoria, where one of the farewell recitals was in the presence of the Governor-General, John omitted his solo performances. Nevertheless, a reviewer commented perceptively on his accompaniment of Beethoven's Kreutzer Sonata: 'Mr John Pritchard contributed a perfect example and throughout convinced one yet again, that good accompanists are born, not made.'

Whilst in Johannesburg on the 'farewell' part of their tour, the two young men gave a charity recital at the Occupational Therapy Centre of the Military Hospital, Johannesburg. In thanking John, the Officer in Charge wrote: 'The patients still refer to your recital in terms of such glowing enthusiasm that it is obvious that it will remain in their memories as one of the highlights in their experience. The general feeling seems to be that you were "just the right sort of people", and every detail about your manner and behaviour – including the swatting of the flying ant – was noted and appreciated. Thank you. We wish you every success in whatever the future may hold for you. We shall always think of you as "our John Pritchard".'

After a 'farewell' recital at Port Elizabeth on 2nd September, the young men set off in an Avro-York Bomber for Nairobi, Kenya on 8th September, where John believed they were the first Europeans to give a recital. Writing to his mother on 31st August 1946, aboard the train going to Port Elizabeth, he described his schedule.

The 8th Sept we fly in the Springbok plane from Johannesburg – at 4am (ouch!). By 4pm we are at *Nairobi* in East Africa, we spend the evening and night, so African Theatres are arranging a *concert* for us!! Talk about a flying visit! The next morning (Mon) we leave at 6am and start the final hop, arriving at Heathrow airport *London* at 6.40pm. (Tues 10th Sept.) Now the next day Wednesday the 11th I would like you to come up to London. I will meet you at the station. I suppose you arrive about midday, I will meet all the trains about that time. I am arranging for us both to stay the night at a hotel in London and you can go back the next day. I expect I shall shoot off to Derby on the Thursday too. We shall talk nineteen to the dozen and it will be lovely to see you just as I return. We have been giving farewell concerts – last Monday at Pretoria the Governor-General and Smuts were at the performance and we were presented.

In summing up the successful collaboration based on their few concerts in England, Yfrah Neaman felt that as there was little difference in their ages, John's attitude towards him was never professorial or paternal: 'He didn't guide me but was receptive straight away and agreeable to what I did.' Admitting that he was not really the sort of person who could draw someone out, nevertheless he was aware that John never spoke much about his family, convalescence or any part of his early life. John never mentioned his father and only talked about his mother. Naturally, John appreciated that Leslie Smart had been very good to him, was his backer, the person who believed in him and gave him whatever a career in Derby could possibly produce. Neaman continued:

> I think though, that when we were together just sitting and chatting or having a meal, he wasn't at all sure if a career on the podium and the post of conductor would come easily to him. It was something that he felt was very much in the mists of possible future good luck. He never really tried in all those three months to get on the podium with a South African orchestra, in any shape or form. There was no worry about living – he was well paid for those days and hotels and hospitality were provided. If somebody had said that they didn't mind him conducting but couldn't pay him, it would not have mattered. Nothing of the sort happened. I think that he must have been, up to a point, a little worried as to how his career would progress.

On his return to Derby, John recorded that the telephone did not stop ringing. Continuing to accompany at recitals in places such as Huddersfield, Leeds and of course Derby he showed the extent to which he had benefited from the opportunity to work in a concentrated manner with a musical equal. At the same time the South African tour had widened his horizon socially.

Whilst in South Africa, John took time to write to the newspapers in Derby about his tour. At this stage in his career, aware of the need for self-promotion and that of newspapers and journals for copy, he befriended newspapermen. However, his opinion of music critics was highly mixed. There were only a few that he truly respected. He and Eva kept all his press cuttings in large scrapbooks. Not occupied sufficiently, he had time to do this and send copies to his mother. Later he subscribed to a Press Agency. When his career had reached the stage at which aspiring musicians sought his advice, either about music or their careers, he would suggest they did likewise. It was always better, he said, not to rush out the day after a performance to buy newspapers on the off chance that they would include a review of one's work, or be very upset by unfavourable comments. One should forget about the previous evening, carry on working and, a couple of weeks later, when the cuttings arrive from the news agency, either be pleasantly surprised by the critics' applause or, if the reviews were disappointing, feel quite unconcerned as sufficient time had elapsed not to feel involved with the performance. That way one could pay attention to constructive advice and discard destructive comment. Interestingly, amongst John's effects was a large box of press cuttings in unopened envelopes. He had been too busy to read them!

Dissatisfied with the Derby Philharmonic, three weeks before their first concert of the season on 30th October, John handed in his resignation and was quoted in the *Derby Evening Telegraph*:

> I attended a rehearsal on Sunday at which only twenty instrumentalists out of the paper strength of sixty were present and a number of these were not regular members but merely brought in for the occasion. It is obviously impossible to carry on in conditions like these, and it would not be fair to those members who regularly attend rehearsals, or to the public, or myself, to do so. In previous seasons I have criticised attendances but this year instead of an improvement there has been a deterioration. It is obvious that the musical standards demanded by a public performance cannot be achieved if many members of the orchestra only put in an appearance at one or two rehearsals before the event.

Even though he had resigned from the Philharmonic, with the backing of Leslie Smart, John continued to work and enjoy the camaraderie of the Derby String Orchestra until 1952. Although mainly amateur in its composition, he established a loyalty amongst his players, some of whom were students from London gaining experience in a wide variety of programmes which would not today be considered 'safe'. Despite his resignation John conducted the Philharmonic for the Derby Choral Union's performance on 13th November 1946 of Saint-Saëns' *Samson and Delilah*. Even though they had reservations about the general standard of the orchestral performance, reviewers considered that John and the Delilah of Gladys Ripley had contributed to the success of the evening. He conducted that orchestra again for the Derby Choral Union performance of *Messiah* in December at the Central Hall, Derby, which attracted, as always, a large audience.

However it was his next engagement, a performance of *Elijah* with the Uttoxeter Choral Society, that was to change his life. The Uttoxeter Choral Society was important in that it attracted good soloists, in this instance baritone Roy Henderson who had had a remarkable career before the war, particularly at the Glyndebourne Festival Opera. Consequently he was on exceptionally good terms with John and Audrey Christie, the founders of that Festival. He recalled the performance of *Elijah* at the Town Hall, Uttoxeter, vividly and with much good humour:

> Maybe it was because I sang it so many times but everything always seemed to happen in *Elijah* and I remember, as if it were yesterday, this particular *Elijah* with John. Perhaps it was ominous that the performance took place on Friday 13th December 1946. Friday the 13th certainly presaged what was to come. The contralto who was singing the Queen had not learnt her part, so I suggested that as a baritone I might sing it. As I didn't wish to be called a 'Queen', I suggested it would be better if I were programmed as an 'Agitator'. Then, when I was getting up to sing 'Oh Thou Who Makest Thine Angel's Spirits', which is a very quiet passage, a lady in the audience at the front started to leave. Having stood up myself, I asked John to wait. John stopped the performance until the lady had left. John impressed me a great deal with the way in which he coped, that he seemed to have the choir under control . . . I suggested that he write to John Christie. Knowing that Christie was slightly eccentric, I told him exactly what to say. Meanwhile, I also wrote to Audrey and John Christie.

This was followed later on 23rd April 1947:

> I didn't suggest Pritchard as a first-class coach. I suggested he should apply to get experience of work under the best conditions in any capacity, paid or unpaid, so that he could learn something of the Edinburgh Festival. He has the makings of leadership, he is keen, he is the right sort of Englishman, but has *no* experience except with

small choirs and a string orchestra. He seemed to me however as likely a lad as James Robertson was his first year at Glyndebourne. His responsibilities should be very small if you take him on and naturally his pay likewise. But he seems to me a boy worth training for future development. I really had in mind a conductor's factotum and general assistant with an occasional chorus rehearsal, or even conducting offstage as is often necessary.

The following day, 24th April 1947, Rudolf Bing, the Administrator, sent a memo to Audrey Christie. 'Please find enclosed a letter from Roy about Pritchard, the young musician who wrote to John Christie and whom Roy recommended. What we need and need badly are first-class experienced coaches. I simply don't know what to do with Pritchard. Have you any views?'

As nobody at Glyndebourne Opera had heard of John, Rudolf Bing sent John to see the Chorus Master, composer Berthold Goldschmidt, at his home in Belsize Park, to find out more about his musicianship. Goldschmidt was still working for the Overseas Service of the BBC, where during the war he had been employed in the German Service Section. His recollection of John was of a very pleasant young man who asked, 'What does coaching for opera represent?' Glyndebourne, feeling unable to refuse anyone who had been sent with such a strong recommendation as that of Roy Henderson, duly took John 'on trial' for the forthcoming season.

John noted in capital letters in his scrapbook,

6th May 1947
SIGNED CONTRACT
WITH
GLYNDEBOURNE
START WORK Monday May 12th

and wrote excitedly to his mother:

I know you will be interested to know the result of my interview with Mr Rudolf Bing, Director of Glyndebourne Opera, today. He has offered me and I have accepted, a lovely job on the music staff. I am to be Coach to the principals and chorus and will undertake general musical duties. The period of my first contract is for eight weeks beginning next Monday the 12th, until July 5th. Then there is a two week break and if I wish I can then probably go on for a further two months which will take in the Edinburgh Festival. We are to be engaged on the production, first, of Gluck's *Orfeo* which

Carl Ebert will produce and in which Kathleen Ferrier will play the title role. As I say, we start next Monday, and as at present there is no accommodation *at* Glyndebourne for the *Orfeo* company, a special train will take us up and down daily from London (they provide us with season tickets for this!). This train leaves each day at 9am from Victoria. They have been very accommodating (at Glyndebourne I mean) regarding such concert dates as I had already booked and which will be difficult to get out of, so everything is in order. Needless to say I am very thrilled about the job – it is just what I want and when you consider I shall be working closely with some of the very finest musicians in the *world*, singers from the Metropolitan, New York, and the Scala, Milan, the opportunity is really a first-class one. It is the first highly skilled professional position I have had as a *conductor*, too. Also when one thinks of that lovely Glyndebourne setting, the great gardens with their fountains and peacocks, the opera house nestling behind an old-world manor house . . . it is really exciting and makes one hope for a fine summer. (P.S. It is very good financially too!)

Am writing this in the train and we are now at Derby, so toodle-oo for now!

Love in haste, John

This was followed by another letter written from Glyndebourne:

On my first day I was invited to stay in Mr and Mrs Christie's house for the whole of the period up to July. Most of the principal members of the music staff are in the house somewhere, so it is very nice and one can get to know one's colleagues in the best possible way.

Now I dare say Mum when writing to you on occasions I have been guilty of enthusing too much about various things I have been doing. If so, it's a shame, because I shall not be able to convey to you any sense of the *wonderful* place which is Glyndebourne. At the end of the first day I pinched myself to see whether this were really PARADISE or no.

Imagine first the rolling Sussex Downs and in these downs a pleasant wooded hollow. Imagine then in such a situation a great country house in Georgian style, with a great drive leading to the front of the house, sloping lawns with chestnuts in full flower and around it acres and acres of landscape gardens, lawns, terraces, quiet rose gardens enclosed with hedges two yards thick, then hundreds of flowering bushes or beds ablaze with tulips: then wonderful shaded walks and paths leading down to a great lake flanked with willows and flowering trees. Very well, you say, I can imagine it – I have seen these great estates, though rarely nowadays. Then picture, built onto this great house, a well proportioned building with a centre tower, around it a cluster of other edifices. This building is approached through further paved gardens and is seen to be a theatre with every modern essential – luxuriously furnished, with a magnificent stage and hard by, a cocktail bar and a large restaurant. Beyond are fine dressing rooms, rehearsal rooms, a canteen . . . Isn't it unbelievable! In these surroundings, work becomes a pleasure: I am busy helping to rehearse the chorus, who travel down from London every day and often my eyes look through the windows to see the grand country outside and again I pinch myself!

Presiding over all this splendour and beauty is Mr John Christie, a breezy, hearty man in a white drill suit, aged about sixty, who married a young opera star named Audrey Mildmay some years ago and spent his millions to combine his two loves in one spot: opera and the countryside. What an achievement he has! He is very friendly to *everyone*, from the least member of the chorus up to the Conductor himself and all the company . . . Christie does not run the Company on the management side, he leaves all that to the experts but he is there as a sort of genial fatherly presence all the time . . .

All I can say is, no wonder all the London élite are fighting to pay their £2.2s. per seat for the production of *Orfeo*. What an experience it will be for them – the special trains bringing them down in an hour from Victoria, then the first act of the opera at 5.30 followed by one and a half hours for dinner in the restaurant (the immaculate head-waiter with his wine list worthy of the Ritz) and a stroll in the evening sunshine in the gardens. Then the second act etc. and leave in time to be back in London well before midnight. Cost you about £5.5s. per head but it's *worth* it!

We have six weeks of rehearsal ahead and already DR FRITZ STIEDRY from the Metropolitan Opera, New York, is here to conduct. Next to him comes Berthold Goldschmidt of the BBC who is Chorus Master, then come young James Iliffe and myself, who are equal partners and are known officially as CO-REPETITEURS: that is we coach the principals, make sure they have their notes and tempo correct – or we may work with the chorus, conduct orchestral rehearsals later – or whatever is necessary. At the moment the day is not arduous: . . . the rehearsal call is at 11 . . . then work till 5 which is the finish of the day for the chorus . . . Then my time is my own at the moment. I can study my Italian down by the lake, or write letters sitting on a lawn, or go for a stroll, or practise the piano, or play the three manual organ in the Organ Room – or just sit!

It's wonderful to think that a great production will day by day grow up under our eyes here – of course it's fantastic in any case to imagine the money it must cost to be able to spend six weeks in rehearsal just for *one* opera – a place like Sadlers Wells would have to prepare fifteen in that time!

Well, dear, I have forgotten doubtless a dozen things but I have said enough to show you that I am very, very happy and – I must say – very, very LUCKY to have such a grand time in the course of my career as it were. You can write to me: Mr John Pritchard, Glyndebourne, Lewes, Sussex.

I was so pleased to hear you have been fixed up as regards the coach: won't it be grand if only the weather holds. I enclose something for your fare and will send some more next week in time for your departure. I *wish* to do this so please don't try to stop me!

All my love and thoughts of you

As ever, John

P.S. The nightingale is singing as I write (11pm).

John's father matter-of-factly noted in his own diary, using the conductor's name:

17th May: John at Glyndebourne, Sussex.

However on the 6th July:

Stanley came home.

3

'Mr John Pritchard, Glyndebourne, Sussex'

The essence and continuing success of Glyndebourne is its teamwork. Its democracy makes it the ideal place for a young person wishing to learn their craft either on or backstage as the conception of a 'star' does not exist. Many great artists today express their gratitude to Glyndebourne as, in the early days of their career, they were judged and accepted on merit alone. In a totally rural setting, without shops, cafés or any form of entertainment within walking proximity, there is no alternative for the Glyndebourne inhabitants other than to 'make music'. In the sometimes claustrophobic atmosphere relationships can become very complex. Nevertheless, derived from the total commitment of the Christie family to the establishment of an Opera Festival of international repute, the overriding factor is the love of music.

It was wonderful for John to find himself meeting some of the greatest musicians of the day. In later years, as Music Director, when the company had grown, he would endeavour to make each new arrival feel welcome. He himself, was made to feel at home by the young stage manager, Harold Chapin. Harold Valetta Chapin, sometimes called Valie, at that time in his early thirties, had contracted tuberculosis during the war and converted to Catholicism in the hope that the solicitude and comfort of that church would help him cope with what was to prove a fatal illness. He had an immediate rapport with John who gave him 'holy water' for Christmas. An actor, sometimes appearing at Stratford, Harold introduced John to an interest that became an essential part of his life, namely theatre. Harold's death in 1950 at the age of thirty-eight had a profound effect on John. Having been close to another young man from Stroud, who was 'killed in action (1943) in Malaya' aged twenty-six, he remarked many years later that he felt it difficult to form either a deep or lasting attachment to anyone. Chapin's mother, Calypso Browning (her second husband's name), was an actress with a remarkable personality. Enjoying a lovely home and garden which she created in Pembridge Crescent, London, she 'adopted' John and would often travel abroad to attend his concerts and operas. He would dine frequently with 'Mrs B' at her house, taking with him his closest friends, first Eva and later, men friends. After performances he took her to dinner at exclusive restaurants and she would confide to friends her concern at his extravagance. In her nineties, when asked what she would like as an aperitif, she would reply in her best Lady Bracknell tone, 'Why, champagne, of course!' Others boast of their great age but at ninety-seven she claimed that she was only ninety-four. Her only child, Harold Chapin was a remarkably intelligent, kind person with a dry sense of humour and great insight into the people around him. One artist remembered him as very self-effacing who, when asked if he would be going to a press conference at Glyndebourne ('You'll be coming along, you're such an important part of us all?') replied: 'Oh no, I flee from publicity in just the same way as Professor Ebert rushes towards it.'

Many artists owe much to Carl Ebert, the Artistic Director of Glyndebourne. Not only a great director, he was also a passionate teacher whose main object had been to get away from the old operatic tradition. In making opera appear real to the audience his influence on both the German and British theatre has been immense. The opera he had staged before the war with the conductor Fritz Busch, had been a revelation to both the critics and the public. Carl Ebert loved working with young people and established acting and opera schools in Germany and Turkey. The organisation of a German theatre was based upon the producer and conductor arranging the entire opera, staging performances from the House's own rosters of singers. Glyndebourne, with its emphasis on teamwork and ensemble was an ideal place for Ebert to work. If Ebert felt that a singer was not doing justice to an aria, he would stand facing them and as they sang he would mouth the words, the expression that he wanted flitting across his own most expressive countenance. It was something one would have expected to embarrass and inhibit but it was not so. With him it made a singer *want* to do it and indeed *could*. Ebert could be very short-tempered if he felt that people were not trying and if they did not pay attention he would fly into a rage. That was comparatively rare because he was so respected that they did listen. It did not matter if somebody happened to be a good singer and was not a particularly good actor; he would make them into a better actor than they thought they could be. Ian Wallace, the singer, never went to drama school or music college and it was wonderful for him to work with the director. 'He had charisma. A very good-looking man with an expressive face; he would comment ". . . you know it's not difficult to produce Mozart. The stage directions are in the music – if you *listen* for them."'

John, who always believed in the practical approach to music, would often quote Ebert. As a repetiteur, accompanying at the piano for rehearsals for the *Figaro* to be presented at the first Edinburgh Festival, John remembered 'acutely every detail of the production, for it was my first acquaintance with the opera in its original language and the first time I could see a typical Ebert production built up detail by detail'. He continued:

I hold firmly that in order to learn an opera completely there is no substitute for the musical chore of playing for stage rehearsals. During the endless repetitions and long waits while Ebert explained things to the singers, I was able, sitting at the piano, in the lonely gloom of the orchestra pit, to read and learn almost by heart the Italian of the libretto. I liked to play from a full score, not from affectation but because da Ponte's stage directions were always given in full (by no means the case in the vocal scores) and moreover the scoring was so entrancingly full of evidence of Mozart's method of thought. I learned with naïve surprise that Mozart had a great instinct for the stage and was a highly *practical* opera composer. I realised that when the chorus entered or made an exit, the operation took time on the stage and therefore a beautiful eight-bar prelude or postlude to a choral number had more than a purely musical intention. I found that in the concerted numbers an effective pause or silent bar, which had always delighted me musically, had an unsuspected significance scenically or dramatically. It became fascinating to watch for Mozart's 'fingerprints' so that by reconstruction one could almost picture the trend of the very first production itself. Under these powerful influences stuffy musical history shed its cobwebs: I read avidly the Mozart letters and Jahn's life, Mozart had become a person.

He felt that it had been of great advantage to him as a conductor to have begun as a repetiteur; to have understood theatre from the ground upwards, so to speak, rather than to have entered an opera house later in life as a conductor, whose only experience was in the concert hall. From Ebert he learnt that what was happening on the stage should only be what was expressed in the music and that it should be mirrored by the individual expression of the voice. Seemingly obvious, a singer should speak the words first, understand their meaning and then put the music to the words.

When John arrived at Glyndebourne the teaching and training of singing was in the hands of a man who became known quite simply to all musicians as 'Jani'. Janos Strasser, of Hungarian origin, was an eccentric in the full sense of the word. He often wore lederhosen and stockings and always carried a large satchel for his music (his home was called 'Sachells'). He was a coach privately and had his own very definite ideas about singing which caused several problems with singers vis-à-vis their own teachers. Recognising John's innate musicianship, the two men soon established an understanding which would last until Jani's death in 1978. John delivered the memorial tribute on 5th August 1979:

One of the great features of Glyndebourne has of course been the fact that artists from all over the world know that when they come here they can rely on wonderful musical coaching, long before the conductor has the chance of messing it up. The very first rehearsals are entrusted to slightly junior musical coaches who run through to make sure and report to the chief coach in charge of that particular opera whether the singer is well prepared, ready to go forward to musical ensemble and generally thoroughly grounded in the part.

Jani used to undertake the ensemble rehearsals before the conductor actually was even admitted to the premises. However when the conductor did take the first musical ensemble, many of us remember as being perhaps the quintessence of preparation of an opera at Glyndebourne, those wonderful sessions in the Organ Room when everybody studied the musical nuance and the dynamics and the balance and the conductor would show them his intentions right through the opera.

I had been conducting *Entführung* which I had never conducted here in Glyndebourne. I had been doing it round the world including the Vienna State Opera and thought it was going very well. I enjoyed the ensemble, we had a wonderful cast, the orchestra was doing well and I was coasting pleasantly on the beautiful music. In one of those sibilant whispers, I heard from about the eleventh row

Jani saying 'when is John going to start making some music live around here?' I didn't say a word to anyone, I had a rotten lunch. It took about three or four days. I felt his clutch on my shoulder from over the orchestra rail and I knew that *Entführung* had come up to Glyndebourne standards which I had regrettably forgotten. This kind of loving musical preparation is today not to be found in the world. All my colleagues here from the great international opera houses will agree with me that only here in this sacred spot can we get that kind of preparation.

The 1947 Glyndebourne Festival opened with performances of Gluck's *Orfeo* in Italian, produced by Carl Ebert with Fritz Stiedry conducting the Southern Philharmonic Orchestra from Brighton. John never forgot the singing of the 'lass from Blackburn', Kathleen Ferrier, with whom he had worked the previous March in a performance of Bach's *St Matthew Passion* with the Derby Choral Union. When a concert was arranged at Glyndebourne in June by the Rio Tinto Company, it was John who accompanied her in two arias from the Gluck opera. They remained friends until her tragically early death.

The other operas performed that summer were given by the newly-formed English Opera Group, under the direction of Benjamin Britten, Eric Crozier and John Piper. Presenting a new opera, *Albert Herring*, a comedy about life in a small Suffolk town, it was John's working introduction to the operas of Britten, whose work was to become central to his repertoire.

Appreciating John's skill as an accompanist and in particular his ability to sight-read, justifying Roy Henderson's recommendation, Rudolf Bing asked him to go with the company to help at the first Edinburgh Festival in 1947.

The Edinburgh Festival was the brainchild of Audrey Christie and Rudolf Bing. Opera at Glyndebourne had been funded by John Christie himself. Although reasonably well-off, he could not possibly sustain a season in Sussex to the extent of pre-war days but in Edinburgh the inevitable losses (estimated between £20,000 – £30,000) were guaranteed by a £60,000 fund put up in equal parts by the Arts Council, the Edinburgh Corporation and private individuals. Even though performances were sold out and the theatre could boast that it had achieved the best business in its history, box-office revenue for the three week season could not possibly pay for the necessary four to five weeks of musical preparation. The argument against the estimated deficit was balanced by the hoped for compensatory profit to hotels, shops, catering and other interests.

The performance of opera at Edinburgh so soon after the war was remarkable. The King's Theatre required the installation of a lighting bridge and the sheer logistics of transporting sixty spotlights together with other apparatus required for the production, from Sussex, is mind-boggling.

For the chorus members there were no seats in the primitive dressing-room and forty-nine stairs to the stage. Once they found fleas and threatened to go on strike and then could hardly breathe because of the powder that was sprayed to get rid of them. They became hot running up and down the stairs, hot on the stage, hot in the dressing-room where the make-up lights were so strong and then went into the icy passages and, after performances, out into the street to wait for trams to take them back to their digs. The end result – all the chorus had terrible colds.

There was a certain difference of opinion amongst the inhabitants of Edinburgh. Some, feeling it was a terrible invasion of their city, tended to go away. However, the majority with the City Fathers, welcomed the Company. Known as 'the Athens of the North', the city was a wonderful setting for an international festival. The Parks Department produced spectacular flowerbeds at the end of Princes Street and flower baskets all the way along. Even the trams' trolley poles had little flags on them. The Glyndebourne ménage was swept up in the general euphoria. Then, as now, misgivings were voiced by the critics that the operas to be performed, *Le Nozze di Figaro* and *Macbeth*, were not the work of a living composer but Rudolf Bing, General Manager at Glyndebourne and Director of the Edinburgh Festival, commented: 'People clamour for new works – and stay away when they are put on!'

The *Macbeth* promised to live up to its reputation as a theatrical 'jinx'. Engaged to conduct, George Szell was very dissatisfied with what he heard of the Scottish Orchestra, which, at that time, was not of the same high quality as his recent appointment, the Cleveland Orchestra. Chorus Master Berthold Goldschmidt remembered going to see Szell in his room. 'How are things?' he asked. The Maestro shook his head. 'I haven't even unpacked' and absconded in the night without telling anybody. The chaos that ensued necessitated a hurried reshuffling of the music staff with

Berthold Goldschmidt conducting the scheduled nine performances and John acting as his assistant.

Thirty years later, in an article in the Glyndebourne Programme Book, John related this story as if it had happened to him personally. It would seem more logical that Berthold Goldschmidt as Chorus Master would have spoken to Szell rather than John, who had only just been engaged as a young man who might 'make himself useful'. On the other hand, in its financially straitened position, Glyndebourne wanted to encourage and make use of a young Englishman who seemed entirely at home either with the harpsichord or piano. His long tour of South Africa as an accompanist was good preparation for his work with singers.

During rehearsals for *Macbeth* which had taken place at Glyndebourne, Berthold Goldschmidt remembered that he had asked John if he would like to try and conduct the chorus, letting him do a half-hour of chorus rehearsal. He found John rather stiff in the arms and taught him a lot of technique.

The performances of *Macbeth* received mixed reviews. Unable to stay in Edinburgh for the last week of the Festival as he had a firm commitment to the Derby String Orchestra for a tour of Haarlem in early September, John flew from Scotland to join them in the Netherlands. This was an exciting tour as, for many of the players, it was their first time abroad. Primarily they played works by British composers such as Elgar, Vaughan Williams and Howells. The soloists were John's old friends, Olga Hegedus, playing the Boccherini cello concerto and Vera Kantrovitch, the violinist. He sent his mother a postcard: 'Today we are in Amsterdam, a lovely city. I went to hear the famous Concertgebouw Orchestra rehearse. We have been having a great success, with dinners, receptions and enthusiastic audiences. Not much time for sight-seeing, should like a real holiday here!'

In his scrapbooks John noted that at every one of the five concerts given in different towns in Haarlem, he had been presented with a bouquet nearly as big as himself. The reciprocal visit by the Haarlem Philharmonic to Derby was greeted with much civic pride.

Permitted by Rudolf Bing to leave Edinburgh to undertake the prearranged Haarlem engagement, John now made himself available to Glyndebourne. With Rudolf Bing more occupied in the planning and running of the Edinburgh Festival, Moran Caplat, Assistant Manager at Glyndebourne, became increasingly involved in the administration in Sussex.

The following year as well as the Edinburgh Festival, the Glyndebourne Opera Company planned to open the Bath Festival with six performances of *Il Seraglio* to be sung in English with a primarily young, British cast and to the Glyndebourne administration, it seemed natural that they should present a young English conductor and began 'talking' with John to this end. The situation was delicate. Goldschmidt had known Rudolf Bing since his Berlin days in 1928 in Darmstadt. It was further complicated by Jani Strasser, who, as a singing teacher, was ambitious for his own pupils. John, a talented Englishman with only a desire to advance himself, had made himself agreeable to everybody. On the other hand, whilst everyone at Glyndebourne knew of him as an accompanist of ability, they did not have first-hand knowledge of his potential as a conductor. After his first concert of the season on 22nd October 1947 in Derby, in which the audience gave an enthusiastic welcome to Léon Goossens, the celebrated oboist, John wrote to Rudolf Bing suggesting that as Goossens was a friend of John Christie's and lived near Glyndebourne, 'Rudy' should perhaps telephone him to 'cut out the delay and hazards attendant upon a visit to far-flung provinces at not too near a date, in order to *see* me! (Also this might put me out of *present agony* . . .).' However, in an ambitious programme, the playing of the orchestra had not been altogether happy. Well aware that Glyndebourne would be taking a risk in employing an 'unknown', John cautioned: 'A further reflection which scares me, in an amused way, is that the man who conducts a "Young English" season of *Seraglio* may be putting a halter round his own neck with employers (like John and Audrey and you) who remember Berger and Kern and Kipnis! It's a good job I *don't mind* tilting at windmills . . .'

Rudolf Bing was very uncertain. He felt that John should be seen at work before a decision was taken.

> It is such an enormously important decision for us. I appreciate your 'present agony'. Please do not rely too much on it yet; though all of us are considering you very seriously indeed for this particular job, it is at the moment not more than under serious consideration, and if it should fall through after all I do not want you to be too disappointed. Whatever happens, however, I am fairly certain

that in one way or another you will be working with and for Glyndebourne again.

Berthold Goldschmidt insisted that after stepping in to conduct *Macbeth* in Edinburgh, he should conduct the *Seraglio* at Bath as promised but agreed that John should be his assistant.

Hoping to form a better judgement of John's ability as a conductor, Audrey Christie went with Moran Caplat to Derby to see a performance by the Derby Choral Union of Handel's *Acis and Galatea* and motets from Parry's *Songs of Farewell*. Advising them of travel arrangements John warned: 'Wear wool-next-the-skin; it's ruddy cold in these northern fortresses!'

The King's Hall in which the performance took place, was really the swimming baths with a floor laid over the bath area in the winter for concerts. Cushions were placed on the stone seats at the side of the baths and chairs in the main hall. It prompted John to write to the local paper congratulating the 'Corporation authorities responsible for the King's Hall and also Derby Choral Union on a convincing demonstration of the fact that Derby now has available a good hall for concert purposes. The recent performance at the King's Hall was, in my view, not only satisfying acoustically, but the facilities for chorus, orchestra and audience were excellent. It is the hope of all associated with music in Derby that one day the town may possess a hall designed and built solely for concert purposes but in the meantime the King's Hall seems to be an adequate and commodious venue for large-scale musical events.'

The performance impressed Audrey Christie and Moran Caplat. His position at Glyndebourne thus secured, John relinquished his appointment with the Uttoxeter Choral Society in 1948 with a farewell performance of Haydn's *The Creation*. Afterwards the Society presented him with a travelling bag and leather briefcase and many formal (and informal) expressions of gratitude. A few days later a performance of *The Song of Hiawatha* signalled John's last appearance as the regular conductor of the Derby Choral Union.

Retaining a loyalty to Leslie Smart and the Derby String Orchestra, John continued to work as Music Director with the Derbyshire Education Committee at their residential weekend orchestral courses in different centres in the Midlands. Throughout his life John liked teaching young people. Again and again people attest to the way that John saw latent talent. Even as an established conductor, he was always approachable, looking for a 'spark' in others which he took satisfaction in developing. It was without self-interest and he never sought gratitude.

The orchestra for *Seraglio* at the Bath Festival was to be on a much smaller scale than the usual one which played for Glyndebourne. The Derby String Orchestra had made a good impression on the Glyndebourne management, who saw in them a possible inexpensive nucleus. Making himself indispensable to Moran Caplat, for whom, as with any good administrator, financial considerations were essential, John suggested on 1st December 1947:

> I think, you know, if you were to give me *ten days* I could get together (on paper, of course!) an orchestra of moderate cost from the younger but excellent players of whom I know dozens in London. I know their abilities and adaptability, and in such a matter I would be quite impartial. To take one example, I know a young fellow (was *third* cellist in *Orfeo* orchestra), who would jump at going if he were offered principal cello, with its little bits of solo, etc! And his fee would be moderate because of the opportunity it gives him. Now I can without trouble think of at least twenty similar cases. If we were to get these people we would have a FIRST-CLASS orchestra, alive with keenness – that rare quality in orchestral players!

Replying the next day, Moran Caplat cautioned:

> The first thing I need to know is its cost and both ourselves and Berthold would need to see a list of names and perhaps even hear one or two of the players before they are accepted. It will have to be worked out which of these plans would be the less expensive (if they were London players it would be cheaper). We could then probably further reduce the overall cost by letting the orchestra play for two Serenade concerts in the Pump Room during the second week on days when there is no opera performance. If these concerts are arranged I feel sure that we should be able to consider your conducting them.

In casting, John praised Richard Lewis whom he had heard recently 'excellent as Grimes' but was hesitant to recommend for the role of Constanze, a close friend whom he had accompanied at the Wigmore Hall. 'This is not the sort of voice to which I personally enjoy listening, but I can quite see she might do vocally for the part. But would the producer like her "type" for the role? I always think of Constanze as tall and dignified!'

While Audrey Christie was involved primarily in choosing the soloists, John was delegated to audition singers for the chorus. Explaining to those not interested in chorus work that the performances of *Seraglio* were designed for them to gain experience he promised that they would endeavour to find as many understudies and small parts as possible from the chorus.

John signed his contract for the productions of *Don Giovanni* and *Così fan Tutte* for the 1948 Edinburgh Festival. The fee of £25 was to cover all preliminary work, including the selection of the chorus, with Glyndebourne paying travel expenses incurred in attending auditions. The question as to whether he should appear on the programme as Chorus Master was left in abeyance 'until the personnel of the musical staff are quite settled. We feel sure you will understand this.'

John's auditions 'revealed an exciting find', Norma Procter, a young contralto pupil of Roy Henderson. 'She looks nice, and sings like an embryo Ferrier.' However, 'contraltos and tenors are the immediate problem: as a general rule I am against large-scale recruitment of tenors from the Welsh – I believe you have had applications – but it rather depends how many applicants we encounter in remaining auditions', and later, in May when the opera was imminent: 'I doubt whether we shall be able to hold any more official auditions for a while, until Nature's supplies of tenors, contraltos and basses pile up on the supply lines.' When one of the tenors in the chorus received an offer of a musical comedy engagement and wished to be released from his contract, John showed his exasperation: 'I don't quite know – there is no other possible or even impossible tenor in the lists, those that are there are almost imaginary they are so bad! I think we ought to ask M—. He should be possible vocally, so the only remaining thing is how does he *look*? If he is impossibly tall or fat we cannot do with him as Mozart does not permit these untidinesses . . .'

Coaching the singers, John acted as assistant to Berthold Goldschmidt for *Seraglio* at the first Bath Festival in 1948, writing to him afterwards. 'I was so sorry to miss you after the performance on Saturday. I had not realised that you were returning immediately to London or I would have come to your dressing-room sooner. You helped me very much in broadening my experience. I was full of admiration for the subtlety and imagination in your approach to the music. Sorry we shall not be together in Edinburgh. I only hope that again before very long, I may be your lieutenant.'

In July 1948, after the Bath Festival, John and Harold Chapin went on holiday together to Cadgwith, a picturesque Cornish fishing village. Staying in a modern bungalow with a 'fine view of the sea' they explored the area, seeing 'all the *colours* of rock and sea for which Cornwall is famous. Saw Landewednack Church [*sic*] (the most southerly in England. Norman porch containing a perpendicular doorway).' Telephoning Leeds he was very disappointed to learn that he was not on the short list for a Conductor's Scholarship and would not be required for an audition. Consoling himself, he and Harold walked to Kynance Bay to see Land's End in the distance. It was on this holiday that John purchased a beret. He was to sport this and other headgear throughout his life. Later it was to hide his receding hairline and finally to keep his toupee in place.

Even on holiday John's thoughts were on *Don Giovanni* planned for the coming Edinburgh season.

DIARY ENTRY:
Thursday 8th July Quiet day, listened to *Don Giovanni* records with full score in morning. Afternoon found a quiet cove where we lazed in the sun. I clambered on the rocks in my pants and paddled in the pools.

Friday 9th July (Returned to London). On Wednesday night I had a long, frank talk with Harold, warning him of my *exact* feelings where our relationship was concerned. Pointed out danger of an emotional liaison which is less intense on my side than on his – every holiday, every happy day makes any later break initiated by me harder for him to bear. I am not, I told him clearly, in a position where living together in my flat would be *anything like* equivalent to what he, in heart of heart, intends. He is very sweet – at least he (for a time) will remember my words. But he is so quietly determined. Watch it! . . .

Saturday 10th July Lunch at Brownings. Tea at Waldorf, then to Savoy Theatre. (Kay) Kendall, (Hermione) Gingold review *A La Carte* goodish. One act was Marcel le Bon, easily the most perfectly handsome man I have ever seen. Supper at Leoni's.

Sunday 11th July Mass at Oratory with M. King. Travelled to Glyndebourne.

Glyndebourne was in financial difficulties. Unable to perform opera that year in Sussex they concentrated on the second

Edinburgh Festival of 1948. It was felt essential to have an international name who would *want* to conduct the planned *Don Giovanni*. Rafael Kubelík had just fled from Prague. Although a conductor of stature, he had not had any experience as an opera conductor. The approach to him was to prove of mutual benefit. John commented in his diary, 'Rafael Kubelík looks a really fine man, he carries artistry in his eyes and his long hands.'

Hoping to entice Sir Thomas Beecham to conduct in future years either in Sussex or Edinburgh and having had problems previously with the Scottish Orchestra, Glyndebourne engaged Sir Thomas' orchestra, the Royal Philharmonic. They became the resident orchestra at Glyndebourne until the mid-sixties. Whilst opera at Glyndebourne itself was not financially possible, concerts were arranged with Sir Thomas conducting.

> DIARY ENTRY:
> *Wednesday 14th July* First day of Mozart Festival – lecture by Sir Thomas Beecham in afternoon. Princess Margaret present and some wonderful performances in the evening including the 'Haffner' Symphony.
> *Thursday 15th July* Henry Holst with the quartet at Glyndebourne – played the G minor quintet. Had tea in the house with the Christies. Playing in the Organ Room when Sir Thomas came through. I introduced myself.

In the early years after the war there were very few British singers experienced enough to sing major roles. A time of 'rebuilding', Glyndebourne was searching the country for any possible young people for the chorus who might develop into soloists. As the season only spanned a few weeks during their summer recess, it suited young singers in their final years at the Music Colleges. The ability to find young talent was to remain with John throughout his life. The experience of John Dobson, who has been singing at Covent Garden for many years, is only one example.

Leslie Smart thought that John Dobson, who had sung at the Derby Music Club, should sing for John and arranged for the young man, still at school, to do so. John Dobson recalled: 'John (Pritchard) actually coached me for my audition at the music colleges. Indeed he went with me to Birmingham, accompanying at my audition. He was so very kind. In 1950 he took me into the Glyndebourne chorus.'

Glyndebourne auditions were held in the Dinely Studios, a hall off the Marylebone Road and the Wigmore Hall, London. Encouraged by Harold Chapin, John moved his home to London, staying with either Leslie Smart or Connie Williams (Pemberton), the soprano, when he travelled north. John had experienced the pleasure of normal family life with Leslie Smart and the people of Derby. Now, as his horizons widened, he began to develop a new circle of friends drawn from his career. Life in the capital, particularly the theatre, became more attractive.

Regarding her with great affection John referred always in his diary to Moran Caplat's secretary, Janet Moores, as 'the dear Janet'. When she wrote to him on 26th October 1950 asking how to reply to a letter, she reminded John of his audition report: 'He has been singing small parts with Vere Laurie's troupe and Carl Rosa. An ox-like bass whom I can do without, poor chap.' John suggested:

> Dear Mr ABC
> Your letter of the 20th Oct has been passed to me and I am bound to say that in accordance with our invariable rule I am unable to give you any detailed opinion on your singing. I can only say that my report to the Glyndebourne Management was to the effect that you were unsuitable for Mozart chorus work.
>
> > Yours truly
>
> > W A Mozart [Facsimile signature]
> > Chorus Master
> Perhaps you will have this typed and sign it in my absence.

The suggestion was accepted:

> Dear Herr Mozart!
> Thank you for your note about Mr ABC. I will send the appropriate reply on your behalf.
> Kind regards,
>
> > Yours ever,
> > Janet

The only work available to a young British singer was at Sadlers Wells, the new company at Covent Garden Opera, the D'Oyly Carte which performed Gilbert and Sullivan, the Carl Rosa Opera Company and the Glyndebourne Festival. Although a number of distinguished musicians began their career at the Cambridge Theatre under Jay Pomeroy, its history was short-lived. Pomeroy had had discussions with John Christie to collaborate and at one time endeavoured to secure the lease of Covent Garden for himself. John was always grateful to Pomeroy as he saw his first *Barber of Seville* conducted by Alberto Erede at the Cambridge Theatre, in which the young Ian Wallace sang Dr Bartolo. Later when Wallace sang in *Rigoletto*, the director was Carl Ebert who invited him to Glyndebourne.

It is believed that Glyndebourne was the first 'House' in the United Kingdom to take appearance and acting ability into consideration when choosing a chorus. Now, a major House, when planning an opera, usually starts with the conductor and producer, 'stars' and major roles. After the war Glyndebourne was working in the opposite manner by choosing a chorus from whom soloists for small roles could be chosen and later, with nurturing, understudy and develop into major roles. The names of those who started their careers in the chorus at Glyndebourne reads like a roll call of honour. Gradually, under John the Glyndebourne chorus did not have or need any students. Considered by young singers as the 'plum' job, by the mid-fifties they were all mature singers, many of whom would not have agreed to be in any other chorus. They were always noticed and when a small part was available, Glyndebourne always seemed to choose the right person, which is how singers such as Dame Janet Baker were given their chance.

She recalled her earliest collaborations with John at Glyndebourne when she was in the chorus. 'We used to do things like "Ingestre Opera" and in 1958 I was singing the second witch in *Dido* there. John Pritchard was conducting and Anthony Besch (Moran Caplat's assistant) was producing. I remember we all went over by train from Crewe to rehearse at Liverpool. John was working with the Liverpool Philharmonic and couldn't get down to Sussex.' She remembers sitting in a carriage with the chorus people, memorising her understudy role, a piece by Rossini, for the following season at Glyndebourne:

> The rest of the chorus were chattering away; one girl was even 'doing' her nails. Anthony Besch came into the carriage. In his quiet way he noticed everything. The following summer I was hauled out of a chorus rehearsal to go on stage. Someone was sick and couldn't take part in the rehearsal that morning. I thanked my lucky stars that I had been working that day on the journey from Crewe to Liverpool and had learnt the part. I was really small fry as the second

witch but John made one feel that, OK you're a young beginner but nevertheless a very important, integral part of the whole and that it would be your turn next. Of course, we were all convinced of that! We were plunged into working with great personalities at a very vulnerable age. John was firm of course but nevertheless his tremendous kindness and warmth warmed the heart. He brought out the best in people with his bonhomie, charm and generosity, the expansion of personality which was absolutely him. A soloist puts a narrow beam of light onto the music but the conductor must shed it over the whole. It was this expansiveness of nature which he had to the utmost degree.

Dame Janet recalled that John prepared his work meticulously. There was not an unimportant bar or an unimportant person and this philosophy has remained with her. 'Wherever one goes one doesn't pass up an opportunity because it's too small.'

Rehearsals for the chorus would begin in the Dinely Studios and then the group would go to Sussex. At that time, most of the men were married and commuted daily. It was a long day as rehearsals began at 10am and often they would not be free to return home until midnight. Others would take digs in Lewes. They were supposed to have a day free but this was rare, especially if they were understudying or had a small part as well. The young singers seldom complained. They were aware of the tremendous competition for the very few jobs that were available but there was always a good atmosphere in the dressing-room which contributed to their performance. They were paid £7.50 per week during rehearsals and £9 during performances. If the opera was broadcast, they received an extra £1. When, later, there were televised performances, they were paid £12 extra which was considered a fortune.

One particular chorus member paid tribute to John:

Absolutely the tops! He would go on and on working with us. He was a very inspiring chorus master. After sight-reading a new opera, John would take the sopranos through their parts, then the altos and finally the tenors. Then we would all work together. He always gave us enough time. Even the slowest sight-readers were sure of the music by the time we reached the stage rehearsal. With John we had to do the words and the music together. They didn't have any amateurs and the sort of people who sing in the big choirs weren't there. A very high standard was expected from everybody and everybody gave their all. He kept himself slightly aloof and we had an immense respect for him.

In 1949 due to the lack of money, the summer season, as in 1948, was to be a series of weekend concerts conducted by Sir Thomas Beecham. John was fully involved in their planning, whilst also rehearsing *Così fan Tutte* and *Ballo in Maschera* for that summer's Edinburgh Festival.

Endeavouring to save a complete week of chorus salaries and fares, which is no small item, Moran Caplat did not want the chorus to arrive at Glyndebourne earlier than necessary. Whilst appreciating the possibility of saving money, John was at first sight a little anxious in view of the big demands of *Ballo* on the chorus. He felt that a chorus which was grimly clutching its music would not be of much use to the Producer.

> I may say I have little confidence in the 'learning beforehand' of *most* chorus members! I should say this preparation, except by the most conscientious, is confined to the first journey between Victoria and Lewes. Moreover until they know 'how the music sounds' most of them lack the musicianship to do much practical preparation. If it is possible to stress any particular aspect in your contractual exhortation (blimey!) it is most useful if they are facile in the pronunciation of the Italian *words*: a great deal of time is saved if they just say the words through to themselves several times beforehand.

At the Beecham concert on 26th June, Brahms' Songs for Female Chorus with Accompaniment of Two Horns and Harp op. 17, was sung by a selection of the Glyndebourne Festival Chorus. On his copy of the programme, John wrote 'conducted by John Pritchard at the invitation of Sir Thomas Beecham'.

During the final rehearsal, Sir Thomas had walked in and stood watching quietly. At the concert, after conducting the first item of the programme, he turned to the audience and announced that he would leave the rostrum to their 'great advantage'. 'The excellence of the choral work you are about to hear,' he said, 'is entirely due to Mr Pritchard's coaching and therefore he should conduct it. John Pritchard is staff conductor and chorus master of Glyndebourne and has done a lot of good work here. He has rehearsed this work for me and if you like the performance – and I am sure you will – it is to his credit.' During the performance he sat in the wings and afterwards congratulated the young man.

The 1949 Edinburgh Festival was quite remarkable for the orchestras and artists engaged. A *frisson* went through the city at the programme: Sir Thomas Beecham conducting the Royal Philharmonic in the Usher Hall, the Busch [Adolf]/Serkin Quintet, perhaps the most famous of its time, Kathleen Ferrier accompanied by Bruno Walter in recital, Rafael Kubelík, Ernest Ansermet, Sir John Barbirolli conducting the Berlin Philharmonic Orchestra and many others of the same calibre. T S Eliot's play *The Cocktail Party* had its world première at the Lyceum Theatre. The inhabitants of Edinburgh could not believe that all these famous people were in their city. There were receptions in the City Chambers for every visiting company and daily press conferences in the Assembly Rooms in George Street. Literary people like Eric Linklater would hold parties to which all were invited. There was the feeling that everything had to be of the best.

When the Glyndebourne company arrived, Ian Wallace, wearing a kilt, welcomed their train. John remembered going with Ian and some of the singers from that year's *Ballo in Maschera* production, to perform in the wards of the City Hospital. Ian brought his ukulele and sang one of his own compositions in his best George Formby style.

Edinburgh gave John the opportunity to listen to music-making and to meet and mix with musicians at the highest level. Working at the Festival in 1950 as Beecham's assistant for Strauss' *Ariadne* (with *Le Bourgeois Gentilhomme* preface), he learnt a great deal from watching the great conductor rehearse. Through the years, developing his own style, John understood how to charm his musicians with the same drawling wit, a kind of ridiculous fantasy. Many misunderstood this, presuming it to be simply a surface attitude, however it was far from superficial. Even when John was not convinced by the music he needed to conduct, in his total understanding of what a work was about, he would persuade the musicians to perform to his conception – without their realising it. He was impressed by the older man's lifestyle; impressed by the independence the conductor had from his profession to sustain himself very comfortably. When he had accompanied a chorus member, April Cantelo, to audition for the part of Echo in *Ariadne*, he noted in his diary:

1950 24th April . . . to see Sir Thomas Beecham in his apartment at Grosvenor House – very comfortable. He was very agreeable. Heard April Cantelo sing and approved her for Echo. Gave me a lift after in his Rolls! Evening – German with Eva.

In recalling the tour of Africa, Yfrah Neaman asked: 'How does a celebrity behave?' More important for John at this juncture was the question, 'how does a young man, accepted as an accomplished accompanist and repetiteur, as a conductor of a semi-professional string orchestra and accepted as Chorus Master at Glyndebourne gain the experience necessary to be regarded as an opera house conductor?' It was a Derby citizen, Alan Turner, who gave him this opportunity.

Many of the young singers recruited for the Glyndebourne chorus had sung with John in Derby with the Alan Turner Opera and Ballet Company, a part of the Welfare Organisation of the Ernest Turner group of Companies existing solely as a charitable and educational society. Alan Turner had a large factory, Spa Lane Mills, from which he would organise spectacular Viennese operetta which he himself would produce and direct at the Grand Theatre, Derby. His large house set well back on the road from Derby to Belper had a recording studio. Not really interested in music but in the town and being an impresario, a 'showman' in the old-fashioned sense, he involved everyone, even choreographing some of the dances himself. The Augmented Theatre Orchestra led by Louise Atherton (leader of the Derby String Orchestra) and conducted by John, gave performances spanning two weeks, of operettas such as *A Thousand and One Nights* (March 1946), *The Queen's Lace Handkerchief* (March 1947), *Die Fledermaus* and *Chu Chin Chow* (March 1949).

For the second act of *Chu Chin Chow*, Turner arranged for a potter from The Royal Crown Derby Porcelain Works to be on stage with his wheel. There was even an elephant and camel, by courtesy of Chessington Zoo, in the performance. One evening walking through the dark passage beside the theatre leading to the stage door, John fell over what he thought was a cannonball. It was elephant dung. Those who saw him immediately afterwards can attest to his ability to swear!

On a train journey Roy Henderson had suggested that he apply to Glyndebourne, now it was another train journey, this time to London in the company of Alan Turner that was instrumental in John's career. Turner introduced him to his cousin, Sir William Walton, who was on the Board of the recently re-formed Covent Garden Opera Company, resulting in a letter to David Webster, the Administrator.

'Mr John Pritchard, Glyndebourne, Sussex'

41 Gloucester Walk
London W.8.

Dear Mr Webster   3rd November 1949
Just before William Walton left to go abroad he dropped me a note
to suggest that on your return from America I should get in touch
with you – I hope you had an enjoyable trip.

I am wondering whether Mr Walton may have mentioned to you
an earlier casual conversation about Covent Garden, which he and I
had: but in any case I would appreciate it if you could find time to
see me for a few minutes with him in the next week or so?

Actually I am rehearsing in Scotland for a few days next week but
shall be back in London after that for a while, and if you have a free
moment I could call at your office.
With kind regards,

Yours sincerely,
John Pritchard

As Covent Garden was in the middle of production rehearsals
for *Salomé*, David Webster's secretary asked John to telephone
some time in the future for an appointment. John persisted.
After a telephone call he wrote again on 4th December 1949 to
David Webster's secretary.

I seem to be now (for the next few weeks), very much away from
London and I think the best thing would be if I give *you* my free
dates, as I am far too well brought-up to write to Mr Webster direct
saying 'Can you see me on the — when I have some free time!' I am
available then on Wed. or Thurs. of this week, or Friday morning
9th. On Wednesday 14th, Thurs. 15th or Friday 16th. After that I
expect things will be getting fairly rushed for all of us so I will not
suggest other dates unless *none* of the foregoing are possible. As I
mentioned to you there is no particular urgency about this interview
but I heard from William Walton and he reminded me I should go
and see Mr Webster when possible. Perhaps you could drop me a
short note?

John was seen on 23rd December and taken on as an accompanist
and repetiteur. 'Pianist' was scribbled in pencil across his file at
Covent Garden. In his letter John had mentioned that he was
'very much away from London'. He was rehearsing in Glasgow,
his first opportunity to conduct opera.

Originally Moira Meighan came across John at Glyndebourne
where she used to attend rehearsals. Her father was President
of the Glasgow Grand Opera Society and she acted as assistant

manager. She asked John to come to the 'Grand' to conduct *The Pearl Fishers* and *Carmen* in 1950, the first operatic productions which he planned on his own.

Like the majority of music societies at the time, the Glasgow Grand Opera Society was run by amateurs as a labour of love. This entailed considerable input by either the conductor or producer, usually the only professional involved. The organisation, an intimate knowledge of what putting on an opera required, was very time-consuming. John's 1949 diary bears testimony to his detailed planning.

Most of the principal roles were cast from singers in the Glasgow region but Moira Meighan remembered that she had asked John to bring the Leila (the soprano in *The Pearl Fishers*) who did not come up to expectations. 'In *The Pearl Fishers*, there are so many difficult starts that she has to make. It was quite ghastly, just unbelievably bad. He was worried about it and so was I because we were paying a very substantial fee to the young lady!' In addition, he was very nervous with the Scottish Orchestra as well as the thought of battling with an amateur chorus of ninety.

During the summer and following winter months John suffered from a glandular problem and became seriously overweight, irritable and depressed, necessitating injections from his doctor. Consequently during the rehearsal period Moira Meighan found John 'a bit temperamental, a little difficult at times. One night, someone came and said "Mr Pritchard's left".' In a fit of pique John had walked out. 'Putting on my coat I went to find him. There were three cafés nearby and I found him in the last one, drinking coffee. "Come on, John," I said. "These people have been working all day and they're amateurs." With a little persuasion he came back.' On another occasion he would not get up and come to rehearsal. The dress rehearsal was a near disaster. 'Taking him some tea, John said to me, "I don't know who you would pray to Moira but I must pray to St Jude." "Who's St Jude?" I asked. "St Jude the hopeless!" he replied. So we did that. In the end it went very well. St Jude must have heard him!'

In his misery John wrote to Moran Caplat from Glasgow on 19th January 1950.

During January I have spent most of my time twixt Glasgow and Derby and now of course the Operas are proceeding to a decisive stage(!), which means that Sumner Austin (producer) and I will spend the whole of Feb. rehearsing every evening in this miserable city. After Edinburgh I find Glasgow extremely *unsympathetic*, too big, too industrial, too serious, without any of the graces of civilisation . . . As for the Opera Society itself, it is a curious mixture of strange ability, prejudiced yet progressive management, and rather touching dependence on its conductor. The advantage from *my* point of view is that I am able to be a little dictator on every artistic question and can really feel *responsible* (technical limitations aside) for whatever results may be achieved. Sumner Austin seems to be very smoothly experienced and imperturbable, but a bit inclined to uniform chorus action (Ladies of the Chorus, hands on breasts . . . PLACE!).

I'm a little concerned about the supplementary (amateur) chorus for Edinburgh. I have been hearing one or two singers in Edinburgh, without noticing much talent. Some of the Glasgow Grand Opera chorus girls are fairly good-looking, and we might easily do worse than import a few chosen specimens in the sopranos and contraltos.

In the week following March 11th we do a studio performance of *Pearl Fishers* (delightful score) for the BBC (Scottish), then I come back to London like a bat out of hell, to rehearse *Serva Padrona* and the David Harris translated *Canterina* of Haydn (*that's* a new one for you – *and* me!). These are being done on the Third at Easter time twice and I'm rather thrilled at being asked to do them with the Boyd Neal.

Have you any idea what duties you will be wanting me to carry out this year at Glyndebourne and Edinburgh? Is the label of Assistant Conductor too difficult of an achievement, I wonder? No doubt however we can *talk* this over in the coming by and by! Spare a thought now and again for your hardly consolable musical lieutenant in the frozen fastnesses (closing time 9.30pm) of the North.

The Pearl Fishers, performed in English, was thought not to have been staged in Britain since the 1924 Covent Garden season. All the music had to be brought over from France and a special translation made for the occasion with every word written painstakingly into each score. Obviously it was a very big undertaking as the company made all their own costumes. The scenery was painted by different artists including Sir Harry (Jefferson) Barnes and some of the students from the art school. Chorus members were expected to sell the tickets. The rarity of a performance of Bizet's early work attracted the attention of the critics, including *Opera* magazine. Excerpts were broadcast from the large studio at Broadcasting House, Glasgow, which was listened to eagerly by John's parents, who never missed his broadcasts.

The other Bizet opera, *Carmen*, was received with great enthusiasm, the music seldom failing to please. Critics praised the chorus work in particular and one remarked that 'the conductor never allowed the large orchestra to play too loudly, and co-operation between singers and players was gratifying'. John always loved the sheer vitality of the music of *Carmen*.

During rehearsals in Glasgow, John was commuting between there and Derby, preparing the Derby String Orchestra for its London debut at the Wigmore Hall on 21st January 1950, celebrating six years since their formation. Leslie Smart declared: 'The intention is to try to show something of what can be achieved by amateurs working "con amore" and willingly co-operating with their professional colleagues in the application of high standards.'

They began with Respighi's *Antiche Danze ed Arie* (sixteenth and seventeenth century) followed by the Adagio from Mozart's Divertimento no. 15 K287. Olga Hegedus was the soloist in the Boccherini B flat cello concerto. The orchestra attracted the critics' attention with the first performance of Divertimento for Strings by the 24-year-old Arthur Oldham, who had studied privately with Benjamin Britten. They ended their programme with Bartók's *Rumanian Folkdances* (arr. Arthur Willner). Almost prevented from conducting by an attack of 'flu, John was praised for the clear lead given to all players and reminded one critic of Sir Adrian Boult's remark that 'a good conductor always gives one the feeling of having a vast score spread out in front of one'. For their first assault on the capital, a group of about twenty supporters travelled with the players. Together with some neighbours, John's mother came from Gravesend for the event. The concert was well attended as the orchestra had become known through broadcasting.

November 1946 was a very important date for British music as it was the start of a music channel called the Third Programme on BBC radio and broadcasting became important for those musicians who did not belong to symphony orchestras. The BBC had a small house orchestra primarily for baroque music which became known as the Goldsborough Orchestra. Although not necessarily regular engagements, radio broadcasting in the years between 1947 to 1954 created a great deal of work for small orchestras. However, by the late fifties and early sixties, they realised that it was the end of a wonderful era because now money would be spent on television.

Every small orchestra is run by an ambitious young conductor with players from his own particular circle. There are many young people who start groups but there are very few like John, who are good enough to keep a fine nucleus of players around them and the ensembles which survive and flourish often do so because they are the most reliable.

Working at Glyndebourne and with the opportunity to watch great conductors at Edinburgh, John was beginning to develop his technique. How one conducts is very much a physical thing and has been likened to the co-ordination needed to drive a car. It is speed of thought in *directing* an orchestra rather than *acknowledging* that the musicians have 'come in' correctly that is important. However it was John's natural musicianship, his sense of rhythm and above all tempi, together with the fine rapport he established with the players with whom he worked, that set him above others. Problems arose because he knew so much intuitively himself that sometimes he did not appreciate that others were slower and without his understanding.

Although the Derby String Orchestra was composed predominantly of amateur musicians, it was able to compete successfully with other small orchestras in the field of broadcasting. Working for the Midland Regional Service since 1946 they became known to the London Music Department of the BBC. Usually programming came from the BBC but there was always a period of consultation so that John had the opportunity to suggest works. Having received a letter of congratulation from Berthold Goldschmidt for his broadcast with the Goldsborough Orchestra of Britten's *Variation on a Theme by Frank Bridge*, he replied effusively on 2nd October 1951 from St Ives, Cornwall. 'Your letter has just reached me away on holiday and I am absolutely delighted that in a busy life you found time to write me such a wonderful appreciation of the recent broadcast. You know *how much* such highly informed and critical comment is valued and from you who in a way started me on my career and gave me early encouragement I regard it as a *special* honour. I do hope we may meet again soon in London – meanwhile my best regards also to Mrs Goldschmidt.'

The first performance on 27th April 1949 outside London of Strauss' extensive but relatively unknown, symphonic work *Metamorphosen*, was an ambitious undertaking for the Derby Orchestra and attracted widespread attention, eliciting a letter from Sir John Barbirolli.

> I was most interested to hear from you that the Derby String Orchestra proposes to give a special performance of Strauss' *Metamorphosen* on April 27th, and I should like to congratulate you on your enterprise and enthusiasm in bringing this about.
> It also speaks highly for the standard of your players that they are able to tackle this difficult but extremely beautiful work and you and they will have my warmest good wishes for a great and well deserved success.

A deeply moving account, in musical terms, of the strife and destruction of Strauss' material and spiritual home, with the words 'In Memoriam' on the last page of the score, the work affected John, draining him emotionally.

During the forties and fifties the business side of music was much more casual than it is today; far less contractual. Exclusivity, which arose through recording contracts, did not exist. John would broadcast with the Derby String Orchestra one day and the Boyd Neal Orchestra the next.

After the war the Jacques Orchestra was one of the most important of the small orchestras. Founded in 1936 by Dr Reginald Jacques, who also conducted the Bach Choir, it was recognised as part of the music 'establishment'. On Good Friday at Glyndebourne the Jacques would play for performances of Bach's *St Matthew Passion*. Not only broadcasting regularly, the orchestra had also made a number of records. Besides a heavy touring schedule, the Jacques shared Summer Serenade Concerts with the New London Orchestra in the William III Orangery at Hampton Court Palace and in 1950 planned to inaugurate a similar series of Sunday evening garden concerts at the Victoria & Albert Museum. The Wigmore Hall was not neglected as a venue either. The Royal Festival Hall and the Queen Elizabeth Hall did not exist yet and a setting such as Hampton Court Palace was a marvellous place to be on a summer evening. Whatever was programmed it was sure of an audience. Nowadays with high insurance and other costs, a regular series of concerts at such a venue would not be deemed financially viable.

'Mr John Pritchard, Glyndebourne, Sussex'

John Denison, who had been at the Arts Council since 1948, attended the Derby String Orchestra concert, conducted by John, at the Wigmore Hall. When he heard that Dr Jacques was being forced by his medical advisors to resign as Director of his Orchestra he spoke to Lord Dudley Gordon, the Chairman of the Board. The wheels were set in motion for John's appointment.

DIARY ENTRY:

1950 Wednesday 26th April evening Had a talk with John Denison – who sounded me out about the conductorship of the Jacques Orchestra. Exciting!

Monday May 15th Had long conversation with Dr Jacques at the Athenaeum for lunch and afterwards saw Miss Collier at the Jacques Orchestra. It seems they really want me to take over but I will conduct a Hampton Court programme first.

Although unable to cope with the strain of touring, Dr Jacques continued as Director of the Bach Choir, the Cantata Singers and as a guest conductor.

One can imagine the pride which John's mother felt as she sat in the surroundings of Hampton Court Palace on 17th June 1950 watching her son. She would stay at Eddie and Win's home in Chingford whenever he conducted in London. For Christmas John gave his father a 'musician's diary' and he proudly recorded on the flyleaf (1950): 'This diary was a present from son "John" of Kensington.' For Amy's seventieth birthday the following year, Eddie, John and Stanley Shaylor bought a 'wireless cabinet' to enable the old couple to listen to broadcasts of John's concerts at home. With Eddie's help they moved to an unfurnished apartment in Gravesend for 14s.7d a week.

Inevitably, with increasing commitments elsewhere, the time which John could give to the Derby Orchestra was limited and an associate conductor, H C Burgess, was appointed. He acknowledged his debt to Derby by putting the String Orchestra first in his *Who's Who* entry. Now, with his appointment to the Jacques, his work focused on the south of England.

With the Jacques Orchestra and the help of the audience, Preston Manor County School in Wembley presented the first amateur performances of Britten's *Let's Make an Opera* and *The Little Sweep* in December 1950 in the school hall. With the experience gained in the Derby Educational Courses, by tact and his personality, John was able to persuade the children and audience to respond to the music.

The Jacques played at the Scala Theatre for the London Opera Club which presented works outside the standard repertoire. Perhaps it was his experience there in performances of the Haydn opera *Il Mondo della Luna* on the 8th and 10th November 1951 with the Kalmar Orchestra that convinced him that despite the good humour and lightness of touch in the music that often foreshadows Mozart, Haydn was not a composer for the theatre. When John was Music Director at Glyndebourne no opera by Haydn was played.

As with most groups, musicians on tour develop a bond of friendship, so within a short time John gained the Jacques players' respect. He appointed as leader someone whose musicianship he could trust. Emanuel Hurwitz had been playing in the Boyd Neal Orchestra as their second leader and John tempted him to the Jacques with the promise of 'doing some interesting work together that might be very fruitful artistically for both of us'. John's appointment was short-lived as Dr Jacques soon felt sufficiently recovered to conduct again and John became more involved at Covent Garden and Glyndebourne.

John did not remain Chorus Master at Glyndebourne for long because with the return of the famous conductor Fritz Busch to Sussex in 1950, he was not only Chorus Master but designated Assistant Conductor. A chorus member recalled: 'With the arrival of Fritz Busch we seldom saw John socially any more as he was always with Busch and he was never Chorus Master in the same way again.'

Fritz Busch had been Music Director in Dresden which had an exceptional orchestra and very good singers. As well as conducting Mozart he had brought about a great Verdi revival. In 1932 – 33 Carl Ebert asked him to do *Ballo in Maschera* in Berlin. The production caused such a sensation in the music world that the *Frankfurter Illustrated*, a weekly paper, dedicated an entire issue to it. Their successful collaboration persuaded the two men to do more work together; that marvellous things could come out of their association. However, the arrival of Hitler on the political scene changed matters. Even though Busch was not Jewish, the Nazis attending a performance in the Dresden Opera House shouted at him because he was not a Nazi. He put down his baton and walked out, advising his Jewish friends to do likewise. He would say, 'I have read *Mein Kampf*, have you?' When she heard what had happened, Mrs Curtis, a headmistress in London, wrote to Busch asking if his children would like to come to her school. In this way, in 1934 – 35, Busch first came to Glyndebourne, where he established a level of quality in music-making. Later, with the threat of war, Mrs Curtis moved her school from London to the Glyndebourne area.

In addition, Busch was working at the Teatro Colón in Buenos Aires which was regarded as a Wagnerian house and decided to take his family to New York which he used as his base throughout the war. In 1948 he had a slight heart attack and collapsed but people were told he had a very bad 'flu. Wrapped up in bed, playing card games such as rummy, only his closest family and secretary, Ellen Morgenthau, knew the serious nature of his 'flu. John was to adopt the same professional attitude during his own fatal illness. Asked to return to Glyndebourne, Fritz Busch flew to London for the 1950 season.

4

The Eingeweihten

1950 was a turning point in the fortunes of Glyndebourne. Not only was the company going to appear in Edinburgh but, with the support and generosity of the John Lewis Partnership, opera was to be performed in Sussex. Assistance too came in a practical form from Miki Sekers who had come to Britain from Hungary just before the war.

One of a number of young men whom the Nuffield Trust persuaded to open their own factory with a government loan, his mill had the most modern looms in Britain. When pure silk ran out shortly after the war started, he devised a method of using nylon, previously used only for bristles and toothbrushes so that it could be made into parachutes. Lady Agi Sekers recalled her husband as 'a sort of "stage-door johnny". It was a privilege for him to do anything for the theatre.' They took a cottage quite close to Glyndebourne, a considerable distance from their West Cumberland home and became very friendly with the Christies.

On the Continent her husband had seen a programme with expensive advertisements in order to support an artistic endeavour. It was Miki (Sir Nicholas) Sekers' suggestion to charge firms about £100 a page to appear in the Programme Book, which was a great deal of money in those days. It seems completely trite now to talk of 'Friends of Something' but it was also his idea to form the Glyndebourne Festival Society. 'We used to give very expensive lunch parties and have what we thought was "la crème de la crème", the sort of people who might be likely to support Glyndebourne. Oliver Messel gave Louis XIV banquets with exotic flowers decorating the tables; wonderful lunch parties, which cost far more than any of the money that was raised! It was Miki Sekers too who supplied most of the materials for costumes at Glyndebourne and Covent Garden at a time when shortages were still the order of the day. 'This was the period when John came onto the scene.'

Looking forward to the arrival of Fritz Busch, Moran Caplat wrote to him on 20th January 1950: 'Regarding Musical Staff, Jani Strasser is still with us . . . and we have another young English coach named John Pritchard, who has been with us ever since the war and who is doing very well; I am sure you will like him . . .' and again on 29th March 1950; 'John Pritchard knows *Così* very well, although he has not, unfortunately, done it with you. However, he has studied your records and I think you may feel satisfied that the earlier preparation in the first week will be along lines that you would approve . . .'

The sensation in the summer of 1950 at Glyndebourne was the *Così fan Tutte* with Sena Jurinac singing Fiordiligi. Having sung Dorabella (mezzo) the previous year, she decided that she would like to sing the soprano part. She and John became great friends. He cherished recorded excerpts of this production.

Taking over the last three performances of Guglielmo from Erich Kunz who had sung the first three, Sir Geraint Evans met John at a *Così* rehearsal. 'He was waiting in the Organ Room at Glyndebourne and we introduced each other. Over rehearsal we got on "like a house on fire". There was an immediate rapport which existed over the years. He was a *very* good pianist.'

Recalling the warm relationship between the conductor and his assistant: 'I shall never forget once when Fritz Busch came into the Organ Room, John was playing and I was singing. Fritz Busch just pushed John off the piano stool and without interruption continued playing, with a little chuckle together, almost as if they were going to play a duet. Fritz Busch saw talent in John who was a singer's delight, a marvellous accompanist and sometimes would ask him to take over the rehearsal.'

John recalled learning from Fritz Busch:

A hundred new and surprising things. Learn, for example, that Mozart of the operas never was pretty even if he might be delicate: that his vein of ardour, of passionate vigour would only be served by playing and singing intensely, not at all by mere precision. Learn that orchestral detail must be made vivid if Mozart's conception of his characters, as revealed in their great arias, was to be made plain in performance. The quality of almost bucolic humour, of masculine directness in Busch's performance, used to keep me, nose in score, in the wings, long after my brief duty to direct an off-stage chorus had been discharged. The rehearsals with the singers were an equal fascination: Busch worked his requirements into their voices with an affectionate eye on the stage portrayals of the character. His infectious love for some particular stage business would be riotously conveyed in an imaginative extravaganza at the piano. He liked playing the piano, had high standards, and at auditions was the terror of repetiteurs who knew perfectly well Busch would be more critical of any weakness in the accompaniment than in the soloist. He continually adjured me to 'play both hands *together*', a thing I had rather imagined I had been doing for years . . .!★

Busch always enjoyed teaching and working with younger, very talented people. Ellen Morgenthau remembered going to the conductor's room at Glyndebourne and Busch saying: 'Go and get that handsome, dark, young man. He is the only one to whom I can talk about this music. He *understands*.' For Busch it was a nucleus of people who saw everything in the same way, on a higher level, with the heart and with the mind; the Eingeweihten, the 'initiated' (*Die Zauberflöte*). He would point at John, 'There goes the Eingeweihten.' Sometimes when John conducted, one realised that he felt that too. Sometimes he did not reach that higher level but the important thing was that he knew it. One can only hope to reach out to that level even if sometimes one hits a different spot.

Ellen Morgenthau felt that Fritz Busch treated John as a younger colleague even though they were in total agreement. 'Perhaps if Busch hadn't died so early in the relationship he might have remained as a protégé considerably longer.' Co-incidentally there are several similarities in their musical background. A fine pianist, Fritz Busch was the son of a violin maker, his teacher, who played in bands in local villages in Westphalia and took his son with him until the younger man went to Riga to become Chorus Master.

Busch was not scheduled to conduct Glyndebourne Opera at Edinburgh that year and went to Denmark to rehearse the Radio Symphony Orchestra for their concerts at the Festival. As the King of Denmark took a personal interest in the Orchestra, he put a ship at their disposal as their hotel. However, the Buschs stayed at the Caledonian Hotel in Edinburgh. The Danes gave

★Taken from an article in the Glyndebourne Programme Book.

two concerts and then Mrs Busch toured the Highlands with them.

Ellen Morgenthau recalled the day when Hans Gal, who was a professor in Edinburgh, came to the hotel and took her and Busch to his home for lunch. 'The flat was dark and sombre with old Viennese furniture. I remember those two at the piano with the score of *Idomeneo*.' After the tumultuous reception in Munich in 1781 of his first major stage work, Mozart had rewritten *Idomeneo* for a concert performance in Vienna. Fritz Busch was forever searching for that concert score and eventually somebody in Vienna found it and gave it to Hans Gal.

Ellen Morgenthau remembers the discussions because Busch felt strongly that the role of Idamante should be sung by a tenor, 'that it was important that the relationship between Idomeneo and his son, Idamante, must sound right. (Originally, it would have been "castrato" singer.) Mrs Gal was such a charming, sweet woman, however I think it was the most spartan lunch I had ever had.' When they returned to the hotel, Busch, who loved his food and wine and was always joking, asked 'How did you like this most fantastic lunch?' Sharing the same dry sense of humour John often said that he learnt almost as much from Busch about fine wine as fine music.

Everybody at Glyndebourne was excited at the possibilities for the season of 1951: opera once more in Sussex with Fritz Busch and Carl Ebert working together again, performances at Edinburgh and hope that this production of *Idomeneo*, the first professional stage performance in Britain, would put Glyndebourne securely on the musical map again.

Idomeneo was first staged on 12th March 1934 in Britain, by the pioneering conductor of the Glasgow Grand Opera Society, Erik Chisholm. The vocal scores and orchestral music were brought from Germany and the English translation was by the Misses Radford of Cornwall. The performance was notable for the use of two tenors in the male roles. A ballet was provided by the Glasgow School of Art.

Whilst *Idomeneo* clearly dominated, planning for the other operas to be performed at both Glyndebourne and Edinburgh was not neglected and Busch wrote to Moran Caplat on 26th November 1950. 'I received your cable telling me of the new arrangement with Edinburgh *Forza* [*del Destino*] and *Don* [*Giovanni*]. I think that *Forza* is a good choice because it has some lively and partly comic situations which are refreshing. Musically the opera is at least on the same high level as *Ballo*, only not as often performed and not as gloomy. *Don* gives me and Ebert more time for preparing and rehearsing *Forza*, as it has been done previously in Glyndebourne.'

Whilst endeavouring to procure whatever material the BBC had used for a recent broadcast, Moran Caplat was not finding it easy to obtain the orchestral material as well as vocal scores of *Idomeneo* in Britain and asked Dr Busch to enquire in Vienna for them. Fully aware of the difficulties in obtaining orchestra and chorus material for the opera, Busch replied from Vienna on 6th October 1950: 'I want you not to worry about it as I am confident that I shall manage to get it. The piano score of *Idomeneo* at Glyndebourne, however, please guard as the rare treasure which it is.' Writing on 17th November from New York after he had gone through the orchestral score, Fritz Busch considered that he had a good impression of the work.

> I am absolutely convinced that together with Ebert we can do an exceptionally good performance and have a sort of sensation if we fulfil all the exacting demands which this work of a genius requires . . . Now as I am catching fire about this opera and the production, I am looking forward with the greatest enthusiasm to perform it. The Mozart 'Ausgabe' published by Breitkopf & Härtel contains a very careful and cleverly written preface by an excellent musician; if Dr Gal cannot get this important score including the preface, I shall copy it and send it to him.

Some months earlier, John had taken Eva with him to the Maida Vale studios of the BBC for rehearsals of the broadcast mentioned by Moran Caplat. Equally excited he wrote in his diary on 18th April 1950: 'What an opera. Was thrilled and in transports of joy. Shall not rest until I have studied the score thoroughly.'

John was involved because Fritz Busch considered that 'the chorus, which plays the main part in this opera, requires at least fifty members' but in order to save expense Moran Caplat wanted to 'engage our special chorus of 24 to 30 and to augment it for *Idomeneo* only with a picked selection of amateur singers from the many active choirs in our area of Sussex'. In appraising the conductor of arrangements, he wrote, 'Jani is no longer at all responsible for selecting the chorus. For the last three years this has been done exclusively by John Pritchard who is so far, God be praised, not a teacher and has no pupils. May I just repeat that all other small parts in the other operas should if possible be cast here. We must keep a fair quota of English singers in all operas.'

Looking forward to the conductor's visit in January, John wrote to Fritz Busch on 14th December 1950:

> I understand from Moran that you would like to hear the chorus and we have made tentative arrangements for a hearing at the Wigmore Hall on January 12th. Actually I feel it is a little difficult to give you an idea of the chorus we shall hope to have, particularly the Verdi chorus, as I am at the moment engaged on a series of auditions with the intention of procuring singers of rather more brilliance than those we have had for the Mozart season and it would be very helpful to me if you would let me know what it is desired to establish at this early chorus audition. For example, we can probably get together those members of last year's Mozart chorus who seemed to be satisfactory and who will wish to join us for next season. Shall I carry on on that basis and, with the addition of any good voices I hear in my December and January auditions, prepare (for example) a chorus from *Macbeth* which you would then be able to hear at the Wigmore Hall? I am also very keen to know all the details of the *Idomeneo* presentation, and doubtless in the intervals of hearing so many singers we shall be able to talk about this.

Writing from Minneapolis on 30th December to Moran Caplat, Fritz Busch asked that John arrange auditions but stressed that they should not interfere with his meeting with Hans Gal on 11th January: 'It is most important that Gal and I will have all material for *Idomeneo*, orchestra material as well, ready to look through at Glyndebourne. I beg you again not to worry about the first-class castings of the principal parts which are still left open. My friends and I are hunting all over the world all the time and the best "animals" will be caught.'

There are differing opinions as to whether the ballet music should be included in performances of *Idomeneo*. Busch considered that they could probably avoid a ballet entirely: 'It seems to me that this ballet music was specially composed by Mozart to satisfy the Duque who was, contrary to me, a great lover of this art, but has actually nothing to do with opera seria. In my score I find the ballet music only in the addenda.'

Fritz Busch was not prepared to leave any musical detail to others and made requests for his proposed meeting in January:

You arrange auditions for me in time, of course with the presence of you and the Christies, Pritchard and Jani. I also want very definitely to hear and see all members who are to be engaged for the main part of the chorus, that means, about thirty. Furthermore I must hear and see British singers who in your opinion are suitable for smaller parts.

I am in daily touch with Hans Gal. I am glad to tell you that we fully agree about cuts, arrangements etc. I think it is not necessary that Gal comes to London, but, for the sake of a most accomplished performance of *Idomeneo*, it will be imperative that he comes to Stockholm. Then, as he is a full-blooded musician, I could go thoroughly through the opera with him, giving him also my opinions about tempos etc. in all detail, which he can afterwards personally transmit to Pritchard and Jani.

17th November 1950

Today I learned from my son Hans, who is for eight weeks stage producer in New Orleans, that he has in his cast for *Don Giovanni* an outstanding Canadian tenor with an Italian name [*sic*] singing Don Ottavio. I am keenly looking forward to the audition next week, when the young man comes to New York.

Studying every day more intensely the score of *Idomeneo*, I believe I can thoroughly talk over the musical problems with Hans Gal if he could come to Glyndebourne during my short stay there. Do not forget to arrange auditions, as many as you can, for minor parts and the chorus, and, of course, only in as much as the singers are worthwhile to be heard.

Commenting on Moran Caplat's suggestions as to singers, Fritz Busch wrote on 2nd December:

After carefully reading all you told us, I sent a cable saying: 'Please stop cast negotiations as am working to get best singers Stop Will be through mid-December, Cordially, Busch.' I sent this cable because you mention in your letter plenty of singers, mostly Italians, unknown to me, whom you consider good for the very important parts, but I do not want singers, *no matter how highly recommended* without knowing them or get the best available reports from various sources. I shall come back to this matter later on in detail, and I am sure that Professor Ebert agrees with my point of view. Both of us certainly will be delighted to get for minor parts British singers, carefully selected in auditions.

Moran Caplat had heard that the French Canadian, Léopold Simoneau, who Busch's son thought would be suitable for

Idamante, was 'absolutely outstanding as a Mozart singer. I think we would agree at once to engaging him for Idamante and Ottavio if we can get him.'

In keeping with tradition, Fritz Busch would usually play the recitatives himself using a piano. However, for *Idomeneo* he decided that a harpsichord and cello continuo was more appropriate for the effect he was seeking and, showing confidence in John, asked that his assistant play the harpsichord. The previous October, John had inspected the instruments at the Victoria & Albert Museum but was having difficulty in finding a suitable one because of the great demand for all instruments during the Festival of Britain. Moran Caplat's assistant, Anthony Besch, wrote to Fritz Busch that 'Arnold Dolmetsch Ltd have one instrument available which we could have this year, but it has only a single manual (a "Single Samuel" Harpsichord with two 8 foot stops and 4 pedals). Dolmetsch tell us that this particular harpsichord, built about 1896, was made for use at Covent Garden and from that time onwards was used in the operas there. John Pritchard says that he thinks this instrument would be satisfactory, but would like to have your approval before we make definite arrangements to have it.'

Anthony Besch had been taken on as an assistant to Moran Caplat for the winter months and allowed to act as 'assistant to the assistant' producer during the summer season. He was the only person working at Glyndebourne familiar with *Idomeneo* as, during his time at Oxford University, there had been an amateur production using the translation by the Misses Radford. John had great respect for Anthony Besch's intelligence and ability and was to work with him later, in other Houses.

The correspondence with Fritz Busch illustrates how the organisation and presentation of opera has changed. Today, with certain exceptions, it is the management of an opera house which organises most aspects and engages artists enabling international conductors to continue 'jetting' about the world. As Fritz Busch's protégé, John can be considered one of the last of the 'old school' of opera conductors. To work with and be guided by people who are at the top of their profession is one of the most marvellous things that can happen to a young person. The meticulous preparation of scores and choice of singers was to be one of the hallmarks of John's work in the opera houses in which he held appointments.

He never forgot that January day in the Organ Room at Glyndebourne, 'surrounded by electric fires', listening to Fritz Busch and Hans Gal turning a concert score into a theatrically viable drama for the opera house: hammering out a version 'unlike any previously made wherein only Mozart would be played. Busch took such artistic responsibilities very seriously and I think he felt a curious air of unreality in preparing himself to conduct, for the first time, a Mozart opera which with every ensuing day's rehearsal revealed itself as more powerful and dramatic than he had ever dreamed. Anxiously we debated whether, in a moment of excruciating stage difficulty unforeseen by the youthful Mozart, an addition of four bars "in style" by Hans Gal could be permitted.'★

At this juncture, it is important to elaborate on the work of the designer Oliver Messel, the third party in the triumvirate of Busch and Ebert, whose work was to influence John.

After the war a number of outstanding students such as Ralph Koltai, Terence Conran and David Hicks were studying at the Central School of Art. The young John Claridge gained a scholarship there. Unfortunately for him, a number of students were young lady debutantes who would arrive at eleven, leave for lunch and never be seen again for the rest of the day. Seeing an advertisement in one of the theatrical journals, 'Young man required to help at Glyndebourne', even though it meant literally sweeping the stage, he jumped at the opportunity to work in a theatre. Showing great facility with his hands and imagination, he was soon in the property department making costumes and scenery. When Messel went to Sussex for discussions with Busch and Ebert he would draw, for example, in a somewhat illegible scribble, sketches for the headdress of one of the soldiers in *Idomeneo*. 'Who can make this for us?' he would ask and John Claridge would be summoned to interpret his drawings. Messel was so delighted with the work that he suggested that Claridge become his assistant. About Christmas time they would go to Glyndebourne and with Busch, Ebert, Christie and Caplat sit and hear the music in the Organ Room, make notes and then research the décor and costumes used in previous productions. This would involve long hours in places such as the Warburg Institute. Messel had a visual archive as to where he could find, for

★Taken from an article in the Glyndebourne Programme Book.

example, a column, furniture or costumes. The costume drawings would then belong in the correct period of time. Then he would think about the colours, the set and making of models.

In musical rehearsals, which is a daily event right up to the first night, everybody knows how the score is being interpreted. Although the designer would liaise very closely with them, the conductor and producer did not really know what it was going to look like until the curtain would go up on a scene.

In the tradition of the great Italian architects who would build models before they proceeded to obtain their client's opinion and guidance, Messel would always create models to scale of each scene in each act to inspire the craftsmen carrying out the work. The scene builders, painters and lighting people would gather in his studio to see what he was trying to achieve. As he was a master of his trade there was rarely any disagreement. Moran Caplat would approve it. His assistant would see the costumier and shoemaker and begin making the jewellery.

Ebert and Messel then went to see Busch in America to talk about the score of *Idomeneo*. Everyone was in total accord about the opera.

Whilst preparations were going ahead for the season, John signed his contract for 1951 to 'serve on the musical staff of the productions and perform any and all of the duties which may be assigned to you as a Coach, Chorus Master, and Assistant Conductor'. As Assistant Conductor he would conduct six performances at Glyndebourne and three in Edinburgh, receiving twenty guineas for each performance.

When Busch arrived, John started to prepare the chorus, which is of major importance in *Idomeneo*. When there is a strong chorus in Mozart operas the balance and emphasis can change. In *Idomeneo*, as in a Greek play, it is a voice in itself. *Idomeneo* was Carl Ebert at his most messianic, a quality which he transmitted to the chorus.

Fritz Busch went to all the pre-rehearsals, joking that he must not let Jani have his way too much. Jani would confide in John that he hoped the conductor would not come too early and spoil it all! This was a very happy time, everybody working well together, joking and achieving. They were all excited and relaxed at the same time. In the still of the evening if one walked across the lawns at Glyndebourne and heard the sound of a piano through the open window of the Organ Room, beautifully played, it was John.

Busch and Ebert would inspire each other. Sometimes Ebert would produce 'trippy' movements in the storm scene and Busch would turn to him and say, 'This is not in the music.' In stressing the need for movement to be inspired by the music, Busch said: 'The pulse of any work comes from the pit. The music is like one's heartbeat.'

The Glyndebourne five week season was sold out before the first night. 1951 was the year of the Festival of Britain and assistance was received from the Arts Council, the only occasion the Festival has received money from the public purse. Miki Sekers not only supplied the materials used in *Idomeneo* but also donated many of the *Don Giovanni* costumes which were especially woven and dyed. The season was not without its social excitement as *Così fan Tutte* was the first opera to be televised. Already familiar with broadcasting, John was very interested in the new medium.

However, for the public the performance of *Idomeneo* was not just a 'sensation', the perfect performance but an emotional experience. Whenever this particular production is mentioned to anyone who was fortunate enough to be in the audience, they recall it vividly as being one of the most remarkable experiences in their opera-going lives. It was like a renaissance picture, which changed as the audience looked on. The chorus moved as if swept by the wind. They swayed with grief and then became another kind of triangle or some other shape. Their movements were like the music. It was lit, not with spotlights but as if there were spotlights, the lighting itself adding to the tragic atmosphere. Present at the first performance, Lady Agi Sekers recalled that the set by Oliver Messel was quite beautiful with its drapes and strange colours. Sena Jurinac, singing Ilia, wore a chrome-yellow dress. 'Colours and costumes looked divine. Her first aria which could be very boring was so full of emotion. The opera was so charged. Richard Lewis was such a perfect Idomeneo. A lady in our party fainted with emotion and when we took her out, which we could hardly bear to do, we found four or five other people had likewise been overcome.' The Idamante, Léopold Simoneau, created great interest, fully justifying Fritz Busch's concept of a tenor in the role.

As arranged, John had been given six performances to conduct that season; two each of *Figaro, Così* and *Don Giovanni*. The length of time and the number of personnel involved in rehearsals and performance of opera produces anecdotes without end but John's career was a gift to the modern public relations man. There were always eventful performances. Unaware of his previous heart attack, it came as a great shock to everyone at Glyndebourne when Fritz Busch was unable to continue a performance of *Don Giovanni*. While the audience enjoyed their picnics during the long dinner interval, Moran Caplat managed to telephone someone who found John lying on the beach at Eastbourne, where he had gone for a swim in the wonderful summer weather. Driving back, his car engine caught fire. Luckily he managed to hire a car and arrived in time for the beginning of the second Act. As in the future, he coped brilliantly. Sir Geraint Evans, singing Masetto, remembered it being very exciting. 'One hears stories of people taking over at the last minute. Really it was the beginning of John's career as a conductor.' In later years when interviewed, John, the romantic, would recount this story with a certain amount of embroidery, when in fact he had conducted *scheduled* performances earlier in the season.

Fritz Busch made a good recovery and was able to conduct at Edinburgh. John took some of the performances of *Don Giovanni* and worked with Busch on the new production of *La Forza del Destino*. Busch then went to London to prepare for a concert with the Danish Radio Orchestra but died at the Savoy Hotel on 14th September 1951. Everyone at Glyndebourne felt the tragedy deeply, particularly after such a remarkable season.

Just as children frequently fulfil their teacher's expectations, John had blossomed and grown under Fritz Busch's encouragement. Reading and re-reading John's correspondence one is aware that it acts as a mirror not of the writer but the recipient. When talking to John, nobody could seem more British but on the podium or with friends, like a chameleon, he would adapt to the company in which he found himself – musically and socially. Within the orbit of Fritz Busch's refined, intelligent, strong but gentle personality, he had found acceptance at Glyndebourne and in return felt that this was the man he wished had been his father. 'I still look back upon the days with Busch as being the decisively formative ones of my career.'

In a long letter to Audrey Christie on 26th September 1951 from St Ives, Cornwall, he attempted to express his feelings:

Sir John Pritchard

This is the first moment I have had to write to you since the terrible shock we have all sustained in the death of Fritz, and reading today your appreciation in the *Times* I felt I couldn't delay a moment more. All I can say is that I really feel I have lost someone who was a wise and kind friend, almost like a father – I learned so much from him, not only musically (that is obvious) but in the *human* sense, in relationships with people and so on. I shall always be glad that I worked on one Verdi opera with him in addition to his vastly experienced, strong and humorous Mozart.

I was saying to a friend only the other day that there is a sort of 'timelessness' about the sudden removal of a great person – one will feel as deeply deprived in ten years' time as one does immediately . . .

What is your view about some kind of memorial function in London for Busch? The ceremony at Golders Green was, I really thought, impossibly painful: none of the consolations of religion (any sort) and no application of those provided by literature or philosophy! Only Dennis Vaughan at the organ playing Bach relieved the awkward tension. Of course it is always difficult to know what to do on these occasions . . . but I do think a public function in London before too many weeks pass would enable so many of Busch's admirers to think of him in the *right* kind of way.

It was inevitable that John should take over *Idomeneo* the following June, conducting a special afternoon performance as a memorial to Fritz Busch. People remembered this occasion for the intensity with which he expressed the tragic and compassionate music before the happy conclusion of the last act. At the end of the opera the curtain was lowered and lifted again for the chorus to sing Busch's favourite passage, 'Placido è il mare, andiamo'. As he conducted, in a moment of spiritual identification, John felt that the mantle of Busch was upon him, that he had been entrusted with the grail of *Idomeneo*. It became his sacred task to introduce that work to major opera houses throughout the world. Through him it has become accepted into the repertoire.

Ellen Morgenthau looked after the score and lent it to Glyndebourne whenever they needed it, until eventually it went to the United States with one of the Busch family. Charmian Hughes, who joined Glyndebourne as librarian in 1973, remembered that even though the Busch Mozart scores such as *Figaro* were in a dreadful condition with holes in some parts and that in the end there were some pages 'in which the pages were attached to nothing', John always used the scores Busch had marked. 'He would rather do that than keep his own score, or have a new score but he always had his own markings as well.'

John conducted Fritz Busch's orchestra the Danish Radio Orchestra frequently and later brought them to London for a concert at the Royal Albert Hall on 25th April 1968 in the presence of King Frederick IV and Queen Ingrid of Denmark. In the eighties, although he was limping because of a hip problem, when he stepped onto the podium, he bore a remarkable resemblance to Fritz Busch. The age gap had closed.

In his Mozart, Busch did not always keep the same tempi in performances. He had a different pulse for each performance; a different feel, relationships were different. He took it always as a whole. The performances never dragged; singers do not like very slow tempi, they always prefer something to be taken slightly faster. Busch emphasised to John the need for a different style for each composer. Some conductors such as Furtwängler might have been great Beethoven conductors but it required something different to conduct Mozart. John never dragged his music. It would always be alive but more flexible in sound compared to Busch's. Some rather large, heavy people are amazingly light on their feet. John was a very good dancer with natural style and it transferred to his music-making. As soon as he lifted his arms for the upbeat into an overture, there was an extraordinary feeling of dancing.

Robert Ponsonby had joined Glyndebourne in an administrative position, initially as Organising Secretary of the Festival of Sussex which Glyndebourne arranged as part of the 1951 Festival of Britain. He became Editor of the first Programme Book and Secretary of the Glyndebourne Festival Society, as well as doing other administrative work.

Glyndebourne in those days was pretty small and one could not be there without finding time to steal into the theatre. Fritz Busch was still alive and John was learning at Fritz's 'feet'. One can hear that in John's subsequent music-making, as one can hear Beecham too; but John had his own voice as a conductor. I think it was more Beecham than Busch. Busch was a more classical conductor of music. John had a more romantic way with music. It wasn't weak, it wasn't spineless ever but like Beecham he had a gift of establishing a tempo and the pulse continued. Even the woodwind solos in Mozart, for example, with the 'rubati' which any musician will make, the pulse was always there. I'm talking now of a John that I came to know much better over many years but one could tell at once, even in those very early years, that here was an innately musical man. He never did an ugly thing; he never overdrove the music; he never let it die. It always breathed.

John had served his apprenticeship at Glyndebourne and in his development it can be assumed that he had a great admiration for Busch's Mozart: *Die Entführung aus dem Serail, Così fan Tutte, Le Nozze di Figaro, Don Giovanni* and, above all, *Idomeneo* and Verdi's *La Forza del Destino*. From Sir Thomas Beecham he was committed to Brahms and Strauss and under Vittorio Gui he had studied *Un Ballo in Maschera*. In addition the music and personality of Benjamin Britten made a great impression on John during his first season at Glyndebourne.

Whilst Mozart has always been the mainstay of the Glyndebourne repertoire, its *raison d'être*, a new tradition, that of Rossini, was established during the fifties and early sixties with remarkable performances by the Italian conductor, Vittorio Gui.

Known generally as Papa Gui, he looked on all young musicians as his children. Trained in the music of Mozart and Brahms, with very strong ideas of what he wanted, both from artists and himself and an overwhelming personality, he influenced nearly everybody with whom he came into contact. Although very strict and demanding when on the podium, Vittorio Gui showed self-discipline in his music-making, never hindering the music in his interpretation of the scores. When Carl Ebert left Nazi Germany he met Gui in Florence where they collaborated at the Maggio Musicale in works by Verdi, Rossini and others, so that when Ebert was to produce *Così* at Edinburgh in 1948, he suggested Gui as conductor.

Covent Garden had *Barbiere, Barbiere* and more *Barbiere* and Glyndebourne was the only place where one could have a broader diet of Rossini. Sir George Christie remembered that Gui had a special knowledge of what Rossini was all about. 'On occasions when a performance was going well, Gui would rest his arm on the top of the orchestra partition, conduct and half turn towards the audience, smiling at them as if to say "Everything's going right". Gui, John adored, I think because of Gui's extraordinary ability with Rossini.' Just as John adopted the style of the reader in his letters, so too with other conductors. Since Gui's Rossini was unparalleled, thinking it worthwhile to emulate, he developed an inimitable style with the Italian 'buffo'. Their styles were almost indistinguishable.

As with Mozart, Rossini requires teamwork with artists of equal ability. Not works with great solo arias, their essence lies in the ensemble, the freshness of the intrigues. The apparent simplicity is deceptive, requiring a depth of perception and understanding to perform the music as if it is alive. Rossini has often been played as farcical comedy but it was elegance, wit and above all, style which Gui and later John, displayed.*

The operas actually brought out the real fun of Rossini and a great deal of that fun was due to John. In those days, something like *Le Comte Ory* which John took over from Gui in 1958, was close to his heart. Rossini's only comic opera, in French, was also a comic opera which has slight traces of sentimentality. There are moments of poignancy which John relished. There was also in *Le Comte Ory* (on record but not conducted by John) a marvellous tenor called Juan Oncina. He was one of Glyndebourne's favourites. One could not hear him in Britain outside Glyndebourne. Oncina had all the elegance and the mellowness that a Rossini tenor should have and the performances of *Le Comte Ory* were very special. Glyndebourne was fortunate that at that time they were able to attract a remarkable group of singers who were capable of singing Rossini opera buffa. Just as *Idomeneo* was a pinnacle of achievement after the war, *La Cenerentola* was to dominate the House during the following years and create a sensation. First produced by Carl Ebert in 1952, the essence of the opera was distilled in the designs of Oliver Messel. The other mood that John brought out well was melancholia and he brought this out in *Cenerentola* – which was enhanced, particularly in the first Act, by another Spanish singer, Marina de Gabarain, in the title role, who had a smokiness and wistfulness in her voice. John was very adept at moving between Rossini's high spirits – the jokiness, the larkiness – and moments where Rossini just takes one's breath away with something that is much more touching.

The intrigues between Dandini and the Prince – 'piano, piano' – and those between Don Magnifico and his daughters Clorinda and Tisbe – moments of whispered exchanges contrasting with

*Glyndebourne and Rossini: 'The Stylistic Approach', p. 351.

the outrageous *importanza* of Don Magnifico – enchanted and captivated audiences. Ian Wallace recalled that Gui was a man of slightly uncertain temper but if one worked hard it was marvellous to work with him. 'From my point of view it was important that he invited me to sing Don Magnifico in *Cenerentola* in 1952. I was lucky to be in the team of singers for the Rossini operas. If you did, for example, the *Barber* with anybody else after Gui, you noticed the gear changes.' It was from Gui that John learnt to create a line with an apparently seamless join.

As Gui was unwell for the 1953 Edinburgh Festival, John conducted the three scheduled performances of *Cenerentola*. Thetis Blacker was a member of the very small chorus. At the end it has a very joyful song. She was standing on the prompt side and as Oliver Messel liked the way she wore his costumes, was put in the very front, right down stage by the orchestra. There is one very quick passage in which the chorus needs to hang on to an F sharp for nine bars. John would count it out with his baton. On this occasion she felt herself to be in exceptionally good voice: 'F sharp was my favourite note – I had a very powerful voice anyway. I gave my all. I gave it so superbly, I thought, that I forgot to count the bars. Suddenly I found that I alone was singing!' Everybody else had stopped and then it was the end of the opera. She was horrified at making, not just a little mistake but a *fortissimo* mistake. 'Nobody makes mistakes at Glyndebourne!' When the curtain came down she was so appalled by what she had done that she forgot to step back. The weight of the curtain can be fatal. Luckily Barbara Gill, another alto, standing beside her, saw what had happened and gave her a tug, just getting her out of the way of the curtain but not before it knocked off the enormous cartwheel navy blue feather hat she was wearing. 'It went whirling like a catherine wheel into the orchestra and I was just saved.' Covered in confusion she could not sleep all night. All the others thought it was 'frightfully funny but terrible at the same time'.

Next morning, deciding that the only thing to do was to go and apologise to the conductor, she took the tram all the way up to the Braid's Hill Hotel where he was staying and arrived just as he was having lunch. 'I went in and stood before his table, "Mr Pritchard, I cannot tell you how sorry I am about what I did yesterday in the performance." He looked up from his boiled cod in parsley sauce, "Well, I was surprised." ' Apologising again, the blushing chorus member withdrew. The following day was the last performance. 'When we came to this bit of nine bars, he looked directly at me and conducted me alone. Then when it came to the end of the "nine" he took me off with a great beat. I was expecting to get the sack. When we came to make the recording I was put in the *back* row!'

Carl Ebert, the producer, knew Willy Brandt, Burgomaster of Berlin. Invited to return to his former position at the Stadtische Oper as Intendant he arranged for Glyndebourne to perform *Cenerentola* there. As Gui could not go to Berlin, John was to conduct.

On arrival Carl Ebert fell ill and his son, Peter rehearsed the cast as it was only a question of adjusting them to a new and different stage. Peter Ebert recalled that on the evening of the performance his father, who was at home, telephoned every fifteen minutes to enquire how it was going. The reaction of the Berlin audience flabbergasted them. 'Normally from the start of *Cenerentola* there is a great deal of laughter at all the things going on in the household. There was not one tiny reaction from them; no laughter, no clapping, *absolute silence*.' Backstage everybody was feeling desperate and could not understand what was wrong or why the audience did not respond. Suddenly, at the end of the Don Magnifico aria, sung by Ian Wallace, there was an extraordinary noise. Ian thought the roof was falling in but it was simply wild applause. The audience had been so stunned by the sets, the style of everything and had suddenly expressed themselves. The Germans have a custom that if there is still some clapping, the artists must go out and bow. The curtain calls went on for more than half an hour. 'I'll never forget this extraordinary experience of a "dead" audience for about forty minutes, who then went totally "bananas".' Opinions as to the number of curtain calls vary between thirty-seven and forty-seven.

The achievement of *Cenerentola* was continued with successful performances of other Rossini operas at Glyndebourne.

Although John took over performances of *Le Comte Ory*, it was not until 1964 that he was given Rossini's *La Pietra del Paragone* to prepare and conduct himself. The opera had marvellous sets by Osbert Lancaster and was produced by Günther Rennert. When Carl Ebert retired from his position as Artistic Director, two new appointments, Artistic Counsellors, were made in the following years: Vittorio Gui as Head of Music and Günther Rennert as Head of Production. John had been slightly in awe of Carl Ebert but he had been at Glyndebourne with Günther Rennert for some time and was more confident. They developed a very good working relationship. He coped well with the differences in their personalities, appreciating the director's ability and practicality.

Rennert was the author of German versions of Rossini's *Le Comte Ory* and *Il Turco in Italia* and introduced his adaptation of *La Pietra del Paragone* to Glyndebourne. It had been produced in Hamburg the previous year and the German text used was translated back into Italian. Vittorio Gui, already seventy-nine (he lived to be ninety), did not approve of Rennert's conception. On holiday at Gui's home in Italy, John found himself caught in the cross-fire and wrote to Moran Caplat on 4th September 1964:

> You were quite right about the cineramic beauty of Maratea – we love the coast and find Gui's domain very delightful, the cottage really cosy, and bathing from the blistering rocks great fun. The old boy is in good form – we had them up here to dinner last night and had an interesting musico-philosophical-political monologue after the scampi fritti. He usually catches me as I pad down past his studio room and this adds forty-five minutes to the five minute descent. He reports on letters from you or Jani and his replies so I am fully 'au fait' with all problems up to date. There is one slight problem for me in being here I'd like you to consider. His leisure is giving him time to chew over *again* the iniquities of *Pietra*, though I got him to agree 'not to be too absolute' in his views about Rennert's version – in other words to vary the verdict '*impossible*' occasionally, just for a change, in favour of 'possible to accept'(!)

Turco was the turning point of John Cox's career as it brought him to Glyndebourne as a director. John and he always had a good relationship. He had wanted to be a straight theatre director until asked to replace Franco Enriquez. Eleven years since their first meeting, by this time he felt strong enough to tell John if he thought something was not going right musically or not revealing the best performance through the amalgam of stage and music. 'We were much more strongly collaborators now.' Already built, the designs were not to John Cox's taste as he felt that Rossini should have more clarity of outline than was expressed in Luzatti's somewhat freestyle cartoon drawing. Although it was not popular with audiences, John was able to show how much he had learnt from the older man in *Il Turco in Italia* in 1970 and was fortunate that his heroine was the accomplished Graziella Sciutti. They met when she sang Rosina in *Barbiere* at Glyndebourne, early in her career. She had worked with Gui a few months previously in a radio broadcast of *Fidelio* in 1954. The *Barbiere* at Glyndebourne was a big turning point in her career. Then Karajan came into her life as an opera conductor and her international reputation grew. In between she went back to Glyndebourne for *Così fan Tutte* with John, the first time she sang with him as a conductor. 'It was always *Così* and *Turco in Italia* that was a part of Glyndebourne and John. Gui had unfortunately been gone a long time. Rossini, with the lightness, the *esprit* of John – this characteristic of John – the smile of the music. It was a joyful occasion and very beautiful.'

She found John a very attentive conductor in rehearsals. Obviously it was easier at Glyndebourne because of living there. In other theatres the conductor always tends to come later but Graziella Sciutti could never remember John not being there. She felt that the musical performance was very much connected with the creative and visual aspect of the work:

> A voice must be beautiful but it must say something. The ultimate is not just the sound. I appreciate it much more now that I do direct. It is very seldom that I get a conductor to come to stage rehearsals. They tend not to and it's hard especially doing a lot of Mozart as I do, the theatre is so much in communion with the musical phrasing and there are moments when you need just a little more breath here . . . It's not changing tempi – but that is what makes the difference between a performance that is good and one that is great. It also made it easy for the director because his phrasing would inspire. It's easy to put on an opera but to make it come alive and be natural is something else.

John had a particular affinity for the Italian temperament. He liked responding to the sudden laughter, the sudden upsurge of vitality. With Moran Caplat, he would go to Gui's home in Maratea. In the words of Sir George Christie: 'Supposedly for work – work made more enjoyable than it merits. It was simply pure enjoyment.'

To John the thought of Italy went hand in hand with holidays. There was something about the Italians' refusal to compromise their pleasures which drew him back continually. Writing to Moran Caplat from Taormina in 1959 he sounded thoroughly relaxed and happy. 'I hear *Cenerentola* may come my way next season so I must look to my laurels because I thought Gui's performance of it one of the best things he's *ever* done! (Funny old man, he pulls it out of the bag with great aplomb too . . .) As you know, I thought the production exaggerated but the cast is very good and I imagine you will keep it fairly intact.'

As the aging Vittorio Gui gradually relinquished his work to John, wanting correspondence, it was to the younger man he turned, sending postcards of his beloved Italian coast, with messages such as 'Do you remember the Paradise lost . . .?!' The younger man put the last letter he received from Fiesole on 4th January 1969 in a safe place, together with an enclosed newspaper cutting. Vittorio Gui wrote saying how pleased he was to receive a letter from John after a long silence. He reminded John of his achievements and the memories they shared of *Fidelio, Così fan Tutte, Falstaff* and last but not least, *Pelléas*.

Gui went on to remark, sadly, that he was getting old now and there were too many memories in his long life and career of more than sixty years' conducting. A recent illness in Rome, just as he was beginning rehearsals of *Turco in Italia*, had forced him to cancel, which was a serious blow for him but he hoped to resume work in a couple of weeks.

He recalled some beautiful concerts during the autumn in Milan, Florence, Naples and, especially, Catania where the atmosphere was very 'nice'. Although mediocre, they were 'full of goodwill' and not 'blasé' as often happens in great cities.

In the anniversary year of Rossini's death, he had conducted the *Piccola Messa Solemni* [*sic*], which he considered a 'masterpiece' and the only religious work by the composer. Proudly he enclosed the newspaper cutting reporting that Pesaro, Rossini's birthplace, in a simple and moving ceremony had made him an Honorary Citizen and regretted that this had not been reported in the English papers. Gui ended his letter by sending his love and asking John not to forget him . . .

Prior to his Glyndebourne debut, John returned to the Theatre Royal, Glasgow as a guest conductor with the Carl Rosa Opera, an itinerant company run by Mrs Phillips and Arthur Hammond. Engaged to conduct *Bohème* in Blackpool and Glasgow, it was an attractive project for him as Oreste Kirkop, a handsome young Maltese tenor was to sing Rudolfo. It was during the preparation for this work that John met Maurits Sillem, who had worked with the company as a coach in the winter of 1949. John spoke to

Glyndebourne about him and after playing for some auditions at the Wigmore Hall, he was engaged as a coach by Glyndebourne in 1951 where he stayed for five years, leaving to work at Covent Garden.

When Glyndebourne went to Edinburgh in 1955 the Company performed *Falstaff* and *La Forza del Destino*. Maurits Sillem was involved in the *Falstaff*. As it alternated with *Forza* and because that opera cast an enormous spell on him, he stood in the wings and listened to it every night. He felt that John identified very much with that particular opera and that perhaps it was his favourite Verdi opera.

This was not only because of Fritz Busch but also because it brought about a change in the attitude of David Webster at Covent Garden towards him. The Bulgarian soprano, Ljuba Welitsch, one of the stars of the Vienna Opera who had sung Donna Anna in *Don Giovanni* at the 1948 Edinburgh Festival and Amelia in *Ballo in Maschera* the following year, was one of the first internationally recognised artists to be engaged by David Webster from 1947 until 1952. She confirmed that during this period Covent Garden only regarded John as a gifted accompanist who had been permitted to conduct a few performances of operas which had been prepared and rehearsed by Fritz Busch.

5

Debut

After the war everyone in Britain was hungry for music. As young singers were only at the level of training and chorus work, foreign singers were imported by Covent Garden and Glyndebourne and Equity was constantly complaining. In contrast, in Vienna, as people did not have food to eat, the politicians decided that the people must be given music so that they would not feel the hunger in their stomachs to such an extent and insisted that their many artists sang.

The year before he died Fritz Busch was asked to Vienna. As always, his performances were received with wild enthusiasm. According to Ellen Morgenthau, the Viennese realised 'this was a serious man. However, frequently the orchestral players were not there for rehearsals and he would become very angry. The Viennese claimed that they had the best singers but they were not always those he wanted. The situation might have changed if Busch had lived and been able to work there longer.' Engaged to conduct *Forza* at Vienna, his death gave Freddie Diez, an agent who knew John from Glyndebourne, the opportunity to promote the young conductor who had worked on the opera under Busch at Edinburgh.

On holiday with his mother in Cornwall in October 1951, John received a telegram:

PLEASE TELEPHONE ME PARK 7930 URGENTLY, RE POSSIBILITY VISIT VIENNA – DIEZ

After lunching together on 25th October at The Wayfarers, John began preparing for his Vienna debut. It was to be a short engagement from 21st January until 14th February 1952. Eva Metzler had been giving him German lessons for the past two years but he was not yet fluent. He took a long list of words and phrases which a conductor might need (together with a translation) which he placed on the podium. Moran Caplat flew to Vienna for the first night on 25th January to give moral support. The singer in the role of Leonore in *Forza* (*Die Macht des Schicksals*) was the Austrian soprano, Hilde Zadek, the Donna Anna in the Glyndebourne and Edinburgh 1951 *Don Giovanni*. There were always parties after performances: Hilde Zadek gave one for the first night, then John accompanied her to others. Zadek was not the only artist he knew from Glyndebourne; in February Ilse Hollweg sang Constanze in *Entführung*.

The Viennese system of rehearsals, or rather lack of them, can be quite terrifying for a young conductor. Ninety per cent of the time, one does not get an orchestral rehearsal, so the first time one stands on the podium is on the evening of the performance, a horrible experience requiring nerves of steel. Fortunately John had *one* rehearsal for *Forza del Destino*, when he was able to try out the difficult parts with the players: 'Being Vienna, the next day not one of the performers from the rehearsal did I see at the performance!' That did not worry him because, at this one rehearsal with the Vienna Opera Orchestra (Vienna Philharmonic), he realised that their standard was so high, the rehearsal was more important for the conductor than the orchestra.

John liked Vienna. Staying at the Pension Aclon in Dorotheagasse, he was looked after by some old ladies who brought him breakfast in bed every morning. Carefully listing those to whom he should send postcards, ensuring that those who 'mattered' were fully aware of his engagement and more importantly, re-engagement for the following season, John wrote letters to Tom Glass of the *Edinburgh Evening Despatch*, Mrs Tillett of Ibbs & Tillett and Mrs Phillips of the Carl Rosa. His engagement was duly reported in the *Strand News*. Writing to John Denison on Staatsoper paper, he wanted London to know that Vienna appreciated his talent. His letter was passed to David Webster at Covent Garden.

It has been a memorable stay for me. Naturally I was nervous and on arrival fearing the redoubtable Vienna fiddle, who are known to have a *very* busy *way* with young conductors, hesitant in any German, totally strange to the ways of the Stanze etc.

However, luckily as soon as the music starts one feels on familiar ground and personally I found bad German a positive advantage as it brought many a smile with a real wish to co-operate to the faces of the players! For my first *Forza*, I had the Zadek, Friedrich (a Tauber-like tenor in the making) and Poell – they do an extraordinary version here with the overture played *after* the first scene, but luckily I had such a shout from the gallery after the overture which went excitingly, that my doubts were settled and I felt happy for the rest of the performance. The direction of the opera are (not unnaturally) *very* sensitive to the reaction of the public and when there was a fine reception backed up by an outstanding notice in the *Wiener Zeitung*, I was promptly offered *a contract for Italian Opera* for next season – a total of five months to consist of not less than a month each time.

Though I have not positively accepted because I *don't* want to be lost from London, naturally, it is *very* nice to be asked! I must ask your advice about it when I return. You see one *can* arrange these things so as to be fairly equally divided between London and Vienna, which could be ideal but I want (entre nous) to keep the Jacques for another year, particularly as I have just appointed the new leader. I have not told the Jacques of the terms of my Vienna offer yet.

By the way, my most exciting evenings were another *Forza* with the wonderful Carla Marbinis instead of Zadek and the same singer doing *Butterfly* which had not been given here for years for lack of an 'Italian' conductor! I have also given *Rigoletto* and *Entführung*.

He wrote to Moran Caplat: 'The women here are such a *lot* better than the men! I did an 'awful' *Rigoletto* which was wildly applauded, the orchestra played well.' He criticised the singers severely but finished his comments with: 'However, everyone but me seems to have been happy, so why should I worry? They said they wanted me to come for six weeks at least at a time, so that they can arrange properly rehearsed performances, but I shall believe that when I see it here! Must stop now – am off to eat a steak tartare, what a good idea of yours, it makes my tempi faster than ever!' As always, food had a place in his thoughts.

John's engagement and re-engagement for a further season in Vienna was an extraordinary achievement for a young, non-German-speaking conductor. Ian Wallace remembered everyone's astonished reaction. 'A lot of people said that it was perhaps "a bridge too far" for the amount of experience he had. I think that at this stage of his career, for a young Englishman to go and conduct at this mecca of opera it was like the old music hall adage about the performing dog who walked across the stage on its hind legs. It wasn't a question of how well it did it but rather the fact that however well John did, if he managed to get through his performances it would be a great achievement.' Looking back on his career, John commented that England did not really take notice of him seriously until he was seen conducting in Vienna.

The persona and characteristics which many associate with John had their roots in the ten years after the war. Many other musicians besides him consider themselves fortunate to have been part of the rebuilding in Germany, Italy and Britain. People were able to attend everything as it was cheap. There was a wonderful upsurge in the theatrical world. With his ability to deliver an anecdote with immaculate timing, John could have been a very good actor of the 'old school', of the variety that played comedy of manners in the wonderful plays that do not run in the West End any more but kept everybody laughing on a Wednesday afternoon. Sir John Gielgud and Hermione Gingold drew huge audiences in Shaftesbury Avenue. Dame Peggy Ashcroft caused a sensation as Cleopatra, reciting her lines lying on her stomach or back and there were long queues outside the Old Vic presenting Shakespeare with actors like John Neville and Richard Burton, making his name as a matinée idol. There were sold out notices for the ballet established under Dame Ninette de Valois and Sir Frederick Ashton and the opera company which was developing at Covent Garden.

The fact that Vienna had re-engaged his young 'repetiteur' and that he might be accused of overlooking British talent caused David Webster, the Administrator of Covent Garden, to act swiftly. Writing to Joan Ingpen (wife of agent Freddie Diez), as he was uncertain as to whether she (as Ingpen & Williams) or her husband looked after John's affairs, David Webster commented that he had spoken to John at Glyndebourne and that he was not interested in him as a Guest Conductor, 'although circumstances force us this year to engage him almost along these lines. What I mean by this is that we hope that Mr Pritchard is in fact in the process of coming to us in a permanent way . . .' Webster felt, however, that his contract in Vienna, 'interrupts his work with us and in fact creates difficult problems for us. He tells me that he is due in Vienna about January 1st and is due to stay there until something like the middle of April. He then feels and again we understand the position, a loyalty to Glyndebourne and his success with them this year means of course that they will certainly ask him to conduct next season going to Edinburgh after their home season.' Webster felt that if John wished to build up a reputation at Covent Garden the Vienna engagement should be kept to a minimum and his Glyndebourne conducting should come at the end of their season rather than at the beginning, which would enable him to return to Covent Garden for a couple of months during the summer. Immediately he processed a contract for the coming autumn season, engaging John to conduct performances of *A Masked Ball, The Magic Flute* and *Norma*, later requesting *Rigoletto*.

Having established Wagner in the repertoire with international artists such as Hans Hotter and Kirsten Flagstad, David Webster realised that the time had come for Verdi to be staged at Covent Garden and decided to mount a new production of *A Masked Ball*, using a translation into English by Professor Dent which returned the setting of the opera to the Court of Gustavus III of Sweden instead of Boston. His policy of encouraging young British musicians would be exemplified by engaging a relatively unknown British conductor to open the season. The conductor may have been unknown but he had the credentials of having worked on the opera, as chorus master, under Vittorio Gui for Glyndebourne at Edinburgh. Planning was at much shorter notice in those days. Today top musicians expect to know their engagements fully for the next two years and often plan in general terms the following three-year period. The Earl of Harewood, who was on the Board of Covent Garden at that time, remembered having a long conversation with John in the garden at Glyndebourne during May or June of 1952, four or five months before the event, when he was asked who was going to sing. ' "Oh," John said. "Well they're all right aren't they. I wonder if we couldn't do better than that. What about somebody like Leonard Warren?" I said that he would never learn it in English as he often does it in Italian and he said, "Well we could do it in Italian then." ' The opera was sung in English.

In the fifties, the Season began in October and preparation would start in September with a minimum of three weeks' rehearsal, sometimes a month. If it was a new work artists would rehearse for at least four weeks with the actual producer and come to stage rehearsals knowing the work thoroughly.

Dennis Goodall, former headmaster of the Sir George Monoux School wrote expressing his pleasure that John had now reached Covent Garden. 'When you are next writing to your people do tell them that I am more than delighted that they are able to enjoy your deserved triumph.'

Mr Belchambers was less formal:

> May I, breaking a silence of many years, offer my warm congratulations on your marvellous achievement! You will, I am sure, realise that I feel, in some small measure, what your emotions must be. There is, I think, no greater joy than that of knowing that one has realised, as a result of hard work and extreme concentration, the intentions of a great composer in a great work. And few have achieved, as you have, the use to the full of musical gifts of a high order. Does this sound poppycock? It isn't to me and I don't think it will be to you.

John wrote to his mother on 31st October 1952, finding an excuse to send her extra money: 'I was very pleased you were at my first performance at Covent Garden and looked so very smart, I am going to give you a cheque when I come down to pay for your outfit as I was *so* pleased with it – good style and taste, you did me great credit! I am enclosing for you to read a telegram from Sir John Barbirolli:

TO YOU AND ALL MEMBERS OF THE COMPANY
MY WARMEST WISHES FOR A GRAND OPENING
– JOHN BARBIROLLI

On the first night of *A Masked Ball* on 23rd October, opening the seventh season of the Covent Garden Opera Company, the audience was surveyed with dismay by those who remembered the pre-war years when Sir Thomas Beecham ruled the House. No longer was the opening of the Season attended by 'society', the 'beautiful one hundred'; the hundred or so people who spent the year travelling to events in the social calendar – Glyndebourne, Ascot, Paris, New York and Monte Carlo; the much photographed one hundred, whose ladies were clothed by couturiers such as Patou and Worth. At Covent Garden before the war white tie and tails had been imperative. Now it was felt that if a person dressed correctly for 'huntin', shootin' and fishin'' and could afford the guinea (one pound and one shilling) for a seat in the stalls, it was carrying democracy too far not to wear a dinner jacket for the event.

Thanking Audrey Christie on 27th October 1952 for her telegram of good wishes, John responded: 'As you know, the cast could not really stand up to the demands of this opera and I had wistful memories of the sort of sounds which we heard from

Welitsch, Silveri and Picchi. But it did the *Garden* an enormous amount of good to be harried by Rennert and in time *perhaps* they will learn various useful things on the musical side!'

The first act disappointed the critics but with the second, Beverley Baxter from the *Sunday Express*, 'realised that in Mr John Pritchard there is a conductor of great promise . . . and inspired and controlled his players.' Others commented on the 'glowing orchestral sound' and 'auspicious debut'.

Whilst John was praised, the production by Günther Rennert aroused mixed feelings. Memories of the Carl Ebert Glyndebourne *Ballo in Maschera* production at the 1949 Edinburgh Festival were not a happy comparison as the opera-going public was beginning to sense that the language of opera was better expressed in the original.

In this instance the performance was handicapped by having as Amelia neither an English nor an Italian soprano but a German lady, Frau Helene Werth. Then a student of design, costume design and architecture, John Copley, the producer, commented that he used to go to the opera every night because he could always get in standing at the back or would have free seats.

> When one was young it didn't really matter who was opening the Season, one went. I just remember it was a pretty awful night. It wasn't terrible musically but it was not well sung, not very distinguished. Helene Werth was the first Amelia and then Wasserthal was very good but they were singing in heavily accented English. 'Venn zee leef vrom zee tree has been shoiken and zee drouft ov oblifion been towken and mine mained hes for efer been shoiken.' When you look back at opera in those days, it was so horrible and nobody complained. When the German repertoire was performed such as *Der Rosenkavalier* and *Fidelio*, it wasn't so bad.

Helene Werth had a throat infection and had to retire from subsequent performances. There was no understudy and the search began for a replacement soprano. Today it is easier to find a substitute at Covent Garden because opera is performed in the original language. Then most established singers had learnt roles in Italian or German, not in English. Direct dial telephone was not in use and Covent Garden was unable to trace two of the numerous sopranos they called. Six others were either working or also ill. Maria Kinasiewicz was brought from Stuttgart to rehearse *Tosca* in case that opera was substituted. Finally Constantina Araujo, a young Brazilian singing at La Scala, agreed to take over the role. There was a slight problem. Although she knew the part, she had never sung it in English and could only perform the role in Italian. She flew to Zurich and thence to London, arriving just before 6pm. Rushed through immigration, she was rehearsed by a repetiteur during the car journey. As the audience knew of the circumstances surrounding her eventful journey across Europe – one must remember that air travel was somewhat different in the early fifties – they gave her a tremendous ovation. She took ten curtain calls with, of course, a photo opportunity for the young conductor to give a kiss of congratulation.

At the last performance the young Australian soprano, Joan Sutherland sang the role of Amelia. She remembered being telephoned early in the morning on 29th December by the Opera Manager, Patrick Terry, who told her Helene Werth was ill and there was no singer for that night. 'I said I couldn't, I didn't know it. I was only just studying it and had quite recently joined the Company (September). There were so many things that I hadn't really mastered yet. He said, "Mr Pritchard said that you'd done half a 'Sitzprobe' and he was very pleased with you." I replied that I'd had the score open, that the music was in front of me but that I hadn't memorised it and didn't know all the words.'

Dressed, ready to go on stage, she went to the conductor's room.

> I felt so sick. John asked me to go through the duets and the big aria. 'Let's just try the duet.' I replied, 'Mr Pritchard, I'm . . . I'm . . . just so confused that I'd really rather leave it and you'll just have to cope. I feel so nervous and awful that I'd rather go to my dressing-room and be quiet before I go on. Please . . .' I was practically in tears. 'If I sing it for you now and find out just how little I know, I'll be that much more frightened on stage.' So he said that I should just go on and do my best. Without John conducting and Ted Downes in the prompt box, I would never have got through. Somehow or other I got to the end of it. It wasn't very good but they didn't kick me out.

Dame Joan Sutherland recalled performances in the fifties. 'Everything was in English and if they had to bring in somebody they were only too glad for them to sing in Swahili if they knew the piece! Even in *Carmen* (I was Frasquita with John) we had Jimmy Johnston, who was Irish, Mike Langdon, very English, two Welshmen, Constance Shacklock [born in Sherwood, Nottinghamshire] and an American, Regina Resnick did some of them too. There were all the regional English accents and my broad Australian, with the dialogue. It was hilarious'. The use of an English text created intense difficulties on stage, as the orchestra would giggle at some of the translations; risqué English words which seemed satisfactory on paper but when spoken in front of an audience would stop the show. John always had control. He would laugh, perhaps, but it was a relaxing laugh and the artist would not feel 'What rubbish I'm singing' and be embarrassed.

As well as the many substitutes for Amelia, the soprano Adèle Leigh, singing Oscar, was ill on one occasion and *Bohème* had to be substituted, the only time John conducted that opera at Covent Garden.

Adèle Leigh recalled meeting the young conductor because they had the same agent, Joan Ingpen, who had heard her take over in *The Magic Flute* under another conductor at twenty-four hours' notice. 'I love to sing Mozart. It's medicine for the voice. When I first started I was a very, very young singer, I was eighteen and Joan Ingpen said, "I have a conductor you must meet. He is the conductor for you."' Adèle Leigh, so full of foreign conductors like Josef Krips and Kempe, did not believe there were any good English conductors. 'She said, "*This* one is different." So we met socially. We were on the same wavelength; we laughed at the same things. In those days, the jokes were a little risqué but it was fun and that's when he asked "When am I going to hear you sing?" Then he heard me and said, "Yes – Susanna" (*Figaro*).'

Adèle Leigh also remembered the continual change of cast for *The Masked Ball* under John, during the autumn of 1952 and 1953. 'In 1953 Jess Walters (singing Anckarstroem/Renato) became sick. They brought in somebody at the very last minute. We had never seen who it was. Suddenly, when I walked on stage, there was Tito Gobbi! That's the way it was in those days. You can imagine – Tito Gobbi was singing in Italian whilst we were all singing in English! It "throws" a performer.' She recalled Günther Rennert, the producer for *Ballo*, always telling her not to look at the conductor. ' "When you are singing your arias you must sing them to the person you are supposed to be singing to or 'cheat', go up front." Then the next day John would say to me, "Yes, it was very good, but you must look at *me* more." So, I had to split myself between the two of them which was not easy. Actually, I think that John won in the end and got his way!'

The Magic Flute was in repertory at the same time as the new production of *The Masked Ball*. The production was not popular, even though the designer was Messel, but it was without the problems which dogged *The Masked Ball* and John's sensitivity as a Mozart conductor, his 'musicianly and sensitive hands', ensured the performances, on musical grounds alone, were praised as of the highest quality. Reducing the size of the orchestra made for a better balance of sound and earned him the singers' gratitude. As the performances ranged from 28th October 1952 until 19th January 1953, it is understandable that there were several changes of cast, many of which make interesting reading.

Dame Joan Sutherland recalled that prior to her performance in *The Masked Ball*, her first meeting with John was when, as the junior member of the company, she went to Covent Garden to start rehearsing *The Magic Flute*, as First Lady.

> I went to my first production call with Christopher West (Resident Producer at Covent Garden) and John Pritchard was taking the rehearsal. There must have been some sort of impression made on John because from that day he 'latched on' to a certain quality of sound that I had. He liked the sound and wanted me to succeed. So he used to encourage and use me. He could see that there was a 'coloratura' quality. It wasn't properly developed then but he could hear it was there and must have thought that I had a voice that needed nurturing.

That winter there was a 'killer' fog in London. One night it was so bad that Sadlers Wells cancelled their performance. Even though the fog had seeped into the House, Covent Garden decided to go ahead. 'John kept on disappearing from view. We were up on the stage, John was conducting and every so often he wasn't there! We had to do it by ear with what we heard from the pit.'

Recalling her early performances with John, Dame Joan touched upon another aspect of opera which has changed. Covent Garden was a company with a nucleus of five sopranos, five mezzos, five basses etc. who were either English, Welsh, Scottish or from the Dominions such as Canada, Australia or New Zealand, who sang the small roles and occasionally, as with Dame Joan, were given the opportunity to sing the larger roles. She felt that this was something which is lacking today.

> Lovely singers come out of music school and are thrown into the big roles in the big theatres – too big for the size of their voices. They

panic and push their voices and in a year or two they are finished. I really have given thanks all the rest of my career that I had those early years . . . The opera house was interested enough to see that I was reasonably gauche on stage and sent me to someone for help. Australian Opera is probably the only place that does that now. I don't think that anybody else bothers any more. One can't do those big roles and survive.

Understanding a singer's needs enabled David Webster to persuade Maria Callas to give her first European performances outside Italy, in *Norma*, in London. Regarded as the soprano operatic equivalent of Mount Everest, she wished to have as conductor the Italian maestro, Vittorio Gui. It was only natural for him to request that his young Glyndebourne colleague, John Pritchard, should assist at rehearsals in the autumn of 1952, conduct a performance on 13th November and then that the younger man should conduct the following summer performances whilst Gui was working at Glyndebourne.

Remembering those performances, Sir John Tooley (David Webster's assistant and on the latter's retirement, General Administrator at Covent Garden) recognised from John's contact with the orchestra that he really understood Bellini – the shape of the phrases, the musical line – in a manner which many conductors have never understood. John was someone who took it very seriously. One of the problems with Bellini from an orchestral viewpoint is that there is nothing very complicated about the music. It does not stretch musicians but John always fired their enthusiasm. 'He was able to say, "Look, you know that this music is relatively easy to play but nonetheless it is music and we must make it sound like music." John did that brilliantly.' Many people have echoed these sentiments, that there has not been another British conductor who was so at home in something so spontaneous and irrational as Italian opera, especially Bellini.

Those performances of *Norma* in Italian are one of the highlights in the history of Covent Garden, with Maria Callas singing the 'Casta Diva' in the original key that Bellini wrote. Looking back, John considered that she inspired him more than any other artist. He felt that though she was not the greatest *singer* with whom he had worked, she was the greatest *artist*. He likened her voice to a string of real pearls whose beauty is appreciated more when there are slight natural imperfections unlike a manufactured article. He was grateful to her for giving him so much understanding of the art of *bel canto* and to Gui for teaching him that Bellini is not only on the surface.

Primarily a 'women's opera', the combination of Callas, Ebe Stignani as Adalgisa and young singers such as Dame Joan Sutherland in the lesser roles, clearly showed Covent Garden was ready for international recognition. John Higgins (later the *Times* critic) as a schoolboy, remembered that the performances were during Callas' overweight days and that the image of two Druidesses of mighty proportions stamping around the stage was highly amusing but 'the fit of giggles that I had was brushed away by the total magnificence of the singing. These are historic performances.' The summer revival with Guilietta Simionato as Adalgisa received equally rave reviews: 'The high spots of this melodious feast are gems of attunement.' John's conducting was also praised: 'The orchestral playing was flawless.' Further performances of *Norma* were given in 1957, the Act II duet between Callas and Stignani being encored at the second performance.

John had great charm and tact in the way that he talked to someone like Maria Callas. He treated her as a queen, a lady, looking up to her but at the same time expected her to behave like a lady, a queen. There was never any trouble with her at Covent Garden. There was clearly a rapport between them as John continued to work with Callas, accompanying her in a scene and aria 'Qui la voce . . .' from Bellini's *I Puritani* for the Centenary Gala of the Royal Opera House on 10th June 1958 in the presence of Her Majesty the Queen and the Duke of Edinburgh.

A rarity in our lifetime until recently at Covent Garden, *I Puritani* was very close to Callas' heart. In the winter of the 1948 – 49 Venice season, she was singing Brünnhilde in *Die Walküre*. Margherita Carosio had been engaged to sing Elvira in *I Puritani*, the other new major production of the season. Carosio fell victim to a 'flu epidemic but Maestro Serafin's wife chanced to overhear Callas vocalising 'Qui la voce'. After hearing Callas himself, Serafin insisted that he could teach her the role in a week. This widely reported achievement that she had sung Brünnhilde and learnt and performed the role of Elvira in the same week, created a sensation.

It is reported that when she arrived at Covent Garden for the Gala rehearsal, Callas was appalled to find that only twenty minutes had been allotted for her orchestral rehearsal. It was explained to her that to allocate more time would make it impossible to rehearse the rest of the programme. Quietly, John led her to a room where they worked together intensely for two hours. He had never conducted *I Puritani* before and his essential strength as a fine pianist enabled her to transmit to him what she needed from the orchestra. Even at this early stage in his career, with his apparently calm manner which hid the tension he must have felt, he was able to communicate her intentions to the orchestra in the short rehearsal time available. At the star-studded Gala, the audience in evening dress and tiaras, with the theatre decorated with spectacular floral and vegetable motifs, her performance was the sensation of the evening. In her musicianship, partnered by what she had communicated to John, she conveyed a madness that fascinated and, at the same time, embarrassed the audience.

Callas, at the height of her fame, was brought to a wider public a few days later through a Granada Television (ATV) broadcast, *Chelsea at Eight*. The specially invited audience had to battle through the police cordons and huge crowds surrounding the converted theatre, opposite the Chelsea Town Hall, where the live broadcast was to take place. With John accompanying, she sang 'Vissi d'arte' from Act II, *Tosca* and the cavatina 'Una voce poco fa' which begins Act II of *Il Barbiere di Siviglia*. Even though the black and white screens could not convey totally the glamour of her French designed red lamé dress, the impact of her performance was the breakthrough for opera on television.

John had been re-engaged at Vienna primarily because of his success with *Rigoletto*. Conducting that opera in London, with Ilse Hollweg singing Gilda, he proved to Covent Garden that he was an asset worth retaining. Although he conducted the orchestra in a seemingly 'easy' manner, nevertheless one critic noted there was a 'mailed fist within the velvet glove'.

1953 was momentous in the development of Covent Garden. Not only were there the sensational performances of *Norma* but, to celebrate the Coronation of Queen Elizabeth II, a new opera *Gloriana* was commissioned from Benjamin Britten, to be conducted by a British conductor.

Writing from Vienna to David Webster, John managed to extricate himself from a tour of South Africa which would come in the same months as *Norma*, *Gloriana*, Glyndebourne and Edinburgh.

Encouraged by the example of Furtwängler and Kraus here, I have recently succumbed to influenza and now that it is departing I have some nice empty days in which to indulge in overdue correspondence! I have served nearly half my sentence now in Dr Hilbert's Reform School, where I feel myself surrounded by arcs of raised eyebrows at conceptions of Italian opera . . . One very worthwhile performance has however been with Jurinac as Mimi – she is very lovely in the role. We are about to plunge into a Wagnerfest with the restored Wilhelm F [Furtwängler] at the helm, so I expect to have a nice lot of free evenings and may take a small holiday somewhere in the snow level. I have received the first act of *Gloriana* in vocal score, and this, displayed in the rehearsal rooms in the Staatsoper on the rare occasions I need to go there, never fails to create an impression.

Feeling that such a very complex score should not be given its first presentation to an audience primarily of court members and politicians, David Webster expressed reservations about *Gloriana* during the period of preparation.★ The situation was exacerbated by the composer's preoccupation in 'creating' the opera.

Adèle Leigh was rehearsing for another opera and used to go to the Crush Bar at Covent Garden to watch some of the rehearsals of *Gloriana*. 'You know, when you are in your early twenties, you feel nothing can touch you. I went to Ben Britten who was conducting the rehearsal and asked, "Why aren't I in this?" He replied, "There isn't a part for you." "But I *want* to be in it. It's an opera that you've done for the Coronation and I want to be in it. Can't you write me something, even the part of the maid?" So he went away and wrote the role of Lady-in-Waiting for me.'

It was rehearsed and performed during the Glyndebourne season when John was living in Sussex and motoring up to London in the morning. The Earl of Harewood, who was working at Covent Garden at the time, recalled the 'intense irritation' of Benjamin Britten because John was always late for rehearsals. 'During the Coronation year the traffic inside London was nobody's business. I think that often he was about an hour late and other people would have to start the rehearsal. He certainly didn't satisfy the composer as he would otherwise have done, because of this circumstance. It might sound incompetent but he

---

★*The Operas of Benjamin Britten*, pp.39 - 40

achieved. He had an "easy" nerve and didn't mind risking being late, very late.'

The Earl of Harewood had persuaded the Queen and the Court to agree to having an operatic celebration of the Coronation. In effect the event was like a State Command Performance. John Denison, representing the Arts Council, recalled: 'It was not a question of whether or not one liked opera, if you are Lord Chamberlain, Master of the Horse, the Leader of the Government – you go. The whole audience was an official list of people, with the Court people wearing Court dress – silk breeches and so on.' Everybody else wore white tie and decorations.

Twenty years later John remembered that the occasion missed being a triumph as the audience had difficulty in digesting the music easily. 'If we'd played the second act of *Bohème* to that audience, they would have said it was highbrow and turgid. The stalls were full of rajahs whose main concern was standing up and sitting down to see the automatic seats tilt.' Perhaps the most significant aspect of the performance was that it was composed, conducted and sung by British artists. It was the beginning of a more public recognition, of opera being part of official life in Britain. Commenting on the evening, the Earl of Harewood thought that the engagement was not a 'wild success'.

After the Royal performance John wrote to David Webster:

You know how rumours circulate around London, and I have heard from two sources which I do not think frivolous a) that William Walton attributes the lack of success of his version of the National Anthem to a fault of mine in the direction of the arrangement and b) that it has been represented to Buckingham Palace that the Conductor made a mistake and caused the Anthem to appear in an unfavourable light.

Of course, if one took notice of every rumour it would be necessary to spend all one's time chasing them to source. But in view of the persistence of this one, I think I ought to say that my performance of the anthem at the Gala which I conducted was precisely the same as that which the composer heard and approved in rehearsal and which you also heard. A slight mistake was made in one note by a double bass player but any suggestion that the rendering travestied the composer's intention is hereby refuted by me and I am letting you know in case the matter is at any time brought to your attention, (when I am sure you can deal with it!).

Debut

Wilfred Stiff, manager of the Liverpool Philharmonic Orchestra, was present at one of the later performances of *Gloriana*, which were more satisfying as they were before an opera-going public. Previously he had heard of John as the bright young conductor of the Derby String Orchestra, associated with Glyndebourne. He thought that he had done a very good job in presenting the opera. During dinner at Kettners, he invited John to Liverpool as a guest conductor for three engagements.

6

Liverpool

ALLEGRO VIVACE

In the fifties, travelling north, the railway line divided at Crewe. Part of the train went north to Scotland, part to Manchester and the centre to Liverpool, crossing the Mersey. Up until then, running through Cheshire the landscape was very pleasant but immediately after the Mersey there was a stretch of about three or four miles which seemed to consist solely of factories all belching out a cocktail of effluence and chemicals. It was long before the days of anti-pollution. Nothing grew, there was not a blade of green to be seen anywhere. It looked like a moon landscape; total devastation.

In the nineteenth century, a major beneficiary of the Industrial Revolution which changed the face of England, Liverpool was one of the richest cities in the British Empire. With a canal from Manchester to facilitate the transport of goods to its port capable of servicing the largest ships and liners, it was the gateway city to the United States of America. The new gentry, the industrial 'barons', expressed their wealth in the creation of large Victorian villas in leafy suburbs and, relevant to the history of music in Britain, in the formation of the Liverpool Philharmonic Society, second only in Britain, in an historical sense, to the Royal Philharmonic Society and third, in a wider context, to Vienna.

A mixture of amateurs and professionals, the orchestra raised enough money to build a hall by selling shares for which subscribers, together with an annual subscription, received boxes and stall seats. In this way they hoped to restrict the audience to 'suitable' and 'respectable' people so that young ladies might attend concerts without needing a chaperone. Musical standards deteriorated. When the Hall burnt down in 1933, many members wanted to disperse the insurance money and give up the idea of serious music in Liverpool. Fortunately it was decided to build a new hall on the same site, on the corner of Hope Street for the then very large sum of £130,000. Completed for the 1939 – 40 season, it survived the war. During its previous history, the Hall had established its name with many great conductors and artists, such as Furtwängler, Koussevitzky, Rachmaninov, Bruno Walter, Melba, Caruso and the young Solomon, so young that in order to play he had to have a permit from the Children's Court. By this time, the completely professional orchestra received financial support from both the Arts Council and the Liverpool Corporation, who had acquired the Hall and granted the Society use of the venue provided that they arranged a number of concerts there. David Webster was Manager (Chairman 1940 – 45) and Dr Malcolm Sargent (knighted in 1947), very much a person who brought glamour to the podium, were fortunate that during the war the BBC evacuated to Liverpool what was known as the BBC Salon Orchestra. Numbering only about fifteen, they were considered the cream of the orchestral musicians. It was in Liverpool that David Webster learnt how to administer a large organisation of musicians, deal with a Civic Authority and the Arts Council.

At the end of the war the ranks were severely depleted as several principals left the orchestra and returned to London. As with singers, training had come to a standstill during the war years and it was very hard to find experienced players. Wilfred Stiff was only twenty-six when he went to Liverpool as Assistant Manager in June 1946. After only three months, asked to take over as Manager, he faced the horrendous task of both building an orchestra and filling the diary with work and realised that it was necessary to employ somebody prepared to live in Liverpool and help create an orchestra. Quite by chance he heard of a conductor, Hugo Rignold, who was playing first viola at Covent Garden. The choice was good, for Rignold revolutionised the playing. After six years, Rignold decided to take up an appointment at the Sadlers Wells Ballet and not to renew at Liverpool. It was at this juncture that Wilfred Stiff heard John and invited him to Liverpool. Another of the guest conductors, Paul Kletzki, was engaged to take over the conductorship at Liverpool. Like John, he was managed by Joan Ingpen who arranged a meeting between the two. When the Ministry of Labour permit did not materialise for Kletzki, without a principal conductor, Wilfred Stiff had some forty concerts for which he needed to find conductors of repute. In a very short space of time he booked Hermann Scherchen, a great personality on the German music scene who wrote a definitive handbook on conducting and was known for his promotion of new music; Effrem Kurtz, who came for three weeks and John, who had already been booked for some concerts, took up the rest of the season.

Joan Ingpen realised that it was a wonderful chance to get John in as Principal Conductor. The following season he went to Liverpool as joint conductor with Kurtz, taking over in the following year. At Wilfred Stiff's last Committee Meeting his appointment was endorsed. Gerald McDonald took over as General Manager and Secretary of the Society.

As well as conductors and soloists of repute and an emphasis on Choral Concerts including Sir Malcolm Sargent conducting Honegger's *King David* and Elgar's *The Music Makers*, there had been first performances in Britain of a considerable variety of works, with Benjamin Britten conducting his *Spring Symphony*.

The Society realised that the many people involved in industry and commerce were unable to attend at the normal concert time of 7pm, so a series called 'Industrial Concerts' began at the new time of 7.45pm. The first concert in 1946 proved such a success that a whole series of wide-ranging music, with several items in the programme, was arranged throughout the season. Tickets costing four shillings were sold through the participating firms which were expected to purchase a minimum of ten seats per concert on behalf of their employees. The demand was such that it became necessary to repeat each programme on four successive nights, playing, in effect, to an audience of eight thousand.

The audience which had been predominantly middle-class, was changing by the start of the fifties. June 1952 saw the first season of summer promenade concerts at the Liverpool Stadium, with an audience of over five thousand. Together with 'Industrial Concerts', a 'Junior Phil' series and concerts out of town, it was attracting a new following.

John's first appearance as a conductor with the orchestra was for 'Industrial Concerts' on the 9th to 12th November 1953, with Gwen Catley as soloist in the Verdi arias: 'Breath of Zephyr' (*Falstaff*) and 'Caro nome' (*Rigoletto*), the 'Doll's Song' from

Offenbach's *Tales of Hoffman*, Mozart's *Alleluiah* and other light music – Verdi's Overture for *Sicilian Vespers*, Debussy's Prelude to *L'Après-midi d'un Faune*, Chabrier, Rimsky-Korsakov and finally, Ravel's *Boléro*, a mammoth programme.

He followed this in one of the 'Saturday Night at the Phil' concerts on 14th November, programmed as 'evenings of relaxation and entertainment' with Paul Badura-Skoda as the soloist in the Beethoven Piano Concerto no. 4 in G together with Mozart's Symphony no. 41 in C, K551 (*Jupiter*), Rossini's *Cinderella* Overture, Turina's *La Procesión del Rocio* and Ravel's Poème Choreographique, (*La Valse*). In a Wednesday evening concert on 25th November, part of a Mozart/Brahms series very much in keeping with the romantic side of his music-making, he conducted a performance of Brahms' Symphony no. 1 (in C minor, opus 68). During the same month in a concert of short pieces with Gladys Ripley as soloist in arias, John conducted Britten's *Young Person's Guide to the Orchestra*, a piece that he was to programme frequently in the future. Wagner's *Siegfried's Journey to the Rhine* (which he also conducted for the Glyndebourne Easter Concert) completed the programme.

His first season at Liverpool as Principal Conductor (1954 – 55) saw John expanding his symphonic repertoire. Bringing a theatrical touch to concert performances of operas such as Puccini's *The Girl of the Golden West* and *Così fan Tutte*, he had the opportunity to conduct rarely heard pieces at that time, such as the 4th Symphony of Nielsen, the *Inextinguishable*, now heard for the first time in Liverpool, on the 1st March 1955, Strauss' Ballet Pantomine *Schlagobers*, choral works such as Verdi's *Four Sacred Pieces* and Kodály's *Psalmus Hungaricus*. Perhaps the most ambitious was Berlioz' *Grande Messe des Morts* in the cathedral with its augmented orchestra and choir with the brass placed dramatically in the corners of the church. Rising to the challenge, the performance was a triumph. As a special Christmas innovation, he introduced two performances of *Hansel and Gretel*, one of which was a special children's matinée. However, the festive season would not have been complete without the traditional Handel's *Messiah*. Leaving the Hall darkened during the pastoral symphony, the only lighting being the Christmas trees on the platform, he enjoyed the 'oohs' and 'aahs' from an appreciative audience.

The north of England has a great choral/oratorio tradition. If one draws a line through the map from Huddersfield across the northern part of the country, all the large towns and cities have well established and active choral societies. Liverpool was one of the best because, unusually, it had its own Philharmonic Hall, 'home' of both the orchestra and chorus, a purpose-built venue in which to rehearse and perform. At Christmas there were always three performances of *Messiah* and three carol concerts.

A chorus member recalled John's popularity. Although very strict he understood that he was dealing with amateurs but did not let them get away with anything. 'He could always put you in your place, pull you up for singing the wrong notes, or singing badly but always did it in a very kind way as if he knew that people were there because they loved singing, loved music, this was part of their life and that they weren't being paid. He never humiliated people if they did something wrong but made it very clear when they had done something wrong and he put it right.'

John brought to Liverpool Covent Garden singers such as Inia Te Wiata, Raymond Nilssen and Dame Joan Sutherland who recalled that the Hall was always packed. 'I don't ever remember it being half full, I did things like *Messiah* and the *St Matthew Passion* in Liverpool Cathedral. Ricky [Bonynge, her husband] and John got on well and we would have dinner at his home. There were some marvellous associations with John and one had laughs.' After the *St Matthew Passion*, Hugues Cuenod, who had sung 'Evangelist' and the rest of the men started telling dirty stories or limericks and she and Norma Procter were blushing to the roots of their hair.

Dame Joan continued that like John, 'at that time, one was so busy learning; intent on the travelling and the learning. One would take the music to learn for the next engagement whilst travelling back on the train. It was like that – I suppose it still is to a certain extent. One rushed to Liverpool to do *Messiahs* and tore back to London to continue rehearsing; did something for the BBC and rushed to Glyndebourne.'

Adèle Leigh recalled the exhaustion of singers during Covent Garden's eight week annual tour. 'Only the sort of thing you can do in your twenties.' Liverpool was a favourite engagement with singers after the war when food was rationed. They need sugar for energy and it was very tiring, trailing around; the train at 3.10 in the morning from Grantham, sitting on a cold station. Those who had relatives living in America were fortunate enough to be sent tinned pineapple. However, after a Liverpool engagement, it was possible to take the night boat over to Dublin. After an enormous breakfast they would walk up and down O'Connell Street, buying boxes of sweets, returning with their bags full.

John was well received by the Liverpool public as he was able to communicate his love of music to the audience but there was one concern for the management and that was his private life which was now openly homosexual. He had grown up and started his career at a time when homosexuality was a criminal offence. The fifties were still an age of innocence and ignorance. In conversation the subject was taboo. Metaphorically John lived his life in two compartments. He would have a circle of friends with whom he could talk and make music and then he would withdraw and turn to another circle of friends, people who belonged to a different milieu. With his sensitivity and good taste he could 'relate' to women and other homosexual men more easily but understood that often other men, even colleagues, found it difficult to accept his behaviour. As in his childhood, hiding many things from his father such as his piano playing, he developed a mask which hid his innermost thoughts. John liked secrets, liked the idea of a private life. Joan Carlyle commented: 'Sometimes he would give the appearance of not being on this planet. It would be as though his mind was away. Seeing one come into a room he'd suddenly come back. My heart used to go out to him.'

Hating unpleasantness, realising they were unfaithful, he would write young men letters saying 'goodbye' but at the last moment often failed to send or give them. Sketching the outline in his diary, he confided his agony.

> The trouble is I do begin to know you and I just can't be a casual acquaintance. You see I understand *so well* how you like to live and I believe that to you, my very seriousness is a sort of obstacle – wouldn't it be nice if I were like all the rest of your friends. I can stand anything from you but not intimacy on Shrove Tuesday and Boxing Day by arrangement. I feel a thousand things about you and all of them add up to the fact you have an odd sort of interest in me but don't want to be with me very much. You must know I like secrecy but then the very symbol of our secrecy disappears. I feel injured by last Wednesday. You can't fool me. I *know* always. The trouble is I have always meant every word I ever said.

A man who knew John well, spoke about their relationship:

Each of us sees each other in a totally different light, a different mood. We are all individual people. You can't say a man is a homosexual . . . There were wonderful, marvellous qualities of homosexuality which John had. On the other hand, there are horrendous, vicious aspects of homosexuality which John didn't have and many people do. He was a wonderful, dear, gentle person who had physical relationships. I was physically very close to him. We slept together. It was not the beginning of a sexual orgy. It was just a warm physical closeness. When one is near someone that one loves and there is a physical warmth, a kind of natural, animal togetherness, wanting to be together, it's not prostitution. One isn't buying or manipulating – just wanting to be with each other.

In commenting about John's interest not only in the music but everything else on stage, Ileana Cotrubas considered: 'He was very cultured, not only musically but he was a man of the world. Many men who are homosexuals, one thinks "Why do these lovely men, cultured men, sleep on the other side of the way?" Who knows? This is something that comes from childhood or family. Maybe in a way he lacked something in life. None of us are perfect but it's genetic. Many conductors and musicians are homosexual. It's a plus, a sensitivity, a *raffinesse*.'

From his earliest years John would look around, encompassing both company and his surroundings with delight. Those who seem to have this ability have from their youth had to find some positive aspect in their unhappy situation. Throughout his childhood, he had known his father only as a very conservative, unbending rigid disciplinarian. Albert had cut himself off from society which referred to him as 'the old man'. Attempting to protect her son from her husband's determination that he should be a violinist, whilst encouraging him at the piano, Amy had connived with John to outwit the old man and to look upon him as 'a bit of a joke'. John's letters to his mother could be interpreted as love letters and as her health deteriorated in the fifties, he needed someone to replace her as confidante. His letters to her became postcards, the most convenient way of keeping in touch. The simple tone of language, contrasting with his letters from South Africa, sound almost as if he is writing to a child, a symptom of her decline.

From: Frankfurter Hotel. Saturday September 19th
Dear Mum,
This is my hotel in Frankfurt, where I am conducting a public

concert next Wednesday for the Radio Orchestra. It is a busy, thriving town, the people very nice. Then on Thursday 24th I go on HOLIDAY!!! to *Rome* for 10 days. After that Oct. 6th, I go back to Cologne (Germany) for another concert.

Much love, hope you are well.   John.

Liking the company of women, several believed that John was attached to them. In later years young women arriving at Glyndebourne would be attracted to him and were disappointed when they found that his interests were homosexual. He was engaged to a harpist for a brief period but the only photographs his mother retained were those of Eva Metzler. She had put a great deal into their relationship, running errands, even collecting the dry-cleaning in Derby. She had taught him all she knew about opera. Always *soignée*, she had followed him to London working at Ibbs & Tillett until her retirement. There are many who believe they were the 'only one', yet unbeknown to each other, he was 'seeing' several people of both sexes at the same time, even visiting Brumas, the baby polar bear at London Zoo, with three different people. However it was only to Eva that he gave presents of equal value to those he gave his mother at Christmas. Seeing John almost daily, teaching him German, she anticipated they had a future together and was dismayed and distraught when he established an association with Basil Horsfield.

His friendship with Basil Horsfield in the fifties was to lead to uncertainty on the part of managements towards him. In the summer of 1952, after a trip to Germany, John appeared at Glyndebourne with Basil. He was introduced as a pupil, a protégé. Resigning from the Derby String Orchestra in 1952, as he could not possibly continue to combine so many positions, John arranged for Basil to work at Derby and Basil officially took over in December 1952. It is believed that there was an occasion at Glyndebourne when John was due to take a rehearsal of the orchestra and he let Basil take it. It caused a great deal of trouble and it is understood was the beginning of a situation wherein John was not totally within the Glyndebourne *famille*.

A similar situation arose at Covent Garden, provoking an apology from John to David Webster.

I must apologise – and thank you for the very understanding terms of your note. *Of course* the arrangement (two isolated occasions) last week was intended, perhaps in excess of zeal, merely to pass on notes of mine to the singers and there was no thought of Basil coaching as such. This enabled me to attend production calls where I was badly needed. However I agree with you it might cause misunderstandings but while *Wozzeck* and *Electra* took up the time of so many of your staff I have found it rather difficult to cope. It was for this reason only that Basil was unofficially co-opted, as he knows the opera extremely well.

I do understand however, the remarks that might be made and shall see that Basil does not do anything that might more properly be done by a member of the staff. Thank you for pointing out the difficulty.

Basil's ambitions as a conductor and the reaction at Covent Garden, worried Wilfred Stiff. The Opera House is relatively cosmopolitan and he was concerned that Liverpool, a rather parochial place at the time, would react unfavourably. In a frank and amiable discussion he warned the young conductor because he wanted to see a man with such musicianship succeed. John understood the situation and neither of them referred to the subject again.

John and Wilfred Stiff drafted the programmes together. It is customary for a conductor to choose the programmes and for an orchestral manager to find suitable performers but sometimes, with great international artists, programmes are based on the particular repertoire that those artists select. Early in John's tenure at Liverpool, for a performance of the *St Matthew Passion*, John made his own very emphatic suggestions as to soloists, from an operatic as opposed to oratorio background. The result was not a normal rendition of Bach and was called 'strange' in the press, alerting Wilfred Stiff to a behind the scenes influence. From the lack of critical approval and his own musical understanding, Wilfred Stiff realised that John would not in future follow others' suggestions without due thought. John needed someone to keep order in his life. Whilst he appreciated beautiful things, the décor of his flat in Knightsbridge had been abysmal so he directed Basil's talents towards providing him with an organised happy background.

John kept two sets of diaries. The first, a standard desk diary in pocketbook planner form, enabled him to see his engagements at a glance. The other was a small diary into which he poured his innermost thoughts, acting as a form of 'confessional'. With the arrival of Basil, it was observed that the small diary became superfluous and unused. Approximately three years later, the phrase 'fings ain't what they used to be' appeared in the 1955 diary. Gradually the small diary came back into use, recording his disillusionment in love and relationships. He understood *Così fan Tutte* only too well.

The other aspect of *Così*, the delicious element of French farce, of doors opening and closing in the night appealed to him enormously. One morning taking a breakfast tray up the stairs, the formidable housekeeper of the Christie household saw bare flesh exit from John's bedroom, run down the corridor and enter another bedroom. She was heard to exclaim: 'My goodness it's just like the Wrens in the war!'

John understood the pressures which he faced and the need to relax. Seldom having tantrums with the orchestral players or artists it did him a certain amount of harm because, for some people's tastes, he was too professional. Many years later on 27th June 1969 as a Governor of the London Opera Centre, the training school for young singers, he gave a talk on 'Professionalism in Music' addressing himself to the various problems facing a young artist. Amongst the untruths about his father, deliberately fostered over the years and romantic stories about his own early career, he perceived that to be a professional musician 'is essentially a decision to be lonely'. A certain isolation is necessary for an artist.★

Commenting on the difficulties which a singer has to face, Elisabeth Söderström remarked:

It's difficult to be only with yourself – to be alone, locked up with yourselves preparing for a concert or a performance – especially as a singer you have to save your voice. You can't meet people and talk too much. So, if you cannot do that, then you have very little chance in this profession, I'm sorry to say. You're nervous and scared, especially when it's a long concert programme that you have to deliver by heart, when everybody sits there with the words in front of them.

I think when you call people 'divas', it's about artists who want to do their job well and they don't want to be bothered with ridiculous details and that makes them seem 'diva-like' to certain people. It's just a practical point of view. I know that if I don't have to worry

★Professionalism in Music, p. 328

about details I can do my job better. I don't think that John was a 'diva' but he was practical.

Reflecting on one summer at Glyndebourne she said:

The weather was very cold, very bad and I lived very far away from everybody else and did not have a car. I felt that we spent all day in prison – rehearsing. That was for *Fidelio* in 1979. I felt in prison also during my free time. I almost killed myself. Everything was terrible. Then I realised that it was very important that you live in the right place and have a car. I think that's something that John knew very well how to do – to arrange a comfortable atmosphere around himself. We all have to find out how we function best. If you sit in a foreign country and long to be home then you don't function as an artist. You must make a home wherever you are. Only a few things that can cheer you up and also to bear to be with yourself. I think that the reason why we did not meet very much after performances was because after performances, most of the time I am drained and desperately tired. I couldn't face all the people that always surrounded John. He always had so many people around him.

The loneliness of the conductor has an extra dimension. Audience appreciation of a performer's talent is inclined to be subjective but it is essential for a conductor to be objective in making decisions. To be a Musical Director of either a symphony orchestra or an opera house, dealing not only with performers, producers and designers but administrators whose decisions are not necessarily made on the basis of musical understanding but are sometimes governed by financial or political considerations, is often to find oneself in an equivocal position. Managements never had any problems when they dealt directly with John. They always found him totally amenable, understanding the practicalities of a situation.

Just before his debut at Covent Garden in *A Masked Ball*, he moved to 14 Vicarage Gardens, Kensington. Later he and Basil occupied a flat at 17 Soho Square, W1. Adèle Leigh remembered that 'everything was so beautifully presented, with the right colour candles on the table, flowers and wonderful dishes that he concocted and Basil prepared. He introduced me to serving dinner by candlelight.'

By 1961, John felt secure enough to purchase a beautiful white stucco villa in Park Village East, close to Regent's Park. Although there is a railway track opposite and a council estate in close proximity, once inside the small house, instinctively one looked out towards the garden. There were endless dinner parties which, with Basil doing the cooking, became gastronomic events. The story is told that when Basil was going to the horticulturist's to buy plants for the garden, enumerating them, '. . . and then perhaps a pergola and a green-house,' he waffled on, eventually asking, 'Is there anything you would like?' 'Just buy me a deckchair!' was the rejoinder.

In Liverpool John's lovely home, Scarletts at Grassendale, overlooked the Mersey but it was with amazement that he recorded in capitals in his 1962 diary: '24 Jan. Scarletts ENTERED AND BURGLED!' Such an event seemed unthinkable at the time.

They kept a dog, Tio and Pepe the cat. When Tio died he was replaced by Sari, a Corgi. John always kept a pet. His preference was for a dog but later the practicality of cats attracted him. There are many photographs of him with large dogs and cats he befriended, from Leslie Smart's Gaythem Spitz to Carlo, the black cat who ruled supreme in the eighties. Carlo, with his 'passport' of vaccinations, travelled the continent of Europe in a beautiful padded basket on John's lap.

In Liverpool John's repertoire and circle of friends was widening. In an Industrial Concert during the 1954 – 55 season for a performance of Beethoven's *Emperor* Concerto (no. 5 in E flat, op.73), he collaborated with pianist Clive Lythgoe, who was becoming well known in the profession. They became close friends. The sympathy between the conductor and pianist was such that they continued to work together later, Lythgoe playing a varied repertoire such as Rachmaninov's 2nd, (op.18) and the Schumann concerto (in A minor, op.54), at the Liverpool Stadium Proms where it was customary to play two concertos a night. The Grieg concerto in A minor on 8th – 10th September 1959 was a great favourite and was the centrepiece for many programmes during a northern tour. Under John's baton Lythgoe played Humphrey Searle's 2nd concerto on 11th December 1956. When John was in Pittsburgh he conducted the second MacDowell concerto and on his return told Lythgoe about it, saying that it was so rhetorical, romantic and with *rubato*. He liked to call Lythgoe, 'Rubato Clive'. They did that concerto first in Liverpool and then brought it to the London Proms.

In trying to analyse the success of their collaboration in a concerto situation, Lythgoe felt that other than making jokes with him about *rubato*, which he took as a compliment, John inspired him to play at his best because he did not give advice and would never lecture. 'What one needs is somebody who understands, is very instinctive and that's what made him a great concerto conductor.' It did not happen to Clive Lythgoe but if John was not happy with what the soloist was doing he would remain silent but his lips would tighten. Although he never appeared nervous himself, he would give a performer support. On one occasion when the soloist was exceptionally nervous, 'he came up behind me, patted my bottom and said I'd be great. I went on and played like an angel.'

Although Lythgoe moved to New York, the friendship continued, John telephoning him the day before he died to say 'thank you'. Even though it was an effort for him to speak, the mind was crystal clear.

The two major orchestras at Liverpool and Manchester helped to satisfy symphony concert audiences in the surrounding districts but Wilfred Stiff felt that John's association with Glyndebourne Opera should be put to good use. He suggested to the Leader of the City Council that they should bring the Glyndebourne Opera Company complete with the Philharmonic Orchestra playing in the pit, to Liverpool's Royal Court Theatre. With full financial support, an extension of the artists' engagements for two additional weeks after their 1956 season at Glyndebourne was implemented immediately.

The possible establishment of a Northern Opera House had been in John's thoughts for several years. During his Derby days, trying to create work, he had started 'Orpheus Opera' with a group of singers from Glyndebourne. The return of Fritz Busch to Glyndebourne and his subsequent career rendered it superfluous. Taking the opportunity of the impending arrival of both Covent Garden Opera and Glyndebourne Opera he voiced his opinions in a talk to the Liverpool Opera Circle on 7th January 1956.★

Long before the company arrived all the performances had 'sold out' notices. Vittorio Gui conducted all performances of *Figaro* and *La Cenerentola* except one by John, who also conducted most of the *Don Giovannis*.

★The Position of Opera outside London, p. 330

Liverpool

The visit by Glyndebourne entrenched John firmly with the Liverpool public who adored the performances. It was a time of celebration, for parties, for fun. At a reception in the Town Hall, the police band played operatic selections and all the singers joined in where appropriate, adding to the rhythm section with knives on wine glasses. An onlooker recalled that Moran Caplat was embarrassed because he thought Glyndebourne was behaving badly, letting their hair down like schoolchildren on an outing. However, the City Council members were so enchanted by this that even though it did not get back in time, a police car was sent to the other side of Liverpool for another selection of opera from their music library.

When Ian Wallace arrived he was buttonholed by Bessie Braddock, the famous, rather large lady who represented one of the Liverpool constituencies. 'I think it would be a good idea if you serenaded me with The Hippopotamus Song. I am like a hippopotamus and I'll be up in the gallery. You'll sing the male hippopotamus part down below and I'll be the female up there you see.' He was highly concerned about doing this to somebody of her size but she thoroughly enjoyed it. 'The whole idea was a conspiracy between Sir Harry Livermore [Chairman of the Society] and John Pritchard without a doubt. John, typically, was so grateful, "So good of you to come and do this."'

The Liverpool Philharmonic gave its own party for the opera company. One of the first violins, Ronald Vaughan would often imitate John. He used to wear a black beret on the side of his head and mimic his walk and speech. During the party, whilst the imitation was in progress, John arrived and the rest of the orchestra made a quick exit uncertain as to his reaction. After a few minutes of talking to each other with the same accent and mannerisms they parted company. However, about ten minutes later John called, 'Ronnie, come over here and do me again!'

John would often add a further unexpected dimension to the fun. It had become a tradition for Fritz Spiegl to produce April Fool's Concerts. At one of these, as the orchestra was about to play, much to everyone's amusement, a latecomer arrived endeavouring to find his seat in the front stalls. It was John, who enjoyed every minute of his late entrance. He detested latecomers at his own concerts and there had been numerous problems with them. At another April Fool's Concert, as usual he came on at the start of the concert to conduct. He then opened the lid of

125

the piano, put the stick in the lid and walked off again. He liked doing the unexpected.

The 1957 – 58 season became a landmark in the history of the orchestra. Wilfred Stiff had initiated the request and the title 'Royal' was graciously bestowed on the Society and Orchestra in February 1957 by Her Majesty the Queen.

In John's first season as Musical Director, the Society introduced a system of family tickets. Believed to be the first anywhere in the country, it was a concession to parents who could not afford to purchase tickets both for themselves and their children. By purchasing a ticket for a series, parents were entitled to a further ticket at half price for children under the age of twenty-one. In Derby John had worked for the Educational Committee, now he conducted Saturday morning concerts in which he would introduce and explain modern music to young people. In 1960, after talking about Humphrey Searle's 2nd Symphony, he announced that prizes would be awarded for the best essays received and, though shocked by the huge postbag awaiting him, read them all and awarded the prize.

The musicians enjoyed playing for his performances of Haydn, Mozart, Berlioz, Debussy, Richard Strauss and Stravinsky but if he felt that a piece was in the repertoire, at rehearsal he would say: 'We did this a few weeks ago, let's leave it till the concert.' This suited those who had played the work concerned previously but frightened others. It kept them alert and sometimes he could produce an electrifying performance. On the other hand, performances of Beethoven and Brahms were not so successful. Once after a very bad performance of a symphony, when the audience was not made up of regular concert-goers, he commented, 'I felt even those mutton-heads wince.'

On another occasion the audience winced for a somewhat different reason, John retaining the account amongst his papers. The main work, Berlioz' *Symphonie Fantastique*, requires an enlarged orchestra. He wanted the Dies Irae played on large tubular bells, amplified off-stage. The part was given to a new recruit who rehearsed in front of a microphone just outside the left-hand entrance to the platform immediately behind the first violins. The door was open for him to watch the conductor.

During the performance John had a premonition that all was not well but, noticing that the door was slightly open, presumed that the player was 'poised for action'. The actual point of entry

126

occurs when the rest of the orchestra is silent. John indicated in the direction of the open door. Silence. At this moment the music cannot be halted as the violins have an important entry. After an even more vigorous gesture at the door, the theme rang out, amplified, several bars out. In the excitement, with extraordinary variations of rhythm, it became a jazz version of Dies Irae. Meanwhile the rest of the orchestra endeavoured to keep up with the bells.

John leant forward to the deputy leader, 'Stop him, Tom.' He put his violin down on the chair and moved towards the door. However, that evening, there were no fewer than three 'Toms' in the violin sections and the audience were mystified to see three musicians jump up from their chairs, one of whom had the unbelievable misfortune to have the fly of his trousers caught in the sweeping bow of a colleague, resulting in him being bent double over the player. At last the original 'Tom' reached and restrained the recalcitrant. The shocked audience heard the hugely amplified explanation, 'The f—ing door closed . . .!'

As Musical Director John experimented with the repertoire, programming works by Prokofiev and Shostakovich, Bartók, Bloch and Sir Arthur Bliss, with several first performances by living composers. It was important for both orchestra and audience alike that as well as visits by international conductors and soloists, composers such as Tippett, Britten and Poulenc went to Liverpool.

John would sometimes comment to the players that he liked new works if they were short. On one occasion not liking a new rather complicated piece, as a practical joke, some of the brass players decided to put a picture of a male nude inside John's score. As he conducted without any change of expression, the players presumed that the offending article had been removed. The next day at rehearsal he thanked them for their performance, 'and also [pause] thank you for your kind thoughts!'

Understanding that an audience was wary of the unknown and to popularise the Industrial Concerts, as a special free event John introduced the programmes using gramophone records to illustrate some of the works and artists to be heard to familiarise would-be concert-goers. He spoke frequently to the members of the Philharmonic Club★ (the predecessor of the present day

★Behind the Baton, p. 333

Friends of the Phil) who met occasionally. One evening, instead of introducing the season's programmes, he started the talk with a recording of Mme Florence Foster-Jenkins' execrable singing of Mozart. He enjoyed watching the expressions on his audience's faces when they thought that she would be singing at a concert but reassured them before the end of the evening that she was *not* on the programme.

Popular with the Club for his relaxed, entertaining manner of presentation, when he saw a concert syllabus from Munich, John seized on an idea to promote modern music and 'Musica Viva' was born in Britain. It is perhaps for this series that he is best remembered in Liverpool, a series which was to give both the orchestra and its conductor an international reputation. Knowing that not only the audience but his players, like himself, enjoyed broadening their experience, he would introduce each work in an informal manner pointing out with quotations any special features and explaining difficulties of performance. An extension of his other pre-concert talks, they became part of the concert itself. When a listener requested that he should talk about the structure of a piece and explain its development, John responded by emphasising his own practical as opposed to academic approach to music and the importance of emotional rather than intellectual understanding. John realised that it was very difficult for the concert public to appreciate highly involved music at first hearing. He was quoted some years later when prefacing a performance on 20th February 1970 of a work by Peter Maxwell Davies in Copenhagen (Sjaellands Sinfoniorkest) with an introduction in 'a very non-technical way'. He stressed: 'The end result must always be aural rather than mental, that it should not need a musical education to appreciate contemporary music but become involved in an artistic happening.'

John's introductions and analyses of the works played were always humorous and never 'stuffy'. In one concert, rehearsing Berg's *Lulu* Suite, he told the orchestra that the story was a 'double X-rated feature'. When the person who was acting off-stage, screamed in German, 'Nein, nein, nein', this had all the players laughing (999 being the British telephone number for the emergency services). John called out, 'No, my dear, I think you must scream in English.' During a work by Peter Maxwell Davies, full of complicated beats for about twenty minutes without a break, John explained to the players exactly what he was beating in each bar and then suggested putting a small pause at a halfway point 'so that those of you who have gone adrift can meet up with us again'. With his clarity of beat, the pause was unnecessary. They did one set of Variations by Iain Hamilton but John wanted them to play the two sets together. 'I don't think the composer knows this yet but these two variations fit very well together.'

By the end of the fifties the compositions of Iain Hamilton were moving in a new direction, becoming much more sparse. His early prizewinning work had been performed under Boult, Sargent and Barbirolli. Introduced by Howard Hartog in 1958 (who took over from Ingpen & Williams, John's agents) he went to Liverpool for a performance of 'A Sonata for Chamber Orchestra', the first of his many compositions which John was to perform. The second work of his which John conducted, the 'Sinfonia for Two Orchestras', had had a controversial première at the Edinburgh Festival under Alexander Gibson and the Scottish National Orchestra. Later John took Hamilton's piano concerto to Berlin in a programme with Humphrey Searle's 3rd Symphony and Sososstris' aria from Tippett's *Midsummer Marriage*.

At that time, Iain Hamilton's work was very avant-garde but John took it up with the same enthusiasm with which he conducted Mozart and Strauss. Britten, Vaughan Williams and Tippett were contemporary composers but the players were unused to Hamilton's style. It is absolutely paramount for a conductor to display enthusiasm for a work to the players. If he finds the music problematic this is conveyed to the orchestra but John was skilful in explanation without being bombastically flattering. They were convinced by his attention to the work that they could play it. Hamilton recalled:

I would spend a little time with him preparing, very little in comparison to the time I've sometimes spent with others. He had a way of not only bringing it off at the performance but the rehearsal was always a very pleasant period. It was always a very, very happy professional relationship. I have very little insight into how he prepared these works but the performances were always lively and one hundred per cent professional. He had a wonderful ear and would always notice every pitch that was wrong. A consummate, natural musician, he belongs to what I would call 'the old school'. His conducting seemed unobtrusive; it was an inner thing. I would sit at a table with the score and occasionally he would ask me something if he was dubious about a note but there would be very little communication. I never needed to go through the score bar by bar, as with many other conductors. John did remind me of Boult. When Barbirolli did my 2nd Symphony, they rehearsed for weeks in Manchester. John did that work at Cheltenham, three days after the première of *Gloriana*.

For players it can prove to be a nerve-wracking experience to approach complicated new pieces sometimes requiring extended rehearsal periods. The orchestra suspected that occasionally John had not opened the score of a new work before the first rehearsal. Nevertheless, with his flair for learning new works so quickly and the reliability, clarity and calmness of his conducting coupled with the relaxation of his sense of humour, they would themselves learn the new works rapidly. After they had played a piece through once, he would give a smile, 'Oh, so that's how it goes.'

As a result of Musica Viva, they were invited in 1958 to the Leeds Triennial Festival for an excerpt from *Moses and Aaron* by Schoenberg, a work by Alexander Goehr and Fricker's *A Vision of Judgement*.

The Earl of Harewood considered that John was '*the* conductor for new music. He was a marvellous learner and was the conductor that anyone who had new music used to commission.' For *A Vision of Judgement* John recommended John Dobson for the tenor as he had done a successful concert in Liverpool. The singer remembered struggling with the piece but on rehearsing with John, the conductor remarked, 'You've done very well with this twelve tone music.' Dobson was amazed as he hadn't thought about it. John reassured him; 'Well, maybe that's the right way to deal with it, not to worry about it and sing it on the ordinary scale.' The work was repeated in the Musica Viva Series at Liverpool.

The next year Leeds planned to do the first English performance of Schoenberg's *The Dance around the Golden Calf* (Act II, scenes iii and iv from *Moses and Aaron*). The opera itself was staged a few years later at Covent Garden. It is very difficult and was cast very carefully. The Earl of Harewood described the occasion. 'He had his rehearsals with the Liverpool orchestra and we had rehearsals there. He'd done a lot of ground work and the chorus had learnt their parts. Two of our Naked Virgins (this was non-staged) were Heather Harper and Janet Baker early in their careers. It's the sort of piece that is difficult. However many rehearsals you've scheduled, you've under scheduled. I used to see John a lot in those days and he was very practical. What he needed I knew how to provide, like engaging people and chorus and things like that.' The early rehearsals were in a place called Beckett's Park in Leeds, with a good University College Hall, which was engaged morning, afternoon and evening. An orchestra tends to do only two rehearsals a day and the amateur chorus could have tired easily. The Earl of Harewood remembered: 'We didn't have much time left and things weren't going well so John said "Right, we'll have an early break for the orchestra – we'll just do two and a half hours and the chorus goes away after the first hour, so it has an hour on its own in another place with the chorus master to try and get this right. We'll break with the orchestra, the chorus comes back, we'll then work through for an hour with them. I'll need a quarter of an hour on my own and then we'll come back and do the last three hours." He organised this to get extra rehearsal time out of the time available. He did the continuous four and a half hours stretch, they had their breaks. He worked like mad and got it going. John had a reputation for not being a hard worker but I have evidence to the contrary that he could work very hard.'

In his ability to study and learn quickly, to illuminate what a composer intended and take an orchestra through complex scores, John displayed a very rare talent. Musica Viva revealed a determination to achieve something which took great courage to bring off successfully. He was willing to trust his players and they, in turn, trusted him and responded with loyalty. It was an extraordinary relationship in Liverpool. On one occasion when dense fog enveloped the town and no public transport was available, all the players, some of whom lived three or four miles away, walked to the Hall. Afterwards John was seen walking down the road, waving a white handkerchief so that the driver of his Mercedes could follow him home.

The orchestra enjoyed going to the highly successful mini-Festival at Ingestre Hall, the Staffordshire home of the Earl of Shrewsbury. In many ways a mini Glyndebourne; there was elegance coupled with the culinary aspect. Instead of a purpose-built theatre, operas were performed inside the house. Governed to a large extent by the lack of space, the repertoire consisted of chamber operas and baroque pieces. Without a pit, in a rather improvised fashion requiring a very much reduced scoring, the instruments were situated on one side of the stage and next to it. Together with players from Liverpool and members of the Glyndebourne chorus, double bills were performed. It was a very short Festival, only three or four performances of each opera but John enjoyed it as he was in charge musically. Alternating on two different evenings, Purcell's baroque *Dido and Aeneas* was coupled with de Falla's more romantic *Master Peter's Puppet Show*, on the other, John Blow's *Venus and Adonis* paired with Bizet's *Dr Miracle*. Anthony Besch directed the Festival and staged a concert version of *Dr Miracle* in Liverpool afterwards.

John's first season there as Musical Director in 1958 was very nearly the end of his career. Writing from the Royal Hospital, Wolverhampton, on 4th March, in reply to a telegram of good wishes from David Webster, he described what had happened:

> I am progressing after going bang through the windscreen on Sunday on our way to Liverpool. Extensive lacerations of the face but I am terribly lucky the eyes were saved by a millimetre! The opinion is that I will have a scar or two but let's hope it'll give a sardonic, not unattractive appearance . . . Luckily I can convalesce for the next couple of weeks in peace. Basil escaped with shock and bruises and has been taken in most manfully by the Shrewsburys who live not far from the scene of the accident. Needless to say I feel *102*!

Enlarging, John replied to Moran Caplat's flowers and queries on 5th March:

> Thank goodness – it might all have been worse. We went at forty miles an hour direct into one of those oblivious Sunday trippers, in an ancient Austin with *one* faded rearlight, *parked* on the crown of the road (two-lane) on the A5. Can you beat it! We had exactly three seconds with it in vision and those three secs. I shall never forget. Basil escaped with shock and bruises but I went like a bullet through the windscreen.
>
> Things are looking up now. I look like a surrealist horror with multiple abrasions, but the opinion is the visage will heal up not too badly scarred – only time can do it. They are sending me up to Liverpool tomorrow to remove some stitches and recuperate. The Shrewsburys turned up trumps and motored over to pick up Basil from the highway, put him to bed, and he's still there. Don't know what we'd have done without them.

Discharged to the Liverpool flat for convalescence, John was 'looked at by a plastic surgeon, with a view to all round improvements! (Long overdue.)'

An artist who knew him well commented that, young and attractive at the time, John was never the same after the car accident. It scarred him and he was never quite as self-assured in public as previously. 'He became very conscious that his looks had gone and seemed to indulge himself because he felt that it didn't matter any more. Whereas he might have kept a trimmer figure, I think he let himself go.' In the concert syllabus for the Season following his accident (1959 – 60), John's photograph shows him in a contemplative Rodinesque pose, chin cupped in his hand, hiding the scar. Other photographs threw shadows onto that side of his face.

He recovered sufficiently for the first International Conductor's Competition in May. Zubin Mehta, who won first prize, was a student in Vienna with, as is often the case, nothing happening. His father-in-law, deputy principal violin of the Hallé Orchestra, hearing of the competition, suggested that he enter. 'I won because William Steinberg [Head of the Jury] liked my opening bars of Beethoven's Fifth.' Winning a competition with several performances as part of a prize is a very useful source of income and experience, as well as exposure for a young artist. As John's musical assistant for the 1958 – 59 season, Mehta's memories are of a punishing schedule. 'He expected me to follow a schedule I would never dream of imposing on my own students.' After his year in Liverpool, their paths did not cross again.

In May 1959 John instituted an International Competition for pianists under the age of thirty, with Solomon as Head of the Jury. Joaquin Achucarro won the first and John Ogdon the second prize. In the year of that competition, John programmed a series of concerts, part of a three year plan, to include all the main piano concertos, including most of the Mozarts. Unquestionably interest focused on John Ogdon's performance of the Busoni concerto in C, op.39.

The competitions spotlighted attention on Liverpool and, in a letter dated October 1959 the Earl of Harewood asked if they could get together for lunch, 'to ask your advice, based on your experience of International Competitions in Liverpool, about a suggestion that maybe Leeds might try to run similar competitions.'

133

The Earl of Harewood recalled that his first wife was one of the instigators of the piano competitions in Leeds.

I think John conducted it for a year or two [He sat on the jury 18th – 21st September 1963]. That he would have been remarkable at because he had a wonderful instinct for accompanying somebody. It must be an awful boring job to work with three different people in the final, without being certain what they would or could do but he did it with enormous tact and skill. In rehearsal, in practical terms, he was a 'non trouble-maker'. He had an instinct for smoothing everything down and making everything as good as it could be. In that sense he was an old-fashioned conductor, an unselfish conductor. I'm talking about rehearsal and performance. He would always fit in with things provided that it made sense. He was an easy collaborator because he was so professional. He could accommodate if it was difficult and make adjustments but didn't adjust over standards.

The following year saw an International Singers' Competition in Liverpool with Dame Eva Turner as head of a jury which included the Earl of Harewood. She was to remain a close friend of John's throughout their lives. John invited Berthold Goldschmidt to conduct the choir. Barbara Robotham won and Kenneth Bowen, later Head of Vocal Studies at the Royal Academy of Music, gained second prize.

During competitions a loudspeaker system was set up in the orchestral bandroom so that the players could hear everything that was being said and played on the platform and would know when they were required on stage. John said that it might be a good idea to have the system working the other way round so that a microphone in the gents' changing room would enable him to hear their comments about conductors. He could imagine 'I think this conductor is —' and then the comment was drowned by the sound of him imitating a flushing toilet.

By 1960, with his contract renewed at Liverpool for a further three years, John was emerging as a conductor of stature with a large repertoire in the concert hall. Today, many young conductors find themselves jetting about the world with just a dozen works in their suitcase until, finally, much later in life, they are able to obtain an appointment and develop their repertoire. John had come to prominence through the world of opera which is very rare. Some start as repetiteurs, becoming 'house' conductors but seldom have the opportunity to transfer to a major symphony orchestra.

The interest in Musica Viva resulted in an invitation to the orchestra for a week at the London Proms. At the Edinburgh Festival John conducted the première of William Walton's Symphony no.2, which although commissioned by Liverpool in the 1953 – 54 season was not performed until the 1960 – 61 season. Invited for two concerts, they gave the world première of Humphrey Searle's 3rd Symphony and were invited to the Wexford Festival in Ireland for a concert in their 1961 – 62 season.

A great fan of Glyndebourne, Dr Tom Walsh wanted to have a festival of that nature in his home town of Wexford, in Ireland, performing operas which were seldom heard or neglected rarities. Consequently they were well attended by the critics. The mainstay of the casts were the Glyndebourne chorus and understudies with one or two artists who were relatively unknown at the time.

The Festival is held at the end of October and beginning of November when the weather is inclement, so unless one flew, people had to cross a very rough sea to attend. Travel arrangements were chaotic. The railway timetable for that period is incomprehensible and there were no taxis. If the Festival were scheduled for the summer months the venue would be highly attractive with white sands, the sea and narrow streets of Georgian houses to the quay. There were only two hotels which were always full. People spent their time either in the theatre, their hotels or the pubs. The old theatre was so small that when artists had to leave the stage they would go out of the door, round the outside of the theatre and back in from the other side. Changing rooms were non-existent. The priest had dispensation for the time of Wexford. 'One would go to the opera. The curtain would creak up at any time between eight and eight-thirty. Young singers would be slipped notes saying "If you're not busy at all, come into the pub next door." Then, into the pub and the priest would take confession from the chorus! Normally the priest would never go to the opera but taking confession from the chorus in the pub, having a drink with them . . . Totally Irish! John, however, was the pivot, a very civilised presence.' Wexford gave him the opportunity to conduct what was then an unknown Rossini opera, *La Gazza Ladra*.

As a Glyndebourne chorus member in her early twenties, Elizabeth Lewis remembered walking along the street lost in a daydream. A figure standing in the doorway of a hotel called to her. She had known John through the tenor Richard Lewis (whom she later married). 'Come in,' John said, 'I'm so fed up. I can't get a decent meal or a decent wine here. *Please* come and talk to me.' Whereas everybody else enjoyed Wexford, John bemoaned the lack of conversation, good food and wines. 'My impression of him was how genuine he was; tough, yes, but very genuine. Later at Glyndebourne he would give me a little twinkle when conducting, a special smile that said, "I remember you from Wexford."'

During his time at Liverpool, as well as Ingestre, he was Music Director in another venture, the Rosehill Theatre. When Miki Sekers learnt in 1953 that he had a heart condition, instead of collapsing with worry he decided to bring art to his home in Cumberland and build his own theatre. Both Moran Caplat and Sir George Christie were involved as Trustees with the Earl of Harewood and David Webster.

Rosehill was situated on a hill so that looking out across a field one's eye could not see the road, only the green of the grass, the blue of the sea and in the distance, the Isle of Man. Originally built as a lean-to to the gardener's lodge, nobody realised that it had been put up without foundations, so that when a wall was removed in order to put scenery into the theatre the whole building collapsed.

Outside, like a farm building with weather boards, inside, designed by Oliver Messel, it was completely silk lined with material produced by Miki Sekers' silk mill. It was like a doll's house. The foyer was all watered silk and inside the theatre there was red, white and gold silk on the walls and seats. There were two false boxes attached to the wall with little toy figures in them to break the monotony of the colour. Lavish in appearance, what looked like gold leaf on the decoration was in fact gold paper glued on by village girls. John Claridge endeavoured to translate the designs of Oliver Messel in the cheapest way by finding *objets*, such as a banister, wall sconces or pictures from demolished Georgian buildings and an old theatre in Whitehaven.

With a completely up-to-date lighting system and sufficient depth with a high ceiling, the theatre, holding two hundred and fifty people, was good enough to put on Britten's *The Turn of the Screw* with the Covent Garden Orchestra playing in the pit. Tickets were about £2 or £3. As they enjoyed performing there, artists charged about half their normal fee. The audience and performers intermingled and there was always a very friendly atmosphere.

Meeting John frequently at Glyndebourne and Covent Garden, Miki Sekers asked him to visit Cumberland, with the oblique comment, 'What a pity we can't have a full orchestra here.' John became Music Director at Rosehill and was invited for the opening of the theatre in September 1959. He thought that the hall had wonderful acoustics as the three materials, silk on hard wood over a brick wall were more satisfactory than concrete.

Despite Miki Sekers' reservations, John believed that it would be possible for the Liverpool Orchestra to perform there and decided to do Purcell's 'Ode to Queen Mary'. The work starts with drums in the March and Canzona, which John placed in the foyer, the doors then opened and the players, walking slowly in, rejoined the rest of the orchestra. A very theatrical touch, it was an unforgettable occasion for the audience who were watching the orchestra on stage and then heard the drums from behind. In addition he worked with Paul Tortelier and Shura Cherkassky. The Sekers lost money on those concerts because it cost so much to transport an orchestra and living in a private house, they were unable to accommodate a whole orchestra! Afterwards Rosehill was used for chamber music and recitals.

The theatre was within easy driving distance of Liverpool for John and he bought a car in easy instalments in 1954. In subsequent years John appeared to be totally amechanical, projecting this image to a greater extent than was really necessary. Like many musicians he had a penchant for gadgets or well designed objects. On entering a room, his eye would unfailingly alight on a new acquisition, wanting to know how it worked. With his co-ordination he was capable of mastering complex mechanical processes but preferred to delegate to others. Being driven allowed him to utilise his time, making lists and writing notes or simply, having a short nap. Never taking exercise, quoting Sir Winston Churchill's reply to questions as to his continuing good health, 'No sport', he would prefer to go everywhere by car. His father had proudly recorded in his diary when his son swam a width in the local swimming baths but in later years, John preferred to stand and converse or watch others indulge in athleticism of the 'Bigger Splash' variety. Another dictum of the great war hero which he emulated was his ability to catnap, to shut out the world with a brief 'snooze', to shut out unpleasantness or realities which he preferred not to face as well as enabling him to cope with an enormous workload.

Enjoying his success in Liverpool provoked an exasperated letter from David Webster on 8th October 1959. 'I have been trying to get hold of you for some little time to talk to you about a variety of subjects. The trouble is you seem to be working so hard in Liverpool and seem to be planning to do so for the whole of our natural lives.' Seeking London engagements, John conducted the London Symphony Orchestra at the London Proms in 1961 and when asked to conduct a concert for the Royal Philharmonic Society commented to Moran Caplat: 'The RPS Concert finally qualified me for membership of the Athenaeum. At the reception afterwards the combined age of the assembled company totalled ·by my reckoning about 4,000 years, so I didn't feel so ancient after all.' Having sought membership of the Savile Club, later he joined the White Elephant Club in Curzon Street, London well-known during the sixties for its cuisine.

Lunch with Eric Bravington on 13th September 1961, Manager of the London Philharmonic Orchestra, was decisive. A concert with that orchestra at the Royal Albert Hall on 1st February 1962, when he programmed Tippett's 'Ritual Dances', Mozart's Piano Concerto K467 and Beethoven's Pastoral Symphony was well received. It was announced at an Arts Council reception that John was to become Principal Conductor to run concurrently with his last year at Liverpool, becoming Musical Director in 1963, at the end of his contract there.

He remained on good terms with Sir Harry Livermore, Chairman of the Liverpool Philharmonic Society and his wife Esther, entertaining them when they visited Glyndebourne. Gerald McDonald, General Manager of the Orchestra wrote on 10th July 1963 after the Annual General Meeting that the Chairman paid tribute to all he had done for the Society during the past nine years and the Resolution was unanimously passed with acclaim: 'That the outstanding services rendered to the Society and to the Orchestra by Mr John Pritchard be formally recorded and that the gratitude of the Society and its good wishes for his future career be conveyed to Mr Pritchard.'

His time in Liverpool coincided with the Beatles 'explosion'. Brian Epstein, whose family owned furniture and electrical appliance shops, asked a friend Peter Brown, who was working in the record department at Lewis', to run a new shop which they had just opened. In those days record shops were only small areas in electrical appliance shops. He and Brian had subscription tickets for the Tuesday night and Musica Viva Series. One of the people who ran the classical division introduced Peter Brown to John and immediately they became good friends, a relationship that was to last until John's death. When Peter visited London he would stay at Soho Square. With the Beatles phenomenon Brian Epstein moved to London and it became obvious that he would need to structure the company so that, even with a large staff, the Beatles were only dealt with by him and Peter. 'We Liverpudlians stuck together! Brian and I had this up and down relationship when we were best friends but always having disagreements. When I didn't live with him, I stayed with John and moved into Park Village East, just after Basil moved out.'

The early sixties marked the end of an important period for John. Although his parents celebrated their golden wedding, he did not have a great deal of contact with them during their last years. Looking at the photographs taken for the occasion, standing in profile John is completely detached from the family group smiling straight at the camera. Commenting bitterly that his father could never reconcile his choice of career as a conductor, he would relate that even after his achievements at Vienna, Glyndebourne and Covent Garden, his father refused to accept his decision. On his death-bed Albert Pritchard's last words to his son, 'You should have been a violinist', remained with John. This does not equate with the awe his father voiced in his diaries, relating that his son was conducting an 'orchestra of sixty-five people' (The Derby Philharmonic), his pride that John had given him a musician's diary for Christmas and amazement when he went to Vienna.

His mother had shared his early success but with hardening of the arteries, was not truly aware of her surroundings during her last three or four years. Living with Eddie, at the very end she was in a home. John recorded quite simply in his diary:

1960 13th March Mother died at Longthorne Hospital.
    17th March Mother funeral.

The diary then went blank until the middle of May – '14 – 15 Rosehill.'

She did not live long enough to know that in the New Year's Honours List of 1962, in recognition of his services to music, Her Majesty the Queen conferred the honour of CBE on him. The Investiture in March was followed by a celebratory lunch at Mrs Browning's (Harold Chapin's mother) and in June he attended a small informal luncheon party at Buckingham Palace.

Since the accident at Ingestre he had put on a great deal of weight and now undertook a strict regime of 1,100 calories a day. Weight, or rather attempts to lose it, was increasingly a necessary preoccupation. It was to be a losing battle between his health and his obsessive epicurean disposition. Never liking to dine alone, the company and his surroundings were almost as important as the food in providing him with entertainment.

Dame Kiri Te Kanawa learnt from John never to book a table for two but for three or five, because 'you never get a good table for two! You can always say the third person couldn't make it.' However restaurant owners welcomed his reservations as usually the table would be enlarged to seven or ten. Once after a BBC concert, remarking that there would be others coming to dinner, John commented: 'But my dear, as "you know who" at the BBC talks enough for all of us, you will sit next to me and then we can watch and talk about everybody else!' John was one of those people whose conversation one remembers – memories of sitting together, talking quietly and an irresistable way of discussing good food. In later years, installing a computer, he programmed the names of all the restaurants and their numbers that he knew before he put in anything else.

During the Liverpool period John found a kindred spirit in Michael Smith a forerunner of British *haute cuisine*, who later designed and planned the menus for Walton's restaurant in London. Although Smith died before John, the owner, Roger Wren, closed the restaurant at lunchtime for a small champagne reception after John's memorial service.

7

London Philharmonic Orchestra

FUGUE

John joined the London Philharmonic Orchestra in Australia on 16th March 1962, halfway through a landmark tour which included concerts in India, Hong Kong, the Philippines and Ceylon. They were the first British orchestra to play in those countries.

Formed by Sir Thomas Beecham, the orchestra had given its first concert on 7th October 1932 in the Queen's Hall, London. The new orchestra played for all the Royal Philharmonic Society concerts, the Robert Mayer Children's concerts and the Royal Choral Society. During the war, it had survived by touring, giving concerts in whatever venues could be found. Sir Adrian Boult was appointed Principal Conductor for the period 1951 – 57 and on relinquishing that appointment, became President of what he came to regard as 'his' orchestra. John was appointed when his successor William Steinberg, conductor of the Pittsburgh Symphony Orchestra, was forced through ill-health to relinquish his position.

Conducting a section of the LPO in Martinů's *Comedy on a Bridge*, a radio opera in one act, for broadcast on the Third Programme on 12th October 1951, John liked to relate what happened at the first rehearsal:

> I always remember at the start of my career I had a trial date. I think it was with the London Philharmonic which was a very different orchestra from the virtuoso group now. I went as a young conductor, a little bit doubtful, to the first rehearsal and my doubts were justified. Have you ever heard of faces carved in granite? That's what I faced. Not the slightest flicker. They played the notes and that was it.

Rather desperate because I wanted a flicker of humanity somewhere, my eye lighted on a young double bass player whom I had known in my chamber orchestra and he was a bright soul and a good friend. At a suitable moment when there was a pause in the music, I flashed at him, 'Hello Charlie' and the whole thing changed. The orchestra said, 'He's got a friend who's a musician' and the rehearsal went swimmingly, in fact I remember I became Chief Conductor of the London Philharmonic.

The significance of this story reveals much about the British social scene. There is a great divide in attitudes between those who began their musical careers before and after the Second World War. As in cricket, it was accepted that there were 'gentlemen' and 'players'. As a conductor Sir Thomas Beecham was a gentleman, a man of independent means. Obviously, with his working-class background, John did not belong in this category but with his height and increased girth, emulating David Webster, would adopt a grand seigneur manner towards strangers. During this period, musicians with whom he came into contact who did not like him, referred to John as pompous, the most frequently used adjective to describe his father. A great raconteur he could charm anyone but would say that it was not his 'thing'. Knowing the truth could be ascertained easily, in London he was reluctant to promote himself to the press or the public, thus avoiding the inevitable questions about his early life.

Many conductors accept an appointment as musical director on the basis of conducting the orchestra they are given but John needed to have people whom he could trust and upon whom he could rely. In Liverpool the orchestra flourished because it had a partnership with its conductor.

John has been considered one of the most important conductors of his generation because of his ability to reorganise and create an orchestra. His meticulous attention to balance of sound originating from his chamber music background with Reg Adler and the Derby String Orchestra, suffused all his work so that even to David Webster he expressed his criticisms on 31st March 1965:

Indeed positive objections to the new orchestral layout in the pit which has been imposed. First of all from whatever good motives, the violins have been placed in front of the conductor, presumably with a view to making them more prominent. Unfortunately, the space between the podium and the prompter's box is insufficient for this, with the result that both sections of violins are spread out in a straggling line and have little or no contact with other section leaders. Then on the right, the first viola is isolated from his section because of an intervening first double bass stand. The greatest isolation is however reserved for the brass who maintain their old position but now of course are completely divorced from the timpany and percussion. This alone seems a very bad idea indeed. As for the woodwind, they no longer can play as a unified section as each line of three players has no aural contact. I cannot think of another theatre where this particular seating is observed as for years the interplay and inter-relation of woodwind principals has been dependent on an accepted principle of seating. The horns are now far removed from everybody (except the percussion) and this again leads to bad tuning and bad ensemble with the woodwind. The players are, according to my judgement, most dissatisfied.

During his time at the LPO he changed about a third of the personnel and engaged as leader a man who became a colleague. Rodney Friend was twenty-four when he first came into contact with John. Having worked at the London Symphony Orchestra as co-leader for a year and a half, he had left because he wished to concentrate only on his playing and teaching. He recalled being telephoned by John early one morning in March or April 1964, saying that there would be a vacancy for a leader at the LPO. Explaining his situation, saying that he felt he had done his 'stint' in orchestras, John persuaded him with, 'Why don't you come round and talk to me, perhaps we could work out a solo schedule for you.' A fine day, they sat and talked in the garden at Park Village East. 'He made the whole thing very attractive for me. I could play what concertos I wanted and offered me enough money for it to be impossible for me to turn it down. He just gave me whatever I wanted.' John was determined to have Rodney Friend as leader and therefore problems did not exist.

In trying to rebuild his orchestra, John realised that there were too many orchestras in the capital competing for too few good players to fill the positions available. There was no London sound. Orchestras in other major cities on the continent of Europe or in the United States of America produce a sound which is immediately identifiable. No one could possibly mistake the Cleveland Orchestra for that of Philadelphia, both of whom are outstanding. His work abroad made him aware of the difficulties under which the London orchestras laboured. The benefits which the Liverpool orchestra gained from rehearsing and playing in the same hall were enormous. The London orchestras were rehearsing in venues not built for an orchestra, with different acoustics, before their final rehearsal at the South Bank on the day of their concert. John considered it essential for an orchestra to have a home, preferably with administrative offices, on the same premises.

The City of London, in its proposed building on the Barbican site, planned to construct a tiny concert hall and small theatre and asked Anthony Besch for advice. He proposed that the City should undertake some research, first to see whether this would be of use to anybody and if so, what size was required. He went to each of the administrators of the London orchestras who responded in the affirmative immediately. John was very interested and Anthony Besch remembers having a meeting with him and Mrs Emmie Tillett of Ibbs & Tillett. In the event, the Manager of the LSO, Ernest Fleischman, put forward the most attractive proposal that won the day. When the Barbican Hall opened on 3rd March 1982, reservations were expressed regarding its acoustics. Hearing that he might have problems, John arrived in London a day earlier than necessary to attend a concert. Changing his seat frequently at appropriate moments, he devised 'his' fan-shaped layout for Haydn and Mozart, to cope with any difficulties.

A solution to the problem of a rehearsal/recording studio was found in the derelict Holy Trinity Church, Southwark in 1972. With exceptional acoustics, it was restored by both the LSO and the LPO, the work carried out by Arup Associates, the architects who designed the Snape Maltings, Suffolk. John, together with the LPO, were photographed in 1975 rehearsing in safety helmets in case any plaster fell in the newly named Henry Wood Hall.

During the period 1963 – 64, the London orchestras began collaborating with the Arts Council to produce more cohesive programming on the South Bank. John remarked on a new feeling of active audience participation which for so long had been lacking in London's concert life, giving the orchestra a sense of the great occasion and helping every man to give his best.

He had achieved prominence as *the* young British conductor, through Musica Viva in Liverpool. In a concert bearing that name on 14th May 1964, the London Philharmonic Society

The first portrait, circa 1944.

John as a choirboy at
St Stephen's Church, Walthamstow,
circa 1928.

The Borough Juvenile Orchestra,
Walthamstow, circa 1932.
Front row, left to right: Bertie Gore, Ronald
Jennings, Percy Timberlake, Bert Kenney;
Back row, left to right: Freddie Forest,
George Barnard, Denis Garbin, Stanley
[John] Pritchard.

Photo courtesy of Percy Timberlake

Aboard the Bonnie Vale during the eleven-hour stopover on the way to Port Elizabeth, South Africa, 1946.

John and Yfrah Neaman on the way to their first rehearsal in Johannesburg, South Africa, 1946.

Conducting the Derby String Orchestra.

With Eva Metzler, circa 1950.

commissioned from Peter Maxwell Davies a new work, *Second Fantasia on an In Nomine of John Traverner*, which John introduced. In 1965 he repeated the talk on the Peter Maxwell Davies work, in analysis making the complicated music seem quite simple.

At another concert in May 1964 the Stravinsky Violin Concerto with Yehudi Menuhin was followed by a performance of the Webern Symphony. As this lasted for approximately fourteen minutes only, John discussed it prior to a second performance, prefacing his talk with the common-sense remark, 'You have just listened to a closely argued piece of musical logic, which like much logic may appear unpalatable until its meaning is really digested. It is no use our complaining that it would have been better, that it would have reached more people, had it been emblazoned on a placard in Piccadilly Circus.'

In terms of contemporary music, more than anyone else, John was responsible for introducing the music of Benjamin Britten to a wider public. The composer's work became central to his repertoire in the concert hall as well as the opera house. *A Young Person's Guide to the Orchestra*, the *Passacaglia* and *Sea Interludes* from *Peter Grimes* and above all the *War Requiem*, were programmed frequently during his time at the LPO and introduced by him during engagements abroad. It was appropriate that when Sir Thomas Armstrong presented Benjamin Britten with the Royal Philharmonic Society's Gold Medal in 1964 it should be at the Albert Hall after a concert under John's baton.

The *War Requiem* was chosen for the celebration of the 900th anniversary of the Battle of Hastings, held in the spectacular Paris setting of the Church Saint-Louis des Invalides. Although John conducted the Orchestre Philharmonique del'O.R.T.F., the soloists were British – April Cantelo, Alexander Young and Thomas Hemsley. Before the concert, with a son et lumière display in a setting dominated by the tomb of Napoleon, tactfully no one mentioned the Battle of Waterloo.

Afterwards Sir Partick Reilly, the British Ambassador, wrote to John on 17th October 1966:

> This is just a line, in which my wife joins me, to express once again our very warmest thanks for all the pleasure you gave us on Thursday and equally our congratulations on achieving an absolutely outstanding artistic success under what must have been difficult conditions. I have heard on all sides how deeply moved the audience was, as you were no doubt aware yourself. You will be glad to

hear that the broadcast transmission appears to have been very satisfactory. In short, I am sure that the performance on Thursday has done much to make better known in France the genius of Britten and to awaken an interest in contemporary British music. We are greatly looking forward to your visit in November and to your concert with the London Philharmonic.

At the end of an extensive European tour in 1966 with the LPO, in Paris John not only premièred the four *Sea Interludes* from *Peter Grimes* but also conducted the European première of Sir William Walton's Symphony no. 2. Tchaikovsky's Piano Concerto no. 1 with John Ogdon as soloist completed the programme.

Whilst John would present all the usual classics, he became known during his tenure as Musical Director for his partiality to French music. Able to conduct all the works of Berlioz, his tastes ranged throughout the French repertoire. In addition, during his time with the LPO he programmed Russian music.

In his will written in December 1971, John requested that at his memorial service the LPO should play the slow march in Mozart's *Idomeneo* and if feasible, the slow movement from the Rachmaninov Symphony no. 2 (in E minor). He had conducted all the piano concertos of that composer with the LPO and the *Rhapsody on a Theme of Paganini* but especially loved the 2nd Symphony. This had been presented at a Royal Festival Hall Concert on 5th October 1965, to open the 1965 – 66 Season and repeated in Watford on 19th October and Eastbourne on 6th November.

During his time at the LPO John worked frequently with John Ogdon as his piano soloist and the violinist Ida Haendel who considered John 'responsible for the rebirth of my career in Europe'. Although still young, as a child prodigy she had been in the public view for some time. 'My parents went to live in Montreal to be near my married sister, so I decided that I would make my career in the American hemisphere.' By chance she was asked by an Indian charity to play at a concert in London in aid of a leper colony. 'As they promised me that I would be performing with a major orchestra and conductor, I accepted. The orchestra was the LPO and the conductor, John Pritchard.' When she had finished playing, John followed her backstage. '"How you played!" he said. "Was it so bad?" I joked. "It was wonderful. Why don't we hear of you more often?"' This concert was the turning point in her career as from that moment John asked her to play with him whenever possible.

In February 1965 the LPO Council was formed to co-ordinate artistic and financial plans. John was happy to report to them on 10th March 1965 after returning from America and listening to the orchestra under Svetlanov, that he felt the LPO was 'over the hump' in its process of reshaping. From an orchestra which had hit a low, under the leadership of Rodney Friend it had become the 'in' orchestra. He noted that the strings 'wherein the main surgery has taken place over the past year are youthful and instant in attack'.

He considered it essential to bring in conductors from abroad, of the stature of 'Krips, Bernstein, Szell, Karl Böhm and Karajan. What we need is a *first class conductor for every concert*' but was concerned that the increased grant, which the orchestra received to provide a new fee structure, would not be allocated for 'Artistic improvements, i.e. specially expensive concerts of high artistic merit with world-famous soloists with star fees and so on.' Fund-raising plans were put in hand as John was determined to 'increase the permanent strength of the orchestra' and finance foreign tours. Appeals for an orchestra would not be complete without a Gala concert.

Promoting the LPO Gala with Danny Kaye to be held the following February, John enjoyed himself with the comedian at the Savoy Hotel – the moment captured, of course, by the cameras. Danny Kaye, who had conducted many American orchestras on their fund-raising occasions, explained that he could not read a note of music but knew every entrance of the strings and woodwind: 'The orchestra think I will just stand up and wave but I am a tyrant. It is the greatest feeling of neurotic power in the world.' John opened the actual concert on 15th February 1966 with the *Mediterranean Suite* by Sergei Barsukov and the Management accepted 'no responsibility' for the part of the programme conducted by the comedian.

Under Basil's influence, John had shown a liking for women jazz singers such as Billie Holiday, Cleo Laine, Sarah Vaughan and Dinah Washington. The Gala for the following year, again held in the Royal Albert Hall, featured the LPO with Duke Ellington and his orchestra. John only conducted the Malcolm Arnold *Tam O'Shanter* Overture and Britten's *Young Person's Guide to the Orchestra*, leaving the rest of the programme to be conducted by 'The Duke'. In his record of the concert: 'Amusing evening. Duke very good form and awfully complimentary. "Wonderful, gracious and hospitable Mr Pritchard." The orchestra made balls-up of Britten, but all loudly applauded.'

John's wide spectrum in music-making, his love of good music without categorisation, was very evident during this period. In a concert in April 1965 in which the LPO played Bernstein's *West Side Story* Suite and Gershwin's *An American in Paris* Overture, the honours went to the jazz orchestra of Johnny Dankworth, also a former pupil of the Sir George Monoux School. John was more impressed by the other musician's brief jazz variations than his large scale works and was highly amused to be shown a newspaper report of a special anniversary of the school, mentioning the two names in one breath. He liked the Howard Brubeck *Dialogue for Jazz Band and Symphony Orchestra* and the following year, in a repeated attempt at a marriage between the two mediums, it proved more successful. After Dankworth and Duke Ellington, John was joined by Jack Benny on 27th May 1969. An evening of sheer enjoyment, recorded by television, the master comedian presented 'his' version of the Mendelssohn violin concerto. It was all part of John's wish to 'blow the wind of change' through the music scene, both in the concert hall and opera house. He was quoted as saying that the days of black tie at Glyndebourne should be over.

In 1964 the LPO replaced the Royal Philharmonic at Glynde-bourne but there was a certain amount of unrest among the rank and file of the orchestra with the engagement. The players needed to drive to Sussex daily in the summer months. This was a period when Glyndebourne was presenting baroque operas requiring only a small orchestra so most of them were idle and unpaid. They seemed to spend their time driving to orchestral engagements outside London as the Arts Council promoted them to co-ordinate musical activities in East Anglia and the Eastern Counties. As well as concerts at the Royal Festival Hall they had been involved in Industrial Concerts at the Royal Albert Hall since 1953, in a scheme which offered concerts at a flat rate admission fee for groups. There were many engagements but the players felt they were without sufficient reward particularly because of a pay differential with the principals.

At the time of his appointment, John had visions about the orchestra but he was not focused in his music-making, in his determination to see things through. He never saw problems because it was the joy of making music which was most important to him. Liking the good things in life; food, company and a glass of champagne, music was one of those good things. When criticised for not having a concentrated attitude towards work, he would quote Fritz Busch, 'When did you last go to an art gallery?' Clive Lythgoe thought that there were many things about the conductor for which he was disliked but that they stemmed from jealousy. 'He was a wonderful romantic, a Renaissance musician, as well as a human being. People like him are often misunderstood. He enjoyed life to the full. The fact that he was able to play at life as well as being such a great conductor made people very envious of him.'

John was ambitious – very ambitious – and when questioning why he did not reach the pinnacle to which he belonged, many consider that he was too easily distracted. In addition he was over sensitive, too easily hurt. It was very easy to take advantage of John, which the numerous hangers-on understood. He would be surrounded after a concert by people who were not there for the music but for the champagne and supper. When one was alone with him, if he cared, one saw the real John.

Ileana Cotrubas added, 'For me, John was one of the finest musicians in our profession. In the end he was quite well known and had a beautiful career but I think that with the years he became a little lazy and indulged in adventures in his private life, so he did not reach the level he deserved musically. There are so many other conductors who did not have the talent and *raffinesse* of John but they made bigger careers than him. This is only my opinion but I don't think I'm wrong. It was because of his indulgences in his private life.' The crowds were a part of the distraction that steered the character and personality away from reality.

John's first visit behind the Iron Curtain was an exciting tour of Poland in 1961. In 1963 an engagement in Pittsburgh marked his debut in the United States of America. Subsequent return visits to America were arranged but there was no strategic planning. John was so pleased to have all these engagements with their financial benefits and was having so much fun travelling that he was tending to conduct works which he had not digested sufficiently. Although he inspired morale in the players through good feeling and affection, he gave the impression that he was not totally committed to the LPO. From becoming the 'in' orchestra, it found itself losing its audiences to the LSO in the latter half of the sixties. That orchestra had some outstanding young players and was attracting the new important soloists.

During the second half of the sixties, due to depreciating sterling, it became financially attractive to make recordings in London. The LPO were doing a large number of concerts but recordings and TV work were not coming their way because of John. Bernard Haitink was with Philips, Sir Adrian Boult and Giulini had EMI and Sir Georg Solti was with Decca. They had exclusive recording contracts and recordings came only if they wished to work with the LPO. John did not have an exclusive contract.

His recording career, moving from one company to another, reflects some of the inconsistencies of John's career in general. Even though he was always busy, highly respected in the profession itself, he never promoted himself in a consistent public relations manner. Whilst some understood that to John the most important thing in life was life itself, he himself, as his looks faded and his health deteriorated, realised that the most disappointing aspect of his career was the somewhat surprising lack of important recordings, particularly of opera. The largest number of records were made later with the LPO in the 1970s for Classics for Pleasure and mono recordings of his early Glyndebourne successes. The opera recordings which he made were done because particular producers believed in him. Even though his 1958 recording of Tippett's *A Child of our Time* with the Royal Liverpool Philharmonic Orchestra and Choir and the Dances from *Midsummer Marriage* are definitive performances, there are very few discs of the numerous works for which he gave the first performance. In spite of the fact that they have done some good work, record companies live off the success of the people that they record and no major company ever felt him to be a conductor they could promote.

In the late fifties and early sixties a conductor needed a contract with one of the major record companies. Dr Peter Andry who was with EMI felt that his company did not consider John as there were many other conductors of established reputations. Although John's recording in 1962 of the Rachmaninov 2nd piano concerto with the Philharmonia was considered the best by the *Gramophone* Magazine, the recording had been made because of the soloist, John Ogdon. On the other hand, others believe that a contract could have been possible at that stage.

Sir Malcolm Sargent and Sir Adrian Boult already belonged to an older generation and Sir Colin Davis and Sir Charles Groves had not yet established themselves. Through Musica Viva, John was the only one of the younger generation who had shown promise at that early time. Sir Colin Davis went to Philips and Sir Georg Solti was taken up by Decca. It may sound cynical but record companies believe that conductors have three distinct periods in their lives: those from twenty-five to forty years when they are regarded as up and coming; from forty to sixty when nobody takes much notice of them and from sixty onwards when they become 'Grand Old Men'. John's disadvantage in the early sixties was that he was 'there' but not on an international level, like a Karajan, nor was he charismatic in a showy way. His conducting was the art that concealed art. As is often the case today, people equated temperament with talent.

Some of the most successful conductors in the world have a touch of vulgarity to them. The public loves the fact that they go a little over the top with the extra gesture, the extra movement partly for their benefit. In the case of Leonard Bernstein he went way over the top but many people adored him because he did. Team spirit and a lack of flamboyance is seen as a negative virtue. Just as music reflects the other arts, with Italians painting in oils, in vibrant colours, the English are masters of watercolour and although he could assume the mantle of almost any composer, there was an essential English colour to John. His style of conducting suited him to be accepted in Britain as a 'Grand Old Man' and by the time of the Last Night of the Proms, he had arrived.

The English in particular are very difficult about all-rounders – Renaissance figures. They want to categorise a person. John was known for his Mozart but it was often forgotten that he was a great Tchaikovsky conductor and gave almost definitive performances of works by composers with whom he was not normally associated. Although John was determined that nobody should stop him achieving, he never appeared to show the kind of hungry drive which has sometimes resulted in the greatest public success and acclamation. He was not that type of person. He has been called the 'musician's musician'. Musicians with whom he worked and who loved him, gave him in return a good performance. Others would complain that he was too able, too brilliant, his sight-reading was lazy and he did too many performances.

More important was the simple fact that from 1955, Basil, who was inexperienced, had been taking on more and more of the secretarial/management side, writing letters on John's behalf to David Webster, bypassing Joan Ingpen, enabling John to cope with a heavy workload.

John met Terry MacInnis at Glyndebourne during the summer of 1963. After a holiday together in Maratea, south of Naples, the home of Elda and Vittorio Gui, Terry moved in to Park Village East. When Joan Ingpen became Controller of Opera Planning at Covent Garden in 1964 Basil took over the concert and later the opera side completely and, assisted by John Davern, became John's agent. Joan Ingpen advised Basil to have other artists besides John 'on his books'. Emotions confused the issue. There was a suspicion that John himself was the source of the unsubstantiated rumours that Basil was exploiting him, establishing himself as an agent with one very brilliant client. On the other hand, Basil relieved John of considerations and decisions which would have taken up a great deal of his time. He understood that John would not take longer rest periods as he needed all the money he could earn to pay for his personal life. At an early age he had learnt that it was possible to buy acceptance, that there was always a price he had to pay. Already the conductor was being called 'the last of the big spenders' because of his extravagant lifestyle.

Although critics were praising their improved standard of playing, the LPO were aware that their position on the music scene was deteriorating and sought a replacement Musical Director which they found in Bernard Haitink, who had a recording contract with Philips. In addition, although the most modest of men, on the podium he had shown the charisma which attracted audiences. Miki Sekers (Sir Nicholas Sekers), then Chairman of the LPO Council, spoke to John advising him to give up his position. At a meeting on 14th September 1965, John told the Council of the LPO that 'in view of his many commitments both as Music Counsellor and Principal Conductor of Glyndebourne' and his engagements abroad, 'the time had come to give more time to these activities.' His contract had already been extended until 1966 so it would not seem as though he was being sacked. Considerable attention was paid by the Board to the statement that would be made to the press. It announced that John would be relinquishing his position in order to devote more time to his career abroad.

This statement appeared plausible as John was accepting a number of prestigious engagements abroad that were reported in the British newspapers. During a tour of South America he had been engaged to conduct *Aida* and *Attila* in Buenos Aires. England had just beaten Argentina in the Football World Cup. The first night of *Aida* was quite chaotic. With a British conductor and Peter Glossop and Marie Collier in the cast, they were booed. John was amused to see his photograph on the sports page in all the British papers, probably the only time a conductor has been featured there. *Attila* rehearsals started immediately after the *Aida* opening. There had just been a revolution in Argentina and the scheduled producer was too nervous to go. Anthony Besch was offered the job at such a huge fee that 'nothing was going to stop me'. Arriving in Buenos Aires on the day of the first night of *Aida*, he rang John who said, 'Don't come to the first night, come to the Gala in two days' time.' So he missed the famous occasion.

The Teatro Colón worked on incredibly tight schedules. Consequently it had become customary for someone to say at the dress-rehearsal: 'We're not ready for the opening night, we'll have to postpone it.' 'Deferred' would be written all over the posters and everything would be changed. John and Anthony Besch had been warned in advance but as they both needed to leave as planned they were determined to be ready. With a good cast who worked well, the conductor and producer said that they were not going to stop during the rehearsals and informed everyone that they had only two days. There was panic in the workshop and wardrobes because they were so used to being deferred that they presumed everything would be delayed this time too. The recalcitrants were summoned to the Board. Anthony Besch recalled: 'They all bowed and we bowed. They said that they knew how well we had been working but were sure we'd like the opening night postponed.' They were horrified when told 'no' and the performances took place as scheduled.

Asked to take over from Zubin Mehta in 1966 for the second half of the series of the Giorgio Strehler production of *Entführung* in the Festspielhaus, Salzburg, the grandeur and splendour of his surroundings combined with the status of the Festival thrilled

John. The cast headed by the famous tenor, Fritz Wunderlich as Belmonte was a dream. There was a wonderful Constanze, Anneliese Rothenberger, a superb Blondchen in Reri Grist and Fernando Corena as Osmin. Harold Rosenthal, in *Opera* magazine, August 1966, considered the performance he attended one of the finest he had ever heard, thanks to John. A performance 'of which his mentor Fritz Busch might well have been proud'. The *Express* in Vienna, 26th August 1966, commented that the conductor, 'knows, loves and feels Mozart.'

Arriving with Terry on 17th August, he stayed at the Goldener Hirsch for three days, moving to the Schloss Fuschl, a short journey from the city. Previously the home of Salzburg archbishops, furnished with antiques, it is in a wonderful setting. He relaxed on the open-air terrace overlooking Lake Fuschl and took walks in the park and woods. Terry remembers boating on the lake, with umbrellas opened in the rain. Moran Caplat and his family were staying on the other side of the lake and Sir George and Lady Christie came to see John conduct. Wooing Karajan, John wrote to the London Philharmonic Orchestra Council that he had had 'my own talks and definite invitations' and 'we have gone very far with Karajan and shall proceed with the plan for a Strauss Festival in 1966 – 67'. John was not asked to return to Salzburg during the Karajan regime.

Enjoying the good things that life in France has to offer, John shared the direction of a series of classical concerts with Serge Baudo during 1966 – 67 at the Opéra de Marseilles. John marked as interesting not the Bruckner 7th Symphony but the soloists for the Beethoven Triple Concerto – Wolfgang Schneiderhan (violin), Pierre Fournier (cello) and his son Jean Fonda (Fournier) at the piano. Jean Fonda remembered the nobility, dignity and above all, 'kindness which emanated from Pritchard to the younger performer I was, and his fatherly look and faint smile during the performance.' Jean Fonda recalled John as 'one of the truly great conductors of our time' and that his father 'had the keenest admiration and friendship towards him'. His father considered a performance many years later with John of the Dvořák Cello Concerto was 'the best "zwammer spiel" he had encountered regarding that work'. After a performance in London with the Philharmonia of Bloch's *Schelomo*, Pierre Fournier's admiration was such that when asked to record the Elgar/*Schelomo* works with the Berlin Philharmonic for Deutsche Grammophon, he wanted John as conductor. Unfortunately he was on a tour of the United States of America.

Continuing to work amicably with the London Philharmonic Orchestra he took them on an important tour of the Far East in 1969 but even this did not compare with their historic tour of China in 1973. As a prelude they participated in celebrations for the first Hong Kong Festival at the City Hall, March 1973. Promoting British music, the first concert on 6th March opened with William Walton's 'Improvisations on an *Impromptu* of Benjamin Britten', followed by the Sibelius Violin Concerto (in D minor) with Ida Haendel as soloist and ended with the Tchaikovsky Symphony no. 4 (in F minor). The piano soloist for the concert on 9th March, Michael Roll, played the Mozart Concerto in C, K503 and John ended the evening with William Walton's Symphony no. 1 in B flat minor and in the final concert on 13th March, opening with the Walton *Capriccio Burlesco* and ending with the Rimsky-Korsakov suite *Scheherazade*, his good friend Ida Haendel played the Brahms Violin Concerto (in D, opus 77).

Walking across the frontier bridge at Lo Wu, twenty miles from Kowloon and Hong Kong Island, they were the first non-communist orchestra from a Western country to go to China. It was as if an English conductor with an English orchestra had landed on the moon. Hospitality was lavish and John was treated like royalty. Theirs were the only cars in the streets, which were lined with applauding crowds. The reaction to their arrival was a revelation. After the initial surprise, the Westerners became accustomed to loudspeakers blaring messages, or music played with seemingly strange instruments.

John went sight-seeing on the Great Wall but did not go with the others to the Forbidden City. When they alighted from the train in Canton, Rodney Friend walked down the platform with John and Terry, followed by Ida Haendel. Always strikingly dressed, she was wearing a large hat and very high-heeled shoes. They were the first Westerners that the trainload of Chinese had ever seen. One has to remember that the average Chinese is considerably smaller than John's six foot six, seventeen stone and size ten feet. The Chinese could not believe their eyes. The train rocked with their laughter. 'You know John,' Ida Haendel said, 'I think they're laughing at my hat.' To which he replied, 'I don't think so Ida, they're laughing at your shoes.'

After lunch they went on to Peking, a city which John found very drab. However, it was here that he and the players began to appreciate that they were involved in a memorable human experience in bringing music to a people who had been starved musically for the entirety of the cultural revolution. Not only enjoyable, it became a very moving experience for all concerned. The halls were leftovers from the old system but it was irrelevant. Suddenly the Chinese were listening to a great orchestra, the London Philharmonic. People would walk hundreds of miles to try to get into the rehearsals which were as crowded as the concerts. In Peking, Shanghai and Canton they played the Elgar *Cockaigne* overture, the Brahms Violin Concerto with Ida Haendel and Beethoven's Symphony no. 7 in A. The Chinese enjoyed the Brahms *Academic Festival Overture*, Vaughan Williams' *Fantasia on a Theme of Thomas Tallis*, Haydn's Trumpet Concerto and the Dvořák Symphony no. 8 in G (which was also programmed for Shanghai). During rehearsals, using an interpreter, John would introduce the works. The audience reaction was such that the players wanted to 'give' music to the Chinese and would add movements from the Sibelius Violin Concerto for their enjoyment.

In composition the Chinese did not have just one composer for a work, but six. They asked if the orchestra would perform one of their compositions. John looked at it. Realising that the players could sight-read it easily, they did so for the packed house. It was as if something magical had taken place. This was *their* music, not blasted and distorted through loudspeakers but the real sound, accurately played. The reaction, the revelation, symbolised the whole tour. Audiences could not have enough of the music and John was wonderful with them. A great speech-maker, charming them, he was the right man for that moment. The orchestra were all looked upon as curiosities but John was totally at ease. Eating well he did not need or want an afternoon rest. He was full of the joy of making music, giving and being received with happiness.

They were entertained at the Chinese opera: stories of serfs and wicked landlords, showing how bad life had been under the feudal system and extolling the virtues of present day society. John was given a booklet in Chinese, with an English translation, of five poems by Chairman Mao beginning with 'Snow', and ending with 'The Capture of Nanking by the People's Liberation Army', part of a concert put on by the Central Philharmonic Society in Peking. The piano concerto 'The Yellow River' completed the long programme which showed the people and the army denouncing and vanquishing the 'enemy'.

John liked Shanghai most of all, especially a cruise on the Whangpoo river to the Yangtze. Writing to Moran Caplat on March 23rd: 'Even you would open your eyes at the various craft on the WHANGPOO here! It's an incredible city, more human and atmospheric than Peking (with its vast avenues, impressive but cold). We have had a fabulous reception everywhere, with crowds appearing in the streets, and real gratitude for the music. Shall be dining out on experiences for months!' The BBC made a film of the tour, *The Red Carpet*, one of the most memorable experiences of John's life.

That summer, back in England, he was invited to a dinner on 7th June 1973 in honour of the Minister of Foreign Affairs of the People's Republic of China and Mrs Chi P'eng-fei, at Hampton Court Palace. In total contrast to their time in China, the musical entertainment during dinner was provided by the Royal Artillery Orchestra and afterwards, the band and bugles of the 3rd Battalion, the Royal Green Jackets, gave a ceremonial display outside the Palace.

The warmth with which the British musicians were received in China could be contrasted with the reception John received some years later nearer home, at the hands of a French audience in Aix. As in Buenos Aires, he faced an audience that booed. The Aix Festival of 1981 was going through a period when many of the operas were not meeting with audience approval. It was a time also when there was a great deal of booing, not only in Aix but in Paris and elsewhere.

The performance of *Don Giovanni* was not bad but there were certain weaknesses both in staging and in the cast. The chauvinistic audience, which had travelled some distance intending to make trouble, objected to a mainly British cast, the Scottish Chamber Orchestra in the pit and the conductor. The only person not included in the audience's displeasure was the Countess, Isobel Buchanan, who sang well and is also attractive. At the end of the performance, wearing his white tuxedo, John took his curtain call. There was quite a lot of booing from the audience. He just stared them straight in the face and gave them a long boo-type 'raspberry' in return. John Higgins applauded. 'I thought it was a splendid gesture of his contempt for an audience, only part of whom knew what they were hearing. It's pretty rare for conductors to boo back. I've seen it three or four times but this was the most resounding boo directed at an audience from a conductor.' News of the occurrence was reported in *Nice Matin*, sending a quiver of pride through the British holidaying on the Côte d'Azur.

For later performances, John would invite friends to stay at the house he rented in the country, just outside Aix. Terry was not around. Even though there was a dish-washer, seemingly no one bothered to clear the dishes for days. He would prepare his favourite summer lunch, eaten on the shady patio, sea bass baked in foil with butter and herbs, salads and fruit, washed down with a bottle of Chablis. At 33°C, it was even too hot to go into the garden and use the large swimming pool. In the great humidity, he was in considerable pain from his arthritic hip and taking large doses of pain-killers. When he walked on slowly dragging his leg to conduct the final act, booing began from one side of the auditorium. With a gesture in the direction of his friends, he conducted the cheers from the foreign audience.

Previously at Aix, in 1963, after conducting *Die Zauberflöte*, there had been confidential discussions with a view to his becoming Musical Director. This did not materialise. His work at Glyndebourne was to become the pivot of his career and the house he bought in Sussex central to his life. *Zauberflöte* was the only Mozart opera he did not conduct at Glyndebourne.

8

Glyndebourne

The musical public that turned to Glyndebourne to see Rossini, needed to go to Sussex for Strauss as Covent Garden was prescribing a diet of only *Rosenkavalier* and more *Rosenkavalier*.

In John's first Strauss production at Glyndebourne, the second version of *Ariadne* in 1954, the Zerbinetta was Mattiwilda Dobbs, a young lady with an exquisite, extremely agile voice whom everybody adored. The sequence used was *Arlecchino* first and *Ariadne* second but for one performance this was changed at the request of the BBC. For some reason this information did not reach Zerbinetta who, when met at Lewes Station by the driver, was greeted with, 'Dobbs, you're on, you're supposed to be on!' 'Oh Harry, don't say things like that, they're supposed to bring bad luck.' She missed part of the performance.

When John repeated *Ariadne* in 1957 it was the first time that he worked with the young Elisabeth Söderström, singing the Composer. Her first impression was that it was 'so fantastic' to have such an efficient conductor treating her kindly. 'The conductors I had worked with were very severe. We got to know each other very well at Glyndebourne because it's a big family affair there and I, arriving with my young children, was nonetheless taking part in all these parties and John was so generous and always included everybody. You felt you really belonged to his family.' Swedish singers coming to Glyndebourne were well prepared.

> We covered all sides of an operatic performance and I think that John liked an artist to know what they wanted to do. It was also wonderful to do my first Strauss opera with him as a guide. We did, among other things, *Capriccio* which was a revelation because it was such a wonderful part and it was an opera I had never heard. Again we went into the Strauss style and his sense of humour was such a

159

treat, especially for that work. My happiest memories of John are of learning Strauss together. You felt that you were very close to John even if you didn't know him so very well because he was so friendly and at the same time, as a conductor, very strong. He knew exactly what he wanted to do.

In her view John was never lazy but gave that impression by his appearance.

Originally *Rosenkavalier* was never wholly successful at Glyndebourne as the stage and pit had not yet been enlarged. Bernard Haitink commented, 'Strauss was a true business man and was not worried to agree to a smaller version for Glyndebourne. There was a reduction of the score by Fritz Busch in which he left out noisy instruments like the E flat clarinet and reduced the woodwinds.' Ryland Davies recalled a performance in 1965 when he was singing the Haushofmeister to the Marschallin. Just before the end of the levée scene, the Marschallin, Montserrat Caballé turned to him and said in Italian, '*Mi dai uno cognac, sto malatta.*' (Give me a brandy, I feel ill). So he walked round the stage and went off. John was puzzled. The producer's assistant rushed out. 'Are you ill?' 'No,' Davies replied, 'quick, she wants a brandy.' With the timing of the piece, there was not long to go. He dived into the Long Bar, grabbed a small cognac, returned to the stage, turning his back to the audience '*Eccola!*' She drank it down and sang her next line to the audience (translated), 'Send them all out'. John commented, 'Well Ryland, you did that in nice time!' This picture remained in Ryland Davies' memory because he felt that John was always very careful with tempi. It was Davies' first appearance on the Glyndebourne stage, the first of many times he was to work with John as a soloist. 'I couldn't really understand the music of that first act and understand what all the fuss was about – people were raving about this piece. After my small part I used to have to hang around and of course, stood in the wings and listened to Edith Mathis (Sophie) and Monserrat Caballé and by the end of the sixteen performances, I was deliriously in love with the piece. It is now one of my favourite operas.'

Vittorio Gui was aging. John's presence and input was needed. Just as David Webster was exasperated at his preoccupation with Liverpool, Moran Caplat felt it necessary in 1959 to stress John's commitment to Glyndebourne under his contract: 'In no circumstances however, can we agree to your release from any of the orchestral rehearsals or performances as set out in the schedule.' As John conducted the Mozart operas, to secure his continued attention he was appointed Music Counsellor in November 1962 for a period of three years. 'This title to be used in the appropriate places on all Glyndebourne literature in a similar way to the use of title Artistic Counsellor given to Dr Rennert and Maestro Gui.' The letter finished with the hope that 'this title will do something to acknowledge publicly your intimate and valued connection with Glyndebourne which everyone hopes may continue unabated in the years to come'.

Sir George Christie summed up the problems of the sixties. 'Glyndebourne was beginning to go through a really quite bad period. My father died in 1962 and I don't suppose it was particularly related to that fact because he had become increasingly inactive through the fifties after my mother's death in 1953 but Glyndebourne did subside to some degree in the mid–sixties. It really took until 1970 in my view, to make a full recovery.' His father had appointed him to the Board at an early age but he felt he was not in a position to assume his role. In addition, the change in orchestra from the Royal Philharmonic to the London Philharmonic in 1964 caused teething problems, the LPO never having worked in the pit previously. Then Rennert left and Enriquez came in with Hadjimischev as producers. His invention was inconsistent. 'John Pritchard was going through a period in the sixties when I don't think he was quite as focused and as serious in his contribution to Glyndebourne as he should have been. I remember Mary and I invited him to dinner when I expressed the wish for more input on his part.'

Emitting a *mea culpa*, John set in train a series of discussion papers in 1964 regarding Glyndebourne's future, expressing thoughts which had been revolving in his mind.★ His final comments were addressed to the 'public image' of Glyndebourne.

> Everyone has his own way of saying 'it's not like the old days' and we know it never could have been anyway! All the more reason to cut through a lot of the tethers holding us back and to present, with all the decent press coverage we can get, a new and exciting picture of our aims and what we want the GB of the seventies to look like. In a way I feel that our public is expecting more from us

★Memorandum – Glyndebourne's future, p. 339

than just a year by year attempt to prevent standards from sliding – because however well we do that, there will always be someone to say 'Sadlers Wells does it better'; the critics being as we know, always prone to praise an inexpensive thing to the disadvantage of the higher-priced article!

He believed that the Glyndebourne Book was a very successful forum to present their case and suggested that there should be an annual press conference to go into the background of the season's planning.

The complaint at the LPO, Glyndebourne and Covent Garden in the sixties that John was not sufficiently attentive to his work came at a time when he was enjoying life. Peter Brown used to spend Christmas with John and Basil and remembered being asked by John to go to Charing Cross station to pick up a young man, Terry MacInnis, in John's new Lancia Flavia. There was an instant disagreement between Basil and Terry. That Christmas it was an argument about potatoes. Terry wanted more and Basil said he was a peasant to eat so many. 'Basil can be as grumpy as hell and Terry was being the "I'm a simple boy from the country, don't put your grand ideas on me." John was stirring his wooden spoon.'

Working as a clerk for the Trustee Savings Bank, Terry was passionately fond of opera. A friend of the ushers, he met John at the dress rehearsal during the revival of *L'Incoronazione di Poppea* in 1963. After their holiday together in Italy, Terry moved in with John. Twenty years older, John regarded him in the manner of an indulgent parent. Hating artificiality, he considered the younger man's innocent honesty more important than the sophisticated deviousness of others. Although Terry stayed in the background, those who worked at Glyndebourne had the opportunity to see and appreciate the great loyalty the two had for each other. When he first arrived on the scene as John's new friend, they thought he was just another of the 'hangers-on' but gradually he became more than that as their relationship developed. Never attempting to influence John in musical matters, it fell to him to look after the household and occasionally deal firmly with the guests and others who wanted to sponge off John.

Whilst many were scared by Terry's driving, John secretly liked the excitement especially when the car screeched to a halt. On 5th August 1964, having drunk a bottle of wine between them at dinner, Terry, then aged twenty-two, drove John in the Lancia from Lewes to Rotherfield to visit Terry's mother. Approaching Tunbridge Wells in the late evening, travelling too fast along the country roads, full of bends with over-hanging trees and hedges, something darted across the road. Terry swerved, went into a skid and, unable to correct it, the car turned over. Fortunately John was not severely injured but his head was bleeding profusely and he was taken to hospital. With two previous convictions for speeding, Terry was banned from driving for six months, a salutary lesson.

John preferred fast, white, open-topped cars and would send Terry great distances even from London to Hamburg when he heard of a particular Mercedes for sale. In 1969 he was noted for the American Thunderbird in which was installed a stereo tape recorder and every possible gadget. However, in America he felt it essential to create an impression by sporting a stylish European car, a Jaguar or Mercedes. When he took up his appointment in San Francisco, his last purchase was a silver Rolls Royce.

Having rented a house in Kingston, near Lewes, during the two previous Glyndebourne seasons, towards the end of 1965 John decided that he would like to live in the country and have his main home in the neighbourhood of the opera house. After several sorties he found what was to become his dream home in Carter's Corner Place. Situated near Hailsham, it had been the family residence of Lord Hailsham who, during the last two years of his occupancy, had completely overhauled the original panelling. Listed as being of historical interest and briefly occupied after his departure, it had been divided into three units. Originally offering £6,000 for Unit 1, John finally purchased it for £7,000 and was able to complete the sale of the lease of Park Village East simultaneously. With Harrods organising the removal he and Terry moved in for the start of the Glyndebourne season, living in the library whilst John lovingly restored the house into a 'first-class country residence'. He would never cease to delight in giving a visitor the 'sixty cent tour', particularly showing the magnificent view from the first floor, which could be sealed off from the ground floor by a heavy wooden door dating from the time when the sea, which had since retreated, might invade the house.

In his *Who's Who* entry, John listed 'good food, wine and

theatre' as his interests but omitted shopping. He loved shopping for his home and furnished Carter's Corner with antiques in keeping with its early Tudor history. Silver and glass purchased over the years were displayed on a huge sideboard. In addition he bought a large four-poster bed, planning the curtains with Michael Szell. The library was full of books and records accumulated to reflect his wide ranging interests, with Elton John side by side with Mozart. It was to the library that he would disappear, locking himself away to study but while working on a score he wanted to know that he was not alone, that there were others in the house having a good time whom he could rejoin when he chose.

If refurbishing and furnishing the house was a labour of love, so too was the care bestowed on the garden. Somewhat neglected, with the aid of Hilliers catalogue he used old Edwardian photographs to re-plant the formal terrace and main lawn but left an overgrown, tree-shaded area extending over several acres. The other two units to the house were soon sold and John was able to buy a disused paddock of extra land adjacent to one side, where, three years later, he put in a large swimming pool. In the summer months the swimming pool would become the focal point, the *raison d'être* of John's parties. Always the person who gave *the* party, it was part of the affectionate way he had of giving to others. There was nobody more generous than John and Carter's Corner Place provided the ideal setting for him to develop and expand that side of his personality which suited the backdrop he created.

In the early years at Carter's Corner, Mrs Mills, the housekeeper, ruled supreme. Her husband had been a civil servant in the Colonial Services and she was almost a caricature of that background, referring to Brian Epstein in a disdainful manner, reflecting her prejudices. Peter Brown confided to John his worries about his partner, feeling that if he had a home in the country it would enable him to lead a more stable life. John saw a house advertised in *Country Life* magazine only five minutes away from Carter's Corner, which Brian Epstein agreed to buy as soon as he saw it. John invited Epstein without Peter to the opera and was able to break down a barrier which had existed between them because of Peter Brown and convince him that his friendship was genuine. Through Epstein, John came to meet many show business personalities, reflecting the continual cross section of people from different parts of the entertainment industry which fascinated him. It was part of his need to always explore whatever was new.

By the end of the sixties, John was overweight, a constant problem for the rest of his life. The dinner parties when there would be eight or ten people from Glyndebourne who knew each other well, or just a small luncheon with close friends on the day of a performance, helped him to relax. He was under tremendous pressure, rushing to London for concerts between performances at Glyndebourne. Particularly on a Sunday and especially if it had been a beautiful day, he would often arrive only five or ten minutes before a performance and he thrived on the knowledge that his friends would still be at his home enjoying themselves when he returned.

Whilst the artists working at Glyndebourne were happy, it began to emerge that the Festival could not subsist on a diet of only Mozart and Rossini, with just an occasional flirtation elsewhere. Strauss was beginning to come through as 'composer number two' but that was not confirmed until the seventies.

When John conducted *Arlecchino* at the Edinburgh Festival in 1960 (part of a triple bill with *Il Segreto di Susanna* and *La Voix Humaine*), one could say it was the beginning of his collaboration with John Cox, who took part as the back end of the pantomime donkey in *Arlecchino*. They had an artistic relationship but Cox had to rely on the front end to take any beats that were necessary from the maestro. 'I think you could say that I started from the bottom!' They developed a strong working relationship during the Festival of 1962 when John Cox assisted Günther Rennert in Monteverdi's *L'Incoronazione di Poppea*. Its success was such that, outside the traditional Mozart, it was the first time that Glyndebourne repeated an opera three years running.

Frequently, those who are able to conduct and sing Brahms and Strauss do not like and find difficulty in performing French music, such as Bizet, Ravel, Massenet and Debussy, together with their heir Stravinsky. In Strauss the feeling is in the orchestration, harmonies and colour and in Cavalli, Monteverdi and Stravinsky the basis is rhythm. Strauss spoke about eighteenth-century French music in *Le Bourgeois Gentilhomme* but he distorted it 'à l'Allemande'. Stravinsky, who in turn did not particularly like Strauss, nevertheless when writing to Ernest Ansermet, the conductor, spoke in awe of the German composer.

The music of Monteverdi was relatively unknown. Vincent d'Indy arranged, or as some consider deranged, the three operas and people went to hear them in 1911 or 1912 but they did not remain in the repertoire. Nadia Boulanger, who has influenced many musicians, did not like Strauss. Beginning with Monteverdi records, she was responsible for the fashion for fifteenth - seventeenth-century French music, building the bridge between Lully and Stravinsky.

Raymond Leppard had done the arrangement of *Poppea* and John Cox commented: 'He was there as the kind of direct line to Monteverdi.' The two men spent a great deal of time in the Organ Room with Leppard doing 'Monteverdi by the yard, or by the minute', with a stopwatch, so that they had enough music to do the onstage scene changes. Then they took it to John and Rennert for approval. 'It was very much building an opera as we went along, with marvellous ingredients that were already there waiting to be brought alive. Raymond never invented. He always knew where to find something, or how to re-interpret or recycle something that was already in the piece just by giving it the variety of the continuo or the ritornello.' There was a very complex and rich continuo in Leppard's versions, which seemed to John Cox to be quite justifiable inventiveness on the other's part.

The general perception was that John did not know *Poppea* and that he had come rather unprepared. It was the first time during their working relationship that Cox had heard this kind of thing said about him. 'I could actually see from my own experience that it was probably true.' It has to be said that this was a very unfamiliar piece and nobody really quite knew how it was going to work theatrically. The sounds that the instruments were making and the sounds that the singers were making were unfamiliar to most, certainly unfamiliar in Glyndebourne. There was an atmosphere of experimental, pragmatic approach to the whole exercise. John Cox was 'aware that in performances John was looking at the score a great deal more than he ever needed to in *Così* or *Idomeneo*'. At the same time he was equally aware that a number of singers on stage needed more help than they were getting because they were also unfamiliar with the material and the style. However, it was a stunning success because John had a theatrical instinct of which Günther Rennert made use constantly, making *Poppea* function as a piece of acceptable mid-twentieth-century music drama.

Although John and Rennert had different personalities, they had the greatest respect for each other but the relationship became strained in 1961 during rehearsals and performances of the world première of Hans Werner Henze's *Elegy for Young Lovers*. Accustomed to a diet of traditional opera, it had a very poor reception from the regular audiences. Nowadays they are more prepared to accept contemporary opera than they were then.

Elisabeth Söderström, who was singing in the opera, recalled that John's attitude and also the way he solved the problems in the score, 'helped a lot to keep the atmosphere not happy but at least endurable.' She remembered Günther Rennert declaring to the authors of the libretto, W H Auden and Chester Kallmann, that it was 'impossible to play' (a polite translation of the German). While she found it a tough experience, John on the other hand approached the singers with, 'Now let's see what you can do with it.'

She recalled a classic story about *Elegy*. Auden had not said 'hello' to John Christie. One day after lunch Auden went in to watch one of the rehearsals and John Christie was in the audience. Squeezing himself into the seat behind, he said, 'Mr Christie, may I say "How do you do?"' Christie turned round. 'I'm Auden,' he continued. 'Who?' said Christie. 'I'm Auden. I wrote this piece.' 'You shouldn't have!' replied Christie. When Howard Wicks, the librarian, was carrying the score through the covered way, Christie stopped him and asked what music he had. On hearing that it was the score of *Elegy*, he was told that he could 'put it in the incinerator for all he cared about it!'

Hans Werner Henze remembered recommending Lila de Nobilis to design the opera. He thought it was a good marriage as the producer, Rennert 'did not understand the opera and wanted a very realistic set which didn't look right as it needed something more theatrical. Rennert and I did not like each other which made everything very awkward. It didn't quite work in spite of the good cast and the marvellous rendering of the score.'

John did not conduct a contemporary score again at Glyndebourne until 1973, the first British performance of Gottfried von Einem's *The Visit of the Old Lady*. It showed how much he had developed in the twelve years since *Elegy*. Based on a Dürrenmatt play, it is a slightly macabre story about the richest lady in the world returning to her old village which is totally dilapidated. Previously all the express trains passed through the town, except for the day when the old lady returned, wearing Hartnell gowns. She blackmails the citizens, paying them a great deal of money to murder the lover from her youth, at the end returning with the corpse to her island of Capri. It heralded a change in the style of Glyndebourne productions. There was a huge revolve on the stage and a Ford Escort car (which was a new model at the time) needed to be driven off the stage into the wings. The effects, symbolising the development of the town from a dreary place to a revitalised one, with skyscrapers, cars and many trains, were quite revolutionary stagewise in opera.

The music was very involved with many repeats and a great deal of percussion. Much was ad-libbed and depended on the conductor. The stage manager running the performance, Tom Redman, had many complicated train cues with projections and John, needing to cue various effects, had to flick a switch on the podium and deal with a huge orchestra at the same time. They joked about it at first as it was a new score but, gradually he made the ad-libs more fixed and they decided how many bars to count.

The collaboration with the composer was such that von Einem trusted John and John tackled the complications raised by the score with great authority and tact. They had a way of arriving at the right solution together for a musical problem. Since it was being sung in English, they were both concerned that it should be comprehensible. On one occasion when the conversation was about some metronome marks at various points in the piece which were proving difficult, John pointed out to von Einem that English 'sings' slower than German. One can sing German at speed and it can sound beautiful but if one sings English at faster than comprehension speed, it just begins to sound ugly. Now Production and Technical Administrator at Glyndebourne, Tom Redman became one of John's true friends. He considers that John's understanding of a work as a whole and the relationships between those with whom he worked were the foundation on which he built an opera and an organisation.

Working as repetiteur on *Visit of the Old Lady* was a young man, Jan Latham-Koenig, who was to become close to John in the eighties. He was eighteen and had just started to study conducting at the Royal College of Music. He was a pianist but knew in his heart that he wanted to be a conductor and wrote to three well-known British conductors to ask for advice. From the first he received a brochure for some future conductors' competition; the secretary of the second replied, 'Mr — will answer your letter in due course but I should point out that he is very busy doing . . .' He never heard any more. John was the only person who replied in a humane way: 'Thank you very much for your letter. I should be delighted to have a talk with you. Please would you call me at my private number from 7th April . . .' 'I phoned when I was supposed to and John knew who I was but couldn't remember what he had said. He told me that he'd try and meet with me the following week. However, a few days later, I received a call from him saying, "I've suddenly got a free seat in my box, would you like to come?" He was conducting *Don Carlos* at Covent Garden. I met him in the interval. He asked what I was doing and if I'd like to come and see him at Carter's Corner.'

Jan Latham-Koenig recalled being invited for lunch at Carter's Corner some weeks later. They talked and then more people arrived for lunch. 'What amazed me was the liberal preprandial champagne and then, the involvement not only of the housekeeper but many of the guests in the preparation of this Lucullan feast. Much wine and brandy accompanied all the courses.' He hardly drank anything at all as it seemed as if he was in another world. As he knew that John might consider him as a repetiteur and that 'he might just ask me to play for him, I had come prepared. At about half-past three I was almost asleep in a chair when Terry came over and said that John wanted to speak to me, alone, downstairs. "Why don't you play something?" He said it in such a nice way. After finishing the Szymanowski sonata I had prepared, he asked me something very important which I have never forgotten, "Can you play to a beat?" I always ask this question now, when I engage a repetiteur. Many pianists can play brilliantly but only on their own and it requires a certain sensitivity and flexibility to follow a conductor. A very special technique is required for being a repetiteur.' He was taken on at Glyndebourne; one of the youngest repetiteurs. 'He never did anything other than put me at my ease and at no time did he try to seduce me either. I knew of his reputation but he was just very kind to me. What struck me already then was a constant need for companionship, I suppose to assuage a very desperate loneliness which beneath the charm and gaiety, seemed to me to be ever present.'

During the early years of John's Musical Directorship, he went to production as well as orchestra rehearsals. In particular John was very patient with people. Although many young people were very much in awe of him as conductor, he was calm about any 'flap' and would just say 'let's get it right', removing the potential heat from a situation. His innate generosity, sense of humour and sense of fun – the 'work hard, play hard' theory – helped. Many criticised John for 'playing' too hard but he was highly respected by the LPO who played at Glyndebourne and still do. Having that musical relationship, conducting them in the concert hall added to the quality of the performances.

In the atmosphere of Glyndebourne, people get to know and understand each other. The attitude of the conductor to the people working backstage communicates very much with the general relationship of the orchestra, who are concealed, in the general sense, in the anonymity of the pit. They need stimulus. John would joke with them and keep their morale high. If there is a problem it can be very expensive to keep an orchestra not playing. When there is a delay on stage, if something goes wrong or, if the production department wants to repeat something, it takes time. Often a conductor will do notes, or sometimes the stage manager will ask for the conductor's co-operation often discussing this before the rehearsal. As Glyndebourne was breaking new ground in terms of technical advancement, the unexpected would happen and the relationship between stage and conductor set the tone of the rehearsal. John was very co-operative in those moments. It kept the orchestra from becoming restless and retained the atmosphere and impetus of the rehearsal, especially if things had gone well. One cannot underrate John's tact because it contributed to everything gelling, sooner rather than later.

Bernard Haitink was impressed by John's manner.

> He was so gentle, also with his musicians, which I liked. I remember attending an orchestra rehearsal and he didn't say much. He worked his way through a part of the score and stopped and they were all practising. We discussed it later and he said, 'Well, I like it when they sort out their problems themselves.' It was a valuable lesson for me. He was really loved by the musicians because he was such a nice man who loved music. John had a lot to offer. I thought that he had a tremendous talent. I thought that sometimes he was

a little lazy and therefore didn't develop his talent more but he had other things in his life that he felt were important and I think that is also a right. People have a right to do the things they like. When I look back and think of John Pritchard, I think of an extremely nice man who loved music *and* his musicians, which is very important. He was a musician's conductor.

The question 'Whither Glyndebourne?' would not go away. The new policy prevailing caused concern amongst its traditional supporters, the Festival Society and Corporate Members who took seventy per cent of the seats available. The former had a long waiting list to pay five guineas annually for the benefit of priority booking. With the added benefit of four free tickets it cost two hundred guineas for Corporate Membership. What they required of an opera and in a sense, of Glyndebourne, was conservative. If the music was boring, the dinner interval, gardens and social cachet would compensate. To their dismay, the newly appointed Musical Director was propounding strong views on the question of dress. He was reported as considering it 'ridiculous' for audiences to wear evening dress after a long journey by train or car, that the ubiquitous floral prints were 'often so inelegant', that the trend in Europe was away from formal attire at festivals and 'anyway young people are against it'. He was offending critics by suggesting that the newly formed Glyndebourne Touring Opera should present their operas in English. However, they welcomed his suggestion that some very cheap seats at the Festival be provided for young opera-goers. Wanting to reduce the large number of performances for each opera in a season, John realised it was essential to present a wider repertoire drawn from more revivals.

Reflecting on the way John expanded the repertoire, Bernard Haitink commented: 'The theatre was his life-blood, his second nature. John was reared in the opera world. I was not. Thanks to Glyndebourne and John, because John *was* Glyndebourne, I learnt a lot from them. Glyndebourne audiences were very special audiences, very good, loyal and dedicated. Of course there was Mozart and Rossini but maybe they were a bit tentative in accepting works on a bigger scale.'

John's love for Russian music in the concert hall extended to wanting to perform Tchaikovsky in Sussex. *Eugene Onegin* in 1968 was very exciting for all those connected with the stage because they realised that they were presenting a new style and a new perception. It was a change in the way of viewing an opera, of combining what has become more obvious latterly, the purpose of the Glyndebourne principle, namely music-theatre. Everything musical is not sacred and the production secondary. John as a conductor was very unselfish in this respect and in his flexibility was continuing the Busch/Ebert/Messel tradition.

Michael Hadjimischev produced *Onegin* and Pauline Grant did the choreography which includes some wonderful dances, the Polonaise and Waltz. In those days the Glyndebourne building was very different and when the dancers had to rehearse the Polonaise, which was to be on a raked stage, the choreographer had to rehearse with an upright piano outside 'transport' where there is a concrete slope. It transpired that the lady who played for those rehearsals and the choreographer had completely different numberings in their scores to the parts for the orchestra and the numbers which John and the singers used. After John had rearranged the orchestral parts, Pauline kept saying to him, 'It's too fast'. Eventually John turned to the orchestra, 'Well gentlemen, Pauline wants it much slower. Now – very maestoso. Let's give it "bags of swank".' He produced a wonderful, majestic Polonaise, the right tempo for a courtly dance. One could hear all the notes. There was a vitality to the music. John had said 'bags of swank' and that is what it was.

The opera was sung in Russian and brought East Europeans to Glyndebourne, some of whom did not speak any English. Virginia (Gina) Popova, singing the old nurse, smiled and communicated with sign language with the Glyndebourne staff but there was a marvellous team spirit and John drew all the people together and, above all, was respected by them.

Every evening Hugues Cuenod as Monsieur Triquet would stop the show with his Couplets to Tatyana. He recalled that John asked him to do something which he has always done since. The second time the Couplets come to an end, 'brillez, brillez', words of endearment meaning 'I love you, I love you', must be sung *pianissimo* (very softly). 'I have done it with several conductors and it was hard to persuade them to let me do that but I never told them that it was *another* conductor who told me to do this.'

Tatyana was another triumph for Elisabeth Söderström. She felt that she would never forget the promenade concert performance of the opera at the Albert Hall. 'We had a very full house and a very enthusiastic audience. John enjoyed leading the performance very much and I was very grateful to take part.'

Onegin was so successful that it was repeated two years later but without Elisabeth Söderström in the cast, performed this time mainly with Bulgarian singers because Glyndebourne could not afford the high fees demanded by Russian singers. Moran Caplat complained, 'Russia doesn't really seem to want any but her very starry artists to come out, except for very starry occasions.'

With his contract as Principal Conductor and Musical Director extended until the end of 1972, the enthusiastic welcome for *Eugene Onegin* prompted John to conduct Tchaikovsky's *The Queen of Spades* in 1971 with Bulgarian performers. It was not well reviewed and was a great disappointment after the previous Tchaikovsky success. Primarily the problem lay with the designs for the production. Complaints were voiced that a dark tragedy did not marry well with the Sussex countryside in mid-summer. However John received rave reviews for his judgement in balancing tempo and dynamics.

John's wonderful ability to cope and the reason why he has been ranked amongst the foremost conductors of opera is best illustrated by the radio broadcast of *The Queen of Spades*. During the run of performances the role of leading tenor was shared by two singers, one of whom, John's preferred choice, was supposed to sing in the live broadcast. During the start of the first act, which is quite long with some very dramatic moments, the tenor disappeared in the middle of an ensemble. Distressed, he just left the stage. It all happened so quickly that the stage management did not realise what had happened. The music is quite complex. John just kept going, keeping everyone together. The other singer was watching from the wings. He scrambled into costume, went on stage and sang the rest of the act and the opera. Everybody was quite astonished at the way John handled the situation. Even the orchestra did not realise what had happened. Only if one knew the opera well would one have realised that there was a gap. Under the circumstances, few conductors would have continued.

It illustrates the difference between an opera conductor and one trained only in the concert hall. It requires a different temperament, sense of awareness and above all, a willingness as much as an ability to deal with and accept difficulties. This was so very much an important part of John and yet was known only to those connected with a performance and not to the general public.

Equally rare was his ability to produce outstanding performances under pressure. When it became known that it might not be possible for Sir John Barbirolli to conduct the New Philharmonia Orchestra in a series of concerts for Expo '70 in Osaka, both the British Ambassador in Japan and the British Council Director made a special request to John to be available. At the time the Manager of the New Philharmonia was Gerald McDonald, previously Manager of the Royal Liverpool Philharmonic Orchestra and the Leader was Emanuel Hurwitz. When Sir John Barbirolli passed away in July 1970, amazingly John commuted to Osaka, making the long journey four times in ten days fitting in five concerts in Athens on his final return journey.

Arriving in Osaka on 5th August, he conducted John Ogdon in a performance of the Beethoven Piano Concerto no. 3 in C minor as well as the Rawsthorne overture *Street Corner* and Mahler's 1st Symphony. On the 7th August, Britten's *Sinfonia da Requiem* was followed by Mahler's song cycle *Lieder eines fahrenden Gesellen* with Dame Janet Baker as soloist, the concert ending with Beethoven's 3rd Symphony. The Britten work, commissioned pre-war by the Japanese and rejected for its Christian title, was an appropriate work to perform to a post-Hiroshima audience. The following day Dame Janet Baker was again the soloist but this time for Mahler's *Kindertotenlieder*, with Britten's *Young Person's Guide to the Orchestra* and Sibelius' Symphony no. 2 making up the rest of the programme. Returning to England, he conducted the Albert Hall Promenade Concert of *Eugene Onegin* before returning again to Japan for further concerts in Tokyo with John Ogdon and Dame Janet Baker.

The singer remembered the occasion vividly. In a terrible state of shock at the death of Sir John Barbirolli she was very relieved that it was John who was taking over her concerts.

> It was a question of personality. As a singer one tends to be blinkered. It is the great conductors and producers who see things as a whole. As a singer you are just a small piece of the jigsaw and you have to make yourself slide into the whole. When we were in Japan, the way that the Japanese public received John made me aware of personalities in the wider sense. It was somehow different, on a deeper level than just the reception of a famous man. It came to me that this tremendously laid back viewpoint of

the world, which was a hallmark of John's, was part of the Japanese culture. He knew exactly what was going on. There was something about his personality, his build. They love rotund people, people who look as if they're enjoying life and food. His physique was of the earth and he would walk onto the platform with his large connected and relaxed figure. He would start to conduct and they understood. They understood what he was trying to say to them musically because of the person he was and the way he looked.

The reception was quite tumultuous. The Japanese manager of the concert hall, rushing round to greet John after a performance, in his excitement stumbled out, 'Glate success, flenzied crapping in the hall tonight!' No less appreciative were the many letters. 'You were wonderful John. I knew you would be but I am always staggered at your enormous vitality, musicianship and tremendous command of the situation.' (Gerald McDonald)

For an artist, being accepted internationally with considerable acclaim is never fully recognised in their home country. Their standing abroad as an international artist cannot be understood. 'Home' can only understand others coming in from outside, when the public thinks they are glamorous, well-paid and famous. For an international artist there are always pockets of resistance, places where they are not accepted, where the doors remain closed.

As John was in Japan, some of the *Onegin* performances needed to be conducted by a substitute conductor. On a previous occasion in 1967 when John was conducting *La Bohème* and *Don Giovanni* at the same time, there was a scheduled replacement conductor. Everyone was shocked to read in an American journal, the *Saturday Review Incorporated*, a slating review entitled 'Music to my Ears' of a rehearsal supposedly conducted by John which had in fact been taken by the other conductor. In mitigation the writer claimed afterwards he had attended a rehearsal for which no special programmes were issued. As John's solicitors were threatening to commence action for libel, David Webster wrote to the editor on 11th October 1967: 'The whole affair is unfortunate but I must admit that if I were in John Pritchard's situation the attempt at apology which you made in your paper is really so appalling that nothing on earth would make me think that I should attempt to compromise. I must confess that your paper has done him an immense injury and your attempt at apology is one of the most pitiful I have seen in my career.' He added in a postscript: 'In spite of what I have written above this does not mean that I am unhappy about anything you have written about our Royal Ballet Company. Indeed we are grateful for all you have done in your paper to help the Company.' The matter was resolved with an apology in the *Times* and costs.

In commenting on John's crammed schedule, Bernard Haitink felt he was a person who could be easily bored. 'Therefore his first nights were always marvellous but he could lose interest if there were a long series of performances, so there was always the urge to do other works. In a way it was a very artistic view. If he felt burnt out then "let's do something else, something stimulating".'

John's constant need for stimulation during a long run of performances was helped when the unexpected happened. Richard van Allan recalled the occasion he was asked to fill in as Pasha Selim in *Entführung*. His aria is fairly high all the way through and at the end of it there is a low 'D' to sing. At this particular performance he realised that there was no bottom 'D' in his voice. 'I hadn't a cat in hell's chance of doing it. When I reached the moment, I knew nothing would come out, so I did a big gesture pointing to where the note should be. Then I leant over and put my hand to my ear as if listening for it. The audience caught the joke and John started chuckling away as he was conducting. At the audience laughter, Rodney Friend (the leader) jumped out of his chair still playing and leaned over, "What's happening?" John simply turned, "Richard's just done something very funny."'

On another occasion Vittorio Gui was conducting Debussy's *Pelléas and Mélisande* in 1963 when Michel Roux, singing Golaud, hurt his foot. The Maestro would not conduct with the understudy, feeling he was unsatisfactory. *Figaro* was substituted with John conducting, one of the very few occasions at Glyndebourne when an opera was changed. Those present felt it was one of the best *Figaro* performances they had ever heard simply because John was presented with the unexpected and the adrenalin flowed.

John's collaboration with Ileana Cotrubas in *Pelléas and Mélisande* was one of the outstanding memories of his time at Glyndebourne. The drama hinges on the moment Mélisande lies and her reasons for so doing. She is frightened by the castle, its high walls and the grand people surrounding her. The portrayal requires a soprano suggesting fragility, a voice like finest crystal. For the 1969 revival John found his inspiration in her. She recalled their first meeting. A London agent had heard her in *Die Zauberflöte* in Germany. Over dinner he explained that Glyndebourne were

Early Glyndebourne.

Albert and Amy Pritchard's golden wedding anniversary, 1953. *Front row, left to right:* Jean, Amy, Winn; *Back row, left to right:* John, Eddie, Albert, Stan.

John with Adèle Leigh at Glyndebourne, circa 1953.

Carter's Corner Place, Sussex.

On holiday with Vittorio Gui in Maratea, Italy.

John with Peter Brown and Mrs Browning.

John with Dame Joan Sutherland, Richard Bonynge, Renato Cioni, Basil Horsfield and some of the cast of *Lucia* during the recording in Rome, 1961.

searching for a Mélisande but she would have to audition for John Pritchard who was conducting in Munich. So she took a train there and sang an aria of Pamina's from *Zauberflöte* and little bits of Mélisande. 'At the end, he said "You are my Mélisande". With this part I made my debut in England in 1969. It was very beautiful.' Her first Susanna in *Figaro* was in England with John, then *Traviata* and *L'Elisir d'Amore* and so on. John was responsible for many of her first steps. She liked him a great deal because he was always very well-dressed, very elegant. 'During the Proms he always had very special jackets, special colours. It was his own pattern. He spoke very, very slowly and lazily and liked to talk to me in French.' Impressed by her recent audition, John wrote to Moran Caplat from South Africa saying he was concerned about the singer proposed for Constanze in *Entführung*. 'I feel her voice is too small for the *three* profoundly varied arias of Constanze. I would prefer to work with the undoubtedly excellent vocal material provided by Cotrubas, especially as the latter does *not* look at all bad on the stage and we may all be surprised by her development in a month's rehearsals . . . Even in the new look we are trying to take of *Entführung*, Constanze will still be the nice girl of noble demeanour and to me that's Cotrubas!'

The first *Capriccio* in 1963, produced by Günther Rennert, which John conducted, was divided into two parts as opposed to the one act without a break which Strauss intended, enabling the Glyndebourne audience to picnic during the interval in daylight.

It was the sophistication of Strauss, particularly period Strauss, which appealed to John's own sophistication. He enjoyed the social niceties to be observed onstage and in the score and it was the partnership between John and John Cox that was crucial to Glyndebourne. The two men had many similarities in their tastes both on and offstage. They were both fairly worldly people and the combination came to the fore in Richard Strauss. In the sophistication which John and John Cox brought to Sussex an audience felt they were watching a play of the calibre of Shaftesbury Avenue.

When people think of memorable Glyndebourne productions, the 1973 *Capriccio* is always high on the list as one of the most magical. Although it was with the ten-year-old Dennis Lennon sets, John had no regrets for the old 1963 effort with its big skirts and powdered wigs. Explaining that if the opera was to be done in a meaningful way for him, John Cox felt that he could not present it in an eighteenth-century setting, Moran Caplat agreed with him. 'Go ahead but you'll have to convince John and Elisabeth.' So he travelled to Stockholm to see Elisabeth Söderström who would be singing the Countess as she had done in the earlier productions and, back in London, met John in Soho where they had a very good lunch. After hearing the other's proposals, John entered fully into doing it in a jazz era conception. 'Why can't we have a white piano as well?' The producer answered, 'We can't have a white piano John, because we'd have to have a white harpsichord as well.' 'Yes, I suppose that would be a bit too kitsch,' he replied.★

Even though it might have benefited by translation, the argument against performing the opera in English one can understand simply by looking at the cast list: a Rumanian, three Swedes, an Argentinian, an Italian and a Swiss, as well as Americans and Irish.

The problem of accents did not exist the following year when in 1974 John conducted Strauss' *Intermezzo*. Although with Swedish and Dutch leads, everyone else was an anglophile and both the principals spoke and sang well in English. Elisabeth Söderström was very keen to have the humour understood, seeing it as a golden opportunity for a major comedy role. Andrew Porter, in Sydney for the opening of the Opera House, was contacted and he agreed to do the libretto in English in the very short time available. The early preparations for *Intermezzo* were enjoyable creative episodes, with John coming to the rehearsals with the singers and John Cox. Together they honed and shaped the translation so that it seemed as though the work had been written for the English language.

There was one point during the season when John's attendance at rehearsals began to be erratic. One afternoon Elisabeth Söderström refused to continue until he was fetched. He had decided to take a long lunch because he had an interesting house guest. *Intermezzo* was an unfamiliar work and everybody needed all the help they could get and knew that the best source of that help would be the conductor. John Cox found himself in the difficult situation of having to telephone and say that the cast was 'on strike and refused to rehearse' without him. Arriving with somewhat ill grace, he did not repeat his behaviour. John Cox commented:

★'Capriccio', from the Glyndebourne Programme Book, p. 344

He wasn't going to risk his reputation by doing that kind of thing too many times. Stories get out! Although I've always been as firm a proponent of him as anybody could possibly have been but when various obituarists started mentioning his streak of laziness, I knew it from experience. From time to time, he would prefer to do something other than rehearse. You could be quite sure that he was never at home in bed. He was not lazy in that sense of the word, it was just a slightly cavalier attitude to what other people thought. He was just very much in demand. I've known plenty of rehearsals when singers have positively prayed that the conductor would not turn up. 'We can't do this without John; he knows the answers; can give us the guidance and do the necessary shaping.' That had to be said and done and it was.

Intermezzo was one of the few times that Elisabeth Söderström arrived at Glyndebourne without knowing her part because it was impossible to find anybody in Stockholm who could teach it to her. 'The score was very difficult, so John was probably a little upset and impatient but still he treated me kindly and it was a real hit. Such a wonderful piece and also a great production. With all the difficulties, it was a very exciting work. I took some liberties in that part because there was spoken dialogue and we talked about whether we should omit it. The orchestra hates to sit and listen to dialogue. I found a way round that – I changed a few words here and there so that they would sit and listen to what would come.' At one performance she was talking about the 'thrills of worldwide travel' and was supposed to say 'Africa, America and . . .', then one day she said, 'Africa, America and the Isle of Wight' which brought the house down. Whether Elisabeth Söderström knew that Strauss himself had indeed taken a holiday on the Isle of Wight or had put it in as a perfect piece of serendipity, it was a coincidence.

Intermezzo involved many scene changes. The first scene was quite long but the second lasted only two and a half minutes and it was a toboggan slope with a snowman. Then after an interlude of a couple of minutes, another scene, the ballroom, lasting three minutes. With so many horrendous scene changes and a great deal of dialogue (much of the words were spoken more than sung), the prompter was a very important person. Calvin Simmons, a young black musician whom John had discovered in San Francisco, was brilliant. As he was black, the inside of the prompt-box was painted white so that he could be seen clearly by the artists and in front of the special gauze curtain that came down to hide the scenery. It needed quite a bright light to show up his hands. Tom Redman, as stage manager, had control of this light from the prompt corner and he and Calvin used to have a game to test the other's musical ability (the music was relatively complicated). Redman would turn off the prompt-light after the singing at the end of a scene but left it until the very last moment, just before the performers actually started to sing, before switching on again. John was very amused by all this.

The offstage fun encompassed Franzl's piano lesson in Act I, scene viii. It was decided that Simmons would play *Für Elise*, very badly in the wings, slamming his hands down on the keys when he could not get it right. Then Elisabeth Söderström would sign off her letter with the phrase, sung through clenched teeth, 'the child is well'. There is a lovely moment at the end of the opera. Christine bakes a cake for her husband when he finally comes home for the great reconciliation and they are going to have breakfast together. The cake is on the breakfast table and she serves a couple of slices in the course of the action. At the end of the opera it was always a scramble to see who would get hold of the cake and at one performance, in the middle of the curtain calls, the soprano was observed passing a slice to Calvin in the prompt-box. Those performances were very happy days; everyone worked well as a group of friends and John presided over that feeling. He was part of it, all the social activities surrounding the Glyndebourne season, all the parties and drinks and everything else that contributed to the wonderful feeling of enjoyment on and off the stage.

John understood something which is essential in Strauss operas. It is to do with the sheer enjoyment of life, of emotion; the sheer enjoyment of appetite and of music-making. A golden irony shines through it but there is a smile as well; sometimes a smile of mockery, sometimes a smile of sheer pleasure but it is always there. John would have a smile on his face most of the time when he was conducting, a fastidious smile.

Così fan Tutte was an opera which John always conducted with a smile. In *Così* was all the uncertainty of emotion, the uncertainty of love, what it could lead to in terms of insecurity and uncertainty in decision-making. The lightness of touch, the gentle irony, the affectionate regard for human frailty which was very much part of John's own character, were all heard together with a bubbling, sparkling wit.

Early in their acquaintance, Robert Ponsonby became very much aware of the iron within John's velvet glove. He realised that the apparently bland man had, if necessary, a very sharp tongue and was very determined to get his own way. Considering that he knew *Così fan Tutte* because he had sung Guglielmo several times in Oxford, not with an orchestra but with a piano, he went to him after a performance of *Così* at Glyndebourne and said '"John that was marvellous but honestly you can't take Dorabella's aria at that tempo!" "Are you sure?" he said. It was quite fierce. He didn't lose his temper. It was presumptuous of me. He knew precisely where he stood on this matter and he knew precisely where I stood. I was very young, very new to Glyndebourne.' People who presumed John was easy-going, easily persuaded to do this or that, very soon discovered that this was an absolutely mistaken impression of a man whose musical goals were always extremely clear. Given the right works, particularly Mozart, Strauss and *Peter Grimes*, he knew exactly what he wanted to do. When he respected the artists with whom he was working, John could be completely charming in persuading them of the rightness of his views.

People tended to underestimate John because he was always joking with the orchestra but it was part of his dislike of people who were filled with their own self-importance. Whenever a British orchestra with whom he worked would have a party, the evening would never be complete without somebody doing an impersonation of John. In a particularly happy production of *Così* in 1969, the cast would not only meet in the tea-breaks but would all go off to a restaurant together for dinner and John would sometimes join them. As in all productions of *Così*, he paid great attention to casting and was one of the first conductors to cast a mezzo, the French singer Jane Berbié, in the role of Despina bringing earthiness to the character to balance Don Alfonso.

By this time, Ryland Davies, singing Ferrando, had perfected his impersonation of the conductor. At the end of the run of performances, encouraged by Terry and several others, he agreed to take part, as John, in the cabaret for a party. He wore a special dinner jacket with a fairy wand as baton. Feeling rather nervous about the proceedings, not wishing to offend or mar their friendship, he approached John and told him what was planned. 'Be sure that you're damn good!' was the reply. With a section of the LPO, Ryland conducted a part from *Così*, preceded by the usual John remarks such as, 'Hello gentlemen, I hope we're starting the season with nice clean parts.' By the end of the exhibition John was collapsing with laughter. The following morning, at the orchestral rehearsal, he walked into the pit as usual with, 'Morning gentlemen, good morning' and pulled out the silver wand which Ryland had used the previous evening.

There are many apocryphal stories about John but they do not translate well into print. It was part of his brilliant sense of timing. With an inimitable voice, nasal and slightly breathless, a diffident manner, his impish humour was easily and often impersonated but it was always with great gentleness. Whilst many know of John's impatience when others failed to give their best, he is never spoken about with anything less than affection. If during a rehearsal he became irritable and showed it towards a musician, he would make a point of going over to them the next day to invite them for a cup of coffee or a drink. They understood he was apologising even when an apology was not really necessary.

Ileana Cotrubus mentioned that John would 'give if it were to somebody who could use it'. If he had a dull cast he would sometimes sit back on his technique and let things go but when he had a good cast and particularly a cast he thought of as friends, not only would they give magnificent performances but it was a joy working anywhere in the vicinity. One could relax with him on stage and socially.

The production of *Le Nozze di Figaro* in 1973 was an example of one of Glyndebourne's most remarkable efforts and just one such occasion. 'The *Figaros* in 1973 and 1974 were the best I have ever seen,' is reiterated often. Even though he could pick up the baton at a moment's notice, John was happiest working in a careful and long-term way, having a wonderful staging collaborator and hand-picked cast. It gave him the opportunity to deepen his involvement when he felt it to be a well integrated project. In this instance he was fascinated by Sir Peter Hall's production and the way he worked with the artists. It was an occasion too when John had a great team of artists in the early stages of their careers. As he wrote: 'Our greater speed in recognising the young singers and our greater cunning in trapping them like Papageno does his birds' brought together Ileana Cotrubas as Susanna, Frederica von Stade as Cherubino, and Elizabeth Harwood sharing the role of the Countess with Dame Kiri Te Kanawa.

Bernard Haitink recalled the magic of this particular *Figaro*. 'I remember sitting in the auditorium during rehearsals and I think it was one of the few times that I was jealous of John because it was beautiful from every aspect: the conducting, the playing, the singing and the production. It was a wonderful moment at Glyndebourne, one of the best productions Peter Hall has ever done.'

Realising that it was essential for a singer to pace their way through a long and taxing aria, John would explain that every great composer would always give an artist the opportunity to rest before reaching a climax. Reiterating that Mozart was a practical composer, he would point out that this was especially so in the Countess' Act III recitative and aria 'Dove Sono' (I Remember) recalling happier days when her husband was in love with her. Usually taken quite slowly, which is more difficult for a singer, he would tell her not to go at 'full tilt' all the way through to the end but to relax at certain moments. John was always wonderful at shaping the recitatives, an aspect often overlooked by other conductors. He instinctively gave the singers the pace to breathe so that they never needed to think about it. They never felt pushed or pressured. One tended to take this for granted because it was absolutely natural. In Mozart, he was very particular about the shapings and observing the dynamics for the text, which seems obvious. Many of the tempi were very fast but he was so secure with everything that one had a feeling of tremendous control and elegance.★

His school-friends had laughed at his large body with disproportionately short arms but Dame Kiri felt that this was an advantage. 'I think I learnt line most of all because his hand movements were very small. His conducting was very small-scale for such a big man. He never over-accentuated anything. The arms never ever went above his head. His orchestra was always under control. A lot of conductors today are waving around so largely that the orchestra feels that they have to do bigger things themselves.' John always made a delicacy, especially in

★The Operas of Mozart, p. 345.

his Mozart, with small movements, almost like knitting. It was so fine that the orchestra became fine and the quality was of that standard. 'In all cases I look at a conductor and he should be short and certainly not too tall and John was very tall for a conductor but with his small arm movements the orchestra didn't go into long, long notes and heavy bowing.' The orchestra will never be too loud if the beats are short, or the spaces between the beats are short. By making the beats like this, the orchestra knew that they did not have much time and had to be there ready for the next one. If the movement is large – arms above the head and then to the chest – the orchestra knows that they have all that time to put pressure on the notes. In his economy of style, quite often John never really had a beat. His hand just went straight across his chest so that a singer knew he was at the end of his bar and it was going to come back down again.

Dame Kiri also remembered that the rehearsals of *Figaro* were great fun. One night when everybody knew it was going to be a very long session, Jean Mallandaine put a bottle of wine on the piano and two glasses with 'Here I am for the night.' Every now and then she would take a little break and take a glass of wine up to John. 'We were up on stage doing *Figaro* and he and Jean were down in the pit with the bottle of wine working and working very hard too.' Her memories of John were always of enjoyment, of doing rather idiotic things, of which he was ready to be part. There was another occasion when she gave him a pair of glasses bought in America with windscreen wipers on the lenses, so loud you could not hear anything wearing them. 'As he walked into the pit he put them on. He was always wicked and naughty.'

As early as 1956 at Covent Garden, John wanted to reinsert both the Basilio and the Marcellina arias. 'I have always disliked the convention of presenting Marcellina as a passé mezzo barely able to sustain the high tessitura of the sextet, and if we were to cast a real lyric soprano (of determined mien) in the part, and give her the coloratura aria it would enormously strengthen and vivify the *galère* of buffi in the cast.' In the Glyndebourne *Figaro* every member of the cast was a person in their own right because the text was uncut and the recitatives given their full weight.

John had come to all the rehearsals as he felt totally involved, prompting speculation that perhaps Sir Peter Hall had insisted in his contract on the conductor's presence. When John was excited nothing mattered except the music and this *Figaro* was going to fulfil all his dreams. From the opening bars of the overture, with the excitement of anticipation it gives, to the finale, the audience was entranced. As the curtain went up on the Norwegian baritone Knut Skram as Figaro, measuring out the half-furnished room in brown and beige hues, with Ileana Cotrubas as his bride-to-be, Susanna, the audience revelled in the music, singing and production, unaware of any single element but engaged by the whole. It was not an opera with the emphasis placed on the arias but a story that was being unfolded. It was not a comic opera played for laughs but an opera where the audience smiled and understood the pathos and sadness of the Countess. Perhaps too, the producer showed the audience that upper-class people have the same feelings as their servants, that we are all the same, that it is only the packaging which is different, something which John appreciated. His conducting never seemed more committed and every performance was a revelation. Several years later John would still play the tape recording of the letter scene with Dame Kiri Te Kanawa and Ileana Cotrubus, commenting that the blend of sound between those sopranos was one of the most perfect he knew.

Through the years, John was evolving ideas about 'his' *Idomeneo*. Unfortunately, the new production planned for 1974 was beset with many problems. Originally intended with Sir Peter Hall as producer, he was having problems with the National Theatre which had not quite opened and John Cox was asked to undertake the work at the last minute. Planned for the same year as *Intermezzo*, he took the designs for both operas to John. Those for *Idomeneo* were an example of very early post-modernism by Roger Butlin, the designer. It was an advanced piece of staging, far from typical of anything that had been done at Glyndebourne before, especially when compared with the earlier, more decorative tradition of Oliver Messel. The set used a long range of concentric silver rings, diminishing in size towards the back of the stage and introduced circular cloths into them, based on Turner's paintings, rather in the way that a juke-box introduces a record, coming into the set on a kind of lift. John was thrilled with this design when he compared this with *Intermezzo*, which was more pictorial in style, saying that he wished those designs had more of the originality and modernity of the *Idomeneo*. In the event *Intermezzo* had the greater success. Familiar with the Messel *Idomeneo*, someone recalled: 'The artists worked within an extraordinary London Underground circular thing. I remember their frustration because the archway through which they were working was very limiting in manoeuvring, so the chorus and soloists became entangled in one another. On the video the monster looks quite ludicrous.'

In preparing this, his own musical version of *Idomeneo*, John's pragmatic and absolutely typical approach to preparation of a score was never more apparent. It is very seldom now that either the Munich or Vienna version is done 'pure' because of decisions whether to include or exclude various parts especially Electra's arias. Like so many other things that were left undecided by Mozart, it is very hybrid in that there are two or three versions. Together with John Cox, John prepared a version which they would both like and want to do. John Cox recalled that it was absolutely fascinating: 'One was working with his musical and theatrical mind, right there on the page, with his ever-ready big pencil.' They married the two versions because in excluding one version completely there is always a feeling of regret at the loss of something. One loses the collective view of *Idomeneo*. The version they created incorporated decoration, not for its own sake but arising very much from John's relationship with the singers. Cuts were made mainly in accompanied recitatives and arias. Arbace's first aria was preferred to the second but they included the recitative before the second. The main difference between the Munich and Vienna version stems from the use in the latter version of a tenor for the role of Idamante. There has never been any question at Glyndebourne of choosing otherwise. John wanted a new scene between Idamante and Ilia just before the great quartet, with an aria for Idamante and again, as in the Vienna version, decided to cut his last aria in the Sacrifice scene.

There were problems in casting; the perennial problem of trying to find good artists to fill roles within a very limited budget, to secure ever younger, up-and-coming singers for more than one season, before they were taken up by international houses. Writing to Sir George Christie from San Francisco in November 1973, John felt: 'We are in danger of allowing our natural pleasure and pride in younger singers' achievements to breed untimely suggestions for them to be over-parted,

particularly regarding your suggestion for Ilia.' He wrote
again later:

> We explore Bulgaria for our Russian wing until we can't stand the
> vocal sounds any more! Italy, once a source of many an inexpensive
> charmer, now produces nothing nor does Germany and as far as
> France! I suppose what has finally sparked off this 'cri de cœur'
> is the whole disappointing outcome of the casting of *Idomeneo*. (I
> needn't stress to you what a unique place in my own scheme of
> things THAT opera has.) No Ilia, that lovely mellifluous creature at
> the heart of Mozart's music, softening the starch of the whole opera
> seria. Even no High Priest . . . Perhaps (though God forbid) we
> shall be forced to say publicly 'Glyndebourne can't afford to have
> the cast it would like for this opera and we won't make do with
> substitutes!'

Just as Fritz Busch would never accept anyone in his casts 'no
matter how highly recommended', John would always prefer
to engage singers whom he had heard personally. To this end
he would audition wherever he travelled, sending back copious
notes, with many humorous comments, to Moran Caplat.
'Medium-heavy build; ingratiating manner (rather like an insurance salesman). Is an adequate buffo, no real style, heavy "vague"
voice. Asked me if I would like to see some "acting" during his
audition. I declined!' Or, 'over the top – if she was ever there!'
Depressed, he wrote again from San Francisco stressing to Caplat,
'the vital need for a glamorous Ilia – hearing candidates here for
Priest and Ilia and still hopeful against odds.' In another letter:
'In *Idomeneo* we are in rarified territory and for much of it I am
suffering.'

George Shirley, performing Idomeneo, was unable to sing all
the performances so John spoke informally to Richard Lewis
and found him 'not only unapprehensive about the demands
of singing the title role but positively oozing with confidence'.
At the first rehearsal John gave the older singer encouragement
calling out, 'Richard, you're better than ever.' He understood that
in reality the 64-year-old was in a vulnerable state and needed
support. His great performance was captured on video and
the communication between conductor and singer is apparent.
Idomeneo is a seemingly static role yet, with a performer like
Richard Lewis, the static was never still. There was an inside life
which communicated the character to others and did not distract
from the opera.

Martin Isepp of the Glyndebourne Music Staff would play the continuo harpsichord in the other Mozart operas but John always played for *Idomeneo*. As Martin Isepp would be abroad during the rehearsal period, John asked Jean Mallandaine to be the main coach. She was very nervous when she went to Carter's Corner before the start of rehearsals to go through the score. John made it clear that it was his favourite opera, that it had very special personal memories. 'I *knew* that it mattered; the writing, the fact that Mozart was so young, that there is so much in that writing that Mozart never really repeated again. He had an enormous affection for the chorus scene and in the opening scene where Idomeneo is shipwrecked – he loved that first aria. John was in awe of the writing.'

Although retired, Jani Strasser was still living near Glyndebourne and came to rehearsals. One day he tapped Jean Mallandaine on the shoulder. 'I have to go home but please give this note to John. It is very important. You know that aria of Ilia's which is being done, it's supposed to smell like a fragrant flower but at the moment it smells like a jungle!'

Unfortunately, the performances were not the happiest because, with the restrictions of the set, the full impact of the chorus sound failed to emerge. John was becoming more and more miserable at not achieving his desired level of performance. One night after a performance, everyone was waiting for him in his office and he did not come. Calvin Simmons, who understood John more than most, found him in a room he never frequented. He was crying like a baby. He had problems with the cast in an opera which meant more to him than any other and he could not cope.

Many people consider that John did not reach the heights because he was too kind and did not have a sufficiently ruthless side to his nature. His depth of feeling towards *Idomeneo* forced him to act differently. In this instance it was quite justified for artistic reasons. One of the major problems was the Electra. She came from Poland and the freedom to be in England was both of enormous value and a culture shock. The problems of singing such a difficult role added to the stress with which she tried to cope. Obviously the possibility of being sent home because she was not good enough was traumatic. John knew that he was going to have to replace the lady and, as the opera was *Idomeneo*, he was not as sympathetic and helpful as usual and in the end Linda Esther Gray replaced her before the BBC broadcast. Previously singing with the Glyndebourne Touring Company, Moran Caplat had considered her for Ilia. As she was theatrically inexperienced, Josephine Barstow took the role for the television broadcast. Caplat had been enthusiastic after the latter's Coliseum success in *The Devils* and the television people were keen because of the ability she had shown the previous year in the televised *Macbeth*.

John had conducted *Don Giovanni* many times since his first performances during the last year of Fritz Busch's life, developing his conception. Open to new ideas, he wrote to Moran Caplat in January 1964 from Vienna.

> I am quite enjoying my stay rather to my own surprise, Vienna remains Vienna and the odd mixture of charm and roguery does seem more interesting after the German serious-mindedness! I had a new cast for the *Giovanni*. The whole thing is black and gaunt in the extreme with Zaccaria booming through loudspeakers as an *invisible* statue – that's one way round the problem! The performance received terrific criticisms but of course one never knows in Vienna how much that is aimed at the General Musikdirektor! (In any case if he reads them I shall probably not be asked back . . .)
>
> One thing deriving from *Don Giovanni* in both Munich and Vienna. I really feel they are right in playing the main minuet of the ballroom (i.e. the big stage orchestra) *in the pit*. The two smaller orchestras are on the stage and one gets a better 'stereo' somehow than when all are up there. Also it spares us many problems as you well know! (Including the *set*.)
>
> On the other hand I am rather inclined to think the supper music should be played *onstage* next time, with a few players in costume awaiting Don G's bidding as it were and then hastening off stage when he calls for music.
>
> Also I have found that the Giovanni serenade gains greatly if the mandolinist can be onstage, so the set requires a black gauze built under the balcony so that the player can see through for the beat.

The *Arbeiter Zeitung* remarking on the guests for the performances; the Stone Guest in the opera, the Shah and Empress of Persia seated in a box and John Pritchard in the pit, considered the latter's contribution, 'the most valuable'. As well as 'the outstanding impression' (*Neue Tageszeitung*) the 'dramatic intensity of the music' (*Express*) coupled with a 'remarkable homogeneity'

(*Die Presse*) were only a few of the plaudits from his return to Vienna.

At Glyndebourne, after the tremendous success of the *Figaro*, John looked forward to collaborating with Sir Peter Hall on *Don Giovanni* in 1976 – 77: 'that intractable hurdle', particularly as it was to be his last new Mozart production there. Privately however, he was rather scathing when the producer arrived at the early rehearsals with books on psychology. John liked to come to productions when the producer knew exactly what he wanted to do, perhaps had even done them several times before – successfully. Sir Peter Hall's way, to use his own words, was 'a voyage of exploration'. He wanted to probe into the opera daily, constantly changing things. John's attitude was much more practical. Preferring a performance to develop naturally between the artists, he felt a production should not be too complicated or impose characterisation on a singer but rather give them ideas they could integrate into their performance. In the event, there were arguments between the two highly intelligent men during this formation period. John had wanted Joan Carden, the Australian soprano, to sing Donna Elvira but as another artist had been contracted she sang Donna Anna instead and disagreed with Sir Peter Hall's view of her persona. He wanted *Don Giovanni* to be dark, not only in theatrical terms of what was happening onstage but also in the actual view of humanity as portrayed by Mozart and da Ponte. John's view of Mozart was a much lighter one.

The first night was a success. John was quoted as admiring the way the producer had probed and probed into an opera which perhaps, above all others in the repertoire, deserves such probing. Privately, he voiced other opinions, saying that up–dating had diminished the emphasis of the church, a very important factor in the opera.

At this particular time, the London opera houses were bedevilled with disputes backstage, with stage-hands banning overtime and having wildcat strikes. Away from the metropolis, Glyndebourne had so far escaped but John was rather nervous that he might become a victim. There was a performance when a door remained firmly closed so that a singer had had to use another exit. On another occasion he was telephoned at home with problems, prompting him to fear sabotage but *Giovanni* survived.

John always looked forward to any new productions, particularly of the da Ponte operas and paid great attention that the production and sets should enhance the music but he became very angry on one occasion. After the public success at Glyndebourne he was looking forward to a *Don Giovanni* in Australia but on opening his post at the breakfast table there was consternation at the photographs of the quite plain set, with a configuration of fruit such as bananas and grapes suspended above in a phallic symbol. It was modified and toned down slightly but is one of the only occasions when John became really upset and was not looking forward to something. It offended his good taste, his love of beautiful things and people, particularly if they were good-looking or dressed attractively. It was part of his wanting everything to be and look right, very much part of the way he lived.

John taught everyone with whom he came into contact that it is within everyone's powers to make each day memorable, not only for oneself but for those with whom one comes into contact. If there had been a particularly difficult rehearsal, he would suggest that everybody should come to his office afterwards and there, over a bottle or two, he would give them their notes. It is a strange life for singers who are, after all, adults, to be told that they are making mistakes or that 'this or that needs to be better'. John understood and never let anyone feel that they were put down in any way. Regret has been voiced that there is not more of John's music-making on disc for future generations but his inheritance is the people he trained and influenced.

Whilst John loved scandal and gossip, he was never truly a political animal. It was more important to him to pass on a tradition, just as Fritz Busch had done. John was a musician who wanted to build, who had the courage to discover new things, not to fight. He liked to keep his options open and could lie quite outrageously, always in the politest possible way, if an interesting new experience were offered. John did this frequently but his friends always forgave him as they knew that sometimes he would make excuses to others to be in their company. He would resort to devious means to rid himself of people who might be giving him unpalatable advice or, the greatest sin from his point of view, they were boring, organising alternative entertainment for them rather than remaining in their company.

Sir John Pritchard

DIARY ENTRY:
Had to be devious as am 'cluttered' with X, who is often very sweet but his presence means I cannot have Y for Easter at the flat, as promised. So on last minute arrangements announced urgent meeting in Brussels. Left X in the flat, went to Three Bridges Station, encountered Y coming from Brighton. Took taxi to Gravetye Manor. Lovely room for two nights only, divine food, villainously expensive.

In his early days at Glyndebourne, Tom Redman won part of the Christie award. John suggested that he study Italian at Perugia University, finding out all the details for him. Although his parents assisted him financially, John and Terry MacInnis spent a week's holiday in Rome with him before the university started. This was typical of John's generosity as he knew that the young stage manager was very nervous about the trip. John's encouragement both in a tangible and moral sense gave the young man confidence, enabling him to benefit from the course. Not only did he learn the language but being away on his own had to make friends and broaden his experience, which he would never have done without John's encouragement.

Jean Mallandaine had first worked with John as a junior coach in 1968 as Jani Strasser would never let anyone supersede him. Although she was taken on with 'You're very good my dear but the work's too hard', Jani admitted five weeks later that she was stronger than the rest. She soon realised that good organisation was very important to John. 'He never overlooked if one made the day go smoothly in the performance or rehearsal or letting him have his party at home and not calling him in until he was really needed!' Working in Houston, John recommended Jean Mallandaine to the Director of the Houston Opera. She is now their Head of Music Staff and Artistic Supervisor of the Opera Studio, a postgraduate training programme.

Much of the planning between John and Jean-Pierre Ponnelle for *Falstaff*, performed 1976 and 1977, had been done when they were working together on *Figaro* in Chicago during October 1975. Their collaborations were always happy. Like Günther Rennert, their personalities were very different but John would understand and appreciate the other's point of view. Understanding that all the eggs were usually put into the basket of a new production, John was always concerned about the quality of a revival and would plan carefully, often conducting himself and sharing with another to ensure continuity of conception. Writing to Moran Caplat from Chicago he suggested: 'We should *ask* Ponnelle to return even for one week in 1977. The production is sure to be very detailed and it will need his eye in revision.' In his attention to reproducing a Tudor background, Ponnelle copied the colour of the brick of Carter's Corner.

Convalescing in Brittany after his operation for peritonitis in April 1976, John was unable to attend the early rehearsals of *Falstaff*. It fell to Jean Mallandaine and Richard Bradshaw to begin the work with the producer Ponnelle, affectionately known as JPP. John sent Jean Mallandaine a postcard: 'Please look after JPP. Give him my office. Make him feel at home and always remember that in difficult times a bottle of Chivas Regal goes a long way!'

With Jean Mallandaine at the piano, Richard Bradshaw went through the score with John at Carter's Corner. Although it was new for John, his assistant was amazed at his ease in reading the complicated work; that he sensed everything a bar and a half ahead, in the way he shaped the music, in the way he himself breathed. He was to be aware again of the complexity of the conductor's mind, that he could work on several levels, later in San Francisco. There, the conductor was doing *Rosenkavalier* under considerable pressure because he was short of rehearsal time and yet before the performance and again during the intervals, he was marking parts for *Ballo in Maschera*, a very different opera. During the interval of the first night of *Rosenkavalier*, Richard Bradshaw found him with headphones on listening to an audition tape of a Finnish bass and writing postcards at the same time.

Purists were unhappy with certain liberties that Ponnelle took but the audiences adored *Falstaff*, especially the moment when the curtain rose after the interval and the hero was seen climbing out of the orchestra pit having been thrown in the river just before the dinner break.

Jean Mallandaine will never forget the 'Sitzprobe' during rehearsals which was going wonderfully. John was in great form because he had had a rest. He loved the cast. At the break she asked, 'Can I go and get you something to drink?' He whispered, 'I really would like a glass of wine. As it's mid–afternoon, I don't think that I should let the lads see me drinking. Go up to my office, take a bottle of Chablis from the fridge, open it and bring it down in one of my best teacups and saucers.' She did this. Some of the players were still around. 'Thank you very much but you forgot the teaspoon.' Of course, some of the players twigged what had happened and whenever she would get him something to drink they would all chorus, 'Don't forget the teaspoon.'

He showed his appreciation in many ways. When Dame Kiri Te Kanawa was singing *Così* in Paris, he invited Jean Mallandaine to join him. Terry was supposed to collect her from her rented cottage. He was late and came scorching up the drive in the Renault and off they all went to Newhaven to catch the boat. As Terry burned up the Sussex roads, John uttered one of his oft-quoted remarks, 'Well after all this jet travel, the boat is going to be positively somnolent.' On another occasion she recalled going with John to stay at Chewton Glen in the New Forest, so that he could meet his brother Eddie who was retired and living in Christchurch, Dorset. She found him 'a lot older than John. He was completely different, not so extrovert. From a totally different milieu, he did not make a very strong impression on me.' John clearly had an affection for his brother, would talk about him and invite him to Glyndebourne.

John kept this last letter from Eddie dated 5th June 1979, recalling the Stroud area where his parents lived during the war. The difference in their ages and interests is very apparent.

Seems a long time since our last communications! I was sorry that we had no chance to meet up on the occasion of your last concert in London. I was on the go all day, with two guests staying the nights 16th and 17th, with a visit to Guildford and back on the latter day. So I didn't have time to listen in. There was a good report in the *Telegraph* and it seems that you had a last-minute predicament with the principal soprano being indisposed. However, Miss Te Kanawa got a terrific write-up – 'in glorious voice' said the *Telegraph*. But, I suppose the change gave you a number of last-minute problems to solve!

I have had quite an active time (for me), with a couple of holidays put in since the middle of April. The first was on the Gower coast in S. Wales. A new district this for me, although I heard a lot about the beauties of those parts when I was working in Bristol. The second week was at Randwick, near Stroud in the Cotswolds – a repeat of our visit there the previous year. I have a great affection (nostalgia I suppose) for that part of the country and the weather was kind, so the countryside really looked at its best. During my stay I met a certain William Shaylor, who, as it happened, lived in a beautiful converted cottage, only fifty yards or so away from where we were staying. I spent an interesting hour or so with him, during which he showed me a family 'tree' of the Shaylors dating back to the 1700s. His grandfather was an older brother of our grandfather, Edward. (The prolific Charles Shaylor – great g.f., married three times and had umpteen children. William's g.f. was the eldest child of the third wife, while our g.f. was the youngest.) William has since written a great epistle to Stan, who will no doubt reply in greater detail!

Well, that's all for now. I see you are in Cologne until 23rd June and then to Paris for a month (you lucky ???).

Hope all goes well, and let me know if you are coming to London again. I am due to spend a few days in Chingford (9th – 12th August), to attend a friend's Golden Wedding celebrations.

All the best, Eddie.

P.S. I am still pondering over Monte Carlo in October!

Mention of Monte Carlo at the end of Eddie's letter refers to the change in direction of John's life and career. Engagements elsewhere were beginning to conflict with the advisory aspect of his work at Glyndebourne. Writing in 1976 from Southampton, Long Island, to Sir George Christie, whilst admitting this was his fault, John complained that he was not being fully consulted. 'I realise the conclusion of the grouches is that I am too rushed and pulled both ways by my schedule to give the necessary thought *at the crucial time* to important Glyndebourne matters. I do want to be fully active as Musical Director right up to the time of my departure both in the conducting of performances and decisions for the future.'

At that time in Britain, taxes were crippling those in the upper tax bracket. Many of these victims were moving abroad and John had been looking into the matter. Given the option to either 'curb your spending, or, if you wish to continue in the manner to which you have become accustomed, you must join the ranks of tax exiles', he decided on the latter course.

Writing to Eric Bravington, Managing Director of the London Philharmonic Orchestra in April 1976 asking to be released from his engagement for 1978 but promising to be available for 1979, he described his situation.

When we last encountered happily on the street outside your office, I was on my way to the second of two important appointments with

Mr Victor Conway, who is a very high-powered and informative Tax Consultant. He has been looking into the tangled situation which faces me in the next few years and to cut a long and painful story rather short, it now looks as very positively necessary for me to absent myself from the United Kingdom for a complete year, beginning on 5th April 1978. You can imagine my feelings when I heard this decision, which I was unable to challenge because of the many technical factors involved but which does *not* necessarily mean that I am taking up residence in another country. You know very well the terribly difficult situation which has faced artists, many of them in the same position as I am, ever since the 'dreadful' budget day of 1975. Those of us who are working almost continually abroad will face absolutely punitive taxation in the future, rendering it almost ridiculous to continue work on any sensible scale.

Conducting in Germany, he was happy to write to Basil that he was being wooed by the Intendant of Cologne Opera.

Hampe seemed anxious to lunch with me and was fairly subtle. (I think he's quite sharp.) First, with the dessert, what operas would I like to do in the future. I said *Capriccio* and then responded favourably when he mentioned starting the House on Monteverdi (*Poppea, Orfeo*). The conversation wandered pleasantly on and we spoke of the (very good) Gürzenich Orchestra. Hampe said because of his own musical background he was managing for the time being without a General Musikdirektor, but 'what this city needs is the *same* music director for the opera *and* the Gürzenich Orchestra, a man who then would have perhaps the most powerful influence in Germany.' He smiled and said, 'So if you're *at all* interested, there's no one whose appointment would delight both the orchestra AND the opera so much!'

Of course I acted dumb, had never even considered such a thing, flattering of course but so much time away in USA and so on . . . however perhaps my forthcoming absence from England MIGHT, just possibly, make the project worth exploring. He for his part said, 'I had no intention of bringing this into the conversation, but do please just think it over . . . etc. etc.'

Afterwards I concluded the whole lunch was *intended* to bring up the matter, ever so casually, because just one day later Hampe said, 'I happened to be with the Burgomaster last night, he is very excited at the *possibility* and begs me to bring you to lunch.'

So, in short, I'm playing it along, lunching with the B/master tomorrow Tuesday and will be careful!

Three things that appeal to me:

A.   It is a dual job – opera and concert.

B. I could start doing the operas that will not be offered me elsewhere, such as *Meistersinger* and *Tristan*!
C. I should like to keep up the standard of the House with good singers and the co-operation of Ponnelle etc. They badly need a non-Germanic approach, but it's a friendly house.

Announcing his resignation as Musical Director at Glyndebourne, his least favourite headline in the British press proclaimed 'Conductor retires!' In Palm Springs, staying with Peter Brown while conducting *Thaïs* and *Peter Grimes* at San Francisco Opera, John wrote urgently to Basil in October. 'I *strongly* feel you must issue something for the British Press' and enclosed the press handout San Francisco Opera had issued, 'to offset all those "retiring from GB" headlines.'

A francophile, John chose to become resident in Monte Carlo and intended that his farewell party at Carter's Corner should be the ultimate. There was to be only a week of rehearsals before the second half of the run of *Don Giovanni*. With Bernard Haitink conducting and several changes of cast, it had reached the dress rehearsal. The cast and everybody at Glyndebourne bundled into cars to Carter's Corner Place for lunch.

The weather at the beginning of July could not have been better. John planned the layout for the party with care: an open-fronted marquee for a self-service buffet. The champagne and bucks fizz flowed. Amused guests watched waitresses, carrying trays and crockery, dizzily walking in zigzag paths across the lawn. It was so hot that everybody sat on the grass under the trees, with little bells, bought in Hong Kong, tinkling in the breeze. Nucci Condo, whom everyone loved, bubbled away. As always the party moved to the swimming pool and borrowing costumes, people flopped in and out of the pool. Rachel Yakar, the new Donna Elvira, stretched out on a deckchair holding court. Everyone was amused by John Rawnsley's (Masetto) and Thomas Allen's (Don Giovanni) clowning in the water and, aping a recent television talent competition, called out marks out of ten, including 'star quality', concerning the diving and swimming ability of the various artists.

John presided over all this in true Don Alfonso manner, orchestrating the afternoon's entertainment which sprang from the interplay between artists, music staff and staff at Glyndebourne, who knew each other well. The party, the setting, the whole spectrum of parties which John held, from the small, intimate dinners to the spectacular occasions which he hosted, are remembered with nostalgia. 'They can never be recreated', 'It's an era that's over' and 'There isn't another man like him'.

Before he left for Cologne, Glyndebourne and the London Philharmonic Orchestra gave him a party in the marquee at Glyndebourne, presenting a beautiful cut glass decanter. 'How very kind of you,' he replied. 'It will come in wonderfully for my "eau" de Cologne.'

He had arrived at Glyndebourne a very good-looking young man, starry-eyed at his surroundings and the people with whom he came into contact. Every year, with his natural musicianship, he had acquired more confidence and his personality developed. Sir George Christie summed up: 'He had the ability to paint any landscape; be it modern, be it baroque; be it a Rossini lightweight or a Verdi heavyweight and everything around that, like Debussy, Massenet and Strauss. He was a man who seemed to acquire the idiom of all composers, effortlessly, at his fingertips.'

Plans were made for him to return but he cancelled a projected *Cenerentola*. Although the summer season was not complete without a visit to Glyndebourne, John did not conduct there again. 'I've enjoyed myself here. Let's move on.' The farewells were over. Gifts and messages of gratitude exchanged, he telegrammed his thanks to the Christies. 'Slept all way to Hong Kong exhausted but happy my wonderful send off. Thank you both cuff links. Brilliant idea fit perfectly. Today ordering yet more Chinese jackets. Having fun but miss you very much. All love John.'

Remarking that Lord Hailsham could sometimes be seen walking along the perimeter of the grounds of Carter's Corner Place looking towards the house, John too would return and gaze wistfully at his former home, his great love. The only time he ever looked backwards.

9

Covent Garden

Twenty years earlier, during John's tenure as Musical Director at Liverpool, there was considerable disquiet amongst the Covent Garden Board because a Music Director had not been appointed after Kubelík's departure in 1958. They had two alternatives. Either they could opt for a star who could present his speciality works which might not be what they planned or choose a conductor on the next level who, even though he might not be a star, might be more suitable as a Music Director. The Board was determined to appoint a star and felt that the only person who had the right experience was Sir Georg Solti. The other suggestions were either pledged to America, which paid higher salaries, or were ensconced in Germany. Initially asked to conduct *Rosenkavalier* in December 1959, with a cast including Elisabeth Schwarzkopf and Sena Jurinac, it was a tremendous success and he was asked to be Music Director.

The Arts Council likes all senior posts to be advertised and nobody likes applying and being turned down. John would never have let it be known publicly that he was disappointed when either Sir Georg Solti or Sir Colin Davis, his successor, was appointed.

Although John had conducted more that eighty performances of eleven different operas in his first two seasons at Covent Garden, he was not considered very seriously. The Earl of Harewood commented that John was an excellent Mozart conductor and he did those works at Glyndebourne.

> Mostly at Covent Garden he was doing things that he'd never done before and was feeling his way. However good the musician, that's not quite as authoritative as doing the things that you come to with the stamp of authority on them. So he was not a sensation but he was a considerable success. I think that the thing that Covent Garden would have held against John was that he had never held an

appointment like that and at that stage (1960) there was a tremendous mystique about the experience and repertoire needed. I think it is a mystique that I would not have discouraged. John came into the category of someone who had worked for an opera house but, as Glyndebourne had a minute repertoire, I think that they would have said that he hadn't the organisational experience. To know the kind of problem that occurs, we thought was important.

Attitudes have changed. Now, a few conductors have become Music Directors in an opera house, without experience or with a small repertoire.

In the early years there was a certain amount of rivalry between Glyndebourne and Covent Garden because in 1939 John Christie attempted to set up a National Council for opera, with a single management for Glyndebourne, Sadlers Wells and Covent Garden, with himself on the Covent Garden Board. After the war it was Glyndebourne that benefited from differences over policy between David Webster and Sir Thomas Beecham. When the new lease for Covent Garden became available in 1949, John Christie was one of those who tried to take over the management of the London opera house. Any ill feeling that existed evaporated with time as many of the young British singers and administrators who received their training at Glyndebourne now work at Covent Garden. John expressed annoyance at the situation. Having conducted *Moses and Aaron* with the Liverpool Orchestra, he was furious that he was unable to present it at Covent Garden and wrote to David Webster. 'I would have done my NUT to have *Moses* if only Solti's enquiry had come even a *week* earlier! But in that week, Caplat made me write down the *Poppea* period and the dilemma therefore posed itself too openly: it would have been a preference too clearly stated, if you know what I mean.'

A number of singers have expressed the view that they would have liked to have seen John as Music Director at some time at Covent Garden and feel that that House treated him badly; that he was the most important conductor to be overlooked. The management were concerned that John did not appear to show enough energy at a consistent level, either during rehearsal or in performance. His musicianship could never be faulted. There was never a standard below which a performance would fall. It concerned them that he seemed so laid-back. They wanted more intensity. He would never let anyone get away with wrong notes but there was something in him which prevented him from shaking a performance out of an artist's complacency. Ileana Cotrubas confirmed this:

> For me John was a very refined musician, very sensitive and when I worked with him I knew that when he liked a singer he gave a lot and he worked. Otherwise, if he was not interested in the people with whom he worked then he was a little uninvolved. He was always very nice and kind and had a noblesse, not only because of his stature. I knew that he liked me very much. I sensed and felt it and so, when we went for phrasing, he was one of the greatest. All the detail, the phrasing, the expression, nobody else except Kleiber now does this. They just think that 'this' is correct and then leave it.
>
> We have to give all the time but who is giving back? For me it is the conductor. I've always felt that the conductor has to be very musical, very sensitive, a very cultured person. I want to take something from him because I bring only my instinct and somebody has to teach me more and John was one of the very few who could. He felt that if he was giving something it would have to be to somebody who could use it. Otherwise, if he was not interested in the person, it was 'yes, nice' and so on but he wasn't so involved. However, I was very happy to work with him.

John believed that if a singer or player was under-rehearsed they would think more and try harder and that if an orchestra went home early they might be in a better frame of mind. Instead they would have been happier if they had felt more confident. Knowing him so well personally, Dame Kiri Te Kanawa found it hard to separate the man from the musician. 'Sometimes to work with him was like working with another person. I felt as if I knew him so well that I had to separate myself from being very familiar as I would have been in a social or private situation.' She recalled a particular instance when he let the orchestra go, not having rehearsed a certain piece properly. 'I was really very angry with him and felt like saying, "Look they haven't got it right yet." Even when it came to the performance it wasn't right. In that instance I felt that I should have stepped in and said, "John it's just not good enough yet. You haven't got it right yet." It wasn't that I had got it right and was wonderful but if the orchestra had had a few more minutes on that particular song, it might have been much cleaner and wouldn't have had me so worried. As it was it really wasn't up to standard.'

A few more sparks might have flown if John had not been so

much in sympathy with his artists but he liked the idea of a clan. Being friends they provided his social life on or off the stage. However, if he took a dislike to a singer or had had enough, that singer was never booked again. Nor did he allow his enjoyment of their company to cloud his judgement. Thinking that his opinion tallied with their own as to their ability, some would be distressed to read his correspondence with David Webster and Moran Caplat and his diaries.

For example, writing to David Webster in December 1953, adamant in his dislike of a foreign artist:

> May I say that I would be very upset if you decided to take her in preference to [XY], for the following reasons:
> 1. [XY] seems to me to have just the sincerity which is always lacking in [AB].
> 2. Whenever I have seen [AB] in performance she has always been vocally competent and at the same time inanely gratified with her own looks, charm and powers of interpreting the composer's wishes (as divinely revealed to [AB]).
> 3. I feel [AB] to be basically a very stupid woman who clings with obstinacy to whatever musical idea of a part she first imbibed.
> 4. I do not stress this in case you think personal antipathy (which I admit) is swaying my judgement but [AB] in the course of the most unpleasant rehearsals with me . . . was so RUDE about Covent Garden and that she never wished to come here again, that I should regard it as an absolute humiliation if she were taken now when we have a gifted singer, who should be of real use to the Company generally in the future, already lined up.

He ended: 'With these kindly Christmassy thoughts', frequently used after a particularly strong letter.

Even under stress John hid his feelings in public, seemingly never losing control. During rehearsals of the 1960 revival of Berlioz' *The Trojans*, which is a very complicated work, singers recalled the producer, Sir John Gielgud, pacing up and down the aisle, working his hands together, declaiming, 'Oh why is there so much music in this piece.' To others, in John's hands, the problems seemed to disappear. Instead, he unleashed his strain on David Webster.

> URGENT *1.15pm* I am *desperate*. Broke off the rehearsal after PERSISTENT, ENDLESS errors in the parts, omissions, wrong

notes which leave me speechless and ill. The orchestra could not be pushed further and now I am left with at least forty-five minutes music *unread*, including a whole new scene. I fear the only thing is to terminate *Monday's* stage rehearsal early to allow for a further orchestral reading session which Matheson must do while I sit there purely for wrong notes. I cannot push myself further for fear of breaking up. In any case I feel we must *give up* the idea of restoring that first *Dido* scene. That will save us some time. I am terribly worried and upset.

His fears were turned into a triumph and press acclaim on the first night.

It was in the new production of the rarely performed *Benvenuto Cellini* in 1966 – 67 that John was able to show himself to be a superb Berlioz conductor. After its disastrous first performance at the Paris Opera in 1838, Berlioz made drastic cuts and revisions for subsequent revivals elsewhere. Hugh Macdonald, a leading Berlioz scholar, resurrected the original score and the earlier orchestral parts. Together with Maurits Sillem and the Covent Garden staff, he restored Berlioz' original idea for an opera comique, with sung recitative not spoken dialogue. In attempting to ensure a dramatic as well as musical reading, Covent Garden brought in a theatrical producer, John Dexter, who had never worked previously in an opera house. He had a superb cast; Nicolai Gedda, Elizabeth Vaughan, Yvonne Minton and David Ward. Unfortunately, the quality of Berlioz' vocal writing did not match the orchestration. Whilst the performances were of significance to Berlioz scholars and the critics, audiences were bored. They favoured the big scenes and here John's ability with the large forces of chorus and orchestra was most apparent. He enjoyed Berlioz, finding its parallel in himself. He loved the vast range of orchestral colour, the lyricism, the unashamed romanticism coupled with refinement in the delicacy of the fine detail. 'All musicians have to make new assumptions when they come to Berlioz. He had a passion for the enormous but some of his finest touches are on a small scale. His music has great tenderness. It is a melodic line which is an acquired taste.' Recalling an opera which she felt was one of the most important she had done with John, Yvonne Minton commented, 'We were always so well prepared in those days.' However, even with the production re-worked for the 1967 revival, the opera continued to dissatisfy audiences.

By the sixties there was an extraordinary nucleus of fine singers at Covent Garden, accustomed to working and socialising together. Good preparation and the benefit of being part of a company under David Webster was remembered by Dame Joan Sutherland:

> At Covent Garden, David Webster had the courage and guts to do things, that I would get my *Lucia* [*di Lammermoor*]. He thought I was ready for it even if some others didn't. He didn't care what the Board said about putting on *Louise*, he was going to give me *Lucia*, with Zeffirelli to make the costumes and sets. That's the way it was. In the old days they didn't spend so much on productions. Perfection is unattainable but there was still a striving for it. Today opera houses want to do something new but pieces like *Merry Widow* and *Traviata* do stand on their own. The producer has to trust them. They're not 'old hat', they're part of a viable standard repertoire. People still adore their little bit of nostalgia. They want to get away from the humdrum, they don't want to see people in leather and jeans.

Although another conductor led the earlier performances, when John did *Lucia* in 1961 with Dame Joan, in the performance dedicated to the memory of Dame Nellie Melba on 9th June, the Sextet was encored – a very rare occasion at Covent Garden. Later that year they repeated *Lucia* at the Edinburgh Festival.

As well as stage performances, John's collaborations with Dame Joan Sutherland were the outstanding recordings of his early years. Liverpool, finding Donizetti's *Emilia di Liverpool* in the archives, put it together. In a concert performance conducted by Fritz Spiegl with Doreen Murray singing Emilia, it was part of the celebrations for the anniversary of the granting of a charter to Liverpool. Three months later, on 8th September 1957, the BBC broadcast a shortened version with John conducting. With some changes of cast, this time Emilia was sung by Dame Joan, with Bernard Miles as the narrator. A private recording was issued on disc, referred to in its publicity as an 'historic recording for Voce'. She and John had a good laugh about this.

John did not make many early recordings for Decca but they are important: an Arias LP with Teresa Berganza, the first *Lucia* with Sutherland. Everyone agreed that he was the perfect conductor for her first *Traviata* as well.

Christopher Raeburn, producer at Decca, met John at Glyndebourne in the early fifties. As he was also 'crazy about *Idomeneo*' they had discussed that opera and in particular, the two versions of the last duet with Idamante. For the planning of *Lucia*, he went to Liverpool. In the process of buying the house in Park Village East, John wanted a flat fee rather than royalties. It was to be a far more complete version than had been put on record previously but nevertheless they decided on certain cuts. The feeling amongst the major record companies was that Mozart and German works should be made in Vienna and that Italian opera should be done in Italy with an Italian orchestra. One singer suggested that many records were made abroad so that technicians could get away and have a good time! When *Lucia* was recorded in Rome, John stayed at the villa of Hans Werner Henze. Working together again in Florence for the recording of *Traviata*, an opera which Dame Joan considers one of the greatest and 'one of my favourite roles, even though I'm not really physically suited to it', with Carlo Bergonzi as Alfredo and Robert Merrill as Giorgio it was acclaimed as the finest available. *Records and Recordings* commented on John's conducting as 'An admirable combination of fire and tenderness' and his control of the ensemble at the end of Act II, 'masterly'. Dame Joan summed up: 'It's strange how we did a lot of the early work so closely and then our paths diverged. Really it was because of our careers, he was getting on with his and I was getting on with mine.'

In Vienna, in 1953, John had recorded a number of works for Philips, such as the Mozart Piano Concerti K456, K459, K453 and K595, Beethoven's Symphony no. 1 and with Ilse Hollweg, the Mozart opera *Bastien and Bastienne* K50 written in 1768. In Britain however, the most significant recording for John was that of the Glyndebourne *Idomeneo*, produced by Lawrance Collingwood. Recorded for HMV in 1956 during the Bicentenary year of Mozart's birth, it was reissued in CD form by EMI for the Bicentenary of Mozart's death in 1991. In the recording John was fortunate to have singers from the original Fritz Busch production; Richard Lewis as Idomeneo, Léopold Simoneau, the French Canadian, singing Idamante and the remarkable Sena Jurinac, as the Trojan princess.

Performances of Mozart were one of the exceptions to the unspoken rule that Covent Garden did not perform the same repertoire as Glyndebourne.

Sir John Pritchard

Although many associate John's name with Mozart, his music-making was far removed from the atmosphere of shallow prettiness with which the eighteenth century has been presented. In his recording of *Figaro*, Fritz Busch stressed the class conflict between Figaro and the Count as well as the ill feeling between them over Susanna. Now there is a tendency to over-emphasise this social comment with consequently a tougher, somewhat hard approach to the music but there was always a light touch, a polish to John's *Figaro*, suiting the Covent Garden production played as a comedy.

In Mozart John measured and allowed enough music for the distance in a theatre. If the distance is longer a singer has problems. During a dress rehearsal for *Figaro* at Covent Garden, in the quiet passage in Act IV for 'Deh vieni', Adèle Leigh as Susanna realised that she could not hear the orchestra as she had been put too far to the back of the stage. John simply pointed his finger up and she knew exactly what he meant. Not even the orchestra realised what he was doing but she knew that she was singing below pitch. John reassured her afterwards about the next performance. 'He said that he would get me further "downstage" because I have the sharpest ear and never sang out of tune.'

Conducting *Figaro* at Covent Garden since 1953, John often spoke of one particular performance on 4th November 1967. That season the Susanna was Elizabeth Robson and Elisabeth Söderström sang the Countess. At the beginning of the week, Elizabeth Robson became ill. Nobody worried very much as they thought it would be easy to find another Susanna. As they had not done so by the Thursday, Elisabeth Söderström proposed that if they found another Countess she would sing Susanna. During the performance she was shown the geography of the scenes in which she had not appeared. One of the ladies with whom John worked in great harmony, she is a miraculous artist. Everything that she did was riveting – irrespective of how well it suited her vocally. Her Countess in *Figaro* was quite different from any Countess one had seen before, so logically thought out. When she took over Susanna, she was totally transformed physically, leaping about the stage like a young colt.

Joan Carlyle replaced her as Countess. She first met John when singing the small role of Barbarina in the *Figaro* of 1956. She

206

hated the part, never having been on stage before. Unlike today when would-be singers go to opera school, she was just taught to sing and had no stagecraft. 'We were rehearsing at the Scala Cinema and I came on to do my aria (at the beginning of Act IV) and the producer screamed at me. John was so sweet and told me not to take any notice . . . It's hard enough for singers to break through inhibitions and display what there is inside us. When somebody gives you flak you go back inside. John just "spun" the music; you were never aware of him, just secure and happy.' Once a fracas on stage between a producer and his assistant was silenced by John: 'It's the *music* that's important.' She found that John would be aware of something and broach the subject to her as 'he had the knack of asking you to do something and allowing you to think that the idea was yours. He was very kind and generous but I found him a very sad person.'

John has been criticised for seeming to lose interest after first nights but Joan Carlyle was always disappointed when a run of performances with him came to an end. She felt that the difference came because singers relax. They 'switch off' after the first night knowing that everything has gone well. 'Relaxing into the performance and losing interest are two totally different things. In the early part of my career I used to feel that everybody was flat on the second night and was always aware that one had to be more alert . . . Some nights, when you're not feeling a hundred per cent, he'd know and be with you whereas some conductors go at their speed and pay no regard to what a singer wants to do. John was so easy to work with that one gave more than with others.'

It is important for an opera conductor, not only to understand a singer's voice but to understand that they feel differently at each performance and breathe with them; to make the second or third beat longer if they need to take a breath. Knowing instinctively when an artist would not be able to reach a note, John believed that he had a sixth sense. This instinct enabled him to anticipate problems.

There were many similarities in his music-making with the German-born Rudolf Kempe, a conductor for whom he had the highest respect. Kempe succeeded Sir Thomas Beecham at the Royal Philharmonic Orchestra, later becoming conductor of the BBC Symphony Orchestra. With an established reputation in the concert hall he achieved fame as an opera conductor. Like Kempe, John would make an imperceptible pause before a climax, with a flick of the wrist, a twirl, the baton would describe a small circle in the air, just as he would 'comma' before delivering the punchline of an anecdote.

John's performances of *The Marriage of Figaro* showed one of his great qualities, namely, that he would never over conduct. The music was never strained. He would give a push in the right direction and let the orchestra coast along under their own steam. Appreciated for this very reason by the musicians, nevertheless the critics voiced dissatisfaction and in his diaries, John confided his mystification in 1968 at Covent Garden's complaints of his 'lethargy'.

Whilst John is remembered for the Musica Viva series at Liverpool, it is sometimes forgotten that he introduced several contemporary scores into the opera repertoire. Always conscious of the technical aspect of theatre, coping with composers altering their scores the day before the dress rehearsal, he earned the admiration of his colleagues. With the composer taking an active part, Michael Tippett's great operas, *The Midsummer Marriage* and *King Priam* were premièred by Covent Garden.

It is reported that the singers found *The Midsummer Marriage* (World Premiere 27th January 1955) incomprehensible and could not understand the story. At piano rehearsals they asked Michael Tippett what it was about and he said it was something inside him that just had to come out. 'Just sing it beautifully, just perform it and it will be all right!'

King Priam was planned for the Coventry Cathedral celebrations in May 1962 with further performances at Covent Garden. Not wanting to work on a new score, John tried to avoid doing the opera which coincided with Glyndebourne rehearsals. Writing to David Webster on 28th July 1961, Joan Ingpen summed up:

> Glyndebourne wants John (not Gui) to conduct the new Rennert production of *Così* and he would like to accept – although it does mean his going there earlier than envisaged. We both know that he is a great one for work but it really does seem impossible for him to combine the rehearsals for *Così* with the rehearsals and performances of *King Priam* (as well as a minimum necessary attendance at the Liverpool Conductor's Competition). John wants to be quite open about this with you and although he would be comparatively unmoved by all sorts of pressures (from composers

and publishers!) he would not at all want to place you personally in a difficulty. Do you think you could let him resign from the Tippett project (he doesn't yet know much about the opera) without hard feelings and too much inconvenience?

Covent Garden insisted that he carry out the engagement.

The most popular of Tippett's early operas, *King Priam* (World Premiere 29th May 1962 Coventry, first performance Royal Opera House 5th June 1962) has never been received with other than acclaim. Produced by Sam Wanamaker with spectacular designs by Sean Kenney, the audience gasped when, as Achilles, Richard Lewis appeared, lifted up into a blood red spotlight at the back of the stage. A difficult role to sing, it is considered one of Lewis' greatest achievements. With the music breaking away from operatic convention – with elaborate orchestral solos particularly in the brass and piano making unfamiliar demands on the players – nevertheless John conducted with authority. At the revival in 1967 he brought strength and intensity to the dramatic vision of the third act, echoing the formidable power of the protagonists.

Although he was conducting a great deal of Verdi at this time, he did not have the innate power for some of the works. He was more in sympathy and is remembered at Covent Garden for the sensitivity of his *Traviata* performances, an opera which he felt was understood by those who had 'loved and lost'.

When it came to conducting *Traviata* in 1955 – 56, he suggested Richard Lewis for the male lead. The Earl of Harewood recalled:

They were rehearsing with Pilar Lorengar, a very young Spaniard of great physical beauty. A beautiful voice, an absolute baby as a performer and Richard Lewis was always an experienced performer. I'm sure that at his debut he was an experienced performer! He was very efficient but had a mildly short fuse and was impatient. They rehearsed and she had no English – it was simply hopeless as the performance was in English. I have a feeling that for the first rehearsal which started at 10am, she arrived at 3pm. That's late! She didn't come to the rehearsal because she said, 'How can one rehearse in the morning. It must be a mistake.' She arrived after lunch for the 'after breakfast' rehearsal and of course there was no rehearsal after lunch. It was heavy going. At some point when they came to the end, when she has to die, obviously they rehearsed it one way and I think at the piano dress rehearsal (a stage rehearsal) instead of falling into the tenor's arms, or whatever they'd rehearsed, she, as a young girl, knew how to fall, so she just crumpled dead. There was the most appalling bust-up because Richard Lewis had expected her to do it one way. Catching a person on stage is very important and it has to be rehearsed. It was amusing and she laughed but he blew his top and there were the most awful tears. John was very good at soothing everything down.

Occasionally conducting *Traviata* with indifferent casts, the exception was the revival of the Visconti production in 1973 – 74, with the Violetta of Ileana Cotrubas, who by that stage was a very accomplished singer. Not having heard them personally, John was worried about the other suggestions for the cast and wondered if perhaps he might conduct another opera. Understanding that the opera is dependant on Violetta, he broke his holiday in Italy to travel to Vienna where Ileana Cotrubas was singing the role. He wrote to Sir John Tooley: 'Convinced that she is in good voice as she could fill the Staatsoper without any feeling of strain. She is such a clever artist and over supper we discussed features of her performance which she honestly feels she can do better with us at Covent Garden. She was very confident in Act I – she knows she is no courtesan – and immensely touching in the rest of the opera. I cannot feel too sure of the reports I hear of the Spanish tenor and if he is not actually contracted, I would like to make a strong plea (after all our anxieties over this revival) for a cast which we can, accidents apart, look forward without premonitions of trouble.' John Tooley replied that he thought José Carreras, 'a good musician with a pleasant voice'. Like Fritz Busch, unwilling to engage a singer whom he had not heard, John insisted that if Ileana Cotrubas should withdraw from *Traviata* if she were ill, he would withdraw too: 'The success or failure of this revival is going to depend a great deal on Cotrubas.' She was a marvellous Violetta. With John's support the performances were very special with José Carreras playing a deliberately gauche Alfredo but with a wonderful freshness to the voice.

On the first night the audience was stunned by the curtains being closed during the second act. Informed by Sir John Tooley of the possibility of a bomb in the auditorium, they left quickly. Returning shortly afterwards all was forgotten, listening to the memorable singing on stage. Ileana Cotrubas recalled: 'When the curtains closed I said, "What is happening? Has somebody in the government died?" Perhaps somebody in the cast is ill and is not going to appear on stage. In full costume and make-up, looking very silly, we all went out onto the streets with the audience around us. The same thing happened in another performance as well.' On that occasion it took rather a long time. With his friends, John went to his apartment in nearby King Street, where they partied until the search was over.

Dame Kiri Te Kanawa in the role of Violetta was the last time John conducted *Traviata* at Covent Garden, the first night on 1st January 1980 providing an excuse for Basil Horsfield and John Davern to host a spectacular party afterwards. Like many such evenings, it ended with John seated at the piano and Dame Kiri, Isobel Buchanan and others singing 'The Twelve Days of Christmas'.

His last collaboration at Covent Garden with Dame Kiri Te Kanawa in October 1981 was one of John's most successful. With its phrasing and climaxes, the two achieved the maximum potential in each other in *Arabella*, an opera dedicated to Fritz Busch by the composer, Richard Strauss. At the end, as Arabella descended the stairs carrying a glass of water, there was hardly a dry eye in the audience. On another occasion, for a concert at the Barbican, John cut out the Mandryka part beautifully so that Dame Kiri could sing the last scene alone.

The historic performances of *Figaro* and *Don Giovanni* at Glyndebourne in the seventies were matched by outstanding performances of Mozart's *La Clemenza di Tito* during 1974 – 76 at Covent Garden. Although John had not conducted the original Anthony Besch production, he was to become associated with one of the most beautiful, popular productions of the seventies, performed three years in succession. As in the other opera seria *Idomeneo*, John insisted on having a cello with the harpsichord for the recitatives, playing the harpsichord himself. He had put on a great deal of weight and his movements were slow. The recitatives were not as taut as they should have been. Except for Titus, the outstanding cast remained unchanged. Inspired by unobtrusive conducting, the big arias, the grandeur of the set pieces and duets between the golden voiced Sextus of Yvonne Minton and the highly emotional, spurned Vitellia of Dame Janet Baker were like fireworks in their impact on the London audience. Together with Anne Howells they were a magnificent advertisement for British mezzos when Covent Garden took *Clemenza*, together with *Benvenuto Cellini* and *Peter Grimes*, on an exchange visit in 1976 to La Scala in Milan. Unfortunately the Italians do not like Mozart. They were bored by *Clemenza* but responded to *Grimes*.

In the Donizetti comedies, *Don Pasquale* (1972 - 73) and *L'Elisir d'Amore* (1975 - 76), together with Sir Geraint Evans, John added a new dimension to the repertoire. For the revival of *Don Pasquale* the following year, the Pasquale of Sir Geraint Evans found his foil in the Dr Malatesta of Sesto Bruscantini, the duet of the two older men needing an encore. The audience delighted in the ensembles, the cameo portraits and the brilliance of Ileana Cotrubas who brought out the pathos in the moment when Norina slaps Don Pasquale's face. However it was John's sophisticated conducting of the trio, partnered by the very polished Jean-Pierre Ponnelle production, with some ravishing visual moments in the household, which remain in the memory. Presenting the opera in English was suggested but although John liked the audience to understand the humour he preferred it sung in the original.

He understood the very whimsical, sly humour of Donizetti. As John pointed out, *L'Elisir d'Amore* has no overture and yet in the first ten bars there are little humorous touches which, if the conductor knows how to bring them out, are self-evident. John had never done *L'Elisir* before but his collaboration with producer John Copley worked well. It had fun; there was a touch of fairground garishness to it which was highly successful. The first night was chosen as the Royal Gala Première, in the presence of Her Majesty Queen Elizabeth the Queen Mother and other members of the Royal Family. As often happened, the revival in 1976, another collaboration with Ileana Cotrubas, was more successful, partly because John did not conduct many of the studio rehearsals when it was new as he was scheduled to conduct elsewhere. John Copley was very worried as he had never done comic Donizetti before. Opera buffa was new to him and he felt quite lost until John came to the final rehearsals and would sit with the score whilst someone else conducted.

John Copley remembered that John not going to early rehearsals had been rather amusing when they were working together on *Macbeth* in Australia. The 'doctor' and the 'damma' who start the famous sleepwalking scene were singers with huge voices with an incredible vibrato. They need to whisper

212

and the producer put them right at the back of the set. Not having been to any of the rehearsals until they were actually in the theatre, John stopped and on one of the rare occasions when he acted as a 'diva' exclaimed, 'It's ridiculous, they're so far away, we want them right down front. With all your experience, why have you put them in such a stupid position?' However, when they came downstage and started to sing: 'For goodness sake, why didn't you tell me!' He turned to the singers. 'I think that where Mr Copley put you is a very beautiful picture indeed and will be very much more effective.' John was quite cross for a few moments but roared with laughter later, confessing that he had never been caught out in that way before.

Aggrieved at the very short rehearsal time allotted to the revival of *L'Elisir* at Covent Garden, John felt he was being treated badly, 'They expect me to perform miracles,' and put his annoyance in writing. 'Over the years I have tried to be helpful on many different occasions to Covent Garden. I am therefore more greatly perturbed to find in the alteration of the dates of the stage/orchestra rehearsals for *L'Elisir* that no regard has been paid to the arrangements which were easy and convenient to me.' He went on to explain that with their 'full knowledge and consent' he was supposed to be conducting *Messiah* in Huddersfield when he should have been conducting a full stage and orchestra rehearsal. 'I face a day of desperate physical strain and responsibility. I feel very aggrieved and cannot readily understand how an important date change such as this can possibly have been approved totally without reference to me or my agents.'

The 'desperate physical strain and responsibility' during the rehearsal period of *L'Elisir*, when he should have been working on *Messiah* in Huddersfield, was to bring about another 'retirement'. After a long talk with Richard Barraclough, General Secretary of the Huddersfield Choral Society, when the latter had come to a Glyndebourne *Figaro*, John had offered to resign from his position as Principal Conductor and Musical Director of the Society. Having held the appointment since 1973 he realised that with his intention of becoming non-resident, he would not be able to appear with them again until 1979 but in a letter dated 1st August 1976 Barraclough 'strongly urged me to retain the title of M. Director provided I would 1) give a little time to guiding them on policy, 2) might consider ways and means to conduct in the interim *abroad* (they are very keen to resume their European or even USA wanderings), and 3) find them one date a year minimum from the 1979 season onwards.'

Primarily because he himself did not have any free dates which could coincide with a projected tour of Germany, in spite of the loyalty of the Committee and members during his interregnum abroad, John insisted that he must resign. In an apologetic letter of 14th October 1978 to W [Bill] Drake, the President at that time, he explained:

> There has been no lack of activity among interested parties in attempts to bring about a Tour in Europe with the HCS and myself. Basil Horsfield has spent hours of his time, and that of his staff, in pursuing the possibilities in Germany and Italy. I have had conversations in Cologne and Hamburg trying to persuade just *one* permanent orchestra to say 'yes we will allocate such and such a concert to this project'. That was all we needed to build up our tour around the one 'lynch-pin'. It has failed, mainly because of the new concert situation in Europe regarding choral concerts – and frankly it is the *example* of the great British choirs such as the HCS which in the past twenty years has at last had its effect. The orchestras, which used to rely on the professional choruses, mainly of the opera houses, for their rare choral-orchestral performances, now have recruited local amateur singers exactly as we have done for generations in the UK. Thus their budgets are necessarily geared to the maintenance of these groups, and I have yet to encounter an orchestra which is ready to 'splash out' on an extra concert of high cost, involving a visiting choir *or* orchestra.

Choruses always liked John. His popular appointment had been at a time when the Huddersfield Choral Society was going through a difficult period and he and Terry enjoyed their time there, finding the people incredibly hospitable. Perhaps the most famous in Britain, to many the Choral Society *is* Huddersfield and it was the first Chorus which sang *Messiah* at the opening of the Huddersfield Town Hall. In the eighteenth century the English choral tradition consisted mainly of works by Handel and the Huddersfield Society was part of the English choral renaissance inspired primarily by the work of Parry and Elgar.

As well as the traditional December Carol Concert and *Messiah*, in which he insisted on using the authentic version, John looked carefully at the wide range of repertoire offered by the Society dating from Andreas Romberg's *Lay of the Bells* (1842). During a period when he was conducting historic performances of operas, the appointment gave him the opportunity to conduct orchestral music expressing his innermost religious feelings. In 1975 the Verdi Requiem, a work he said was 'in his bones', *Messiah* and *Dream of Gerontius* were treated in an operatic manner, hardly surprising when the soloists were habitués of Covent Garden. Many important soloists went to Huddersfield during John's time; Dame Kiri Te Kanawa for *Messiah* and Ian Wallace, who was invited with the words: 'Come and do a Carol Concert with me. It would give them such a lift if you came.'

Dame Janet Baker believed, 'John was one of the most loved artists because he never treated young inexperienced singers as cannon fodder.' Many young singers are rehearsed too hard with subsequent vocal problems in performance but John was like a father, nursing their voices. Engaging Ryland Davies for *Dream of Gerontius*, performed on 5th April 1974, John realised that it would be a nerve-racking occasion for the young inexperienced tenor. Meeting him at the London railway station, John advised him to go into a carriage on his own: 'Save your voice and relax.' His solicitous manner continued during the rehearsal itself. At the back of the hall, he advised the tenor to 'have a little warm-up. There's no chorus here, just the orchestra.' At the later rehearsal: 'Now Ryland, don't sing every note full out but warm up so that, if you want to, you can. Don't worry about the Huddersfield Chorus breathing down your neck. I want you to give them the cues in full voice and, for the rest, keep them guessing. Don't let them have the chance of summing you up before the event.' Ryland Davies considered: 'What he had to tell me musically about the work will stay with me all my life. He obviously had a great love of the piece. What is tempi? Everybody has their own feeling about "andante". I came to understand through his taste and musical experiences.' As in speech, John imparted his own feeling for words and expression in his letters, his understanding when to lean on a word and when to stand back. There are many such moments in Part Two of *Gerontius*.

It was shortly after a concert on 17th March 1976 of Dvořák's *Te Deum*, Vaughan Williams' *Serenade to Music* and Tippett's *A*

Child of Our Time that, feeling he must resign, John spoke to Richard Barraclough.

After his performances of *Figaro* at Glyndebourne, John wrote to Basil, mentioning that Paul Myers of CBS was interested in making some records with him.

Paul Myers had become Vice President of A & R (Artists and Repertoire, a division of CBS) in 1974. Up to that time the company had made only four opera recordings in twenty-five years. He recalled that the man who had been President, Goddard Lieberson, was not particularly fond of opera. He was a composer and CBS maintained the Philadelphia Orchestra, the New York Philharmonic and the Cleveland Orchestra, produced the complete works of Stravinsky conducted by the composer and Copland conducting all of his so there was not much availability for opera as well. When the President left the Company, the New York office was run by Marvin Saines who was very eager that CBS should get back into opera and signed up Renata Scotto, who was currently enjoying great success.

Happy to pursue this idea, Paul Myers pointed out that to develop a public image the subject should be approached rather cautiously by recording operas that had been neglected for a while, rather than standard repertoire. In addition they were eager to take advantage of prepared performances, such as recording *L'Elisir d'Amore*. The only difference between the recording and the Covent Garden production was Placido Domingo who asked if he could sing Nemorino, the title role. A singer whom John admired, he had been very good to CBS in its early days and Paul Myers had to placate José Carreras who was a little upset not to be doing it. 'It proved to be rather a problem because Placido had difficulties with his schedule and we ended up with a duet with Cotrubas in which they never met. We had to record by over-dubbing.'

Paul Myers had found John 'a joy to work with' and when the latter took up his Cologne appointment, CBS arranged to make *Hänsel und Gretel* in Germany. The sessions were successful in the main but the chemistry between John and a different producer was not very good. When one considers the cast: Christa Ludwig and Siegmund Nimsgern as the Mother and Father, Frederica von Stade and Ileana Cotrubas as Hänsel and Gretel, Elisabeth Söderström as the Witch, Dame Kiri Te Kanawa as the Sandman and Ruth Welting as the Dew Fairy, everything should have gone like a dream but they were not terribly happy sessions. It was just a bit too tense and John hated that because he liked to work in a relaxed atmosphere.

The prospect for John of more opera recordings at CBS was affected by the signing up of Lorin Maazel who wanted to conduct opera and developed an interesting idea, namely the complete operas of Puccini which were about the same length as 'The Ring', even putting it out in one boxed set. This fitted in with the New York plans and suggestions to use Renata Scotto as much as possible. Most of the opera budget was then taken up with the Puccini project. These were the main factors that prevented Paul Myers from making more opera records with John who did not have a contract.

John's main contribution to CBS lies in a number of important solo recordings: Frederica von Stade's first big solo record 'French Opera Arias' and one with Ileana Cotrubas of Mozart, Donizetti, Verdi and Puccini which was very successful.

Dame Kiri Te Kanawa remembered going to Cologne for a recording of Verdi and Puccini arias. She had recently moved house, was exhausted and had 'flu. The producer worked for half an hour and then said they should 'try again tomorrow'. As any good, professional producer would he was worried about the costs of cancellation because, although in Britain one can postpone because of ill-health, it is not possible in other countries. He therefore kept coming back each day, 'Let's try again', making her feel all the worse. A few months later when they heard the first playback, John was instrumental in abandoning the recording totally. Re-recorded in London, it was very successful and a great part of those recordings have been used for commercials. Dame Kiri remembered: 'He spent two or three days finding all the proper takes of the ones that the producer decided to do, on both occasions.'

> I think John was very pleased with the final recording but it took his influence and strength to say 'No, it's not going to come out.' I think that this is what I am most grateful for. If I have to be thankful for anything that he ever did for me, it had to be that one incredible gesture. No other conductor in the world would have done something like that – only my husband. Only somebody who really, really loved you. I think John stepped out of his own skin and became my guide, my mentor, my Svengali for a very, very precious moment. Without telling me, he quietly went away and

did this. In order not to tell anybody that they were incompetent, they didn't know what they were doing, he would say, 'I would like to come in and do something about it . . .' The person didn't actually hear that they were not very good at making the choice but only that he wanted to take a personal interest in it. He didn't have to or need to do it but he made the time. That was why he was such a special person for me.

10

Germany

'WHAT HARBOUR SHELTERS PEACE'†

In 1975 John was awarded one of Europe's most valuable and prestigious cultural prizes, the Shakespeare Prize; the first time the FVS Foundation★, established in 1932, had given the award to a conductor. Ralph Vaughan Williams (1937) and the Poet Laureate, John Masefield (1938) were the first recipients. It was re-started in the sixties, to commemorate Her Majesty the Queen's first official visit to Germany after the war. Even though a person might be a household name in the UK, the recipient needs to be well known in a pan European context and in German-speaking countries particularly.

John, developing under the aegis of a German conductor, Fritz Busch, with his introduction of Musica Viva to Liverpool, an idea he had garnered from Munich, in the words of the citation, had 'grafted modern German musical works into the British repertoire'. Introducing *The Visit* by Gottfried von Einem and Henze's *Elegy for Young Lovers* to Glyndebourne, he had conducted that Company in the 1954 Berlin Festival, given concerts with the Berlin Philharmonic and Dresdener Staatskapelle and taken the London Philharmonic Orchestra and the BBC Symphony Orchestra on tours of Germany and had been a guest conductor at the Munich Festival. In addition he had worked with the Stuttgart Philharmonic and was well liked by the Bonn Symphony Orchestra. At the time of receiving the prize, he was conducting *Figaro* in the Cologne Mozart Festival. Above

†*Peter Grimes*
★John was recommended for the honour by Keith Jeffery, a committee member.

all the committee felt that with his performances of *Idomeneo* at Glyndebourne and subsequent recording he had 'helped Germans to rediscover a musical treasure which was in danger of fading into oblivion.' John received the Prize in Hamburg together with a large tax free cheque. In turn, given a scholarship to award, he gave his to a young composer from Munich.

In his acceptance speech, John expressed many of his own views on conducting:

> We may concede the need for a kind of musical traffic policeman, who starts musicians playing and keeps them on course by an agreed code-system of motions in the air. These physical motions can of course become organised and made glamorous to typify the personality of the conductor and make him more interesting to listeners, or rather viewers, who like to associate what they are hearing with some visual portrayal: thus we are familiar with the demeanour of crouching menace which betokens a *pianissimo*, the wide flung arms which herald a great climax. But is this all the conductor's art contains? Sir Adrian Boult used to tell me that when the great German conductor Nikisch was on the rostrum, the movement of his arms was so small as a general rule, that the orchestra was forced to watch with great concentration and that the magnetism he exercised was so great that you felt if he clenched his fist a thunderbolt would fall. I was brought up in a musical background provided by my father, who for many years played the violin in various symphony orchestras, and I remember he told me he had once dared to ask Toscanini, at the end of a rehearsal, which part of the physical being – meaning arms, hands, facial expression and so on – were most important to him in conveying his intentions to the musicians. The incisive and often menacing movements of Toscanini on the podium were well known, so it was a surprise to my father when the maestro replied, 'the eyes'.
>
> When a new guest conductor meets for the first time an orchestra completely unknown to him and has to rehearse, frequently not in his own language, there is a moment of truth right at the beginning which affects both sides. Useless at this point to make beautiful movements in the air, perhaps rehearsed at home in front of a mirror. At this moment the man is judged by his fellow musicians, in a matter of minutes.
>
> One of the best conductors of our time was Guido Cantelli. One day rehearsing the Philharmonia Orchestra in London, he stopped and talked in rather halting English about the way he wished to have a passage played. Becoming very poetic, he wanted the players

to imagine they were on the shore of a great and secluded lake in the still of the evening, with the sun just setting, the birds growing silent, scarcely a breeze disturbing the surface of the water and from the far distance an intangible mysterious sound stealing towards the senses. There was a silence, then the concert master stood up and said to his colleagues: 'He wants it more *piano*.'

It cannot be repeated too often that it is what the conductor does in the rehearsals which is crucial to what you hear from the orchestra in the concert. If the musicians have not been interested during the rehearsals, the chances are slight that you will be greatly interested in the result, even if the conductor puts on a show, dispenses with the score, and vibrates with a passionate belief in himself. After all, whatever public attention and glamour surrounds a conductor, he is in basic function something quite simple to understand. He is a teacher and by standing up in front of the complicated instrument of the symphony orchestra, he makes public the fact that, as a poet uses language to express a truth we had only half observed, so the conductor has thought deeper and longer into the music he is performing and has something distinctive to say about it.

The English music critic, Ernest Newman once tried to express in a single English word the innermost gift or attribute of several world famous conductors then appearing before the public. Thus for Toscanini the word was 'Rhythm', for Furtwängler 'Profundity', for de Sabata 'Passion', for Beecham 'Style'. Without the slightest intention of placing myself anywhere near such a gallery, I could dare to say: for Pritchard 'Fidelity'. This sounds boring and out of fashion as a word and an idea but I do think we conductors must exercise fidelity towards the composer and the music-loving public. From what I have said, you will realise that I am unsympathetic to the concept of the 'jet–set Dirigent'. I do not really understand how so many conductors nowadays can accept the directorship of more than one orchestra, often thousands of miles geographically apart.

I cannot end my remarks to you today without mentioning one name, which represents to me the best in the art of the conductor and somehow of all the humanities. The fact that I stand before you today, honoured by Germany and deeply appreciative of the facilities Germany provides me to exercise my art, the greatest influence on my musical career was my work under Fritz Busch. His ideal combination of extreme thoroughness in rehearsal, plus unbounded confidence in the talents of his men, his 'brio' and his love of life itself: all this represents a type of musical leader I should dearly love to be. Your confidence in me and the award of this Prize will help me enormously on that road.

Great music has been created and performed in Germany continuously for the last three hundred years. Whilst there are more opera houses in Germany than anywhere else in the world, there is a 'class' order in which the flagship houses have always been Hamburg, Munich and possibly Berlin, followed by Cologne and Stuttgart. Whilst John was there, together with the Intendant, Professor Dr Michael Hampe, Cologne became the place in Germany to which the opera-going public looked with interest.

In terms of an audience, Cologne is in a very favourable situation, being the centre of the most densely populated region of Europe. If one draws a circle around the city encompassing about sixty miles, there are as many inhabitants in the region as in Greater London but there is a cultural difference. In the area around Cologne there are at least fifteen opera houses. With excellent rail and road connections, its audience comes from as far afield as Brussels. Arriving by rail one is struck immediately by the Gothic architecture of the Dom (Cathedral) which took several hundred years to complete and is the focal point of the city. The Oper der Stadt Köln comes as a surprise. Its austere modern brick exterior reminds one that it is a *city* opera, a civic institution belonging to a democratic tradition, in contrast to the baroque splendours of theatres in the court tradition of many other European houses.

To run an opera house successfully requires considerable technical knowledge. In Germany the Intendant is often a conductor or producer/director who has overall charge of all aspects of the theatre whether it be artistic, financial, technical or administrative. Like Vienna, the traditional way of presenting opera in Germany, the repertory/ensemble system, dates back to the seventeenth century. Twenty or twenty-five years ago in the opera houses, it was quite normal during the course of a month to play fifteen or sixteen different pieces, performing not only German repertoire; Wagner, Strauss and Weber but Puccini and Verdi as well as Russian, Czech and French operas. Often the singers and orchestral players were not there for rehearsals and only arrived for performances. When John worked in Vienna, he had had to cope with the unnerving situation whereby on arriving at the theatre he would see a strange face and be told, for example, 'I am your Rigoletto for this evening.' John would introduce himself, 'I am your conductor. How would you like the performance

– fast or slow?' This can be quite terrifying for a conductor as he does not know what is going to happen from bar to bar. For a young man it has its excitement and stimulates the adrenalin. For John, twenty-five years older, having experienced the preparation at Glyndebourne, it was frustrating and during his time in Cologne, with the co-operation of the Intendant, Professor Dr Michael Hampe, he transformed the system to a certain extent. Now Cologne works on the semi-stagione system whereby pieces are rehearsed, played over a two month period and then put away again for a time. Although each system has its advantages and disadvantages, it is not really systems which are unworkable, it is the relationship between the people running the House which is all important.

If one buys a season ticket in Germany for eight performances a year, one does not have to accept the same opera twice in three years. The effect of this subscription system means that the public must be offered a wide range of repertoire and this enabled John to do two or three new productions a year, which would never have been possible in Britain.

To the outsider, German opera houses seem like a financial paradise but they overlook the great number of performances to be subsidised. They are like factories; every day there must be a performance. Cologne Opera gives about 200 – 220 opera performances a year, plus ballet and other events, consequently people do not realise that for a House with 1,350 seats, the subsidy per seat is only 90 – 100DM. In a stagione system, where only one work is studied every six weeks, it is possible to rehearse and leave a production on stage but in the ensemble tradition in which each opera house has its own singers, it is necessary to take down, for example, the lighting and set up again within three hours. The optimum number of productions during John's time at Cologne was twenty-three or twenty-four a year. No longer able to afford to maintain enough singers in its Company, guest singers needed to be engaged. If there was a revival with perhaps six or seven performances there would be several new singers in the cast who had never attended rehearsals, which led to chaos. The famous guest artist would arrive just before the première. He does not need coaching and he will sing 'his' Otello. Consequently young repetiteurs who would like to work with an artist who wants to learn Otello or Hans Sachs do not have the opportunity. As the subscription audience can return tickets if they have seen an opera during the last three years there may not be a revival for a few years. Young orchestral players have a problem in learning scores, as with this system they may play five or six performances of an opera and then not have the opportunity again for another five years. The music is not in their blood. John faced this problem when conducting *Rosenkavalier*. Both 'leaders' were ill. Nobody knew the work sufficiently well. *Rosenkavalier* is a very complicated piece and can fall apart quite easily. Fortunately, the management remembered an old man who had retired years before. He was asked and played without any problems. John always said that by the time one was fifty it was essential to have some composers and operas in one's 'blood'. One should not learn either Mozart, Beethoven or Bach at that stage and he was fortunate that he had had so many opportunities at the right moment, both to learn and conduct.

He was very excited about Cologne. Many young singers such as Lucia Popp, Edith Mathis, Yvonne Minton, Margaret Price and Julia Varady were engaged for a Mozart cycle in the early seventies. The Gürzenich Orchestra which played for the opera was considered one of the best in Germany. It was a very idiomatic Mozart orchestra and most of the Mozart operas had been very well prepared originally, mainly by István Kertész. With his tragic death by drowning in 1973, John became involved in the presentation of *Le Nozze di Figaro* in 1975. In addition, he would present the Mozart cycle, Strauss and the baroque operas he had done at Glyndebourne. Cologne had a great Wagner tradition as well as a reputation for contemporary work and was going to give him the opportunity to conduct works which he had not or could not do anywhere else. It still irked him that he had been unable to conduct *Moses and Aaron* at Covent Garden. In Cologne he would present *Meistersinger*, *Parsifal* and the Puccinis, operas which were not necessarily thought suitable for him.

Like all conductors he had his little disasters mainly due to lack of rehearsal or because he was not particularly interested.

In Puccini, John conducted *Manon Lescaut* and *Madame Butterfly*, of which he said once: 'In this *realism* of Puccini, one's power of poking fun at our beloved operas recedes.' He was supposed to do *La Bohème* but it never happened. He was more successful in Verdi than in Puccini because he was primarily an accompanist, allowing the singers to create the line and following them. This works in Verdi. However, in Puccini it is the orchestra which says everything and the singers must follow and it can prove dangerous to wait for singers as it slackens the tension.

The Gürzenich Orchestra gives some concerts too but is much more involved in opera. British orchestral players look with envy on their German counterparts. A British player needs to play to earn and has to work sessions. In Germany, after a year's trial, players are engaged for the rest of their working life. The social net is so safe that unless a musician commits a serious crime, he is secure. At the last main rehearsal for *Arabella* in 1976, the first violinist came and did a first sight-reading of it. John stopped, went up to his room and said that he would not conduct again with substitute players. It took a full half hour for him to be persuaded that he had to continue.

He came to Cologne with many ideas about reforming the orchestra but when he found that even though he pushed against the door it would not open, rather than be unpleasant about it, he walked away, regarding Cologne as only one part of his life. 'I would sum up the position by pointing out that it is NOT in my plans to appear less frequently in Covent Garden and much *more* frequently in Köln – delightful as that might be.' He was not there enough to fight over something he would have had little chance of winning.

In recalling the problems John had in Cologne, one should also mention that he could never understand why others could not feel that to make music was pleasure and fun. He was too much of an English gentleman for the musicians. Initially Günther Rennert had found it hard to adjust to the democracy of Glyndebourne and vice versa John could not behave like a dictator. German players like a disciplinarian conductor and to be told exactly what to do. At John's Memorial Service in Cologne, Claus Henneberg told the story of a conductor who said to the orchestra, 'If there is anybody who wants to leave, do so' and they all stood up and left. One of the singers had said to John, 'Oh, they would never do that with you' and he had retorted, 'Sometimes, I wish they would!'

In one incident during *Falstaff*, at the end of Act III [XY] was singing and forgot her offstage part. John beat and a few people started playing. Some stopped and a few more started playing; a few stopped and some others came in. There was a terrible din! John threw down the baton. 'Well, you just finish it yourselves' and sat there arms folded, as they struggled to the end. 'You made the problems, you sort it out!' This was a rare occasion.

Wisely, John insisted that he did not wish to have the title General Musikdirektor and was called Chef Dirigent, a completely new title in a German opera house. Not only is the former involved in conducting his own performances and solving any problems which arise but he is also occupied in resolving the difficulties of other conductors. John had no intention of being involved in this way as it would have interfered with his work elsewhere and his decision led to problems for a company which had been accustomed to functioning in a particular way. When it was known that this was his intention, the Kappelmeister, Georg Fischer, tried to persuade him over lunch that a piece such as *Arabella*, which was going to be John's own new production, should, for revivals, only be conducted by him. If another conductor were to conduct the revival, he would change the orchestral markings, such as the bowings and the piece would be altered so that it would lose the stamp which John had brought to the work. Before he took up his appointment he insisted that he should be fully involved in his productions from their inception and wanted to see models and designs at an early stage.

At the beginning, John tried to work in this way but gradually it became more and more impossible. He had had such a wonderful dream about Cologne. On a practical note, the Deutschmark was the strongest European currency and an appointment to a German house made financial sense, as it would allow him to continue living in the style to which he had become accustomed. Musically, he intended to programme perhaps two Mozart operas, one twentieth-century piece, some Verdi and Russian composers but the reality showed him how impossible it would be to realise his intentions. The sets would be too expensive, the technical possibilities limiting, problems having nothing whatsoever to do with the artistic and musical side of a presentation. If, for example, one performs *Turandot*, it is not possible to rehearse *Don Giovanni* either on the morning before or after such an opera. The reality of the situation was that he did his own rehearsals and his own performances which is the way most companies are being forced to work now.

In Cologne John's major achievement was always when he was in the pit, not during rehearsal but in performance. He never conducted the piano dress rehearsal but would always watch, as it was his last chance to concentrate on the production and make his final comments. Very often he did not take part in the early scenic rehearsals either as his many engagements took him elsewhere. It was his ability to come in at the final rehearsals that really made them work. Unfortunately singers sometimes found it difficult that Jeffrey Tate had prepared them as his beat is very clear, in marked contrast to that of John. Even when he had firm ideas, if something really was good he was easily convinced. Nevertheless he had the discipline not to intervene when it was bad but concerned himself with the music. The exceptions were *Idomeneo* and *Peter Grimes*.

At Glyndebourne he had been able to rely totally on the preparatory work of the music staff. Likewise at Cologne he had assistants whom he could trust. He wrote to Georg Fischer on 7th November 1978:

> We have more hope of a settled working plan. BUT, and this is the main purpose of my letter to you, we must counterbalance the administration with an impressively strong musical team. In my view the triumvirate of Jeffrey Tate, yourself and myself would be more than able to look after the musical values which in the end will determine the standard of the House. Even more importantly, Georg, I would feel much happier if *during my absences* you would represent me totally in the House.
>
> Another point I consider important is greater feeling of involvement by our repetiteurs and associate conductors (staff) who at present go about their tasks in a sort of vacuum, and of course like all people working a little far from the centre of events, don't know what is going on and tend to grumble and feel dissatisfied.

John had met the third party in his triumvirate in the late sixties when Jeffrey Tate was a medical student at St Thomas' Hospital, London. He invited the young man to a performance of *Benvenuto Cellini* and then to a party at Carter's Corner on Boxing Day. Jeffrey Tate remembered driving down with John: 'A motley group, as you can well imagine. John invited me because although I was a medical student, he knew I was interested in becoming a musician.' The young man really came to know John at Covent Garden as his assistant for *Clemenza di Tito*. A few years later he received a missive from Cologne that they would very much like him as John's assistant. 'I think I went as much because of JP as to get away from Covent Garden. Knowing that he was there, I thought it would be easier to cope with the change of scene, the language which I knew but not very well, a completely new way of life. I realised that this was probably the right moment to go away from Covent Garden, widen my horizons. I didn't even think of being a conductor at this moment but thought of myself as an assistant, a coach. I arrived at exactly the same time as JP.'

As his musical assistant he came to know John under the apparent nonchalant surface, just how much work went into giving that impression. 'We would sit in the library for hours marking up parts in the score that he wanted, so that when it came to rehearsal no time would be lost.' His assistant was always being given huge lists of notes to go and mark into parts or into the score. Making sure that life ran as smoothly as possible, as well as lists when they were rehearsing, John would give huge lists for shopping and things to do. 'We know that very well because Klaus Kuhlemann and myself shared a little house in the Eiffel with John.'

John liked the idea of having a country cottage. Although Cologne is by no means a huge metropolis, nonetheless if one lives in the centre, it is fairly oppressive and after a while they wanted to share somewhere in the country. Jeffrey Tate remembered spending a whole day driving around the Eiffel, a hilly region to the south of Cologne, looking at various places which Klaus had found in the paper. The last cottage they saw was a Hansel and Gretel type house, three-quarters of an hour's drive from Cologne, which they shared for two years until Jeffrey Tate went to America.

It was a tiny hunting lodge built just before the war. In the basement, where the garage was situated, was a furnace which heated the rest of the house but had to be made up when anyone arrived. 'A hot air system which if you couldn't do, you froze. We always laughed because when we arrived after John had been there a day or so, he was going around swathed in clothes because he had *no* idea how to do that – neither did Terry. They were very practical when it came to cooking and that sort of thing but give them things like boiler rooms and they were absolutely useless.'

For all that John liked the idea of an arcadian retreat, he could never be away from the big world and wanted a telephone. He always feared there might be a phone call from San Francisco or somewhere else that he might miss. He was an inveterate telephoner. 'Klaus and I fought against it like mad! We made sure the bills were itemised! We shared all the expenses but we were worried about the telephone. They actually had to lay a special line. Can you imagine what it was like forcing the General Post Office to lay the line!'

It always amazed Jeffrey Tate that John never seemed to settle in one place, coming to believe that it must be part of his nature. Carter's Corner was an exception. 'All the time I knew him there was a feeling of restlessness, that he never wanted to settle in one place. He had a lovely flat and then moved out to a bigger flat, always on the move. There was Monte Carlo and then France. He never seemed to stop thinking of buying something. We thought it was a mania of John's, houses all over the place.'

A home in the South of France appealed to John. Somehow the sun and warmth seemed to bring out an expansion of his personality. On his first visit to Juan les Pins, one August evening at the height of the season, he squashed himself into a stalls circle seat at a pavement café. Bathed in psychedelic coloured lights in the blaring sounds of a band vying with a similar venue across the road, John watched the crowds milling around, beaming, 'I'm *in* a Fellini film.'

It was during this period that a pair of two-toned coffee and cream coloured co-respondent shoes spoke to him from a shop window. Having bought them he would sit with his legs crossed at the ankle, leaning back, enjoying them. Admiring a navy and white pair worn by singer Helga Dernesch, shoes in those colours also joined his wardrobe. They represented summer in the South of France.

Every time they went to Monte Carlo, John and Terry would drive around the surrounding area looking at properties for sale. Eventually in 1984, set on a hillside, the Manoir de Nenfré replaced Carter's Corner Place as home, the place where John could display his treasures. Seated next to the large pool, he would play a César Franck organ concerto at full blast enjoying the sound reverberating around the hills, knowing that he was not disturbing any neighbours.

There are few artists able to function by travelling from hotel room to hotel room. Most need to stay for a period in one place; to take an apartment or, if they need an hotel, always the same hotel, preferably the same room. They need to create a home, a place where mementos or photographs can be laid out on a dressing-table, not to return to the bleak impersonal tidiness of a hotel bedroom. Always rushing about, without true family, more than anyone John needed somewhere to call home.

Graziella Sciutti commented: 'John didn't like to be alone, was afraid to be alone, surrounding himself with people, going out after performances. We all feel the same. After a performance we are too wound up to finish. For us the curtain doesn't close the performance, our metabolism goes on. You need to be together with people, to eat, drink, talk. If you had a home to go back to it might be different but a hotel room, or a rented flat is not the same. So we try to go on, create a little warmth and then little by little we get tired and we can go to sleep – ready for the next battle.'

John learnt to party in Vienna. At the end of a performance he would never just say 'Goodnight, that was very good.' It always had to end on a high note. Many of the parties he hosted were secretly referred to by heterosexual friends as 'gay nineties' parties – the men were mostly gay and some of the women over ninety. John would sit back watching personalities such as close friends Elisabeth Welch seated on his right with Dame Eva Turner opposite, enjoying the repartee across the table.

Driving everywhere with Terry, there always seemed to be disasters such as the occasion when the Jaguar completely burnt up on the Italian motorway. The engine had literally solidified, burnt itself into a solid mass. They were lucky to escape. John had to be flown back. Klaus and Jeffrey Tate looked after John in Cologne when Terry was not there because if he needed to get anywhere they would always drive him. 'It was quite a sight to see the enormous bulk squeeze into our little car to go shopping or to a restaurant.' John loved restaurants and Jeffrey Tate loved eating, so he was commandeered to eat in various restaurants. 'It was a very happy time. We were very fond of each other.'

John seemed to have a love/hate relationship with Cologne, saying that he found it very dour. He came to like living there because in Cologne he found a certain freedom and was at ease there. People did not mind what he was or what he did. Once used to the idea that there would not be ready smiles and witty replies from the Germans, he enjoyed it. Initially it was through his two friends when he was getting to know the place and then afterwards began to feel an enormous affection for the city.

John always wanted to move on but he needed a few stable points.

Klaus and I felt that he often surrounded himself with people who weren't very stable. We didn't mix with his other circles at all, keeping ourselves apart. We often wondered how someone who was cultivated and sensitive could sometimes mix with some of the people he did. It was difficult for us to feel what he saw. I'm sure we were wrong, that among these people some were probably cultivated and sincere but it seemed to us as though there were too many people who used him. It used to upset us enormously that people were exploiting him for aspects of his personality and we could never understand why John, being far too clear-sighted not to see what was happening, didn't put his foot down and say 'stop'. As a last resort he drove himself to work like mad, to keep up a lifestyle that was only partially his, apparently supporting a whole sub-culture. There was a 'band' who lived on John's energy and abilities. We only hope that he got something out of it that made it worthwhile. There were times when we thought it wasn't the case. Of course, this was just our reaction, not John's.

It irritated John that he was always expected to pick up the bill but he understood that it was a price he was expected to pay.

> DIARY ENTRY: Took [A,B,C,D,E] to supper. At first [A] said he would cook dinner at home and I said 'Isn't it too much?' and he replied, 'Yes, OK let's go out'. Went to lovely — restaurant with [A,B,C,D,E]. After all the hospitality given them since Sunday and my paying for dinner, which I expected, they didn't even put their hand in their pocket, for a few coffees at —. I was livid! I swear NO MORE HOSPITALITY, NONE!

Although he expressed his thoughts on paper, when it came to possible unpleasantness, he preferred to pay. Easily bored, wanting to be the centre of attention, he did not like other musicians who talked shop.

The freedom which Cologne gave John to live his private life publicly, distressed many of his close friends who were all aware that he preferred a gay milieu now. It is important to reiterate that there are many types of homosexual. Even at Carter's Corner he had excluded women, as far as possible, from some of the private dinner parties. In Cologne John became a very, very lonely man because gradually he excluded even his genuine homosexual friends and only had 'hangers-on'. The fear of loneliness was always uppermost in his mind. Although he knew he was being exploited by these people who were virtually prostitutes, he still felt that it was better to be exploited than to be lonely. There was an element in John that liked all these people around him, fighting for attention. He loved controlling and commanding. Almost a professional vice, it was as though he was used to telling people all day what to do and then continued doing the same thing out of conducting hours, revelling in it.

Jeffrey Tate wondered, 'if he stopped having his hair woven and accepted his age, what he could have done. John was always wanting and trying to be younger than he was and yet in a sense was so much more distinguished than the people around him and could have got away with blue murder. It disturbed us that he needed "the beautiful people" around him. It was not necessary.'

The sadness increased the older he became, not just because of his physical problems. He needed a hip replacement operation and suffered considerable pain for several years because he was overweight. The operation was delayed as it is necessary, for a full recovery, for the patient to be leading a less active life and to have lost weight. Eventually the doctors realised this would never happen. He discussed medicines and treatments frequently, telephoning excitedly about a new miracle drug, a wonderful pain-killer but, like the rest of his life, disillusion would set in. In hospital he became very depressed.

Similar to his reaction after the accident at Ingestre, the thought that he was no longer physically attractive upset him very much and seemed to drive him to compensate with greater excesses. That and the pathetic search for love with youths who could never provide it for him. Catching a glimpse of a young man at a party he would hope that this would be the great love for which he had searched. It was an extraordinary, immature hope. Likewise, with every new musical project proposed, he believed it would fulfil all his dreams. Gradually reality would impose itself and his hopes would be eroded. The star would be ill and one by one all the reasons for which he had accepted would evaporate and it would become only work. Once, visiting in France, there was a new, quiet, intelligent young man by the swimming pool. Alone with John in the kitchen preparing lunch, I commented that I liked his guest, the first time I had ever done so. Very quietly, after a pause, 'Yes, my dear. He is without interest.' In that moment I knew that the pity I had always felt was the truth. However, waiting longer than the others, the youth soon asked to 'borrow' an exorbitant sum.

The tragedy of his life, the boys, demeaned John. He became

mentally lazy. Instead of reading and having friends who stimulated his mind, he appeared to pass the time with what amounted to the lowest common denominator. They wanted to watch television all the time and made him do the same. He did not want to be too tested by them. As his health deteriorated, the effort involved in his work, the travel, exhausted him. John made a conscious choice. He liked to see physical beauty and surrounded himself with it. He loved farce and all those naughty things happening. A great deal was 'imagining'. John enjoyed his friends being malicious as it meant that he could be malicious too. He knew exactly what was happening. He was interested in family life, wanting to know about friends' children and their hopes for the future. These young men were his family.

A man with more friends and acquaintances than possibly anyone else, he was aware that he was the loneliest. Bernard Haitink commented: 'This profession breeds lonely people. We live day and night with what we have to do and we have to isolate ourselves to be able to do it. It's a terrible balancing act to also have a private life. John was an example of that! I think he was a very lonely man and very easy to hurt. In that situation a person sometimes leans on the wrong people.'

In his Memorial Tribute, Professor Dr Michael Hampe summed up:

> Like every great personality, John Pritchard too had dark sides and abysms and this should not be left unmentioned. There was about him an aura of great loneliness, deep sadness and sometimes forlornness, helplessness and need for assistance. He made no secret of it, nor did it ever occur to him to complain about it or ask for sympathy. He ignored it. He was aware of his abysms; he knew that every great personality is made up of tensions, tensions of strong antitheses, some mastered and some still unmastered. His cheerful Dionysian approach to life was matched by deep grief, and sometimes probably also by dark despair. Anybody who could make music like him has – like any other great artist – to pay for it to the last penny. For basically music is anyway something for people who are urgently in need of it, something which is a bitter necessity for them.

Dr Hampe preferred to remember John's warmth and the way he could make people feel at ease. As at Glyndebourne, after a rehearsal which had not gone well, in Cologne John would say 'Come up to my room for notes'. There the singer, director or whoever was concerned would find a wonderful buffet laid out. After helping themselves, he would call them, relaxed, one by one and quietly speak with them.

The first five years in Cologne were very much part of the happy memories, the honeymoon. Money was forthcoming and John attracted many great artists to the house. Jean-Pierre Ponnelle was the leading director. At Cologne there are still eighteen of his productions in use but it is the Mozart cycle with John, for which he is best remembered.

John was happiest using those scores. They were old and lovingly inscribed. As he did not often go to the early rehearsals he would send the score ahead, writing in tempo markings. He had a particular code for this. With scores he was learning he would put the exact tempo markings and all minute changes. They did not necessarily mean what they said but gave an indication of changes for his assistants.

In the Mozart cycles, taking great care with casting, John would always insist on having top-rate singers. For *Figaro*, in the role of Countess, he had artists such as Dame Kiri Te Kanawa and Margaret Price who commented, 'Every artist that worked with him remembers him for the musician, the superb Mozart conductor and the ability to accompany a singer so perfectly.' In 1980 Anna Tomowa-Sintow sang the Countess and Ileana Cotrubas, Susanna, of whom John remarked laughingly, 'She is one of the only artists who doesn't just accept that the producer tells her to enter and exit through a certain door but wants to know *why* she should use that particular door.' He was very fond of Ann Murray, singing Cherubino. Originally she had been invited to Cologne by Georg Fischer and this was not her first *Figaro* there. She and John became very friendly during this period and he would often include her in his supper parties after a performance.

DIARY ENTRY:
5th June 1980. Lovely first night of *Figaro* – just like my first days in Cologne – great cheers. The public wild about it all. Ann Murray is a delicious Cherubino . . . N.V. came – was my personal Cherubino!
15th June 1980. The last *Figaro*. Great triumph – the public throwing whole bunches of flowers at the ladies, who deserved it. (Esp. Ann Murray has confirmed all promise.)

In the last series Margaret Marshall replaced the singer cast as Fiordiligi in *Così*. The need to concentrate brought out the best in him. Previously, as he was always flying in from America, *Così* had disappointed those who knew of his achievements elsewhere. In this particular performance, he paced everything so precisely that many consider this to have been one of his greatest. Hilary Griffiths had replaced Jeffrey Tate as John's assistant. Not knowing the conductor was so ill, he sent him a letter thanking him for such an evening. After John's last performance of *Zauberflöte* when he went up onto the stage, his assistant slipped into the pit and the orchestra played 'Land of Hope and Glory' when he came out to bow.

There were many important productions for John in 1980. He had come late to learn the full score of Strauss' *Die Frau ohne Schatten* for the Jean-Pierre Ponnelle production the previous year. Not fluent in German and with no great love of the language, unlike his ability in French, he had his problems in mastering the opera. There were a couple of disastrous orchestral rehearsals as he did not know the work. Orchestras hate conductors who talk a great deal, so they were happy with him getting by with his basic German but he had difficulties with the complicated text. On the Scarsdale Diet, he had just lost seven kilos in eleven days and even though he sought consolation with 'Perrier and stuff', he missed wine and did not have the patience to follow the text completely as he was lost in the grammar of the language. However, singing the Nurse, Helga Dernesch only had happy memories of the first time she worked with John. 'I had just changed from a dramatic soprano to being a mezzo-soprano in 1979 and it was my first big part in a real première. Sir John knew about the change-over and he helped me and we talked together. He always had his eyes on the stage and the orchestra followed his gentle movements. He never had rough gestures, always gentle, as he was as a person, giving a smile when everything went quite well.' Helga Dernesch is Austrian and there it is usual for a gentleman to kiss a lady's hand but otherwise it is very rare nowadays. 'It's a lovely gesture and Sir John was one of the gentlemen who used to kiss my hand.' The première was not a good performance but it improved and the revival was successful.

When rehearsals and performances went well, John would dispense happiness but like most people, would blame others when things were not good. When he saw the huge set, all red and gold, for *Ballo in Maschera* he was upset about the lack of fantasy. He approved of luxury on stage but not when it did not lead to fantasy or inventiveness. He had liked *Die Frau ohne Schatten* because there was almost nothing on the stage, only red roofs which would go up and down.

Ballo came after disappointing rehearsals for *Il Matrimonio Segreto* and he confided in his diary that he was feeling 'very "off" Cologne'.

> *22nd April 1980.* I was in disagreeable mood (Sitzprobe of *Ballo* – Aragall in lovely voice but Tomowa-Sintow ill).
>
> *23rd April.* Felt weak-kneed all day, weather cold and rainy so have given up Scarsdale Diet pro tem. Meeting with Hampe.
>
> *26th April.* Good satisfying Act I with the orchestra, rich in sound. All singers in happy state.
>
> *28th April.* The usual stage goings on, with threats of 'nothing ready in time'. Hampe fairly distracted and we have little contact. T-Sintow will be lovely.
>
> *29th April. Walked* to Rodenk for shopping. Hate the plastic bag syndrome. Evening Act III. Usual confusion with the stage music and the celebrated Menuett – which began my conducting career in Edinburgh 49? [Conducting the stage music in the Glyndebourne *Ballo* under Vittorio Gui.]
>
> *2nd May.* Dress rehearsal went well.
>
> *4th May.* Opening of *Ballo. All very good* except lighting! Michael H. did not take bow so I took the brunt of a few boos from a loving public. Orchestra superb, rich and colourful.

Die Meistersinger in 1979 and the revival in 1980 was masterly. Reactions were mixed, largely because he was not German. He ignored the traditions and it worked, prompting a letter from Sir Oliver Wright, the British Ambassador in Bonn.

> *11.30pm 29th April*
> Before I go to bed and while I am still 'under the influence', I must just drop you a line to repeat what I told you in your dressing-room: it was tremendous. I do congratulate you. Well done!
>
> You have clearly now a special place for yourself in the hearts of the people of Cologne. As a connoisseur of applause, it is especially heartwarming for one of your fellow countrymen to register, as you enter the pit and before you pick up your stick, the extra warmth with which your Kölners greet you. As for your final appearance on stage – well, I can only hope that it must make all that effort worthwhile.

Again, thank you for a wonderful *Meistersinger* – a *Meistersinger* to remember. I believe Wagner did not mark the speed on his scores saying that conductors either felt it instinctively or would never get it right. I reckon you got it right first time and that old Klingsor would be content.

John's conducting was very light, lyrical and fast-paced, and the comedy emerged. Preparing for the first night, he sighed, 'Wagner wrote some of the most marvellous, lovely music ever but oh, those long boring bits in between! I shall have to devise a conductor's stand with a shelf that slides out, so that I can have a glass of champagne and a plate of smoked salmon sandwiches.'

Jeffrey Tate recalled: 'He had an incredible constitution. I have seen John in the middle of *Meistersinger* happily consume half a bottle of white wine in his room. I would have been out. I wouldn't have been drunk, just not capable of going on with the second Act. You wouldn't notice anything with John. He was an enormous man who could eat an enormous quantity of food. Abused is the wrong word but he didn't worry about his body, that had to take care of itself and it did – an incredible constitution which, I'm sure, is the reason he survived his own lifestyle.' John was up all hours, endless hours but would be up before anybody else; at 7.30 or 8 o'clock, padding around in his red silk patterned gown if one stayed with him. Anyone else who was staying was of course snoring in bed, as they were not in bed before 3 o'clock the night before. John was *always* up.

The opportunity to conduct Wagner again presented itself in 1983 when he and Jean-Pierre Ponnelle presented *Parsifal*, a first for both men.

From the first time he heard *Peter Grimes*, the opera meant a great deal to him. An outsider in many ways from his childhood, with his sensitivity and later through his homosexuality, he identified with Grimes. The tragedy in Grimes is inevitable. So too with John, as his friends tried to reach out and help him in his loneliness, he only retreated further. Unlike Grimes, in his last year John tried to pull himself back from the abyss but it was too late. The fates destroyed him. In the opera as Grimes takes his boat out to sea in the fog, one hears the sound of the horn and then it fades and disappears, it is heartbreaking. Some of the most beautiful moments in the opera stem from Britten's evocation of the sea. From his family background, John understood the sea-faring communities, that they are very close-knit. In the stark reality of life the people are different from those living inland. They are frugal and often harsh, like the weather and the wind.

In Cologne, it was decided to perform *Grimes* in German. Germany is the one country in the world where it has never been a real success. They prefer *Albert Herring*, that opera perhaps according more with their view of the English. John was not happy that *Grimes* was to be performed in German but decided that if it were, then Claus Henneberg was the expert to do it. They talked about the environment and about George Crabbe from whose poem the opera is derived. In planning the performances for the following year John was involved totally. Writing to Michael Hampe on 23rd February 1980, John wanted to decide on a producer.

> Now that you have decided against doing it in English, may I make crystal clear that with a predominantly *German* cast, I do not want any bright adventurer of the German Schauspiel, or indeed any innovator at all. I would like someone who knows the opera and the *background* and this resolves the choice in my view to the following:
>
> | | | |
> |---|---|---|
> | (English) | a. | John COPLEY. Not now free, I think. |
> | (English) | b. | Anthony BESCH. Good German and has imagination and a very good designer, John Stoddart. |
> | (American) | c. | Bodo IGESZ. Has done the opera many times at Met and has fluent German. |

In the event none of these produced the opera.

John, who cared passionately about the opera, was appalled when he saw the proposed designs for the set. They were by a good modern painter who saw *Grimes* with a painter's eye and used a painter's means. It had big splashes of colour, very impressionistic with several crucifixes. John looked on *Grimes* in a more realistic way, symmetrical and stark with the conception of a formal façade hiding a can of worms.

> DIARY ENTRY:
> *12th May 1980.* Had such a depressing meeting for *Grimes* with rag, tag and bobtail. So depressed.
> *13th May.* After sleeping on events, I typed a long letter to Michael H *resigning* from GRIMES project. No confidence in Neugebauer or casting.

The huge volume of correspondence with Michael Hampe expressing his worries about *Grimes*, reveals more than any comments how deeply he felt about the opera.★

Michael Hampe remembers that he was not happy either but thought that when the set was actually on stage, the result was convincing, as it created a very poor village with normal everyday people. When it came to the first stage rehearsal and John was doing the storm scene, he noticed they had not built the door on stage. 'I have to have a door. When it opens I play the storm music.' At the reassurance 'there'll be one tomorrow', John took off his glasses. 'Ich gehe zuhaus' (I'm going home). The rehearsal did not take place.

John's distress was based on knowledge not whim, writing to Dr Hampe. 'Rodenkirchen, *5.15am* 27th May 1981. It is rather a long time since I actually wept real tears but I did last night, have been unable to sleep and now in the early morning have to face once again the dismal remnants of a great opera to which Cologne has reduced one of the significant works of our time.'

Despite his fears, John looked forward to the first night. There was no mistaking his breathless excitement when he went out to conduct. It is considered that there is a great deal of Britten himself in *Grimes* and John was very conscious of all the underlying rhythms and meanings. The performances of 1981 were a great success and he was particularly happy with Hugh Beresford, who had replaced William Lewis in the title role. It is a very tiring opera to conduct, almost non-stop for three hours. After all the problems, the success was doubly satisfying with a feeling of achievement. He had succeeded in creating something which people understood.

It is easy to understand that Britten played a very important part in his emotional life. Yet, on the other hand, performances of *Figaro*, *Idomeneo* and Schubert were equally good. In a radio interview, John was asked 'Which composer and which music is most important to you?' Frequently asserting that one cannot live always on Olympus, he began talking about Mozart but after a couple of minutes moved on to Britten, Verdi and Rossini. When one asks why he was never fully appreciated, it is because his musicianship was highly sophisticated. *Falstaff* will never be as popular as *Rigoletto*; nor *Così fan Tutte* or *Idomeneo* as *Zauberflöte* or *Figaro*. Beethoven string quartets do not attract the crowds.

★Correspondence with Dr Hampe on *Peter Grimes*, p. 360

Moses und Aron was one of the operas John had proposed to Dr Michael Hampe before he took up his appointment. While he was in Cologne, Jeffrey Tate considered it was John's greatest musical achievement. 'He conducted that with such consummate ease – for me that was his high spot.'

Like his Wagner, John's approach in the performances of 1978 and 1979 was quite different from any previous conception in Germany. Suddenly the seemingly grey music was suffused with colour, a colour so lively that, even though John felt some reservations about the production, the audience enjoyed the performance. Apart from the sensational aspects such as the Golden Calf orgy, the opera concerns the relationship between G – d and mankind. It is in this opera that the Schoenberg twelve-tone scale appears for the first time – when G – d is quoted – a comment on the inventor of that system who appears to equate himself with the system and G – d. In John's hand one forgot any unhappy feelings about this. Conducting it like a Verdi opera, it had a freshness. Unfortunately when he came to the first rehearsals he had not really looked at the score.

John not looking at the score before rehearsal became an 'in' joke with his colleagues, both Jeffrey Tate and Ann Murray recounting the same story. Tate recalled that they were doing a very complicated version of *Tales of Hoffman*.

> It had been a long struggle because Michael Hampe had gone to the sources and investigated all the possibilities and put together a very complex version without dialogue, using a lot of discoveries by Oeser and produced a pasted-up score with a lot of inserts which I presumed John had looked at. He was enormously quick and would say, 'Yes, yes, yes.' I had been rehearsing some people and John came in to the rehearsal which he was due to conduct. He brought the huge score and went to open it and it wouldn't open. Finally after bending, it opened with an enormous 'crack' and John said, 'Oh dear, I have given myself away haven't I?' Typical John! He had of course, the speed of mind to cope with it. I wonder how many occasions he had turned up at rehearsal, with his extraordinary busy life, not having had time to look at the score and of course always about two or three bars ahead of any singer or any orchestra. It was a very funny moment. We all screamed with laughter. One couldn't resist that sort of comment from him. *Hoffman* was an enormous success. It went on being played and played and the audiences loved it. They could not get enough of it. It was one of the great things.

Rehearsal at the new Henry Wood Hall, Southwark, 1972.   *Photo courtesy of Arup Associates*

John and Professor Dr Michael Hampe in Cologne. *Photo courtesy of Köln Oper*

John with Anna Tomowa-Sintow after the performance of *Un Ballo in Maschera*, Cologne, 1980. Giacomo Aragall and Dr Hampe in the background.

John with Peter Nestler, Julia Varady, Ann Murray and the Manager of the Israel Philharmonic Orchestra at the Cologne Opera Press Conference during the Tel Aviv tour, 1982.

Photo courtesy of Köln Oper

John talking at the Théâtre de la Monnaie, Brussels, 1983.

Photo courtesy of Théâtre de la Monnaie

Outside Buckingham Palace after receiving his knighthood, with Ian Wallace having received the OBE, 1983.

Photograph: John St. Clair

John with His Serene Highness Prince Rainier, Princess Caroline, Princess Stephanie, Dame Kiri Te Kanawa and His Royal Highness, The Prince of Wales in Monte Carlo for a gala concert in aid of United World Colleges, 3rd August 1984.

Photo courtesy of UPI/Bettmann

Ann Murray added: 'At the next rehearsal – did he know it! He knew it backwards and upside down. He was very, very quick. It was a marvellous *Hoffman* and perhaps one of the best things Hampe has ever done.'

Unknown to Jeffrey Tate and Ann Murray there is a story behind this joke, revealing how John came to use an unopened score. During the summer of 1980, receiving an urgent request from John Drummond, who was running the Edinburgh Festival, to take over André Previn's two London Symphony Orchestra concerts, he managed to clear things in Cologne to go there. However on his return journey disaster struck.

> DIARY ENTRY: Ray Holden [an assistant] took me to the airport. Left in such a hurry, he took off my two vital scores for Hoff. needed for tonight's orchestra. Alone in Cologne was so vexed and nervous after this silly accident, the day was spoiled. Managed to rehearse with another score. The whole assembly of the Hoffman score has been a *hideous* chore. Scores arrived air freighted by Ray. Cost 177DM!

Dr Hampe considered the theme of *Hoffman* as the 'creation of art; the transformation of life into art; not a drunkard and his affairs as it has so often been played. The opera *Hoffman* does not exist. It is all bits and pieces from various composers, with parts added from various versions and various people in the different stages of the composition of the work. Offenbach paid a very large sum to get the rights from another composer. It was decided in Cologne to follow the line of the drama *Les Contes d'Hoffman* by Barbier.'

In the summer of 1980 John took Cologne Opera to Edinburgh. The two works he conducted, the highly successful *Il Matrimonio Segreto* and *Così* both have a great deal in common; apparent comedies but an element of tragedy within.

> *15th August.* Early plane to London. Horrid wait for Ray Holden. Terry met me at Edinburgh Airport. To the George Hotel, usual *British* inefficiency with room not ready. Finally gained access to a large suite like a dentist's waiting room. Evening to the dear old Kings Theatre with *Così* from Köln squeezed onto the stage. I fear the technik will have great difficulties. Dress rehearsal difficult and tiring but Varady impressive (*Così*).
>
> *17th August.* The première quite exciting, could not always move the artists along, everyone is nervous.

18th August. Tired but had to rehearse Scottish Chamber Orchestra in *Matrimonio* at King's Theatre. (Hilary Griffiths help.) Dined at Cramond Inn (nostalgia again). Looked at the boats on the creek in the dark.

19th August. Rehearsal am. Scottish Chamber Orchestra at their new Edinburgh HQ. Queen's Hall a nicely converted church with good sound. They are an excellent bunch but at the moment lack homogeneity of chording and attack. Performance in evening much more relaxed.

20th August. Left George Hotel, impossible communications, for Greywalls Hotel at Gullane near N Berwick. Lovely and spectacular Lutyens House, just like staying in nice country house of friends. Very civilised and quiet. Lunch simple but good. Evening. Run thru' of *Matrimonio*. Singers all very tired from plane journey but orchestra coming on. Supped with Michael Storrs (manager of orchestra) and W Decker. Home to Gullane at 12.30am – lovely bed.

21st August. Last of three *Cosìs*. Gurz. Orchestra has really not distinguished itself – very out of time with winds. Not best of players perhaps. Think they enjoyed Edinburgh however.

Dress rehearsal *Matrimonio*. Long, very disorganised on stage. (Two singers replaced by Runge and veteran singer from Hampe's Stockholm.)

22nd August. Lovely day at Greywalls – it is the most beautiful house and just the right size for a *personal* hotel. Food simple but wholesome, therefore one eats too much!

23rd August. First of the two *Matrimonios* – really a raging success. The Scottish Chamber O. notably good.

The following year at Edinburgh, using the version which had belonged to Vittorio Gui, with his own parts, John introduced what was to German ears, a new *Barbiere*. In the Mozart operas he would have his own parts for most of the orchestra parts which he carried around with him wherever he went. Likewise with *Barbiere*. It was a mixed version based on the old printed version and then changed. The orchestra in Cologne had been warned about John's version. 'What is he doing? We have played *Barbiere* for fifty years, we know every bar but this is not the same piece.' After the performances though, the players commented that it had been wonderful playing for him. The negative comment one could make is that it came from a style which had its roots between the two World Wars, when the music was being reappraised and perhaps the newer so-called authentic attitude is from a strictly musical basis. With his experience, musicianship and understanding of theatre, John did not have time for purists or authenticity. His great strength was that his music-making was not distracted by the thought that the music should be performed in 'this' way because it comes between 'this' and 'that' year.

In his attitude towards 'authentic' instruments, John felt that composers like Mozart would have revelled in the sound which modern instruments can make and that concert halls and opera houses today are different buildings from the past. We are listening with twentieth-century ears. The problem is that many conductors treat the historical instruments as normal which is a mistake. For John it was a question of style, of interpretation. He was a complete professional. Therefore it irritated him to waste time with what were, especially in its early days, little more than enthusiastic amateurs who played early instruments. Although the technique of playing these instruments has improved in the last ten to fifteen years, at the time that this movement was developing, John would have tired very quickly of having to constantly go through the same piece because the orchestra could not get the notes right, the intonation correct. In order to work with those early instrument players, especially during that period, one needed to have the patience of Job. Despite the passionate advocacy of his friend Peter Wadland, who through the L'Oiseau Lyre record label has done perhaps more to promote the early music movement, John remained unconvinced.

Whilst not happy with period instruments, John was very enthusiastic about the use of 'sur-titles' and suggested them for a possible production of Handel's Italian opera, *Agrippina* which Dr Hampe proposed to give in Germany (but which would not fit into his schedule). John wrote from New York on 14th October 1983.

> There are several things wrong about translation of comedies. 1. The words are not *really* understood unless there is *spoken* dialogue. 2. There is more than a suggestion of 'provincial theater' about it. 3. If (as often happens with your productions) we are asked to take the production abroad – Edinburgh, Paris, Holland etc. – then the cast have to learn the whole opera again! 4. Handel operas have a 'special velocity' in melodic line, and German *slows this down*. (This is important.)
> Even better *Cendrillon* has been given in NY, at the City Opera,

with '*sur-titles*' in a running translation into English which is projected ABOVE the proscenium arch and was so well done that the audience's laughter *exactly* coincided with the moment in the French text! It is *inexpensive* to do and I am sending on to you the very favourable article in the *New York Times* which describes the method. Would this not be a *very* good thing for *Agrippina*? – it would be a sensation and a FIRST for Europe!

I do *in any case* feel that as a Handel expert (perhaps) I could not really conduct one of his Italian operas in a different language.

Edinburgh had been a time for nostalgia. To most of the participants, their visit to Israel was a landmark for Cologne Opera. The idea had developed between Dr Hampe and some members of the Israel Philharmonic Orchestra who were visiting Cologne. At the time Zubin Mehta had wanted to perform *Tristan* in Israel with the Israel Philharmonic. He wanted Cologne to do the production whilst he prepared the Israeli orchestra but there was a big scandal in Israel during a concert when he programmed some Wagner. It even involved the Israeli Parliament, the Knesset. Clearly Mehta's ideas could not be put to use. However contact had been established and an alternative co-operation between the two institutions materialised.

The Mann Auditorium, home of the Israel Philharmonic, is not an opera house and needed equipment, which Cologne, being the twin city of Tel Aviv, donated, leaving it there. The programme was included in the subscription series of the Israel Philharmonic. Dr Hampe worked out a financial arrangement with the German Foreign Office and the Israel Philharmonic. It was really 'private' enterprise between the two institutions, costing much less than previous normal arrangements. Hamburg and Berlin had been to Israel previously, giving only a few performances. The Cologne arrangement cost about a third but instead of four performances they were able to give eleven or twelve. Apart from the artistic success, it was a great financial success and became the model for many subsequent activities which the German Foreign Office subsidises.

The effect of the visit was incomparable. It is important to realise that, unlike European or American orchestras, the Israel Philharmonic works in isolation, without tours of its neighbouring countries. At that time, programming was usually unadventurous as the orchestra is totally dependent on full houses for its subscriptions. On one occasion when a modern, unknown work was put into one or two programmes, the series was unsold and the whole subscription schedule had to be changed. A national institution, founded in 1936, it is one of the world's busiest orchestras, presenting over two hundred concerts annually in its subscription series alone. Absorbing many immigrants into its ranks, particularly from Eastern Europe, the colour and warmth of its string section is outstanding. Zubin Mehta has been associated with them for over twenty years and with others such as Isaac Stern, Arthur Rubinstein, Leonard Bernstein, a strong relationship developed.

Cologne proposed *Così* and *Wozzeck*. The Israelis demurred about the *Wozzeck*. Dependent on all the performances selling within their subscription series, they were afraid it would not sell but Dr Hampe and John particularly wanted to perform a work which had been forbidden under the Nazi regime, by a composer, Berg, who was persecuted by the Nazis. Compromise was reached. Only three performances were put in the programme. Needless to say *Wozzeck* was sold out before any of the others. The performances were outstanding as, whenever John faced a challenge, he really pulled out all the stops. During one of the rehearsals in Tel Aviv, there was a terrible storm. At a big clap of thunder, John relaxed everybody with, 'Whoever made that terrible noise, please be quiet.' Summing up, Dr Hampe felt that 'the experience of bringing *Wozzeck* for the first time to Israel was one of the great experiences of my life and John's too, I believe.'

John found himself conducting concerts in Israel. Writing to Victor Conway on 23rd November, he attempted to clarify what had become a very complicated exercise in Tel Aviv.

> While conducting quite happily my six scheduled performances with one section of the Israel Philharmonic, Lorin Maazel scheduled to conduct the *other half* in concerts in Haifa and Tel Aviv, cancelled at the *last* minute and in a desperate crisis the Orchestra begged me to give up the smooth-running opera performances (to a deputy conductor), i.e. the last three of my six performances, and take on the whole *six concerts* planned for Maazel – extending my stay by four days here.
>
> The weather is *quite* wonderful here. I sat on the terrace in

sunshine like July. It's a beautiful country – but you want to watch out for 'that Israeli charm' among the people!

The artists were able to do a great deal more sight-seeing than John, who was only free to go to Jerusalem for a day, where he had a splendid lunch looking out at the wonderful panorama of the city and then stopped again for tea, before returning to the Orchestra Guest House. Not only did he approve of the Israeli breakfasts but enjoyed 'what the conductor says goes!'

The Cologne/Israel co-operation was a blueprint for the future. Cosmopolitan John and Dr Hampe introduced the idea of co-operating and co-production in various forms into the German system, which was not prepared for it at all, ten or fifteen years ago. It is now. Even so, Cologne is doing more in this field than any other German house. They have co-operated with Covent Garden many times and still give their productions to San Francisco, not only those which John conducted.

Frustrated by the repertory system in Cologne, John often focused his resentment on the Intendant, Dr Hampe, not feeling animosity towards him personally but the position he represented. The problems of the system are not only endemic to Cologne but exist all over Germany and the stress John felt was created by the other appointments he held.

Conducting *Figaro* in July 1979 in Paris, he was approached by Gerard Mortier and told confidentially that Brussels wanted to establish itself securely as a major centre for the European Community and that money would be available to refurbish and recreate a vibrant opera house, opening with a spectacular production in the autumn of 1981. For John it was like a new love affair.

There could not be a wider difference between the two houses. In Brussels the opera would give about sixty performances a year contrasting with 200 – 220 plus ballet etc. in Cologne, so although the overall budget in Brussels is lower than Cologne, the budget per performance is three to four times as much. In addition, they used the stagione (as opposed to repertory/ensemble) system in which they concentrated on one work for six weeks, rehearsing and leaving it on stage so they could create wonderful effects with lighting and scenery as it did not need to be taken down. For John the difference between Brussels and Cologne was like leaving the sauna and then taking a cold shower.

Germany

Shortly after his opening in the Théâtre de la Monnaie in Brussels he wrote in December 1981 a confidential memorandum to Dr Hampe. The first five years in Cologne had been idyllic. Now he complained about the support received but suggested how they should work in the future. 'The purpose of this memorandum is to explore ideas in which you and I can hold our heads up and feel we are supplying a worthwhile standard of opera to those, still in great numbers in this city, who will gain from our actions.'*

Very popular in Cologne, he had imparted a sense of 'style'. Difficulties for the management were created not so much by the financial crisis but the announcement in 1981 in London of John's forthcoming appointment to the BBC Symphony Orchestra as Chief Conductor. He tried to extricate himself from commitments to Cologne.

> I am sure you will wish to initiate your own Mozart cycle to replace Ponnelle's and it is only right to give you time to plan it with a conductor who has not been so closely associated with the existing cycle . . . I hope we can meet soon after my return. WHATEVER the conflict of my 'other organisations' might be at that period . . . You know there were conflicts with my BBC Symphony dates at that period and now this is complicated much worse by the likelihood of a USA TOURNEE of the Orchestra which could ONLY take place with my direction. You know very well that I am (perhaps) one of the artists in the world who has the *greatest* difficulty to fit in all the dates I am asked to do . . . I think it would be best for us to decide now that my work as Chef Dirigent *should conclude in June 1985*.

Given the opportunity, he forgot his acceptance speech for the Shakespeare Prize ('I do not really understand how so many conductors can accept the directorships of more than one orchestra and often thousands of miles apart.') by accepting appointments in Brussels, London and San Francisco.

With so many appointments it was obvious that he would not and could not give sufficient time to each institution. He had a lack of direction in management. Basil was sick and it is no coincidence that both his work and private life were in chaos. To Cologne the Monnaie from which he withdrew was not the problem. As the San Francisco season was from September to December, he was unable to open the Cologne season for which the first production had a luxurious rehearsal period. Returning

---

*The Financial Situation, p. 365

to Cologne in December, the month in which *Zauberflöte* and Christmas performances for children were given, it was not the best time for rehearsing. Carnival followed with its own special performances and John's main productions were between March and June, his presence concentrated on the second half of the season. This was not balanced. It was a problem for Cologne and a problem for John. The San Francisco appointment created the most difficulties because of communication; not only because of distance and timing as to telephone calls but also because there were clashes in rehearsal time. John tried to answer the criticisms writing to Dr Hampe. 'Personally I don't believe the public care all that much about the opening production *as such* because Cologne is noticeably free from '1st Night' snobbism and all the top-hat-and-tails to be seen for example at the Met.'

However, John wanted to continue his association with Cologne. He and Dr Hampe had developed a good working relationship and he wished to maintain a position in Europe but Cologne became a 'job' and he contracted forward to remain as Principal Guest Conductor from 1989 until 1993, conducting a minimum number of twenty evenings per season.

Writing from Brussels on 9th January 1986 to Dr Hampe, John stressed that he had been giving considerable thought to 'the problems of my work in Cologne and nothing is EASY!' He summed up:

1. First let me *concede* that MANY DIFFICULTIES were caused by the serious illness of Basil Horsfield at the end of 1984. My schedules fell into disarray, I was quite unable to cope with the organisation . . .
2. I saw you some months ago in Cologne when this confusion was at its height and was so desperate I said it would be better for me to *resign*, or take a Sabbatical leave for the Season – but it is not fair to take a Sabbatical from one Theater in order to work elsewhere, of course! You told me you *by no means* wanted this, and begged me to try and free myself from BBC, Brussels or S. Francisco commitments in order to give Cologne more time.
3. With S. Francisco I have the great difficulty that, in accepting the Music Directorship, I want in the next six years to orient my work MORE in USA (where there is still MONEY FOR OPERA!) and moreover S. Francisco is a season, *Sept – Dec*, in which there is *not much room* for manoeuvre in dates!
4. The BBC are always the *first* with dates and consider themselves

to possess the PRIORITY of those who are first in the line: but sometimes we can manipulate the periods. Nevertheless for 1986 – 87 there is an *expensive* USA Tournee which makes changes very difficult.

5. Brussels is much *less* of a problem: after *R'kavalier*, I have NO COMMITMENTS whatever to the Theater, and have *refused* as *Entführung* would have cut into a Cologne period . . .

6. In some respects, '86 – 87 is not too bad from the Köln standpoint. I offered three weeks in November which are no use . . . – a pity.

In December we have *Rosenkavalier*. In April '87 I can undertake *Bohème* with the possibility, not certainty, of *Fidelio* in May. Although I am *not happy* at the limitations of my time in this half of the Season, from the public view JP will be *sufficiently* in the Spielplan.

7. *In '87 – 88* I admit and concede that the opening of '87 was promised to Cologne but we wrote *many months ago* to request a deferment to *'88 – 89* (which is still reserved in fact). Therefore, it was not agreeable to be accused recently of 'sabotaging' the projected *Macbeth*! I was *not* kept informed of the *Macbeth* plans.

[Confirming that in 1988, he would be back in Cologne on 23rd February and remain with them until 4th April it was] one of the longest consecutive unbroken periods I have ever spent in the House! And what has happened? – the *Manon Lescaut* dates were changed without reference to me, so that the première on 27th March permits me only *three* performances before my essential departure! I still think, if that cannot be changed, I should give up this production. Why cannot we have a series of Mozart in the whole of March?

8. It must not be forgotten that with Brussels excluded and the BBC terminating in August '89, '89 – 90 Season should have fewer problems – *if* you and I decide I should continue in Cologne so long! (This can be openly discussed between us of course – my thinking will be coloured by *your* remaining as Intendant??)

9. To conclude, as we have been colleagues and *friends* for so long, I would like eventually to talk to you about the organisation of the Spielplan as it very much affects me. Moreover, I don't always admire the way MY repertory is disposed of to other conductors: WHY, for example, was the successful MOSES AND AARON not fixed in a period I could be available?

I always enjoyed the days when I sat in your office and you discussed with me the Season's operas and the future, writing down the Repertory and inviting consultation. I have *not lost* my enthusiasm for Cologne's artistic progress but sometimes feel my absences are weakening my influence. My happiest operatic moments have *very often* been with *your* productions!

In taking up his appointment, John wanted to conduct the Gürzenich Orchestra in concerts as well as opera and possibly assume control of the orchestra, as well as being Chef Dirigent at the opera.

In a letter of 24th September 1983 to Peter Nestler of Cologne opera, he repeated that he had had a long discussion, after the summer recess, with Michael Hampe, and 'heard from him of the modification of your plans for the future of the Gürzenich Orchester and the music direction of the Oper. I am still happy to assist your plans in any way best for the artistic life of Köln, to make the following *proposals* for your consideration. I have assured myself that these proposals would have the agreement in principle of Michael Hampe.'*

It is customary to refer to music as an international language. However, John felt that whilst performances in international opera houses were becoming standardised, borders were more closed in the concert hall than in many other art forms. Even today if one were to programme a recital of songs by Fauré or Poulenc in Germany, or if one tried to perform a Bruckner Symphony or even Belgian music in France, nobody would attend. Most people are only aware of Italian music from the opera house and only a small number know works by others besides Scarlatti, Vivaldi or Monteverdi. John was very angry on several occasions at the lack of public interest in his frequent attempts to programme English music such as Elgar and the Dances from Tippett's *Midsummer Marriage* and came to realise that people would not accept his wish to promote Delius. He realised the difference in literary taste too. Once, needing to be interviewed for television, he asked Claus Henneberg if he might use his apartment. 'I put him in front of the bookshelf containing the English literature. When it was over Henneberg asked, "Did you know where you were sitting?" "Yes. In front of the dirty diaries of Byron but between us, nobody will know."'

Situated in a cobbled precinct behind the Dom and overlooking

*Proposals for contract, p. 367

the Rhine, the Philharmonie Hall, opened in 1986, gives about three hundred and fifty concerts annually, of which forty are by the Gürzenich Orchestra and twenty-five by the Radio. Every year they hold a benefit concert. Offering his services, John asked Franz Ohnesorg, Director of the Hall, if the money from the 1988 concert on 12th September might benefit AIDS. 'The idea came from him. A friend of mine is head of the University Clinic Centre and I knew of his wonderful work and that he needed money. We visited the hospital together.' John was very concerned and asked that the money should be divided between that hospital and an organisation he knew, 'AIDS Hilfe', a voluntary group concerned with helping sick AIDS patients at home. It was an act of humanity which, together with the musicians, he wanted to carry out.

11

Brussels

The Strehler production of *Figaro* at the Paris Opera in July 1979, with an outstanding cast, was a great success but John was excited about something else. Enthusing about the performances, Gerard Mortier wanted him to reorganise the Théâtre de la Monnaie in Brussels and that the money would be available to make it worthy of a European centre. 'I am so sure that we would realise wonderful things together. I would do everything to make Brussels for you, as Glyndebourne.'

Later, interviewed in San Francisco, John expanded:

The Belgian Government felt that what had been a sleepy, charming House where the standard of performance was such that it would be much easier not to cross the road and visit it, was not quite in line with the pre-eminence of Brussels as a political centre with international visitors. By hiring at the same time a very go-ahead administrator, Gerard Mortier, who had had a distinguished career already, assisting Rolf Lieberman at the Paris Opera and is himself a Belgian, they did entrust a new team with a very difficult spring-cleaning job. When I say spring-cleaning, we actually did that. They hired those special vacuum cleaners which deal with large factories, and something like twenty tons of dust was removed from the stage area alone. It doesn't mean to say that it had never been cleaned – but pretty near that. This was a symbol of the kind of action which went on. From my earliest days as a pupil of the renowned Fritz Busch who was a very hard taskmaster but a wonderful musician and conductor, the insistence on perfection within human possibilities was one which was instilled into me as a young man and a young conductor. This was a very simple criterion to follow in the early discussions.

If any of you have ever visited Brussels, you will know that the Théâtre de la Monnaie is one of the most beautiful examples of the first half of the nineteenth century. It's a ring-shaped arena – not a circular one but horseshoe shaped and it's beautifully decorated in slightly baroque style and it's a charming auditorium to play in. Therefore it seemed right as we started on this rejuvenation process to set operas, early Verdi, Mozart, Rossini and this sort of thing. The orchestra has been greatly increased in size. This was a planning job which I undertook at this particular period five years ago. In my mind psychologically, I was ready to undertake this job with a very gifted administrator who got on well with the politicians which was important.

Gerard Mortier remembered going with John to the Monnaie to see a performance. 'Afterwards Sir John said to me, "You asked me to come to Brussels – you were joking!" I replied that I knew what he meant but that it wasn't a joke. "Well then," he said, "we must contact the unions and talk to them."' Inviting the Orchestra Commission to Paris for lunch, during another series of performances, John convinced them that they must make some concessions and then he and Mortier would help them. It ensured Union collaboration for a new orchestra.

It seems unbelievable but Gerard Mortier, the conductor Sylvain Cambreling and John auditioned some 1,400 musicians. The first two would arrive in Paris on the first train in the morning and take the last train back to Brussels thinking it would never end, that they would never find good players. 'It was very depressing because on the first day we could only find four musicians but slowly we built up an orchestra of ninety-six.' John brought in one of the best London oboe players, Derek Wiggins and Sylvain Cambreling brought in a top cello player from the Orchestra Nationale, in Paris. The cutbacks by the BBC in their provincial orchestras helped in the string sections but the woodwind were mainly Belgian players. As well as the hiring of musicians, John paid considerable attention to the technical aspect, suggesting that Gerard Mortier buy new instruments, himself arriving off the plane with beautiful cymbals that he had bought in London. In order to improve the sound and also the rapport between orchestra and stage, the floor level was raised about forty-five centimetres.

Writing from Houston, where he was conducting *Otello*, John wanted a Verdi cycle, beginning with *Don Carlo*. In Mozart he hoped to start with *Zauberflöte* 'but *Idomeneo* fairly soon.' He also wanted Strauss but esoteric Strauss and a Britten cycle. Regarding contemporary operas, John thought it 'pathetic that the German theatres rush to do world premières by third class composers purely in order to have an Urauffüehrung [world première] . . . we should not waste money in this direction.' He suggested importing the Cologne *Moses*, 'as it is such a simple set and the lighting, I was told, was based on the neon lights of the Belgian autoroutes.'

Even though the orchestra was not completely ready it was decided to open with *Don Carlo* on 10th November 1981. A very distinguished occasion, the British Ambassador, Sir Peter Wakefield, held a party afterwards. Although a Belgian, one of the great artists of our day, José Van Dam had never felt able to sing in his 'home' and it was a mark of the quality for which the Monnaie was aiming that he sang the role of King Philip.

Many people have accused John of being outrageously lazy but Gerard Mortier thought otherwise. 'It didn't mean that he didn't work hard. Some say he was lazy because he was gifted. Lazy? He didn't think it was necessary to work on things that the musicians should learn themselves. The orchestra was there to make music with him, not to learn the notes. He was well disposed to work, not only with the big stars but also with younger singers, as at Glyndebourne and we worked hard together with the stage directors on casting.'

Unrestricted by the technical problems inherent in the German system it was possible for the Monnaie to achieve opera performances with more possibilities of aesthetic success. Although not interested in day to day problems, with his knowledge of running a house John would bring a sense of proportion to questions which arose.

He had the ability to make everybody feel as if he had seen them yesterday. Whenever he arrived he and Gerard Mortier would go out for a wonderful meal 'to work out our plans and collaboration. Sometimes I had to explain my views on opera on the scenic level but he agreed with them and understood. I am not an avant-garde man but we both wanted to get away from the clichés of some stage acting and were not interested in Puccini.' John felt Puccini was 'not refined enough', preferring the great classical works of Mozart, Verdi and Wagner and landmark operas of modern times. 'I would have liked to do *Peter Grimes* with him. It was never possible. As far as Cologne was concerned we didn't really clash.' When John went to San Francisco in 1986, his role in Brussels became that of First Principal Conductor. 'We went on with one new staging every year with plans for a Rossini opera in 1992: *Guillaume Tell* or *La Donna del Lago* were the two we discussed.'

John became enthralled with Brussels, with its wide boulevards and squares, its pavement restaurants and cafés reminiscent of the *belle époque* of Paris: the old city with its narrow cobblestone streets; its arcades with elegant boutiques and rival *confiseries* enticing and seducing the senses with the smell of chocolate. Suddenly he evinced an interest and a taste for Art Nouveau and Art Deco. He found a home in Art Deco style reminding him of his suite at the Savoy in London, a favourite hotel. At the Savoy he insisted on showing guests the huge shower unit, just as he revelled in his black marble Art Deco bathroom in Brussels.

At the Monnaie his office was in the old building. As it was not renovated, it had complicated security measures. There were many small windows with a rope and he was told that if there was a fire he should throw the rope out of the window and use it to jump out. So there was a big joke at Brussels Opera that he had to fly.

Although John did not conduct many operas, they were all new productions. In what was a 'new' house, as the presiding spirit he gave it a sense of style. Very popular, everyone felt honoured by his presence. There was never anything snobbish about him. Yannick Vermeirsch, Press and Public Relations Officer of the Théâtre commented: 'How simple he was compared to many other people who are less important but are so much more pretentious. He had every reason to be pretentious but he wasn't. I remember giving a party at my house for people of my own age and said that he was welcome to come but I didn't expect him. He came. People who were impressed by him found it made them uneasy – he knew how to talk to them, liking to talk about things other than music, such as films, theatre, travelling. At a dinner party he was the one who kept the conversation going even though he had more reason than anyone else to be exhausted.' John would draw back immediately if anyone was artificial and being polite for its own sake. Yannick Vermeirsch thought, 'people didn't deserve so much generosity from him. Always inviting one to go to eat with him, he would then be so immensely grateful when once in a while I would invite him to my place or a restaurant. It was embarrassing.' They had some telephone contact when John left

255

but less in the last year. 'Perhaps he sensed that maybe I didn't feel too close to some of the people he was with at the end.'

Through the years John conducted many different casts in *Così*, some of them absolutely top casts and some of them examples of casting at its weakest. He liked the way the pairs assembled, dissembled and then, at the end, reassembled or not according to the producer's whim. He liked the game playing, the deceptions, the wit and as in Rossini, he liked the changing moods where one is suddenly moved from a purely cynical comment or aria from a Despina or a Don Alfonso into a Ferrando singing 'Un aura amorosa' (My love is a flower) where the whole mood of the opera changes and it was this quicksilver, mercurial ability to mix elements and change which he was so good at conveying through the orchestra. This needed his two great qualities: professionalism and sophistication. In the lightness of touch, the gentle irony, it was the affectionate regard for human frailty, very much part of his own character, which was most evident in any performance John ever conducted of *Così*.

Recalling his relationship with Fritz Busch, he explained to Gerard Mortier how much he had been influenced by and discussed every detail of the score with his mentor. Concerned about the proposed Brussels *Così* for June 1984 because the producer, Luc Bondy, having come from the spoken theatre, had only worked on a couple of modern operas such as *Wozzeck*, John asked him to come specifically to New York. In Peter Brown's spacious apartment overlooking Central Park, he offered the producer a glass of white wine. Luc Bondy gained the impression that he drank a great deal of white wine, that he was a man who enjoyed very much the *'plaisirs de la vie'*, that he was 'hedonist, from the world of ancient Greece'. They spent the afternoon talking only in vague, general terms about *Così*. He formed the impression that he had been asked to New York 'just so that we could get to know and understand each other, rather than actually talking about what we were going to do'.

Later, in Brussels, Luc Bondy became very worried as John was not there a great deal during the musical rehearsals. When it was on stage 'he arrived and told me in English that he was surprised because the movements I asked the singers to do would not be easy for a conductor as they were sometimes standing far apart'.

Gradually a chemistry developed between them. Contrary

to his previous opinion the producer found that when John conducted he had an eighteenth-century rapport with *Così*. Having conducted the opera so many times, at first he seemed superficial. Slowly he himself became part of that music, became Don Alfonso himself. The musicians and stage became one and he was Don Alfonso orchestrating the action. Conducting that music was not routine. As it began to please him more and more, it became more fluid and the musicians sensed this and truly loved to play for him. Luc Bondy commented: 'The slight touch of decadence of Don Alfonso, giving the impression of boredom, his own way of life, drink, the boys but above all the love of music – one heard all these things in that *Così*.'

It was the first time John had seen such an approach to the opera. Previously the two sisters, Fiordiligi and Dorabella had been treated as rather grand ladies but Luc Bondy made them seem like two seventeen-year-old girls in love. The first scene, initiating the intrigue between Don Alfonso and the two young men, took place in the auditorium (the Royal Box). It was then acted out on the stage. The extraordinary set with a continuous cyclorama of seascape, then landscape, unwinding throughout the performance, emphasised what was happening. The singers made their entrances up a ramp placed in the orchestra pit, as if the story grew out of the music. At the beginning, the young girls, unaware of their sexuality and the truth of their relationships, momentarily confused their fiancés, stood apart and did not even touch them.

It is customary for the role of Fiordiligi, the soprano, to be the focus of attention but Luc Bondy stressed the importance of Dorabella, who has the first solo aria in the opera. More mature by the end of the opera, the two women were condemned by convention as a house descended, surrounding and trapping them. The singers were enthusiastic and John responded.

Considered the Monnaie's most successful production, revived frequently, it was taken to Nanterre and later Vienna for the Wiener Festwochen. As part of their tribute to John, the revival of *Così* conducted by Sylvain Cambreling was dedicated in his memory.

For John, Mozart at Brussels would not have been complete without *Idomeneo* and he wrote a full introduction himself for the Brussels Opera magazine in September 1982. Recalling the first time he heard the music at the BBC and the Glyndebourne performances under Fritz Busch, he discussed previous performances.

Carl Ebert had felt the pivot of the opera was the promise that Idomeneo made to Neptune, to sacrifice the first living thing that he met and that that person was his own son, Idamante. 'Ebert was convinced of the difference in psychological and physical impact of this confrontation on the spectator between a young man or a woman in travesti – as well as trying to put it into the context of the eighteenth century.' He was pleased that the producer with whom he had worked on *Don Carlo*, Gilbert Deflo, was in accord in using the Viennese (tenor) version. However, he was unhappy that the stage was covered in rice. John wrote to him constructively in September 1982 before the première.

> Because after that (however well or badly IDOMENEO may be received) opinions become 'coloured' this way or that, this is the last moment of *professional* detachment one can have.
>
> I am now concerned solely with the eventual *revival* of IDOMENEO, to try to put to you my point of view. You MUST NOT think that I am always taking a contrary position to you: especially with a work I know as well as IDOMENEO, I very much like to be stimulated by the Stage Director to new approaches and different presentations. Thus with DON CARLO you created a deeply impressive stage presentation working from a very *untraditional* approach to a Verdi opera: with strong principal artists you succeeded in bringing out the elemental power of the opera. But in IDOMENEO, after beginning so well with the principals (all of whom found your ideas stimulating) you gradually ploughed yourself into a deeper and deeper furrow in the soil; pinning your artists to the dead centre of the stage; utterly restricting their freedom of movement (this too when many of the arias are passionate utterances of the like Mozart scarcely dared to attempt ever again!); worse still, NEGATING THEIR CHARACTERS, so that the public cannot be sure what they represent. For example, what real importance did you give to Elettra? You have merely made her a dark, nearly invisible, lady, moving onto the stage, with vague indications of her jealousies, rages and *strength* of personality! Naturally, by this method, in the most *violent* aria Mozart ever wrote, everyone on the stage looks on motionless as rather pained, silent statues. I admit the part is too low for her; but it is useless to point to the success of her final aria: NO ONE can fail in that!
>
> I do ask why have you been so constricted, as though opera seria was a worthwhile concept, when Mozart was striving with all his soul to break its bonds like the chains of the Trojans?! I tell you frankly, you have threatened *half the impact* of the opera by treating the chorus (in *this* opera) as classical, motionless commentators – a

thousand times no: they are the protagonists opposed to Idomeneo himself! No wonder I have been criticising the chorus master about their PALLID singing . . . 'o voto tremendo' must be a great *physical* outburst with its tremendous music and there they are in 'choral society' formation as throughout the opera!

Another great objection I have is the uninteresting treatment of 'Nettuno s'onori'. I feel you could not recover from the cancellation of the Ballet (which you were quite right to cut) and the 'family photo' end which you originally planned. But it is clear that this Chorus is a *hymn of praise and thanks* to Neptune for the salvation of Idomeneo: in the *absence* of the king, who seems to be engaged elsewhere? Had you brought on Idomeneo and Idamante, you could have shown the troubled feelings of the king, who is forced by the public occasion to see his son in a formal setting. Omitting this makes the end of Mozart's first act very weak (which musically it is anyway!).

You have been ill-served by the stage set:

1. All the doors are too narrow and insignificant, so that you are in trouble with the chorus exits and entrances;
2. The IMPOSSIBLE PLEXIGLASS, which distorts reflections from every seat in la Monnaie. It is typical of modern stage 'technique' (so-called) that we are *forced* to look at this piece of expensive nonsense, just because of one good idea – that we can see other fantasies through the glass, such as Ilia's garden, the shipwreck (very good) or those peculiar figurants during the 'devastation'; yet we are denied the *monster* which Mozart wanted – why? All these effects could be seen *just as well* through a gauze at the back. I do counsel you to scrap the plexiglass, perhaps just keeping the Pediment, which does not reflect, on the revival.

And is '*that rice*' worth the trouble, hampering as it does all movement?

But the main aim of my proposal to you for next time is:
   a) to vitalise and liberate the soloists and
   b) to use the chorus as actors (Carl Ebert used to go to every singer and tell him what his reactions should be, how he should move, etc.).

I do appreciate that you had not enough time – but next time we *must* give you more!

As always the love he bestowed upon the score convinced the Brussels public. He revelled in the music. Whilst it will never be popular like *Zauberflöte* and the da Ponte operas, Mozart lavished seemingly more on this score than on others. There is more in the bass line and melody, with harmonies more worked out, more 'dense' than anything later. Interested in all *Idomeneo* performances, John sent a telegram of good wishes to Sir George Christie at Glyndebourne for their new production: 'For another beloved *Idomeneo*. May your monsters be small ones.'

He had had great hopes in Germany but it was in Brussels that he realised his dreams for Strauss with performances of *Capriccio* (1983) and *Rosenkavalier* (1986). The Monnaie later took the John Cox production of *Capriccio*, with Felicity Lott as the Countess, to the Chatelet in Paris. With Dame Kiri Te Kanawa as the Countess and new costumes, it was repeated in San Francisco and London under different conductors. John Cox recalled going to Brussels at John's request. 'He knew it was a good production, liked the concept and persuaded Mortier to take me because I don't think I typified Mortier's particular brand of director. John understood that it couldn't be done on the same intimate scale as Glyndebourne, as indeed did I, which is why we had a much grander look at the piece; more elaborate and richer, to keep it as beguiling on the eye as possible for a relatively long spell of looking at the same set.'

The Countess, Felicity Lott, had started in the Glyndebourne Chorus in 1976 and then, when John left, took soprano leads in *Figaro, Rosenkavalier, Arabella* and *Intermezzo*. 'There was obviously more social life at Glyndebourne than in Brussels where everybody returned to their little rented places.' John invited her and Sarah Walker, who was singing Clairon, to dinner and sometimes took them out to tea. 'I've never been in a cast of *Capriccio* that hasn't got on well together. It's that type of piece. He always had a few people around to cook for him and produce exotic meals. Wonderful wine! I was very touched to be asked to dinner.'

The times they worked together are marvellous memories for her. 'He was very loyal, very supportive. Not a beating conductor – all very smooth and liquid. The accompaniment would flow along beautifully and you fitted in over the top. It was wonderful to be so free and not have somebody saying "Will you follow this", which is very inhibiting and unmusical. Music isn't written like that – it can't be divided up into chunks. His music was quick-witted too. I was very much in awe of him; he wasn't the sort of person that I thought I could hug. For me conductors are somewhere "up there" and I am somewhere "down there".'

The Monnaie was ideal for *Capriccio*. Not a huge theatre, the voices do not need to ring out. A singer does not need to force their voice and John was able to reveal, in a relaxed and easy manner, the full beauty, warmth and lyricism of the score.

Rosenkavalier, in a very beautiful production by Gilbert Deflo, was the first time Felicity Lott sang the Feldmarschallin. The theatre was reopening after work to the fly tower. At the first dress rehearsal, she remembered making her entrance in Act III in black, wearing a black veil in order not to be recognised. 'I looked a bit silly and when I came down to the front of the stage he said, "My dear, you can't possibly wear that, you look like somebody from Majorca advertising cheap holidays!" He was very worried about that costume.'

The production was televised and a huge TV screen put in the cobblestone Place outside the theatre. It was deferred so those who were not singing in Act II went outside and watched Act I.

John split the preparation of *Meistersinger* in June 1985 with Hilary Griffiths, his assistant from Cologne. One day, lunching together after morning rehearsal at a table outside a very chic restaurant, John noticed 'the group of Italians at the next table have gone off without paying!' There was a wonderful scene which John adored, lots of shouting from the waiters reminiscent of the end of Act II in *Bohème*. They were football fans and it was the day of the Heissel Stadium disaster. Returning for a scenic rehearsal, they heard a noise outside. It was like a mob chanting, strange and ominous. It was nothing serious, just rival groups of fans. What had happened at lunchtime was fairly good-natured. Hilary Griffiths recalled: 'I went to one place to rehearse the strings and John went to another with the winds. Suddenly he came over, "Stop the rehearsal - now! We must go, something awful has happened." We took a taxi back to his place and heard the news. We were stunned.'

As in Cologne, John took *Meistersinger* away from the German tradition, making it more *bel canto*. Although attention focused on the performances of José Van Dam singing his first Hans Sachs and Karita Mattila, enchanting as Eva, John drew warm applause for the clarity and lightness he brought to the score, one reviewer noting the marked improvement in the Opéra National Orchestra.

The San Francisco appointment caused complications in Cologne. Problems of a different nature brought dissension in

Brussels. John, loyal to Basil Horsfield, was unwilling publicly to blame the latter's illness as one of the reasons for his break with Brussels. Originally he welcomed Sylvain Cambreling's assistance, writing on 23rd December 1981 to Dr Hampe, after a performance of *Wozzeck*. 'What Sylvain Cambreling did with this (inexperienced) orchestra was a revelation: I have not pressed him for something in Köln because it might be thought I was favouring him just because of Brussels. But there is *no doubt* of his talent and we should try to get him for a suitable opera, as soon as possible!' With John's peripatetic appointments, Sylvain Cambreling was shouldering not only the major operas but also the concerts. John became resentful. The break with Brussels was inevitable. He wrote to Gerard Mortier on 27th January 1988, suggesting how to handle the press announcement.

> Before the passage of time and possible developments at La Monnaie may confuse the issues, I think as a matter of order in the public view, we should devise a statement for the Press regarding the conclusion of my contract as Directeur de la Musique at Opéra National. I would think it appropriate for this to be announced before I conduct the concert in Brussels on 5th June 1988. You will remember that one and a half years ago, when I had rounded off five years of collaboration with you, in the production of *Rosenkavalier*, I suggested it was no longer realistic for me to hold the title as we had then no concrete future operatic plans together. However, in view of the problems you were encountering politically and economically, I had no wish to give any impression of disunity and we carried on, I must admit sometimes in an atmosphere of some bewilderment in the house, especially on the part of the orchestra, who could not make out what my position had become.
>
> I think now that an entire Season has passed without my directing an opera, it is the moment to make the situation clear and both sides can do so with excellent grace by referring to my participation in the 1988 – 89 Season in the performances of *Norma*.

He suggested a possible draft for the Press Announcement.★

After an outstanding concert performance of Bellini's *I Capuleti e i Montecchi*, John wanted to conduct *Norma*. The concert performance in 1988 with Sharon Sweet as the Druidess was the last work he gave to the Brussels public.

★Draft Press Announcement, p. 369.

Summing up, John Higgins thought that John's European career did not get sufficient coverage in the British press.

> People tend to forget that he had a longstanding and very professional relationship with Michael Hampe in Cologne. The two men together really put Cologne on the map. To those on the international opera circuit, Germany tends to mean Hamburg, Munich and Berlin but there is also this Opera House in Cologne which under Hampe and Pritchard became famous for its Mozart performances and indeed in bringing a large number of Mozart singers to the fore.
>
> The other town is of course Brussels and it's a source of regret to me that I didn't go to Brussels more often. Maybe his work there was also underestimated. *Meistersinger,* an opera that one does not associate with him was a very, very considerable success which went virtually unrecorded in his native Britain. There was also a pretty impressive *Rosenkavalier* which of course goes back to the Richard Strauss love developed by Glyndebourne. *Rosenkavalier* and Pritchard were pretty firmly welded together. The stroke for this welding came out in that *Rosenkavalier* at the Monnaie. In an opera house which is on our doorstep, with an Englishman as its Music Director, did the English critics go across to see his performances? No they didn't. I think we have far too powerful a vision of John Pritchard in Europe conducting Mozart, Mozart and more Mozart, when in fact he was doing a very considerable range of operas.
>
> He was insufficiently honoured operatically in his own country but if you went to San Francisco – to the Opera House – he was a very considerable hero. The same applied in Cologne and Brussels. I feel that insufficient recognition was given to him after he left Glyndebourne.

In Brussels he was well known, liked, easily recognised. Gerard Mortier summed up: 'Mozart was loved more by his musicians than his public. He composed music for them and not for the public. I think that's the way it should be. You should be a conductor for the musicians and then the public can like you or not. It's what you are giving of yourself and the public who came to the performances liked it.'

Together with Gerard Mortier and Sylvain Cambreling his achievement is a simple statistic. When John started in Brussels subscriptions numbered 1,200. When he left these had grown to 15,000.

12

BBC Symphony Orchestra

'I AM A NATIVE, ROOTED HERE'†

When John left Glyndebourne to commence his 'Wanderjahre', it was thought by many in Britain that careerwise he had stayed there too long. Continuing to work with the LPO as well as the other London orchestras, he conducted the Hallé Orchestra regularly. During the late seventies John was attracted to the possibility of a position with the Bournemouth Symphony Orchestra which had London engagements and made six records annually.

Through the years he conducted interesting programmes at the Proms. Giving many first performances, his name had become synonymous with Britten, Tippett and Iain Hamilton. No less was his commitment to the work of Sir William Walton and he was considered 'one of the outstanding interpreters' of *Belshazzar's Feast* particularly. On 20th August 1968 he had shared the podium with the composer when the latter conducted the BBC Symphony Orchestra for his *Johannesburg Festival* overture and *Façade* suite, with John conducting the Violin Concerto in B minor with Ida Haendel as soloist and *Belshazzar's Feast* completing the programme. In a Royal Philharmonic Society concert with the BBC SO on 1st April 1970, he presented a concert version of Weber's romantic opera *Oberon* which did not meet with critical approval. John had wanted to conduct it at Covent Garden in the sixties. Maria Callas had been interested but as she was always keen to give a work in the original, in this case, English, it presented problems.

†*Peter Grimes*

By 1970, the high professional standards of David Munrow and his Early Music Consort and the Carl Dolmetsch Ensemble were attracting larger audiences to baroque music. However, uncertainty was voiced about the BBC's new policy towards contemporary music. The Third Programme, 'one of the greatest contributions to culture made by any country since the war' (John Warrack, *Sunday Telegraph*, 25th January 1970), decided to widen its audience by broadcasting more mainstream standard repertoire. The performance of Iain Hamilton's *Circus* commissioned by the BBC with a first performance on 22nd January 1970, prompted the writer to echo the concern felt by musicians that as it was safer and cheaper to broadcast recordings by the great international musicians of the day rather than live performances by young artists, they and young composers would find it harder to find a forum. Not only composers but young artists at the beginning of their career owe John a debt of gratitude.

Dame Kiri Te Kanawa remembered singing the Strauss *Four Last Songs* with him in a BBC Gala. 'Basically they began my career. My mother had died whilst I was learning them. Every stage of my life has been around that particular Strauss and death and at the time John and I talked about death.' In remembering the man together with that music, she feels that the association is what makes 'the music so wonderful – that I did my very first performance with someone I adored'.

After a concert with the BBC Symphony Orchestra on 7th April 1976 at the Royal Festival Hall, he hit the headlines. It was a difficult programme comprising the Walton *Capriccio Burlesco*, followed by John's friend, Hans Werner Henze's Piano Concerto no. 2 with the Bartók Concerto for Orchestra in the second half. On his schedule John wrote, '*Note* – During *this* concert JP taken ill, completed the performance with difficulty and was operated on in emergency during the night for peritonitis.' The 'myth' relates that an ambulance was waiting outside the Festival Hall which whisked him to hospital as he finished conducting. Actually his doctor, Gordon Atkinson, had seen him that morning in his apartment in King Street when John referred to stomach-ache, that probably it was caused by something eaten in a restaurant but that he 'had to do the concert' as there was nobody else to do it. His medical friend, Ian Weir, was staying with him and if anything happened, he was in good hands.

That evening, listening to the announcement of the radio

broadcast, his doctor believed that he had recovered. However, having attended his concert in Glasgow, John's cousin, Eric Shaylor, was bewildered when he heard the live broadcast of the same programme from London a few days later. At 2am Dr Atkinson was called. Diagnosing peritonitis, he immediately called a surgeon and assisted at the operation in St George's Hospital, Hyde Park Corner. Dr Atkinson remembered visiting him the next morning. 'He was sitting up in bed, his toupee slightly crooked, which suggested that he wasn't 100 per cent. The surgeon could not believe that someone could have conducted a concert with all this going on.' Hans Werner Henze commented: 'I do not know anybody else who would have done that but with his sense of duty, responsibility and solidarity, he knew this performance meant a great deal for the progress of my music in Britain. It was amazing. I understand from Paul Crossley, the soloist, that the performance was full of panache and *very* fast. John wanted to get to the end!'

As early as 1970, John was inveighing against the poor subsidy meted out at home, comparing it to the system of private patronage encouraged by tax concessions in the United States of America. It was not only the financial but the social anomalies that he felt were relevant. In a long talk on the BBC radio on 'Artistic Patronage' he remarked: 'I have been gratified (in America) that a symphony orchestra conductor is called "maestro" even by bell-boys and among people who wouldn't cross the road to go to a concert.' Working regularly with the BBC Symphony Orchestra, as it was more secure in terms of subsidy, it was understandable that he should prefer to have an appointment in 1978 as their guest conductor.

Founded in 1930, the largest symphony orchestra in Britain, the BBC Symphony Orchestra was the first in which musicians were employed with full-time contracts. Under Sir Adrian Boult it set new standards especially in the field of contemporary music. John's appointment delighted the older man who wrote warmly on 22nd September 1978.

> It is great that the BBC looks like really putting the clock back, and going back to 1930 – and I want to send heartiest congratulations. Did you know that when Hitler (1932) [*sic*] went into Vienna and ejected Bruno Walter, I went to Reith and suggested that Walter should be engaged for six months to help train the orchestra but Allen (who was the Chairman of the Music Advisory Committee)

vetoed it 'because they were doing quite nicely as they were!!' And *look* at all those foreigners since!!

May I just give you a word of advice? Don't let the BBC SO give you too much work – I did and I think we should have done better with a little less – it would have enabled me to see *always* that every show was better than the last and I do feel that is important. But you know all about that sort of thing I'm quite sure – opera houses are a bit tempting in that sort of way!

Best of luck and let's hope you'll soon be absolutely on top there and no more Russians.

This needs no answer – I just wanted to wave the Union Jack a bit!

Remembering the effect Sir Adrian's conducting had on John as a young 'prommer' at the Queen's Hall one realises the many qualities they shared. The older man had a remarkably wide repertoire and had encouraged and promoted the work of the then contemporary British composers; Elgar, Holst and Vaughan Williams. In his integrity, he never acted in a temperamental manner on or off the platform. Forced to retire as conductor of the BBC Symphony Orchestra at sixty by the Corporation's rules, the LPO had been delighted to engage him and he continued to work with them, accepting the office of President in 1965. During this period he liaised closely with John. Perceptive commentators hoped that, unlike Sir Adrian, John would not have to wait until he reached his eighties before the British public truly appreciated him.

The following year, Sir Adrian wrote again on 29th March 1979. 'I am indeed touched that you are coming over specially to do those LPO concerts to celebrate my birthday (90th). I'm pretty well under the weather now (top half not too bad but legs are hopeless – I can't stand or walk!) so I will ask you to do the kindness of also thanking orchestra soloists and chorus as well as any "back room boys" who may have helped to boost the performance – I am sure it will be *most* impressive under your direction.'

Then, in a final letter of 18th April 1979: 'Eric [Bravington] has just rung me up and told me that you made a speech before you conducted those concerts and so I feel I must send another line to thank you for doing this as well as going through that great work twice. Well, once again I say thank you very much indeed and also I say again – please do not dream of acknowledging this – you have done a very kind act and it is I who say thank you.'

Taking up his appointment, John revived several pieces from his repertoire, such as Maxwell Davies' *Second Fantasia on an In Nomine of John Taverner* on 21st January 1980.

In John's successful working relationships there was respect on both sides; not simply because people were colleagues, fellow musicians but because there was never any question musically. Everything was always possible. Very often John neglected the detail, it was not in his character, so he needed to trust those who were working with him to insert them. His talent was for architecture, not breaking down a work into bars or individual notes. Rodney Friend recalled that in all the years he worked with him, the conductor never chose the wrong tempi. The music was always natural; a natural *rallentando* or *accelerando* and a natural dynamic. His strength was in his capacity to produce something that sounded absolutely natural but with a hundred people. 'Eyes, to hands, to orchestra was enormously fast. It hit the brain in a very major way. It was never a problem nervewise or technically, however complicated the rhythm.' Somehow, even when John played harpsichord recitatives, there was always time for a smile and a nod to those players or performers who had done something well.

In his professionalism, John prided himself on his reliability as a timekeeper. Therefore he was surprised to receive a letter from a listener expressing annoyance that his concert on Radio 4 of 15th May 1979 overran the time allowed, delaying the weather forecast which featured an important frost warning. She added that many years ago Sir Malcolm Sargent had had the same problem and she had made some suggestions. Firstly, that there should be an alarm watch, a light to signal time or one of the orchestra to draw his attention when he was loitering. She did not know which he had employed but Sir Malcolm did manage after her letter to end on time and the concerts were broadcast on Radio 3 which was where the writer felt they should be. She appreciated that the BBC could fade John out but that he had been paid well for a full performance and eight minutes was a long time to lop off. The writer wondered if the musicians were trying to get paid for an extra hour and that in an amateur bad timekeeping is understandable but not in a professional. Finally, she commented that during a large part of his life they referred, in a not very complimentary manner, to 'the late Malcolm Sargent'.

The question of 'tempo', metronome markings or the lack

of them, was considered seriously by John on more than one occasion. In an essay, part of which was first broadcast in 1971, he appreciated that the question of 'tempo', the speed at which music is performed, is vital.★ John believed, 'It's Mozart who best repays study to see if we can establish any useful guidelines to speed.' Without the invention of the metronome, Mozart 'relied on basic Italian terms and he must have thought, in a fairly small and aristocratic musical world of the eighteenth century, where style was rather like dress – a question of the good taste of gentlemanly people – (later stated by Wagner) that "the inner content of the music is sufficient to establish fairly exactly, the pace".'

He had been irritated, after a Promenade concert with the BBC SO, by a Birmingham reporter's recent criticism of his choice of tempo for the first movement of the Mozart Symphony no. 40 in G minor. It had been compared disparagingly to the 'cheerful, uncomplicated attitude of the pop version which gave a quite artificial impression of greater speed and what the critic found dragging and perhaps dreary in the concert performance, was occasioned – I admit it proudly – by my view of this symphony as an exceptionally serious piece with strong undertones of pain and resignation. Einstein described this symphony as "this fatalistic piece of chamber music", and descriptive of the "abyss of the soul", Otto Young spoke of it as a "piercing cry of anguish".'

John was to feel actual anguish rehearsing *Peter Grimes* in 1981 in Paris. Amongst musicians there is a saying: 'If you can work in Paris, you can work anywhere in the world.' The head of L'Opéra, Bernard Lefort wanted to present the Covent Garden production of *Grimes* which had not been seen in Paris since 1948 when Covent Garden, on tour, gave two performances of it. Then home to Paris Opera, the Palais Garnier with a relatively small auditorium (1,800 seats), nevertheless has a wider, higher stage and the imported sets needed to be adapted. It was reported that a language problem between the British producer, lighting designer, the Paris Opera Chorus and stage staff complicated matters in a house notorious for its out of date machinery and personnel, chosen by the unions rather than the technical director. In one instance a rehearsal was halted for forty-five minutes until

★ Tempo, p. 370

the correct man could be found to put some nails in a carpet whilst eight other stagehands stood around. During the soliloquy John wanted the lights to dim but the lighting people could never get it on cue. Finally, in desperation, he said, 'I'll do it myself.' During rehearsal, when the soliloquy was reached, touching the rheostat he received a devastating electric shock, was flung into the air, crashed to the floor of the pit and finally was taken out on a stretcher. Carried through the stage door, he turned to the doorman, 'I always thought you used the guillotine in France, not the electric chair!'

A highly respected and popular figure abroad, John's performances in London were not such a triumph. Elisabeth Söderström recalled her own anguish during a concert with John at the Royal Albert Hall with the BBC SO on 15th April 1981, singing the Berlioz song cycle *Nuits d'Été* (op. 7), 'one of my most horrible experiences ever'. Arriving from Sweden in the spring, the leaves were just appearing, something to which she is allergic. With a sore throat, rehearsing in the difficult acoustics of the Albert Hall did not help, so after the dress rehearsal, she tried all sorts of medicines which made her throat even drier. 'I didn't quite realise my problems until I walked onto the podium. It was a live broadcast and after two minutes I felt that my tongue was stuck in my mouth. If it had been a normal concert I would have said "I'm sorry I have to go out and find some water" but I thought, "I can't stop the broadcast." I forgot every word and every tune, I just had to survive and it was sheer horror. I had sung the piece before, enjoyed it tremendously and I love it, so the problems were not on that level. It was just practical problems.' There was rather lame applause. Afterwards as she said goodbye to John, she apologised. 'I'm so terribly sorry.' 'Well Elisabeth,' he replied, 'may I suggest that next time you sing this piece you learn it by heart.' He said this because she had brought the score with her. 'Another conductor would have scolded you or ignored you but he just suggested that next time I should learn it by heart. A review said, "We don't believe that this was a concert that Miss Söderström would like to remember in the future" but that's a concert I shall remember for ever. Unfortunately, it was the last time I sang in concert with John.'

There was a complicated situation at the BBC SO in the early eighties. The Austrian Chancellor, Kreisky, wrote to Mr Brezhnev asking for Gennadi Rozhdestvensky, Chief Conductor of the

BBC SO, for the Wiener Sinfonica and the BBC SO had a difficult time trying to get the Soviets to extend his contract. When finally Rozhdestvensky had made up his mind not to continue, the BBC's Controller of Music, Robert Ponsonby was able to ask John who fortunately had a titular association with the Orchestra, to step into his shoes. 'John was able to say and I was able to accept that he could do enough to justify the appointment soon. Then obviously we developed more.' Robert Ponsonby remembers their meeting, having a Chinese meal together, just off Mayfair. 'He said, "You know you mustn't expect me to bring you a good press." He knew what the score was where the critics were concerned, who are themselves corrupted by the superhype of the big recording boys. Not all, but a lot of the younger ones were and are unable to appreciate natural musicianship at its most humble and professional; humble in regard to serving the composer.'

In Brussels, John had created an orchestra. Now he understood that his task would be one of recreation, of orchestral retraining. It is a long process, miracles do not happen overnight. The essential clause in his contract 'to undertake the building of programmes' prompted him to present a Memorandum on 1st September 1981, attempting to devise a recognisable direction to the repertoire.

1. a) Works other than Contemporary which in an artistic sense are NECESSARY at this point for orchestra building or training – for example, the general eighteenth-century repertoire, espec. Haydn and Mozart. JP with suitable Guest Conductors will expect to give particular attention to this vital department.

   b) It will be more difficult with JP than with Gennadi to give a 'personal slant' to the composition of programmes, for the reason that our Russian colleague has at his back the immense realm of Slavic music, much of it already known and appreciated by British audiences and presenting the conductor with any number of interesting 'sidestream' works which he can graciously introduce at concerts. (Thus, to take an example to hand, it is easy to schedule *Swan Lake* Act II at a PROM and obtain an ecstatic reaction from public and Press, but frankly if this were in the charge of practically ANY British conductor, the most likely adjective used would be 'routine'! Moreover, a certain British self-disparagement makes us grateful and flattered when Gennadi ventures into the British scene, with major works (Britten, Tippett, Elgar and so on).)

c) I do not mention these attitudes with rancour, but merely to point out the difficulties of presenting a British conductor, who has in his own right a very large European repertoire. In a similar light to the public eye to JP himself, the position is complicated by his own great interest in Russian music, instanced by successful performances over the years of Shostakovich, Prokofiev and Rachmaninov. It may be difficult in programming to give these works a sabbatical period but we must avoid 'confrontation' with memories of Gennadi's own performances.

d) JP's own solution to these problems would be, *generally* speaking only, to make a habit of scheduling 4-item programmes as opposed to the universal trend towards one item on 'mammoth' works. The latter he would reserve for the big choral concerts where applicable but the concept (of which Sir Thomas was a great begetter) of inserting a lesser-known fifteen to twenty minute work after an overture, at once makes available a whole host of works, perhaps not absolute masterpieces, which nevertheless need careful preparation, interest the orchestra and public and (if given in the second half) force the critics to stay after the interval. I can instance many items of French provenance which to my certain knowledge have not been played in the Festival Hall for years. Another example – I wonder (though I have not checked) how long it is since the BBC Orchestra gave the César Franck Symphony at a public concert? The choice of this as a main work necessitates careful planning of the rest of the programme on 4-item lines.

e) Finally, JP thinks that an analysis of the programmes of Adrian Boult over the years might be interesting and instructive. After all, he trained the original BBC Orchestra and JP is in sympathy with his humane but exigent approval. What we need to do is present the new Chief Conductor's extreme catholicity of musical taste in the most favourable light: it will be hard to invent a genuine title for his type of programme; they should however emerge as non-egoistic exercises, championing intensely the eminence of the BBC Orchestra itself.

John sent greetings to the players. 'I would have liked so much to be there with you when the announcement of my appointment has been made but it was impossible. Nevertheless, you must know there is no job in the entire musical world which could give me as much pleasure as this one. I am very happy and I hope

John with the author in the kitchen at Nenfré, 1984.

John with a 'sixty-fifth' birthday cake modelled on the score of Brahms' First Symphony before conducting at the Brahms Festival, The Barbican, 1986.

Photo courtesy of the BBC
Photograph: Kenneth Saunders

John, as conductor of the First Night of the Proms, meeting Andrew Davis, conductor of the Last Night of the Proms, at Broadcasting House, 1988.

Photo courtesy of BBC

With Sir John Tooley and Margaret Price, receiving the Covent Garden medal after the final performance of *Norma,* 1987.

Photograph: Featureflash

Thanksgiving in Palm Springs, California with Bill Oakes, Terry MacInnis and Peter Brown, 1989.

Talking to the audience at the Last Night of the Proms, John's last UK performance, September 1989.

Photograph: Alex von Koettlitz

Sir John Pritchard

Bottom photograph: Godfrey MacDomnic

you will be. I look forward to our next meeting – meantime be good!' They cabled back: 'Looking forward as always making music with you. Have tried being good being careful failed both. However backing you to the hilt. Welcome BBC SO.' No less welcoming were the letters from composers, their widows or publishers. Throughout his appointment they would endeavour to interest him. He replied to their letters personally.

Rodney Friend, returning to London from working with the New York Philharmonic joined Bela Dekany as leader.

The programmes for a tour of Australia and Hong Kong beginning 2nd May 1982 were well prepared, John having conducted at the Royal Festival Hall on 7th April the Britten Violin Concerto with Ida Haendel and Mahler's Symphony no. 4 with Heather Harper as soloist. Conducting that symphony together with Beethoven's *Egmont* Overture and Williamson's *Hammarskjöld Portrait* in Melbourne, the programme in Canberra featured Ida Haendel in the Britten Violin Concerto. After repeating this programme in Sydney, John departed for Hong Kong to visit his tailor to whom he had sent explicit instructions from Cologne.

At a time when he was supposed to be making an effort to diet because of his arthritic hip, changes needed to be made to the sizes – upwards, asking for 'a very good length to the pleated section' for his evening shirts. Known since his Glyndebourne days for the elegance of his black figured Chinese silk smoking jackets, he would purchase the material himself before sending it to the tailor.

Once, visiting a recommended tailor in London, discussing tail-coats, he was shown, as the 'ultimate', what the tailor was making up for another conductor – then not known for having either an international career or style. John pursed his lips and raised his eyebrows, 'No, *that* will not do.'

Away from Sydney for Ida Haendel's birthday, he arranged for a member of the orchestra to take her out into the countryside to a particular restaurant for a memorable meal looking out on beautiful scenery. When it came to payment, she was told that John had settled the bill. Somehow in his crammed schedule he found time for such gestures of generosity. Recounting this story after John's Memorial Service, Ida Haendel explained it was one of her many reasons for flying especially from Florida to London to play for the occasion.

Full of enthusiasm for his new appointment, the Proms that year were marked by reviving Harrison Birtwistle's *Triumph of Time* in one concert, Giles Swayne's *Orlando's Music* in another and a very beautiful performance of Strauss' *Don Quixote*, with Yo Yo Ma as soloist.

His first concert as Chief Conductor, a performance of *Gerontius* on 10th October 1982 at the Royal Albert Hall, received mixed reviews. The critics were awaiting the forthcoming first European performance of Concerto for Orchestra by the American composer, Roger Sessions. A very beautiful work in three movements, it was commissioned for the Boston Symphony Orchestra's centenary. John did it competently but it did not appeal to his heart. The performance was rather dry and did not make much of an impression. He did not repeat this in a Prom, presenting instead, in 1985, to a better reception, the same composer's *When Lilacs Last in the Dooryard Bloom'd*, based on a setting of Whitman. With the help of Robert Ponsonby in planning, he resurrected some of his LPO and Liverpool Musica Viva repertoire. There he had introduced work by Alexander Goehr and on 25th July 1983 gave a successful Prom performance of his largest choral composition, *Babylon the Great is Fallen* and presented again Peter Maxwell Davies' *Second Taverner Fantasia*. Even under John's guidance, this last revealed flaws in the orchestral playing. Conducting a beautiful performance of Delius' *A Mass of Life* in a Royal Philharmonic Society Concert on 5th December 1984, marking the fiftieth anniversary of the composer's death, with meticulous tempi he paced the music to give the words clarity and meaning.

Amongst the many interviews for his first Prom season as Chief Conductor, he was invited to be a castaway on *Desert Island Discs*. Recommending a particular wine from the Montepulciano area, where he had rented a house for summer holidays for two years in succession, he was amused to learn that sales had risen after the radio broadcast.

Jokingly he commented frequently that in Britain football club managers were held in more esteem than conductors and bemoaned his lack of recognition. Now, as a result of representations being made, a knighthood was announced in the New Year's Honours List of 1983. This was *the* achievement, *the* acceptance. When he went to the Investiture, he was delighted to see his old friend Ian Wallace receiving the OBE. Immediately after the ceremony John planned to go to France where toilet paper was expensive and it was customary for Terry to fill the car boot with as many rolls as possible. In the shiny, freshly-cleaned car, they halted at the gates of Buckingham Palace for security. The policeman glanced at the crammed boot, 'I see you have come well prepared, sir.'

Among countless congratulations full of warmth and happy memories from the past, his cousin, Joseph Pritchard from Dovercourt, Essex, detailed the musical talent of his grandsons, who had been recommended to pursue music professionally. In reply John invited the three boys to a Prom rehearsal and concert.

More honours followed with the Charter Centenary Concert at the Royal Albert Hall for the Royal College of Music, by 'the College's distinguished students' in the presence of Their Royal Highnesses the Prince and Princess of Wales. After conducting the College Orchestra in Britten's *The Young Person's Guide to the Orchestra*, John confessed to the organiser that he had not in fact been a student. Having received the honour of a Fellow of the Royal Academy of Music in 1976, that summer he was invited to become a Fellow of the Royal College.

In a post-Vietnam age, he was able to express pacifist convictions openly and in the Britten/Tippett Festival of 1986, involving the BBC SO amongst others, dedicated to 'the cause of peace' he conducted Britten's *War Requiem* at the Royal College of Music.

The year had opened auspiciously but Beethoven's *Choral Symphony* on 7th February 1983 disappointed. 'The orchestra was often alarmingly sloppy. Sir John Pritchard will not again want to lead his forces under such circumstances.' (Paul Griffiths, the *Times*, 8th February.) However, the Proms opened on 22nd July 1983 with an outstanding performance of the Beethoven Mass in C major, inspired by soloists of high calibre: Ileana Cotrubas, Kathleen Kuhlmann, Robert Tear and Gwynne Howell. The rest of the programme was equally distinguished with marvellous performances of *Trauermusik*, Wagner's piece in memory of Weber based on *Euryanthe* and Berlioz' *Symphonie Funèbre et Triomphale*.

Associated with both orchestras to which Sir Adrian Boult had been affiliated, on his death (23rd February 1983), John was the obvious choice to conduct the concert at the Royal

Festival Hall to celebrate his life on 9th December 1983. In a programme of Parry's *Blest Pair of Sirens* and Elgar's *Enigma* variations, the performance of Mahler's *Das Lied von der Erde*, with Dame Janet Baker and William Lewis as soloists was deeply moving. Lady Boult wrote, 'You and the [his] Orchestra gave him a fine tribute indeed – the tone was lovely – the playing splendid. Could Dame Janet ever have sung better? Her finale was out of this world, one hoped it might never end. I am profoundly grateful to you all.'

Ensuring that the conductor's room at the BBC Maida Vale studios was refurbished, John spent a great deal of time recording. This sometimes involved taking up previously free days on which many key players were engaged elsewhere and recordings needed postponement. John determined to increase the personnel. However the recordings he did make do not match his live performances in the concert hall. In an interview he explained: 'It would take an orchestra of saints or rabid enthusiasts to give of their best in that rather dead atmosphere. I've insisted that we get in a studio audience, even a small one of twenty or thirty, for studio concerts: it makes a great difference to morale. And to have the concert announced live from the hall, though, alas, because of radio planning, our studio concerts very rarely go out live on the radio or indeed with any real sense of occasion, which is a great shame for the players.'

In the studio listening to a contemporary work with the composer present, the warmth of tone from the strings which John produced was beautiful, alive. However, sitting in the producer's box one was immediately aware that the sound which listeners would hear was dry and without colour. John shrugged his shoulders. 'They tell me he is the BBC's best producer. Is it any wonder that contemporary music is considered boring?'

His many studio recordings compensated partially for the lack of a contract with one of the major commercial companies. From this aspect, career-wise, the BBC SO appointment was a mistake as, from a record company's point of view, they have always been hesitant about recording radio orchestras. People tend to think of them as second class orchestras. The name puts them off. Polygram (Decca) does record one radio orchestra, the RSO Berlin but it's called RSO and does not suggest radio. The other orchestra that is successful on records is the Bayerische

Rundfunk because the English-speaking world does not know that it means Bavarian Radio. Looking at a catalogue for the eighties, the bulk of all London recordings were made by the other London orchestras and rarely by the BBC. Recordings were made earlier with the BBC when Pierre Boulez was Music Director but record companies, as a general rule, are inclined to avoid radio orchestras, so when John was in charge of the BBC, companies were more inclined to talk to him about recording non-radio orchestras.

When it came to recording *Idomeneo*, Christopher Raeburn of Decca chose John because he 'believed in him'. The opera was going to be presented at Salzburg and Luciano Pavarotti wanted to record the role of Idomeneo and was agreeable to having John as conductor. In the Glyndebourne production of 1964 he had sung the role of Idamante of which John had only wonderful memories. In turn Luciano Pavarotti remembered that his kindness and affection towards him was 'a great source of inspiration'. He looked on the conductor 'not only as a colleague but a true friend'.

That was in the old Fritz Busch, Viennese version but for this recording, Christopher Raeburn went back to the Munich version, insisting on a mezzo-soprano voice as Idamante but adding two arias; one for Idamante and a final aria for Idomeneo. Although written at that time they were not performed in the first version at Munich. 'We simply put them in because they're such lovely music and they fit.' John did his own version with recitatives and so on to make it a whole and it worked out that it was as 'a performing version'. In a live performance some of the additions would have had to be cut. Idamante's part would have been too heavy and too long – so would the evening. Consequently, the record is probably longer than any performance. As it was thought that there might be some session time unused, it was decided to record a final aria with Luciano Pavarotti. John thought he would like to run through a couple of arias with the tenor, who had a piano in his room. On discovering that there was no pianist available, like a true professional, John sat down and became a repetiteur again.

John Fisher, who had worked with John in Cologne, was a very good assistant for Christopher Raeburn and Peter Wadland made up the trio who went to Vienna to make the recording.

Arranging a schedule to fit in with the artists' engagements was very complicated and the recording was made in two separate groups of schedules.

It was twenty years since John had conducted the orchestra in Vienna. He confessed to not feeling at ease with them. 'They were terribly nice to me and, of course, I put my bowings in but I was a bit afraid of them and at the beginning asked them to "Please change any of the bowings you don't like."' Christopher Raeburn felt that the Vienna Philharmonic did not really respond to John. 'It was all perfectly friendly, everything went off all right. On the basis of the recording they wouldn't have offered him concerts or more work.' One or two did appreciate that underneath his very easy-going demeanour was somebody who really knew what he wanted. As he did not display temperament, most of the others just played through.

The aim of the recording was to be part of a tradition. 'It had everything that Fritz Busch wanted.' There was the marvellous sound of the Vienna Philharmonic, the chorus work was good and an outstanding cast; with two Italians giving an enormous Italianate 'lift' and Lucia Popp singing Italian very convincingly and Agnes Baltsa as Idamante. John worked very hard with them. On the telephone after enumerating excitedly his wonderful cast, he paused, then added, very quietly, 'I think it's the best recording I have ever done.'

It received an enormous hammering in Britain. The critics wanted old instruments, the so-called authentic approach and John's recording had been made seemingly at the wrong time. Some critics wanted something different from John but one suspects that what they expected is something superficial. Abroad the reaction was different and in America it was nominated for a Grammy award.

With the major London orchestras projecting their image and that of their conductors to attract sponsors and full houses, John felt that the BBC SO was losing ground. Understanding the power of television, he wrote to Aubrey Singer, Managing Director for Radio that he did not want the BBC to look upon promotion as a 'pious cultural exercise' but rather that 'the BBC SO should gradually take its place in the programmes (and in the public eye) as an essential but not boring side of the medium. The need is to establish *quickly* a certain "inevitability" about the combination Pritchard/BBC SO which will gain in time the instant recognition of the public.' John suggested a regular winter series for television. 'I would not be averse to a general title, perhaps a *bit* corny, such as "Sir John introduces . . ."(!) I have quite a few young soloists in mind. The public I feel loves astonishing virtuosity and with a soloist the camera is not so bound to search out instrumental "leads" (of doubtful visual interest) in the course of the music. In the middle of the series I would propose one orchestra ONLY programme devoted to brilliant showpieces (not too long) of the repertoire.'

Unfortunately the forward planning of a contract orchestra, particularly a broadcasting orchestra, is out of scale with planning for television. The BBC SO has hugely demanding schedules: foreign tours, Royal Festival Hall, college concerts, studio work and so on – and by the time television made up their mind the BBC SO Management had committed themselves to something else. With the greater authority of being Controller of Radio 3, John Drummond★ had more success than Robert Ponsonby. This came too late for John.

There were seldom 'sold out' notices for his concerts. We have all been corrupted to a certain extent by television. Lacking visual stimulus to the public, it was the same problem that had dogged him at the LPO. The players felt differently. They adored him because he knew how to interpret the music, to talk to them, when to make a joke. His jokes were always amusing, very dry and witty, sometimes very naughty. For the musicians he was the perfect communicator. The beat was clear, the left hand eloquent and did not do anything if there was nothing required. In his interpretations he never distorted the music, never drove it unduly. The paragraphs were always long and beautiful. He seemed to produce the unexpected for which one never suspected that he had an affinity such as an amazing Shostakovich 11th Symphony with great force and drama.

Orchestral players like to recount the many stories of life with John, particularly on tour, his gargantuan appetite providing most of them but a favourite anecdote stems from the occasion when Terry telephoned the Royal Festival Hall to say the car had broken down. In full evening dress, John boarded a bus asking the driver for the Savoy. 'I can't drop you at the door but we stop nearby.'

★ John Drummond took over from Robert Ponsonby in 1985 but the Proms of 1986 were planned by the latter.

Finding his pockets empty, 'Do you take American Express?' has become part of his legend.

The occasion when Ann Murray felt poorly, she received only help and sympathy. Telephoning in the morning to see what time she would like to come to the afternoon Prom rehearsal, she confessed to feeling 'very grotty'. When she arrived John briskly informed the orchestra, 'Now ladies and gentlemen, Ann's just got out of bed for this rehearsal and, much more importantly, I have to be at the hairdresser's at four o'clock!'

In his nineties, Sir Robert Mayer was persuaded by the BBC to let them take over his Concerts for Children. It was John who conducted A Salute to Sir Robert, to celebrate his life at the Barbican Centre on 14th October 1985, in the presence of Her Royal Highness the Duchess of Gloucester. The programme began with the fanfare Sir William Walton composed for Sir Robert's Hundredth Birthday Concert in 1979. The two lady soloists were Ida Haendel playing Schubert's Rondo for Violin & String Orchestra in A major and Sarah Walker in Mahler's *Des Knaben Wunderhorn* both of whom John chose for his last Prom Concert. The third soloist, John Lill playing Beethoven's Piano Concerto no. 1 (in C, op. 15) had been sponsored by Sir Robert for his journey to Moscow in 1970 when he won the International Tchaikovsky Piano Competition.

Like Sir Robert Mayer with his interest in young people, John often served on a competition jury.

> DIARY ENTRY: 1980. Budapest. Stayed at beautiful Intercontinental Hotel, lovely views over Danube. It's a wonderful city. Watched videotape of six young conductors. Nothing spectacular in talent. Finals: I graded the six finalists 1, 2, 3, 0, 0, 0, which caused a stir (before the TV cameras). When pressed I said Nos. 4 to 6 totally without talent, should be graded alphabetically.

In the prestigious Arturo Toscanini competition of 1987 in the Boito Conservatory, Parma, the two competitors to whom he gave the highest marks were summed up with: 'Good beat. I feel he is a musician. The orchestra followed him with pleasure' and 'I felt he has clear ideas and is ready to insist on them with the orchestra. Is a professional.' Unfortunately, many received damning comment. 'The music is simply beyond him. Why choose conducting?' and 'Extremely boring and uninspired', or

'Completely useless, drab, unable to rehearse. The lady *suffered* through all three pieces producing tension but not comprehension.'

Frequently, composers attend rehearsals. If in John's view they 'interfered' too often, he would always support the orchestral players in their difficulties. Whilst rehearsing *Punkte*, a difficult work with some wonderful moments, he refused to be intimidated by the presence of a composer of the stature of Stockhausen. The performance was absolutely competent and fully justified his title 'the musicians' musician'.

With his reputation as *the* protagonist for contemporary music and his ability to illuminate a work for the players, he was expected to conduct pieces which he was beginning to feel should be given to younger conductors. No longer wishing to educate himself, now he was seeking fulfilment. Although he spent considerable time repeating past successes or searching out new work, John's intention as Chief Conductor was to bring the orchestra (post Boulez) back into the mainstream repertoire, believing that training was most successful when working in the Brahms/Bruckner/Mahler *œuvre*. In order to produce the sound he sought, additional strings were added. Gerard Mortier changed performance dates in Brussels to enable him to conduct all the symphonies in a Brahms Festival at the Barbican in February 1986. In those performances he provided the architecture but even with distinguished solo playing, detail lacked the precision which more thorough rehearsal would have given. However, with the augmented strings and ten double basses providing a foundation for the sound, John was able to show that he was the master when it came to sonorities. At the first concert the orchestra produced a cake iced to represent the score of the Symphony no. 1, to celebrate John's 'sixty-fifth' birthday. Reading newspaper interviews it is noticeable that his age remained at 'forty-four' for some time. Displaying a little creative accounting, he was older than stated in his *Who's Who* entry.

Understanding the morale-building effect for the players of rehearsing and performing in the sometimes magnificent venues on a prestigious tour, especially when accompanied by a welcoming reception without too many speeches, John embarked on a series of tours. His restless nature, coupled with the ability to always say the right thing when needed, made him one of the first conductors a British orchestra would ask when they contemplated necessarily rigorous travel schedules. His stature and the authority of his musicianship was appreciated abroad. Now with the added cachet of a knighthood, he was delighted by the speed with which the maître d' of the most popular restaurants would find a table, sometimes even setting one up in a private room, not to keep him and his guests waiting.

John continued to behave as an ambassador for British music. Opening his programme in the Zurich Tonhalle with Sir William Walton's *Partita*, it was the ideal venue for such a work. With a high ceiling and baroque décor it has a brilliant acoustic and is perhaps one of the better venues the orchestra encountered on its Swiss tour of April 1986.

Wishing to develop his career in the United States, following his appointment as Musical Director of San Francisco Opera, he insisted that a proposed tour by the BBC SO of the United States of America the following January, supersede all other engagements.

In Europe, radio orchestras are an accepted part of the music scene. Apart from the NBC Symphony which was created specifically for Toscanini, in America radio stations use music provided by existing orchestras. To survive they need private patronage and sponsorship and consequently are mindful of the need for popularity in their programming. Equally, in London, with the orchestras fighting for survival, it was being left to the funded BBC SO to explore the repertoire.

The BBC recording supervisors accompanying them planned to record seven of the ten performances on the tour, so they took ten works plus two encores. The young Nigel Kennedy was the much praised soloist alternating between the Sibelius and Tchaikovsky Violin Concertos. Although John had often been to Florida, Miami and Key West in particular, for vacations, he had never conducted there. Beginning the tour in Fort Myers, 'showing the flag', John presented *Spring Music* by Nicholas Maw. Travelling on to Daytona he conducted David Mathews' one movement Symphony no. 3 giving these works their US premières, both of which whilst contemporary are not avant-garde. A letter from Ashville, North Carolina, expressing a family's gratitude that the orchestra had not treated their 'small town engagement' as such but had given a performance such as could only be heard in a major city delighted John. Now playing to a consistently high standard, he felt they could be judged with any of the other internationally recognised orchestras. The final concert in the Avery Fischer Hall, New York was broadcast live. Opening with Walton's *Portsmouth Point*, followed by the Tchaikovsky Violin Concerto, he conducted an intensely strong performance of the Shostakovich Symphony no. 11.

Two months later he hired clothes from Moss Bros suitable for a Russian tour from 21 – 29 March 1987. With soloist Natalia Gutman playing the Elgar Cello Concerto (in E minor), John repeated the same programme in both Moscow and Leningrad. Opening with Oliver Knussen's Symphony no. 3, he balanced this in the second half with Scriabin's Symphony no. 3 choosing as encores the lively *Marriage of Figaro* Overture and a Brahms' *Hungarian Dance*.

With his contract ending in 1989, not wanting to see his achievements dissipated, John determined to take an active part in the choice of his successor. He had met Andrew Davis in 1972, the year prior to the young man's first engagement at Glyndebourne to assist and conduct some performances of *Capriccio*. Over lunch John enumerated the pleasures and uniqueness of working in Sussex and the beauty of the surrounding countryside. The spell has not been lifted and Andrew Davis is now Music Director at Glyndebourne. Through the years John had watched his career and, more importantly, wide range of repertoire during his Toronto Symphony Orchestra appointment. A deeply moving performance of the European première of Michael Tippett's *Mask of Time* at the Proms on 23rd July 1984 with the BBC SO showed that Andrew Davis could control the large forces involved. When he was introduced as John's successor at a lunchtime press reception in April 1988 at Broadcasting House, it did not come as a surprise. After press photos, John made a quick exit. A successor appointed, the BBC belonged in the past.

13

San Francisco

'It is absolutely essential for an artist, particularly a woman singer, to have an American career because then she can go on "milking the cow" into her old age.' Thus put rather crudely in the late seventies, John stressed the importance of an American career, the great loyalty of the American public and the huge variety of engagements available.

The conductor of the Pittsburgh Symphony Orchestra, William Steinberg, had chaired the jury for the Conductor's Competition in Liverpool. Although comparatively young, the Pittsburgh Orchestra is rated one of America's top orchestras. Making his American debut with them in 1963, John was determined to put aside part of his schedule for them annually. In 1965, while still Principal Conductor of the LPO, he was invited back for a five-week period culminating in his New York City conducting debut with them at Carnegie Hall on 20th January 1965. The maestro of an American orchestra rarely conducted any other during his tenure. When asked how he could leave his own orchestra for such a long period, John excused himself. 'In England, the resident conductor isn't really resident – the musical public is more fickle and likes to have many visiting conductors.' Following his time with Pittsburgh, John went on to conduct the San Francisco Orchestra, from 10th – 12th February 1965. Opening his programme with the overture to *Così fan Tutte*, one reviewer commented that they would like to hear him conduct a Mozart opera.

However John's opera debut in America was with Rossini at the Lyric Opera, Chicago in November and December 1969 in *Il Barbiere di Siviglia* with Marilyn Horne as Rosina and Sir Geraint Evans as Dr Bartolo, artists he knew well. John was always happy in Chicago because the Lyric Opera fully justifies its reputation as a house where preparation and ability are of the highest level. He is remembered particularly for the Cologne production of *Idomeneo* in 1977 with Jean-Pierre Ponnelle. John's love for that opera encouraged the orchestral players themselves to study not only the music but also Mozart's letters to his father about the composition of the opera. *Don Pasquale* (1978), *Don Giovanni* (1980) and *Ballo in Maschera* (1980) were other highly successful productions. However, *Arabella* in September 1984 was special as it was the Lyric Opera debut of Dame Kiri Te Kanawa in the title role.

The rapport between the two artists was shared offstage. John found he could tell her his problems. Dame Kiri did not believe that he was a difficult character to understand but, 'I do believe that he had quite a nasty temper.' It was to his closest friends that he would express annoyance. Sometimes they were about seemingly unimportant, petty things, even voicing annoyance several hours later because a maid had left a pin in the jacket she had been given to press and he had pricked himself. He understood human weakness but refused to accept unprofessionalism at whatever level. Not a complicated person, there was a solid, firm streak within. When John determined on something, he was hard to dissuade.

When Jean Mallandaine, from Glyndebourne, went to Chicago to see *Arabella*, she stayed with Dame Kiri at the Doral Plaza, the same building as John. He had gone to Michael Jackson's concert in Comisky Park and was not 'at home'. Having recommended her, when Jean Mallandaine did her first production in Houston, John flew there from Chicago.

His own debut at Houston was in *Peter Grimes* in 1977 with Jon Vickers and produced by Ande Anderson. Before the large theatre was built, rehearsals were in a hall with appalling acoustics and the Sitzprobe in the basement. With a large cast and an extra chorus plus the orchestra, the only way to work was to put John in the middle of the basement with everybody around him. Many others would have refused to work in this manner but he made light of it. When faced with a difficult situation, he would always take the pressure.

In the early days, one of the difficulties in America was that few of the opera houses had a permanent chorus. They were permanent but most of them were business men during the day. In *Peter Grimes*, in essence a 'chorus opera', the rehearsal problems were enormous and this is probably why it is seldom performed there. Most conductors would have become quite hysterical. Never John, he would be practical. 'Listen to the sound they make!' Never raising his voice, they paid absolute attention. Somehow, in that hot, sweaty town the semi-professional chorus, augmented by the totally amateur extra chorus, related to the cold, grey English shore and gave the work an enthusiasm and attack inspired by John.

After a difficult rehearsal, knowing his gourmet taste, Ande Anderson was delighted when John promised to take him to one of the best restaurants in America. He ushered the producer into the restaurant at the Hyatt Regency. 'He had the biggest hamburger with all the trimmings, that I'd ever seen!'

Jon Vickers also sang *Otello* with John in Houston in 1979 and, in *Werther* the same year, he was working again with Frederica von Stade. One of her favourite collaborators at that time, John was responsible for many of her important first steps.

Although he conducted *Il Turco in Italia* in a concert performance at Carnegie Hall with Met soloists in 1965, his debut at the Metropolitan Opera in New York in *Così fan Tutte* was not until 1971 during Rudolf (ex-Glyndebourne) Bing's last season as General Manager.

After an early whirlwind of achievement, every good musician has periods of self-doubt especially when the furore has settled. John's rise had been meteoric; first Vienna, then the youngest conductor to make his debut at Covent Garden and now he was to conduct at the American mecca of opera. Interviewed in New York about his forthcoming engagement, he lied, revealing his insecurity. Apart from his family background, he explained his time in Derby as a war service posting with the 'tommies'.

Preparing for his debut John stayed in the studio attached to the apartment which his friend Richard Gaddes rented in the Ansonia Hotel. With the American paranoia for security it had two keys, one to enter and a different one to exit from inside.

John always lost keys. By the evening of his debut, he had already lost two sets of keys. At the Ansonia he was still checking his appearance at 7.15pm. Richard Gaddes was straightening his bow tie and brushing his coat. He then left for the start at 8 o'clock. 'I jumped into the shower – the Met was only 8 mins away by cab – and rushed to the front door, only to discover that he had locked me in! This was the day that we had waited for, for years. I had gone through the whole rehearsal period with him, every person that he knew had been to my home, here was the big night and I was locked in the apartment.' There was nothing he could do. 'I just stayed home and missed his debut.' At 1am he received a call from John at the Gingerman restaurant. There was a lot of noise in the background, suggesting a big party. '"My dear, where are you?" I very grittily said, "I am locked in my own apartment, having waited four years for your debut at the Metropolitan Opera." There was a small pause and then, "My dear, that story is worthy of us!"'

On his return to the Met in 1977 he himself rented an apartment in the Ansonia. John loved the baroque embellishments on the 'great, big ice cream cake building'. He would explain that the uncarpeted corridors were wide enough to drive a coach and horses. Belonging to an American singer the apartment suited the romantic, theatrical side of his personality.

Fully preoccupied with their own performance, most conductors cannot find time to attend those of others but John would go to everything possible staying only a short time. Looking at the wide repertoire at the New York City Opera during that period, many singers in the most minor roles later found their way into his own cast lists at Glyndebourne and Cologne. Conducting *Grimes* with Jon Vickers and Heather Harper singing Ellen Orford, he found time to see the Met *Rigoletto*. In this his first year as a non-resident, the poor staging and consequent necessity for singers to move to the front of the stage to be heard in the auditorium, made him feel very homesick for Glyndebourne and Covent Garden.

That year, as well as *Grimes*, John had the pleasure of working with Beverly Sills in a new production of *Thaïs*. Cyril J Magnin, who owned the department store in San Francisco was a great fan of the soprano and offered her this production which was first performed at San Francisco in September 1976. Sybil Sanderson who inspired Massenet to compose *Thaïs*, taught the role to Mary Garden, who in turn coached Beverly Sills. Having sung *Lucia* with him at Covent Garden in 1970, asked whom she wanted to conduct, she had replied, 'John'.

John was thrilled at the publicity for *Thaïs*, especially as he was photographed with William Rockefeller at dinner after the benefit performance in January 1978. Commenting on their collaborations, the soprano recalled, 'John always put on this front of being very cool and calm and very little could agitate or upset him but actually he was a very deep feeling man and did get very excited. He teased me a lot about *Thaïs* and we both referred to its size, calling it "thighs".' They did many things together but Beverly Sills considered that 'most of all I really treasure his friendship. We had so many good times together. The nice thing about my memories of John is that in everything I look back at, I can never remember having an unpleasant time with him. I loved him dearly.' She recalled their first meeting in the late sixties or early seventies. 'We took to each other immediately. He had a dry sense of humour that appealed to me and said that he'd never heard anybody laugh the way I did, so he spent much of his time trying to make me laugh.' She felt that once John became interested in a project that 'so-called veneer of standing apart and commenting rather than participating, disappeared. He became a real collaborator with the *Thaïs*.' When she and John did a concert in Paris of primarily French music, they created a sensation.

> The newspapers were extremely kind which was less important than the fact that the French public embraced both of us. This is a rare compliment to an American and Englishman. I was aware of the fact that something extraordinary had happened in terms of the attention it received. We were both very pleased and proud. I can remember that one of the things we did of which we were both enamoured, was 'Depuis le Jour'. The other that we giggled over a little was one of the arias from *Huguenots*. I also did the gavotte and the recitative from *Manon*. That created quite a stir. John and I prepared that programme together and it was broadcast too.

Referring to the changes that have occurred, Beverly Sills recalled a performance at the Old Metropolitan Opera House, where there was a *suspicion* that a microphone had been used. 'This goes back possibly forty years. Imagine, today it is not a question of singing before 2,000 people in an auditorium, it's now a question of whether you can accommodate 100,000 people, with thirty microphones. There are things that are acceptable today that would never have been acceptable in John's, or my time.'

Shortly after Joan Ingpen became Assistant Manager at the Met at the end of 1978, John intimated that he would like to work there more. She said, 'John, I've been trying to get you for about three years now and Basil makes it so difficult. He wants this, that and the other and it doesn't sound like you.' John replied, 'It's not true. Let's talk together. I like working where the conditions are good.' She remembered that Basil Horsfield was apparently saying that John could not afford to go to the Met unless he was given two operas. It needed to be on a very commercial basis to support his lifestyle. In the time it takes to rehearse and conduct an opera a conductor can always earn more doing concerts. She and John started talking about the future and arranged for him to conduct *Grimes* in October 1983. She then spoke to James Levine who agreed that John should prepare *Traviata* for the same period. In addition, he took part in the Met Centennial Gala.

John had made his debut already in San Francisco with *Così* in 1970. There was never a need there for a Musical Director because of Kurt Adler. Born and educated in Vienna he had worked in small opera houses in Germany, Czechoslovakia and Austria and as an assistant to Arturo Toscanini at the Salzburg Festival in 1936. With the war he went first to Chicago and then was hired by Gaetano Merola, the founder of San Francisco Opera. Appointed Artistic Director on Merola's death in 1953 and in 1957, General Director, he influenced the development of many young American musicians, among them, Calvin Simmons.

John recalled his first meeting with that young man. On his own arrival, Kurt Adler had greeted him and whisked him into the elevator to the sacred precincts of the fourth floor, where his office was. Just as the door was closing, a tall, slender black boy slipped through, with the greatest of ease.

> That was Calvin. Adler informed me he would be my assistant for *Così* and thus began this unforgettable relationship. I cannot think of a moment when Calvin and I did not look at a score with the same vision. Yet his perspective was individual because it was always informed by his scintillating humour. I loved that. And to hear him play from an orchestral score, particularly one by Mozart, was remarkable – because he thought in terms of the stage. His concern was not getting things right in his fingers; he was taking in every aspect of what the conductor and singers were doing. Those dark eyes would flash. After the experience of only two seasons, I asked him to join the team at Glyndebourne.

John became close to the six-foot-two black man. Unlike most people, Calvin Simmons was able to get behind John's mask. They both wanted to escape from their past. Like him, he was the young man who had 'made good'. Starting in the San Francisco

Boys' Chorus in the early fifties when Merola told Kurt Adler that he needed some children for the opera, Calvin's musical gift was discovered whilst he was still at school and he was hired at the opera. As well as working at Glyndebourne with John he was assistant to Zubin Mehta at the Los Angeles Philharmonic in 1975. Appointed to the Musical Directorship of the Oakland Symphony, in a predominantly black city, it was interesting for a young, black man to be taking over a cultural organisation. His droll gangling humour, his gossipy, gregarious, clowning manner cheered John. Like the older man, an accomplished pianist, opera was his first love. Tragically drowned whilst holidaying at Lake Placid, New York on 21st August 1982, the news of his death shattered John on holiday with Terry at Gian Carlo Menotti's home. He never really recovered from it. In John's early days at San Francisco, the energy created by him with Calvin and Jean-Pierre Ponnelle produced exciting performances.

Ryland Davies made his American debut in that *Così* as Ferrando. Having worked for several days with the producer, he recalled leaving his hotel one morning to go to the theatre. A voice hailed him. Looking back, across the street was John whose first question was, 'How are things going?' There was Capecchi who later sang Falstaff at Glyndebourne with him, Margaret Price singing her first Fiordiligi, Graziella Sciutti and Alberto Rinaldi, all of whom John knew well. He continued, 'Is everybody having tea and the odd meal together? Jean-Pierre Ponnelle – how do you like him?' 'Oh, I think he's marvellous,' Ryland Davies answered. 'Very interesting and stimulating.' John continued, 'Are you comfortable here? Your first time in San Francisco. Where are you staying?' 'Well John, I'm staying just over there in the El Cortez Hotel. Where are you staying?' 'Just around the corner at the Gaylord.' Ryland Davies asked, 'That one at the back?' 'Yes,' he replied. 'If you'll pardon the expression, we're backing onto each other!'

Those who have worked together at Glyndebourne, when they meet again in other parts of the world, still maintain the family feeling. It is more than just a question of sharing the musical experience, they share their lives. So for this *Così* everyone went out together and laughed together. Knowing it was Ryland Davies' first time in California, John introduced him to his first Mexican meal and first Californian wine. It was natural for John to say, 'Jean-Pierre's doing something and you're not involved. Terry – where's the car? Let's go to Sausalito and have lunch.'

Graziella Sciutti remembered: 'The last performance is always very sad. Although we shall meet again, it is as though something has died. So on the last night, I decided that we should all have a dinner party in my flat. We had the greatest fun and as it became late, little by little, the other singers left and just a couple of people, including John, remained. I had with me the tape of *Turco in Italia*, taken at one of the Glyndebourne performances and we listened to this. We were so happy and laughed so much and this music reminds me of that beautiful night.' They stayed up till 7.30 in the morning and she prepared breakfast because everybody had to leave the next day. 'I was going to Tokyo, John to New York. We all needed to pack and yet we were eating bacon and eggs at 7.30 in the morning.' If she saw John was conducting, or he saw she was singing somewhere, they would try and get together even if they were not working together. 'He would always ask when we could have another night like that one because it had been so much fun. We never managed to repeat it. These things can never be repeated because they just happen.' The last time she saw him he was conducting *Lucia* at Covent Garden. 'I went backstage afterwards and he said, "When, when? Let's get together, let's organise it." It's the most difficult thing actually between artists . . .'

Kurt Adler was a brilliant musician, linguist and stylist and would hire conductors for specific operas, not because they were well known but because it was repertoire to which they were most sympathetic. The fact that John returned to San Francisco so many times during his regime speaks sufficiently of his recognition of John's ability. He was to conduct eighteen productions of fourteen different operas for the Company.

Returning to San Francisco for the *Così* revival in 1973 with Frederica von Stade singing Dorabella, he was also her collaborator for her first performances of *Cenerentola* in 1974. Produced by Jean-Pierre Ponnelle, the Rossini just bubbled along. Nothing was ill-considered. The triumphant first performances of *Grimes* in 1973 and 1976, a production shared with the Chicago Lyric, were under his baton and the first performances of *Thaïs* in 1976 with Beverly Sills and Sherrill Milnes thrilled the audience at the flower-bedecked Gala opening night.

Idomeneo in San Francisco in 1977, marked John's third important staging of that opera and a further collaboration with Jean-Pierre Ponnelle. He knew how to handle the temperamental, egocentric and very brilliant director who, in turn, thought highly of the conductor. John had given his score to Richard Bradshaw, now Chorus Director in San Francisco, who was conducting rehearsals because, as usual, he was not there. Ponnelle insisted on making various cuts which Richard Bradshaw felt John would not like. When eventually John arrived, appraised by the Chorus Director of the situation he said, 'Don't worry, just leave it to me.' They went to see Jean-Pierre and by the end of the meeting John had his own way completely, in the most gentle and friendly manner.

Feeling that the public in San Francisco should be aware of the different versions of the opera, John expressed some of his thoughts on *Idomeneo*.

> In the later version for Vienna, which Mozart himself rearranged, the Idamante was sung by a tenor; originally a castrato role but with the tessitura lying very high. The principal difference between the Munich and Vienna versions lies in the role of Idamante and Mozart, with great care, altered the notes, for example, in the quartet, making sure the tessitura was right and the chords properly balanced. The problem of the role for contemporary mezzo-sopranos is that much of the role, especially the first aria, lies very high.
>
> For me, it will be very interesting. It's only my association with Jean-Pierre Ponnelle that has convinced me to do it with a mezzo Idamante. I used to feel that, although a modern opera audience was accustomed to the Strauss trouser-roles and had no trouble accepting Cherubino, they would have difficulty in believing a noble prince 'en travesti' who in turn had to sing a love duet with a soprano.

He fully concurred with Fritz Busch's opinion. 'The ballet is second-class Mozart, at best.' The current production in San Francisco derived from Ponnelle's in Cologne, originally prepared by István Kertész. Previously John had voiced regret at some of the cuts made by Fritz Busch and Hans Gal and wanted to do a fuller version. 'I do regret the loss of the tenor-soprano revision of the Idamante/Ilia duet in the Vienna version, which is superlatively beautiful.' This time John considered that the advantage of utilising the Munich version far outweighed recourse to the 1786 (Vienna) revision, for instance, in the character of

Arbace, a kind of prime minister figure. 'Here, we will do at least one of the arias. When we did the opera with a tenor Idamante, Busch felt that a third tenor was too much of a good thing. So the role of Arbace was given to a baritone and was severely cut. His music is very beautiful, including the third act accompanied recitative, which is simply superb. To my mind, there's a great division in this opera between the unique voice of Mozart and the places where we have what you can only call a conventional operatic conclusion.'

John explained the way Mozart transcended the opera seria form.

The first act chorus 'Nettuno s'onori!' is simply the kind of thing that was being written at that time. But then looking at the beginning of the same act, he began with an orchestrally accompanied recitative, 'Quando avran fine omai', which is an innovation. Then, following it with the aria, 'Padre, germani', gives immediately the full character of Ilia. Soon comes the B flat major aria for Idamante, 'Non ho culpa', (that's the high one). Here's a case of Mozart's suddenly remembering that he's supposed to write an opera seria. Now the first aria for Electra 'Tutte nel cor', is a precursor of the Queen of the Night (*Zauberflöte*), the intense character of the woman established in only a few bars. Then, Idomeneo himself arrives from the shipwreck. His first solo, 'Vedrommi intorno', is perhaps, you could say, an opera seria aria; it's beautiful but we have to wait, in a way, for the development of Idomeneo's character until he encounters his son. At that point, Mozart has written this great recognition scene, cast in the form of a tremendous dramatic recitative. This is the full character within the framework of the opera seria form.

If Idomeneo himself is the obvious link to the older style (opera seria), the other characters reveal a remarkable histrionic range from section to section. There is an amazing contrast in Electra between the Act II 'Idol mio', with its soft high coloratura, making it all but impossible to cast and her third act exit aria, 'D'Oreste, d'Ajace', done in a more extrovert, more florid style. The accompanied recitatives with orchestra hit a level that is absolutely unsurpassable. Really, they disrupted the whole focus of opera seria. Haydn could also write some interesting accompanied recitatives but he did those only after hearing Mozart's work.

We must see Mozart's genius as water flowing from a faucet. In the case of the earlier operas, it is as if the water were flooding out, like a waterfall. Later on, it was all channelled within the composer's experience, within his knowledge of the theatre, within his desire to write beautiful music and within his mature concept of easily identifiable characters. *Così fan Tutte* was the first perfect placement in the balance of characters.

In the third act chorus, 'O voto tremendo', when the king finally takes the populace into his confidence, the way in which they respond with pity for him is so profoundly moving. After Busch died, as a memorial to him, I led the F major March of the Priests. It's truly amazing – how terribly affecting a major key can be.

Generally against the use of cadenzas and embellishments, except in opera seria, John thought the difficulty of writing and conceiving decorations which do not make any knowing musician sit up and say, 'My G–d, there's a cadenza' was the problem.

We're listening with twentieth-century ears and we have lost the performing style in which the singers conceived them on their own. Mozart himself wrote decorations into the vocal line, which may indicate that he was opposed to overly florid embellishment of his music. The vocal line is so wonderfully pure and expressive that what we do with our modern and our rather clumsy hands is bound to be worse. Take the 'Dove sono', (*Figaro*) and the return of the first theme. I have yet to hear a bridge passage which didn't seem to be banal and extremely anti-climactic. I would feel that the silence and the *pianissimo* return of the theme are equally evocative. But appoggiaturas, yes. One must insist upon them more and more with singers. These very banal phrase endings are wrong and simply out of tune with the times.

When Kurt Adler retired Terry McEwen became General Director. He had met and had dinner with John and Basil at Soho Square when he worked for London Records (Decca) in the fifties. Invited to Liverpool to give lectures about operatic records and their history, he remembered it as the largest audience he had ever addressed. They kept in touch through the years and now he approached John to become Musical Director. He was conducting *Traviata/Grimes* at the Met at the time, staying at Peter Brown's apartment on Central Park West. A marketing person, the latter always felt inwardly cross with John as he would listen and not do anything. At this point John's friend told him that in America no matter how many operas he did at the Met it was useless career-wise unless he held an appointment in America.

Ten years after his acceptance speech for the Shakespeare Prize,

San Francisco

John held positions in Cologne, Brussels, the BBC SO and now he accepted the Musical Directorship of San Francisco, hoping to rebuild his reputation in the United States.

One never quite knew what John thought about America. He liked it, to a point. When he first made his debut, attitudes were different. Twenty years previously, in May 1967, the Supreme Court had ruled that under the 1952 Immigration Act, homosexuals were excluded from entry into the United States. Originally the law had prohibited applicants 'afflicted with psychopathic personality' and was amended by Congress to exclude aliens suffering from 'sexual deviation'. Now, in the major cities, life has changed. John loved San Francisco. It was so much his sort of place: the climate, the atmosphere, the freedom. He felt very much at home. Coincidentally, Jeffrey Tate and Klaus had a great deal to do with his finding a home there because when John first arrived, they had taken over a little house in Sausalito which he thought delightful. The landlord had a little 'house' downstairs which he rented out. John fell in love with it and redid it completely with antiques from a lady they discovered in Union Street. Writing to Victor Conway on 3rd December 1985 about 'a nice little *pied-à-terre* for me in Sausalito, the yachting village just over the Golden Gate Bridge (yes ANOTHER apartment! – but it's only $800 monthly next March) – very picturesque and JP-ish.' Telephoning: 'It has a little patio, just the sort of romantic spot where I could finish my autobiography.'* John intended to end his book with these excerpts from his brother Eddie's diary, describing the latter's visit from September to October 1976. In its matter of fact realism, this passage contrasts their different personalities and lifestyle.

At San Francisco 27.9.76 – 7.10.76

Hasn't been possible to keep this diary in detail sufficient to cover the many activities of these ten days. On *Tuesd. night (28th)* I attended the last performance of THAIS by Massenet – fine performance by Beverly Sills and Sherrill Milnes. Wore my white jacket and dress trousers but felt generally overdressed as most men wore lounge suits (women all well-dressed however). Good reception for the principals at the end. A wonderful Opera House with excellent facilities for refreshments, etc. (reminded me much of the Théâtre at Geneva).

*See Introduction

295

Sir John Pritchard

Afterwards to a big hotel for late meal. Throughout my stay we were constantly going to super restaurants mostly with panoramic views of the Bay and S. Francisco. At the weekend we went to a swell place called BOLINAS – home of a Mrs ALBERT, a rich friend of John's who had put a villa on the coast at his disposal. Bolinas approached by a hair-raising coastal road where one had to put trust in Terry's undoubted skill as a driver.

Just before they arrived (late), an elderly lady arrived. I thought she was just a local character who had dropped in but it soon transpired that she was there by appointment. She was the owner of another coastal villa (called 'The Look-Out' and built in the shape of a lighthouse). John made out that he was just acting as an intermediary, to assist her in obtaining a valuation of the 'Look-Out' which she wished to sell – but *not* to the present occupiers. All very mysterious and typical of the way I am brought *just partially* into John's affairs – my guess is that he is interested in buying himself, though why he should want a place in such a remote district I cannot imagine. Incidentally, the village of Bolinas was about as scruffy and sordid a village as anyone can imagine – full of flea-bitten dogs!

Food continues to be the drawback in that I rarely find anything which I really enjoy, due to overflavouring and exotic sauces etc. Never-the-less [*sic*] have had some memorable meals in marvellous situations. John has footed the bill usually – what he must spend on meals out, for Terry as well as himself, must be enormous.

Originally the San Francisco Symphony Orchestra performed in the Opera House together with the opera and ballet. All three were separate companies with separate budgets, organisations and managements. In 1980, the new Symphony Hall was completed and the Symphony Orchestra moved into that building freeing the Opera House for more opera performances. At the same time a new rehearsal building was built adjacent to the Symphony Hall, across the street from the Opera House. Now most of the opera rehearsals take place in three large rehearsal rooms, one of which is an almost complete replica of the Opera House stage with an orchestra pit. Prior to 1980, rehearsals were held wherever possible – warehouses and a place called the Armoury, which continued to be used until quite recently. Like other American opera houses, the entire chorus were only available in the evenings. By 1981 it had developed into a full-time chorus of about fifty people which is still augmented with people who are only available in the evenings.

296

John liked the idea of going to a place where he would have direct control over the quality of performances. Intending to spend four months a year in San Francisco, including the summer and autumn, he felt that there should be a distinctive House style, a concept he felt fast disappearing in Europe primarily through financial constraints.

The essential difference between Europe and San Francisco lay in the fact that the latter was a concentrated season, a 'constellation of star singers plus orchestra and chorus gathered for only part of the year, a festival with a wide repertoire'. John understood that to be Musical Director embodied 'a great deal of forward planning and is not just the fact I am here to conduct operas each season. The role of the Musical Director is not merely to concern himself with the operas he conducts. That is a major fault around the world. It can be solved, addressed by a Musical Director such as my friend Jimmy Levine at the Met in New York, and that is to conduct practically everything himself.' The Met is a repertory opera house but San Francisco uses the stagione system which John preferred. He foresaw that his major problem might be cancellations. 'We are all affected by this and we can't live in our own little island, still less out here on the West Coast, where in both time and travel we are far from Europe and we can't replace singers.'

As always his first aim was to raise orchestral standards.

> The financial conditions, too, will change. I'm all for the players getting good money and for having a better schedule of work. I'd like to improve the wretched room the players have to relax in. These are physical things, concrete things I'm working on. What I also want is to show the orchestra on full mettle, not just at gala concerts but in three or four performances a year of, say, the Verdi *Requiem* or Beethoven's Ninth Symphony. I'd like to see in the programmes, photos of members of the orchestra as well as the singers. The obscurity of the pit is the greatest enemy of the individuality of the orchestra.

Alterations are easy on the concert platform but the pit poses difficulties. 'Every conductor has his own way. The La Scala tradition at the Chicago Lyric Opera has it that the first flute has to be under your left armpit. There's no way I could accept that, the woodwinds sitting in pairs behind each other. The bassoon (in the back) couldn't hear what the flute was doing.' The effect of his intentions would not be felt for three years. 'I want to improve *all* orchestras, including the BBC Symphony Orchestra.'

When asked what he felt about programming modern works, John replied: 'Why do *Lear*? Contemporary opera the calibre of *Midsummer Marriage* or *King Priam* interests me but where do you find it nowadays? I think the American scene is more promising, actually, than the European one. I'd be hard put to name five composers in Europe who would have a future in opera.'

He opened his first season in 1986 with *Don Carlos*, using a composite of the 1867 Paris version in French and Verdi's later revision, which was not musicologically pure. There were four or five versions performed in Verdi's time or shortly afterwards. Sitting down with producer John Cox, with a good bottle and a sharp pencil he put together the 'San Francisco version', which in retrospect will be viewed as an history-making event. It was John at his most intrepid. John Cox recalled: 'I know that there are some commentators and critics who are very sensitive about these things and, of course, they are entitled to their view but when I was working on a piece with John, there was never any question but that the theatrical effectiveness of the version was what was uppermost in his mind.' They both decided what parts they liked whilst bearing in mind the availability of singers.

The major question in *Don Carlos* is whether to do four or five acts, which usually depends on whether the company in question can afford overtime for the orchestra. They opted for five acts as they wanted as full a version as possible with the Act I chorus. Their intention was to restore the central relationship of Carlos and Elisabeth, which is lost if one does not do a strong Fontainebleau act.

The very last Verdi version, usually heard in Italian in four acts, Verdi rewrote into French. The prima donna in San Francisco, Pilar Lorengar, had sung Elizabeth in German and Italian but never French. She said it was an absolute revelation. Suddenly she felt comfortable with all the notes and all the words. Everything fitted together.

It had a rather complex and difficult modern design by Stefanos Lazaridis with which John was reasonably happy. Unfortunately they had to rehearse in the Armoury, a gigantic aeroplane-type hangar with a dirt-floor and impossible acoustics. At the other end of this immense volume of space, the police would come two afternoons a week to play volley-ball and there was nothing John could do to stop it. The piece was too long to forgo rehearsals. The circumstances under which he worked were indescribable but he behaved impeccably. The others involved would have thrown a fit and refused to work there. That was an occasion when John went meticulously to all the rehearsals. He and Pilar Lorengar made it quite clear to their colleagues that there was going to be absolutely no protest, nothing other than the most positive approach to this work. Clearly very much in love with *Don Carlos* he was determined to make this version successful.

The following year, 1987, as well as a revival of *Salomé*, John conducted *Fidelio* in a new production by Michael Hampe. Commenting on the music John confessed the first time he conducted the opera:

> [As a] dyed in the wool Mozartian, I had to face that Beethoven doesn't do things all that smoothly but we're used to these things from the symphonies and we know the message that must come across. Over the years I have found in this work incredible tone painting, as in the beginning of the second act, that long orchestral prelude in which we're introduced to Florestan in his misery. It's a major symphonic assumption and not at all easy to do. I find that with *Fidelio* you have to insist with the orchestra the whole time that they do what Beethoven sets out. His *sforzandos*, for example. There are hundreds of them and *fortepiano* accents, in this score and all of them relate to the dramatic content. They cannot be played mechanically. Each has to be expressive in a particular way and the orchestra must be on the alert for them.

When John conducted *Fidelio* in Cologne, he had used the *Leonore no. 3* Overture instead of the traditional *Fidelio* Overture and decided to repeat this in San Francisco. As always his decision was practical.

> At the very first performance at the Theater an der Wien, the overture we now know as *Leonore 2* was played and thought by everyone to be too long and too obscure. A year later, after many other changes in the opera itself, the same theatre mounted the opera again, with what we now know as *Leonore 3*. It was an instant success – and it's hard to see how it could not be. A year later, in Prague, the overture we know as *Leonore 1* was performed and again the critics were disapproving. It was only seven years later, in Vienna, that the work we now know as *Fidelio* was performed, with the *Fidelio* Overture and the work edged its way into popular success. For ages, stage directors and designers

have found it very difficult, technically speaking, to pass from the second act dungeon set to a totally different one, with its open skies. To meet the sheer physical demands of changing the set without a long and very anti-climactic wait until the trumpets have sounded to announce the arrival of the minister, technical people have needed ten minutes, which *Leonore* 3 nicely fills. Conductors have not been able to resist the acclaim they and the orchestra receive for this wonderful piece. We've all thrilled to this superb moment . . . *Leonore* 3 is much closer to the eighteenth-century overture form, which, for the benefit of the audience usually laid out some of the principal themes of the opera – which the *Fidelio* Overture does not do. And *Leonore* 3 puts people in the mood for the music they are about to hear. Since now we all want to proceed as directly as possible from the darkness of the dungeon to the brilliant light of the final scene, placing the overture there is wrong. But why should we deny ourselves in the opera house the effective outline of the plot which *Leonore* 3 gives us? And as music director and conductor, I must remember that it puts the orchestra on its mettle from the word 'Go'. Those are the artistic reasons for my decision: the aptness of the overture, its symphonic brilliance and the fact that I think that it will be a great *coup de théâtre* when we move from the dungeon into the final scene.

Holding the monumental, unrelieved epic together was not something John cared to do. There was not the sense of absolute intense sweet vision one needs to feel. Whilst he had a certain success there was conflict between the idealism of Beethoven and John's own personality.

It always hurt John when the producer or performers were praised but that a reviewer might end simply with the line, 'John Pritchard conducted'. At this stage in San Francisco, he was still putting his imprint on the house but his intention to conduct *The Ring* became a focus for critical disapproval. One of his stated reasons for accepting the appointment as Musical Director in San Francisco – technically the only place at that time where he held such a title – was his respect for the General Manager, Terry McEwan. However, the latter's diabetes deteriorated, necessitating his resignation in the spring of 1988. Lotfi Mansouri, Manager of the Canadian Opera Company, began working in San Francisco on a part-time basis in July 1988 until he could replace him completely.

14

Full Circle

From the time he left Glyndebourne, John intended that his work should expand at Covent Garden and the possibility of presenting a new production of *Norma* in February – March 1987 excited him. Having only a very old printed full score of the publishers Ricordi, he saw that it referred to the legendary Callas performances. 'Which makes me realise that a lot of water has passed under the bridge. However, the version could hardly be improved upon. The only exception is a verse for Adalgisa in the Trio which I shall include.'

Unfortunately, Margaret Price, singing Norma, was ill during rehearsal and in all was only able to rehearse for three days during the entire period. Every morning John would re-schedule. Without adequate rehearsals, the set was a problem, as the stage was divided up into very small areas and people did not know where they were supposed to go. It was so utterly unrehearsed that there were some scenes that had never been staged. People were just crashing about into each other. John was doing his best, trying to smooth everything over but even he could not make the production succeed. As not only the artists but the technicians were unrehearsed, the performances themselves became a nightmare for the backstage staff. Throughout the performance period, *Ariadne*, which is a long, technically complicated opera, was in rehearsal during the day, with the consequence that the House Manager found himself apologising for a late start.

There was a tent on stage in Act II, scene ii which made for a difficult scene change, taking longer than it should have done. Disaster occurred one evening when it had to be lifted and flown out. The 'OP' end of the tent became caught in the metal holly cut-out attached to the ceiling. The House tabs had to be closed, the tent freed and then flown out. The Stage Manager telephoned John and established a starting point in the music. As the House tabs were opening, there were four people frantically trying to lash the metal holly upstage OP. They fled.

Having studied Bellini with Vittorio Gui, John felt that it was under the baton of Italian conductors like him, Toscanini and Serafin that one realised the true expressiveness in the typical Bellini arpeggio accompaniment. Although everything in opera is interdependent, 'in Bellini, the orchestra is half the apple'. It was the beauty of the orchestral playing which flowed firmly and with subtlety, with John breathing with the singers that saved the performances. Later performances, when Margaret Price had recovered, were a profoundly moving experience. In the finale, John's preparation for the double climax, the overwhelming beauty of the orchestral playing matched the singing. It prompted Rodney Milnes in the *Spectator*, February 1987, to advise readers to 'use every possible subterfuge (you should try marrying a critic) to obtain tickets'.★ At the end of the series, on stage, Sir John Tooley presented John with the Covent Garden medal in honour of the twenty-five years plus ten he had been associated with the House.

After *Norma*, he hoped that *Lucia* in April and May 1988, might recapture memories of his past success with Dame Joan Sutherland. He wanted to reinstate the Wolf Glen scene which had not been included in the original production, because it had been done badly in a revival in 1980 and entailed eight minutes overtime. Funding problems prevented it from being included for this set of performances.

John showed that he was one of the few conductors with the ability to understand this particular music intuitively. *Lucia* is a technically complicated opera, with problems which need to be digested and solved well beforehand. In particular the great ensembles need to be pulled together with authority. The mad scene was a complete *tour de force*. At the end of the great aria with a superb flute accompaniment, John leant back smiling, joining in the applause for Edita Gruberova (Lucia). Surprisingly he drank lemonade, not white wine or champagne in the interval. Everyone at Covent Garden was aware that he was unwell. Pale, sweating profusely, every step seemed to be an effort.

★The article first appeared in *Opera* magazine

His tour of Germany, East and West in May 1988, with the BBC Symphony Orchestra, inspired John to declare the orchestra capable of becoming one of the greatest in the world. In the magnificent acoustics of venues such as the Leipzig Gewandhaus, the colour of the sound he produced was apparent even in broadcasts. Alternating Wagner's *Siegfried's Rhine Journey* and the Overture to *Rienzi* as the opening piece in the last concerts, it was very daring of him to programme the overture in Dresden, the city in which the opera was first performed. The musical benefits accrued during a long working period such as this and previous tours, were shown in the Orchestra's playing during the Prom Season and in the Schoenberg series during the autumn of 1988. A marvellous performance of *Moses and Aaron* at the Royal Festival Hall was achieved through John's positive commitment in getting that work performed.

Interesting engagements were being offered. His BBC appointment became a 'tie' and he vented his resentment privately. He considered the BBC's music station too esoteric and that the public was not being presented with the finest recordings available. He found Radio 3 a poor relative in comparison with French broadcasts in which the audience could hear Callas, Tebaldi et al., nearly every week. Outwardly, John never seemed to want any fuss or adulation but we all want to be loved. He enjoyed having an audience, being recognised, just as much as anyone else. Internationally recognised and, on a personal level adored by musicians, he felt deeply frustrated by the apparent unwillingness of the BBC to appreciate the new stature of its own orchestra and conductor. Having a powerful publicity machine at its disposal, he was unhappy at the empty seats at the Proms that season. He reported how absolutely furious he was when on telephoning 'his' secretary at the BBC, he was asked, 'Is it important because I'm rather busy?' and slammed the receiver down. The same day he had heard from Dame Eva Turner, who normally attended several Proms, receiving tickets direct from the BBC, that they could no longer supply her. 'After all that woman has done for British music!' he fumed as he signed his post backstage. Yet, on the podium, no one would have guessed that there had been anything to ruffle him.

During this period in Cologne he conducted such widely different operas as *Aida* and, on the following evening, *Wozzeck*. Returning to San Francisco for the autumn season of 1988, he

303

was conducting three operas, *Manon Lescaut, Parsifal* and *Lady Macbeth of Mtsensk*, two of them concurrently, putting him into the category of true music directors, those who have the ability to conduct almost anything in the space of one week. The success of the performances of *Parsifal* and *Lady Macbeth* turned John into a very popular figure with the San Francisco public.

John loved Wagner. As a young man, he cherished the recording of a synthesis of live performances under the baton of Hans Knappertsbusch at the 1951 Bayreuth Festival. Regarding *Parsifal* with special veneration, he considered that it had 'the most remarkable orchestration in the whole output of Wagner. There's nothing to equal the refinement of *Parsifal* in the treatment of the orchestra. When I conducted *Die Meistersinger*, I came to the last act thinking "Even if we hadn't had the first and second acts, what we hear in Act III would be a complete musical experience." I apply that attitude to the whole of *Parsifal* without any exception.' He felt that he was 'walking down endless paths of beauty.' As in *Meistersinger*, he wanted to avoid any sense of heaviness. The Jean-Pierre Ponnelle production he had conducted in Cologne, with sets of Gothic columns receding into the distance, used the whole depth of the stage. In San Francisco, he was happy to find a producer, Nicholas Joel and designer, Pet Halmen in sympathy with what he considered to be the great transparency of the score, the feeling of light which infuses the music. This production had columns too but they were translucent, 'with no annoying period touches.' In *Parsifal* the audience was overwhelmed by the incredible experience which can happen with this opera. Exhausted by the sheer length, he lay on his sofa in the dressing-room during the intervals, eating smoked salmon sandwiches to restore his strength.

Alternating *Manon Lescaut* with *Parsifal* in the evenings, *Lady Macbeth* was rehearsed during the day. The leading lady, Josephine Barstow, had sung the role of Katerina Ismailova at the English National Opera in English. Studying the role beforehand in England, it was the first time she had attempted something in Russian and, after a day of crisis, telephoned her manager saying she would have to cancel as she could not possibly learn the role. When she in turn telephoned San Francisco, she was greeted with laughter at the end of the line. 'We've just had Michael Devlin [playing the male lead] on the phone in tears, saying he couldn't learn it either.' As John was working on the other operas, the cast did not see him a great deal during the early rehearsals. It was his first *Lady Macbeth*. Not really familiar with Russian either, it was quite a struggle for everyone but he was excited and fell in love with the piece. By the first night he knew the work intimately, commenting to Josephine Barstow after one of the early performances, 'I went gooseflesh after one of your arias. It was wonderful.' She felt he was always kind and supportive but with a quiet discipline. 'He freed you. Some conductors dictate everything and others, like Karajan and John, created the music but inside what is happening, there was room for me as an individual to express myself.' John had the ability to take what the artists gave and absorb it into the whole. 'You felt free to do something, free to express something that maybe you had never talked about before, in the security that he would know why you were doing it and be totally with you. It's not even a conscious thing. It's something that happens in the creation of a moment. He was very much like that and those are the great conductors for singers. John would also know when you were going to forget something. Those people who are so in tune with everything, they've a kind of instinct that something is going to go wrong. They know before it does.'

Many believed his punishing schedule was responsible for John's exhaustion. He was coughing and himself diagnosed sinusitis or asthma and used a Ventide inhaler. Some investigations were done but this did not include a chest x-ray. He had refused. If John did not see any reason for something, he would refuse to do it.

The Grammy nomination in 1989 for his *Idomeneo* recording coincided with the disc he was making of Mozart's one act comedy with music, *Der Schauspieldirektor*, with Dame Kiri Te Kanawa. The producer, Christopher Raeburn, suspected that John had never conducted it before. Although the tempi were very leisurely, John coped with the work. At the end of the long CD is the *Figaro* overture, the last recording he made.

Travelling to Cologne in the spring of 1989 to conduct *Traviata*, *Entführung* and *Figaro*, John underwent extensive tests in April, including, for the first time, a chest x-ray. This revealed a cancer in his chest and a specimen was sent for pathology. Not knowing that the problem was extensive and would need not only radiotherapy but chemotherapy as well, that same day he went to London to conduct Dame Kiri Te Kanawa in a Barbican concert. In London, Peter Brown heard secretly from John's close friend in Germany that John was terminally ill. They went to the opening of Andrew Lloyd Webber's *Aspects of Love*. Unaware of the situation, John enjoyed himself.

It is a tragedy that his supposed asthma had never been investigated fully but John never pampered himself when ill, just wanting to be patched up to carry on working. Perhaps he instinctively guessed its seriousness but pushed the possibility out of his mind, allowing a full investigation only when he came to a full stop. It was 'inconvenient'. Later, John was told by four doctors that the tumour was not operable; that he had only months to live but that his age was in his favour as cancer is less aggressive in an older patient. Obviously the cancer had been missed but, irrespective of when it had been found, perhaps two per cent of patients might have up to two years' life expectancy. To his doctors it was not a question of mapping out the rest of their patient's life. John took things in a parochial way and continued to plan for the future. It was an old habit – not to listen, shut out unpleasantness and continue to do exactly as he intended.

Jeffrey Tate heard the news from a close friend of Peter Brown. At a meeting at Covent Garden to discuss the Japanese tour in 1992, he put forward John's name to take over *Così* because 'being the doyen of British conductors, if not the greatest Mozart conductor in the world today, I think he should do it but I've heard a terrible thing, that he has lung cancer'. Then, turning to John Cox, 'I'd like to know if it's true because if it is, we must seriously think about an alternative.' John Cox investigated and came back with a totally negative answer, that he knew John did not look very well but that there was absolutely no truth in the rumours going around.

John commenced therapy in London but interrupted treatment to make a studio recording with the BBC SO of *La Mort de Phèdre*. Written by Iain Hamilton for Helga Dernesch, it was the first time the mezzo-soprano had ever seen John impatient. The composer had not worked with him since 1985 and was very concerned because John seemed so unhappy. They did not know that it was an accumulation of annoyance. Like others who experience life-threatening illness, he no longer bothered to hide his feelings or maintain a calm outward manner. Always the first to promote contemporary British music, he voiced privately his impatience with the fact that the BBC, because they had public money available to commission works for the Proms and concerts, were presenting music that was constructed intellectually rather than created. The burden had been on his shoulders to make their compositions intelligible to the players.

Originally when appraised of Iain Hamilton's project, John was keen that it should be done in English but the composer thought it would be hopeless to translate Racine and made extracts from the French. Written very low, in a 'Clytemnestra' register, it is a very dark piece. Many contemporary composers are more approximate in their work with singers but, trained as an engineer, Iain Hamilton's music is very precise. It was difficult arranging dates suitable for both John and the soloist. Finally they both came up with the 26th and 27th May and John felt duty bound to honour his obligation. Although seated most of the time, it did not affect the vigour of the piece. Aware of an underlying tension in John, Helga Dernesch was nervous. Iain Hamilton had hoped there would be a piano session before but that was changed. John and the soloist, being very professional, worked well after more takes than expected but John knew there were places that were not accurate and he was unhappy.

Known primarily because of Mozart, now he was associated in the public eye as a champion of Strauss operas. During his time at the BBC, this extended to the Strauss symphonic poems. It was almost like pop music for him, particularly the tone poems, *Don Juan* or *Till Eulenspiegel*. Not only loving the colours in the orchestral sound, John identified with the characters they portrayed. Listening to a tape of *Ein Heldenleben*, which had been performed on 2nd December 1981, at the end, in a moment of great pain, the hero sees his whole life before him. It is all over: the battle, his wife has finished being terrible to him, his heart, breathing in the music, has floated away. John could hardly breathe. It was in moments like this, particularly during the Strauss 'last works' conducted in that last year, when he too was aware that he was dying, one knew that this was not a superficial man. When the pain was in the music, in Mozart or Strauss, in concerts or rehearsal many people missed it but he would hide his tears, not wanting anybody to know.

Conducting *Metamorphosen* on 1st February 1989, a very emotional piece written when Strauss was dying, performed in the Royal Festival Hall with solo players from the BBC SO, John was sucking cough sweets and trying to clear his throat.

The music was driving him crazy. It was very painful for him. 'Can you imagine it. This man was dying when he wrote this.' There were tears in his eyes.

In his last concert at the Royal Festival Hall on 14th February 1989, Felicity Lott recalled the orchestra playing the sextet and finally she sang the 'farewell' from *Capriccio*. 'We were both in tears at the rehearsal. There was an extraordinary atmosphere about the whole thing. I didn't know he was so ill. I had no idea. The sextet is so beautiful anyway, then they dimmed the lights and just had the lights on the music stands; a very theatrical touch.' The audience was so moved that the final notes floated away into silence. In the Green Room, sweating and pale, John seemed almost too emotional to greet the huge crowd that gathered.

Conducting a concert in Montpellier, John realised that he had a serious problem with his leg but nevertheless went to Salzburg for the revival of *Cenerentola*. Produced by Michael Hampe, it had been conducted originally by Riccardo Chailly but there was a difference of opinion as to who should conduct the revival. Recommended by Michael Hampe, John was the last minute preferred choice in the spring of 1989. Although he should have been in San Francisco, he was determined to conduct at Salzburg.

Arriving on 10th July to stay at the Goldener Hirsch in the Getreidegasse, just one hundred metres from the Festspielhaus, Count von Walderdorff, with his usual thoughtfulness towards guests, accommodated him in a very quiet part of the hotel. The Getreidegasse is a very narrow pedestrian shopping precinct converted from old, painted houses. Mozart was born at Number 9. Now a Mozart museum, on the ground floor several rooms contain models of stage sets of productions reflecting landmarks in either music scholarship or technical advancement in his operas. The first model is the 1951 Glyndebourne *Idomeneo*.

July 1989 was very hot throughout Europe. Suffering with his leg, the heat of the town centre became unbearable. Only two days after his arrival, John moved across the Salzach river, into the hills above Salzburg to a chalet apartment in Sonnleitenweg near the Haus Ingeborg.

John's favourite 'homes' have always been hideaways, secret places. Roads were easily missed and that to the chalet he rented was no exception. Up a steep zigzag, the overhanging trees left the road barely wide enough for a car; on the one side a sheer drop, on the other a brook rushing down the hillside. Parking the car, if one walks to the other side of the chalet it is easy to see why John chose this place. No stage designer could ever create such a set. Many countries have outstanding panoramic views but combined with a special clarity of light this memory is unforgettable. In the far backdrop, to the left, lies the Untersberg mountain; to the centre, below, the city of Salzburg with the spires of its many churches in the middle distance. There like some enchanted castle, the fortress Festung Höhensalzburg, seated atop the grey rocks that rise like enormous tree trunks, is spotlighted in the early morning sun. It was memories of the image of this fortress escarpment when they visited Edinburgh and looked up at the castle, which inspired Audrey Christie and Rudolf Bing to create the Edinburgh Festival.

In Salzburg to conduct a Mozarteum concert, Jeffrey Tate remembered going to the Hirsch restaurant in Parsch. 'That night there was everyone – Carol Vaness, Georges Prêtre and there in a corner was JP.' He and Klaus rushed over. 'He was delighted to see us. I looked at him and thought, "Oh God." I didn't like the look of him at all. He said, "I haven't been very well. I have had a thrombosis in my leg but I'm getting over it."' They made arrangements to get together. John went on his own. 'It was just like old times, the three of us.' He was sweating and coughing, very yellow, sunken and the clothes were hanging on him. 'Of course my mind went back to what I'd heard. I didn't say anything. I thought, if John wants to tell me, he will, I don't want to force him. He knows I'm a doctor – but of course he didn't at all. He told me about the little things, little by comparison, about how he'd had to abandon a concert, hadn't been at all well but was on the mend, would do the Last Night of the Proms and was looking forward to it.' John talked about the lovely time he had been having driving around the English countryside with Terry MacInnis. 'I couldn't believe my ears because John was being nostalgic. He was *never* nostalgic. Never reminisced about the "old days" with a tone of regret in his voice. He'd talk about them perfectly normally: there was never the impression "Oh, wouldn't it be nice to be back there!" He lived very much in the present. I could tell then, in a strange sort of way, although I didn't think he was conscious of it, he was probably aware that we were meeting for the last time.'

John talked about their time in Cologne, commenting that it was sad that they had not seen more of each other in the last few years. Increasingly, Jeffrey Tate realised that the evening had a valedictory feeling, that he was already aware everything was drawing to a close and was saying goodbye.

> It was very beautifully done in a way but it was definitely goodbye. My one sadness was that maybe something more could have been done medically: remissions are known. But John was a fatalist. I was convinced in Salzburg that he had decided in his heart of hearts that this was the end and he was going to go on working until he stopped and that was it. This is not the way John's life should have ended. I felt very angry with the Fates that they gave John that particular card. It didn't seem right to me because at the BBC he was beginning to enjoy an Indian summer and how awful not to have reaped his well-earned glory.

Singing the role of Cenerentola, Ann Murray was thrilled to be working with John again as she had not seen him for a few years. He telephoned her saying modestly, 'I think they asked everybody else and they were either busy or on holiday, so they came to me.' She thought he looked very tired but he did all the rehearsals. 'The orchestra loved him because he brought to the Rossini all the fizz and sparkle that only he could create.'

Peter Brown arrived in Salzburg two days before the dress rehearsal. John did not seem to have deteriorated but was having problems of a personal nature, in the management of his business affairs. Seeking to disentangle himself from a complicated, unwanted situation, he showed him a letter he was writing to an agent whose advice he sought. Since Basil's illness it had become necessary to make other arrangements regarding management. 'To try to get some order into the confused situation facing me, I had few alternatives available at the time.' Taking on a friend in Cologne to look after his business affairs he realised he had made a mistake. 'In a way, because of a general mix-up of the demands of personal friendship and business procedures, I'm afraid I sowed the seeds of a confusion which now persists.' Problems had arisen because John was careless with his money. He was so busy making music that he did not want to know about finances. Never wanting to think about organisational aspects in a business sense, refusing to look upon schedules and money realistically, he needed to have deadlines for decisions imposed upon him.

The paradox of John's life, the claim that he liked the good life and consequently was lazy and laid back is given the lie by one glance at his schedule. In the last years before his death he was probably working harder than at any time. A healthy person of his age would find it almost impossible to cope. One might almost believe that working too hard was connected with his enormous appetite; his tendency to eat too much, to make liaisons with too many people. John wanted to work hard, wanted to get up in the morning and say 'to which airport should I go?' Now he needed to pay more attention to his career but he did not have the time.

Restlessness remarked upon in early school reports, was inherited from his seafaring grandfather. His own father, Albert, had travelled around the British Isles. On marriage, it manifested itself in continual arguments with managements and the subsequent search for a new job. Unemployed, he had taken long daily walks in an attempt to deal with the restlessness within. Occupation helps blot out unpleasantness. It is not surprising, in his unhappy childhood, with constant friction at home, that John, like many sensitive people, sought refuge and solace in religion, the arts and in creative activity.

The impression that he was bored easily, the apparent need for stimulus and occupation, was part of his other problem, loneliness. In John, the continual search for fulfilment and the need for love with young people, even with those seemingly unlikely, represented the 'fresh start' for the unfulfilled part of himself. It was convenient for him to have friends who were to a large degree dependent. He could enjoy himself with less complications and, to paraphrase Oscar Wilde, 'Put his genius into his life and his talent into his work. When, through ill-health, he had periods of enforced rest, John suffered acute depression. The peripatetic nature of his career was given impetus by the increasing facility and speed of air travel. He was afraid to stop.

Never having worried about his body, it took care of itself. Not now. Just before the dress rehearsal of *Cenerentola* he went very discreetly to the hospital for treatment. On the first night there was a doctor on standby. John had trouble walking down the corridor. Ann Murray was very frightened. 'I don't think

311

I've ever seen anybody look so ill. He was a waxen colour; hot but freezing cold.' Yet, in performance, it was as though he was transported to a plain above physical suffering.

After the second performance, Terry MacInnis received a call in Brussels on 3rd August from John, saying that he would like to go home to Nenfré for a few days. Arriving in the early morning, he was surprised to see how bad John looked, as on the telephone he had not sounded so ill.

John sat in the back of the Mercedes with the front seat down so that he could rest the leg with the thrombosis. It was a hair-raising, horrendous journey as he had a very high temperature and was rather weak. Glad to be home, he enjoyed being in the house and for a while seemed to be getting better. Ten days later, Terry became very alarmed as John had a terrible fever and was coughing and shaking. He telephoned the doctor in London, who thought that pneumonia was the cause. Very worried, they went to the hospital in Nice where he was given antibiotics and advised to go to London. There he was admitted to hospital immediately.

Knowing that only something very serious would have caused John to cancel performances, especially Salzburg, I tried to contact him. He called from the hospital. 'My dear, it's so wonderful to be back in the arms of British medicine.' 'Well,' I replied, 'French medicine does tend to begin and end with the liver.' As always we began with a joke. Visiting him, his face was very pale and he used a wheelchair. I had sent him yellow roses for which he thanked me with a knowing nod. We always sent each other yellow roses after discovering, by chance, a shared preference. He talked about his medication. Terry mentioned that John would need to do less. He seemed to shrink, weaken and almost sink into the pillow at the thought that his *raison d'être* would be curtailed. 'But Terry, why should John cut back, there's nothing he wants more than to make music,' I said. John's eyes sparkled and he came to life again. Promising that when he was better we would go to Fortnum & Mason, I left. There was no doubting his happiness and contentment that Terry was with him, caring for him.

Ellen Morgenthau (now Mrs Philip Thurman), wrote requesting his participation in the memorial service in Germany to com-memorate the centenary of Fritz Busch's birth. The reply of 21st August 1989 was on hospital stationery.

Your 'voice from the past' reached me during a spell of check-ups and tests here, as I have finally realised there are limits to the pressure one can submit one's body to! I am leaving today, gradually to resume (but very gently) the career . . .

It was nice to hear from you after all this long time and of course your words aroused so many memories.

Asked by his doctors what he wanted to do, John had replied, 'the Last Night of the Proms

It was terrible for him to have to cancel the Prom performance of the Beethoven *Missa Solemnis* which he had never conducted. Revering the work, he never considered himself ready to give it the performance it merited. Although the Last Night is not musically more important than the *Missa Solemnis*, it was to have been his last concert as Chief Conductor with the BBC SO, the culmination of his achievement.

His doctors were in a quandary. Whilst wanting to give John every encouragement, there were many outside factors involved. With ultimate responsibility for the Proms, John Drummond telephoned the doctor frequently. He in turn would speak to the conductor. 'John, I've just had another talk with Mr Drummond.' 'Oh,' he would reply, 'you just leave him to me.' The doctors felt able to assure John Drummond that the conductor would not be perfectly fit but would be able to conduct the concert.

Released from hospital, he was readmitted immediately as an emergency and his medication changed from Warfarin to Heparin. It was explained that in spite of his lung cancer it only needed a little clot of blood to float up from the leg vein to the heart or chest, a pulmonary embolism and he would die. John understood everything quite clearly. He did not need extra details. He adjusted to the situation. If any doctor had been a disciplinarian, John would never have seen that person again. He wanted sensitivity and good advice and then made his own decisions.

Out of hospital and regaining his strength, he telephoned his old friend John Cox. 'You remember you said I could come down to Greenwich [his home] to tea, I'd like to come one day next week.' John, with his new friend Christof Paetzold and Terry, called for him at the stage door of Covent Garden. A brilliantly sunny day, the hood of the car was down and John wore a broadbrimmed black hat. They tootled off in the debonair manner he liked to adopt. John Cox remembered: 'It was a fabulous day. The garden was delightful. We found a footstool for his leg. It was the last time I saw him – waving goodbye as he was swept off to Blackheath.'

Amongst the many good wishes for the Last Night, few can have pleased John more than the phone call from Paul Myers asking him to make a recital recording with Dame Kiri Te Kanawa and Frederica von Stade singing duets. Even in happier circumstances, it would have been very difficult to find dates when all three were available. Future plans in London included more work at Covent Garden, the Japanese tour and *Bohème*. He was also scheduled to conduct *Die Fledermaus* for the English National Opera.

The audience of 7,000 filling the Royal Albert Hall, some of whom had begun queueing twelve days earlier for the privilege of standing through the music party of the year, had brought with them flags and banners of greeting of all sizes. To the millions watching their television screens at home, this was the first year in which the Last Night of the Proms was being broadcast on such a worldwide scale, even introducing Japanese viewers to a very British institution. It was the night when everyone in the audience could lose their inhibitions and enjoy themselves. Little did the audience of party-goers know of the nervousness amongst players and management. If the clot broke away from where it was lodged, the conductor might drop dead before the television audience. John made no secret of the fact that he had a thrombosis in his leg but there were rumours that he had lung cancer and had already lived his predicted time.

The planning involved was immense. John's three doctors had seats close to the exit so they could move backstage quickly. There was a strong young man crouched behind a potted palm by the platform to watch the conductor, who was seldom shown in close-up. At the least sign, he could leap onto the rostrum, put John over his shoulder and carry him offstage. Terry remained backstage watching the television monitor in case he was needed. Sir Charles Groves, in evening dress, sat at the back of a box ready to take over the performance. The conductor's room at the Albert Hall is rather narrow and is divided into small areas, so John was given the large soloists' room and oxygen was ready for use. He did not need it but it was there as a psychological boost. Although confined to a wheelchair offstage, John insisted that he would walk onto the platform himself. Wearing a new jacket made for the occasion by a German tailor, although intentionally loose, it hung from his shoulders. Apprehensive, the doctors remained with him until the beginning of the concert and then went backstage in the interval. Despite their nervousness, the performance was very moving for everyone. It was a tremendous effort and it was clear to all who saw him that the end could not be far away.

Anyone who has only seen the Last Night of the Proms on television, cannot imagine the heat and haze generated by the dazzling lights for the cameras. With the aid of a walking stick, John walked slowly onto the platform to the podium, greeting the roar from the audience with a wave of his hand. To an extra cheer he stood to acknowledge the applause, waving to the gallery but then sat down after the first few bars.

As well as being a gesture during the bicentenary year of the French Revolution, the first half of the programme could have been classified as a homage to Sir Thomas Beecham. Very fond of French music, John had often played the Beecham 'lollipops' from Chabrier and Massenet as encores on his tours with the BBC Symphony Orchestra. They began with the overture of *Le Corsaire*, which Berlioz wrote whilst on holiday in the South of France. With John's home in Nenfré, it seemed an appropriate piece. In addition the Promenade Concerts had originated in Berlioz' own time in Paris in the 1830s, an idea which was soon adopted in London.

The soloists had been chosen with great care. Standing to applaud the entrance of Ida Haendel in a red dress, John sipped from the glass of water under his desk while she tuned her violin. She had been invited to play the Saint-Saëns 3rd Violin Concerto. 'It was the greatest honour that John asked me to play for him. He was so terribly ill. I could not think about the music and my playing. I was only aware of him as I could see the terrible effort he made. The sweat was pouring down his face. I shall never forget that evening.' Afterwards, presented with a bouquet, not looking him straight in the face, she laid it on his music desk as her gracious salute to him.

Written five years after the Saint-Saëns, the *Carmen Suite* followed. As often happened with John, one would watch him begin conducting. Gradually his back would tense as he became involved in the music. Bobbing up and down in time to the Toreadors' music, the audience were roused to cheers by the performance.

During the interval the young man, whose job it was to look after John, gave him physiotherapy, pummelling and tapping his chest to bring up the phlegm which had accumulated during the first half, so he could make his speech without coughing.

The Eric Coates *Knightsbridge Suite*, written in the early thirties, began the second half. Like John in his early years, Coates had been a viola player but in Sir Henry Wood's Queen's Hall Orchestra. The audience were in high spirits, bobbing up and down in time to the music and the balloons being tossed about were already bursting. Fearing the worst, the cameras seldom sought the conductor and then not in close-up.

The second soloist of the evening, Sarah Walker, in a black gown with a purple bodice and velvet coat, sang in English 'Softly awakes my heart' from Saint-Saëns' *Samson and Delilah*. John was only conducting with his right hand, turning the pages slowly with his left but for Delius' *Summer Night on the River* which followed, used both hands. An exquisite performance with great delicacy in the strings and a beautiful cello solo encapsulating in miniature the essence of the composer, more than anything else it showed the great improvement he had made in the orchestra. No Last Night would be complete without Elgar's *Pomp and Circumstance* March no. 1, with the added words of 'Land of Hope and Glory'. Distinctively British with its contralto solo and chorus it roused the audience. They were getting noisy in preparation for joining in the chorus but John, putting his baton under his arm, half turned. There was an immediate and absolute silence in the huge auditorium at the presence and natural authority he always commanded. During the last verse when the audience stood with their flags waving, he began to use both arms, turning two-thirds towards them and then finally, when the yells for the reprise reached a crescendo, stood smiling broadly. John had placed the bugles for the opening of Sir Henry Wood's *Fantasia of Sea Songs* in the gallery, a typically theatrical gesture which the vast audience appreciated. Half turning to them, he spoke into the microphone, 'See if you can catch us in the last bar.' Of course they finished ahead. He wagged his finger, 'Shall we say six out of ten?' After the good-humoured laughter there was silence until Sarah Walker reappeared in a white dress with a cloak which was red on one side and blue on the other, suitable for 'Rule, Britannia', the second 'national anthem'. The audience rose during the performance, at the end of which she put her hands behind her neck, unhitching her cape and sleeves from the back. The cloak opened with the Union Jack flag on the front and back of the sleeves, prompting John to say in a sotto voce aside (fully miked), 'I want to let you into a secret. This is the last of Miss Walker's costumes for this evening. So to make it worth her while to give us such a beautiful display, let us do that last verse again.'

It is customary at the Proms for a number of presentations to be made. To John the promenaders gave a bottle. The BBC Symphony Chorus gave four silver-plated wine goblets and a bottle of champagne and the orchestra presented a Waterford decanter.

Sucking sweets, John prepared himself for his speech. He began quietly, hesitantly. 'Now you must be tolerant with me if my very brief remarks tonight have a slightly different tone from those other Last Night conductors. After all, for you this is a really joyous celebration of a wonderful series of concerts and it should be fittingly celebrated. For me, number one, it's my first Last Night.' John warmed to the applause. 'I could never get a ticket!' With the laughter, he relaxed and the raconteur surfaced. 'Secondly, you must allow me a certain amount of sentiment, a nostalgia, as it is my last concert as Chief Conductor of the BBC Symphony Orchestra. That's an important occasion. I have been with them, I could almost say, through thick and thin. It's worth thinking just for a moment about the nature of the relationship between a great symphony orchestra and its regular conductor. It's something very special. You know, although they look quite nice, orchestral musicians are a hard-bitten lot!'

John began to talk as if he were confiding in everyone individually, recounting as if for the first time, his often repeated anecdote about his first rehearsal with the London Philharmonic. The punch line 'He's got a friend who's a musician' delighted the spellbound audience. He went on:

> There is a certain danger for conductors which I sometimes stress, and that is, with great respect to my dear friends here, if the conductor or the artistic leader, is too much one of the boys – you know what I mean – if he's seen at the local pub after rehearsal, quaffing a few pints, there's nothing wrong with that I suppose but there must always be a gulf fixed, between the man who's carrying the can back at the end and earning all those gorgeous notices in newspapers and the artists who produce the musical sounds.
>
> What I've learnt from the BBC Symphony Orchestra and I'm

proud to say it, is that they willingly go along with what I want. I know that sounds a dictatorial attitude – it's not that – we have what is unique in my experience, an artistic rapport. I have only to look and something happens to the phrasing, to the dynamic. I don't like conductors who give lectures all the time. I like to be very practical. The orchestra gets used to the fact because in Maida Vale, the rehearsal begins at 10.30 and finishes at 1.30 and then at 2.30 to 5.30. Anybody who comes to the hall, for most programmes I do, at 4 o'clock the orchestra and I will have gone. It doesn't mean we don't like to rehearse a lot of music. This orchestra is incredibly adept at contemporary music – as sometimes you've had to suffer [applause] - but there are of course a great many symphony orchestras who enjoy playing to an audience such as yourselves, who respond to everything they do; who have responded throughout this long and tiring season. I would like to go round the orchestra now and pick out – they'd be Christian names – all my friends who deserve so well of you, and whose playing you have learned to appreciate. I give you now the BBC Symphony Orchestra. Let's stand them up [much applause]. I'd like to finish on a personal [someone starts singing 'For He's a Jolly Good Fellow'] – I'll conduct that in a moment! - a small personal statistic you'll all love. Apart from the revered figure of Sir Adrian Boult who was the founder of the BBC Symphony Orchestra, there's one other conductor equalled the length of time I've had conductorship of this orchestra and he occupied the throne, if I might call it that, for seven years and three months, Sir Malcolm Sargent. So I looked up the records to see if I came somewhere near his record and I did. Chief Conductor for seven years and only one and a half months. I then said to Mr Drummond, who was helping me with the statistics, 'Surely, I was Chief Guest Conductor at least two years before that? Undoubtedly this must count!' So, if you want to get some phoney figures, just get the Chief Conductor and the Controller of Music together! That's all – I hear you sing a very tidy *Jerusalem*. Would you like to have a go?'

He appreciated very much that Sir Charles and Lady Groves congratulated him afterwards. Normally after exertion John would have a dry coughing spell but this evening he was quite well, seeming to get a charge out of his achievement, unaware that those who knew and had worked with him spent the evening watching their televisions in tears. As his doctor said goodbye, John smiled. 'I didn't cough once.' Highly elated he went to the orchestra party in a wheelchair for a short time and then was taken back to the rented apartment in Pont Street.

The next morning Peter Brown, who had come to London for

the performance, was surprised when John telephoned. 'I thought it would be nice to have lunch.' Knowing how ill the maestro was, he suggested his suite at Claridges. Recognised by the concierge, it was a wonderful meal. In the evening Dame Kiri Te Kanawa and her husband, Desmond enjoyed the champagne in the goblets John had been given. 'It was a lovely hour that we spent. I thought then that I might not be able to spend much more time with him.'

Over the weeks, the farewells had been made. The morning he was leaving for San Francisco, accompanied by Christof who looked after him for the next couple of weeks until Terry arrived, Dr Atkinson went to see John to give him his Heparin injections. He was in great form. He was going to conduct *Idomeneo*.

When one realises how ill John was, it seems unbelievable that not only did he conduct the Last Night of the Proms, which entails so much more than any other concert but travelled to San Francisco to conduct *Idomeneo*. As everyone knew the only reason for him to live was getting on a podium, no one dared say 'no'. Immediately on arrival, contact was made with Doctor Colman Ryan, a former colleague of his London specialist, who was supportive.

Having seen the models and designs, John was happy that *Idomeneo* was being done in a classical manner. John Copley felt that working with him on such an extremely powerful, passionate opera was 'one of the greatest experiences of my life'. Unlike previous collaborations, the producer was amazed that John came to all the rehearsals. It was obvious that he was adoring every minute of an opera which he knew probably better than any other and of which he was still the master. With difficulty in breathing, desperate to keep going, he seemed to believe that by actually being there, sometimes walking, sometimes in a wheelchair that he was making progress. He was not.

As usual, he intended to play the harpsichord continuo but after the first big rehearsal, acknowledged that his assistant, Patrick Summers should. John had loved the Glyndebourne performances with Pavarotti and decided to use the tenor (male) version for Idamante, feeling that it was crucial to the emotional impact of the opera. The combination of Karita Mattila (Ilia) and Hans Peter Blochwitz (Idamante), both making their San Francisco debut, was very moving.

Even with his terrible cough and obvious weakness, moving about very slowly and in great pain, many of the cast were not aware that the conductor was dying. They knew about the leg, that he was having daily blood tests and continually taking medication, yet when he sat down and conducted, his concentration was such that none of his musicality and involvement was affected. In front of the score he seemed to come to life, knowing exactly what he wanted to hear and conveying his love of the music. That John had not lost his 'touch' with the music most impressed Karita Mattila. After winning the Cardiff 'Singer of the World' competition, she had auditioned for him in 1984 and appeared at Brussels singing Eva in *Meistersinger* with a predominantly young cast, also singing their roles for the first time. She recalled that her first solo album was with John, for Philips in the autumn of 1987. At San Francisco she was singing Ilia for the first time, again with John.

During rehearsal he wanted her to 'enhance the beauty and simplicity of Ilia. In performance, for him, time stopped during the miracle moments of beauty in the middle of the more dramatic scenes.' There was a special feeling in her last aria. At that point the staging was very simple and she could 'feel the "zeffiretti lusinghieri", the winds, in the theatre.' A long and taxing role, she was amazed not to be tired at the end of the performance and realised that this was due to John's ability, even then, to breathe with a singer. After the series she could not understand why *Idomeneo* is so seldom performed.

Nancy Gustafson, singing Electra, had met John previously at a dinner party and knew him socially but not professionally. She is married to Brian Dickie, who as assistant to Jani Strasser and later Administrator, knew John well from their Glyndebourne days. She remembered: 'Watching John, my heart was breaking . . . I would never forget my first musical rehearsal in the ballet room on the fourth floor of San Francisco Opera.' Orchestral rehearsals, just standing in front of the conductor and musicians, are difficult for singers as they are often happier in costume. 'I was a nervous wreck because I knew John was *the* expert on *Idomeneo*.'

She had sung Mozart roles before but found difficulty with decisions about appoggiaturas and what is not written in the score. Mozart stylistically is not like other operas in which every note is written. Electra has three arias. The middle one in Act II, 'Idol mio' is the most difficult because there is a soft, high coloratura, quite different from the other two. Nancy Gustafson had worked on it but was petrified. 'Of course John said, "Let's start with 'Idol mio'."' She remembered panicking and John laughing, 'What's the matter?' 'I replied, "Who told you that this is my least favourite? Somebody told you. You're doing this on purpose!" John was so kind – "No, well we'll make it your favourite."' It became a little joke between them.

Michael Hampe recalled the last time he saw John at a rehearsal of *Idomeneo* in San Francisco. 'I think it was clear to both of us that he wouldn't live much longer. He knew it and I knew it. It wasn't necessary to speak about it. It was my last sad meeting.'

John missed a rehearsal, just before the opening night and people sent him flowers. A special handrail was fixed so that he could climb onto the podium.

On the opening night the cast heard that John was so ill it was questionable whether he could conduct the whole performance. Mark Haffner sat at the back of the pit to take over from Patrick Summers, who was playing the harpsichord, so that, in turn, he could conduct. Every one of the singers felt that the opera was unimportant. There was no question of opening night nerves. Nancy Gustafson explained: 'We went out on stage and I'm sure that if something had happened to John, every one of us would have stopped singing. We wanted to do a good job for John; wanted it to be a success for John. Every one of us was thinking only about John.' The main problem was that he could not raise his arms very high, so that the singers had to look down continually. Even though he could not do all he wanted to do, he used his face and his eyes. 'He was with us every second. Every time we heard a cough, we would look quickly to see if he was all right. It was clear amongst all the singers and his colleagues that this was the greatest man for *Idomeneo*. He shaped the music, forming it exactly as he wanted and was one hundred per cent with you.'

Despite familiarity with *Idomeneo* there was never any question of 'I've done it, let's close the book'. As he conducted, the music brought him back from death as his face radiated happiness. Listening to a tape of a performance one would be unaware of any differences in terms of the harmony produced. Commenting about the performance he attended, Paul Findlay, Head of Opera at Covent Garden, felt that everything in it was 'right'.

Staying close to the Opera House in a modern apartment complex with a swimming pool and garden courtyard, John was resting in bed before the evening's performance of 17th October, when suddenly the building shook like a shoe-box. It was *the* earthquake. All the lights went out. Patrick Summers, Hans Peter Blochwitz and Nancy Gustafson ran out into the courtyard. Pipes had burst and water was gushing out. Fire alarms were ringing. 'It looked like hell, mass confusion.' Hans Peter felt that he had to see if John was all right, if he could get down. In the total confusion it was uncertain if there was going to be another earthquake, that this was just the beginning of something worse. Everyone was nervous about going into the building in case they might be crushed but with great courage, Hans Peter ran up all eleven flights of stairs to the top floor to find John, only to learn that he had changed apartments that day to the fourth floor. Later others came to see if he was safe. The performance was cancelled. The next performance, in concert form in the Masonic Auditorium, upset his colleagues because the audience could see him brought in a wheelchair to the conductor's podium. The circumstances and intimacy of this concert inspired an especially beautiful performance.

Whilst *Idomeneo* presented problems for the San Francisco Opera administration, the truly difficult situation was *Orlando Furioso*. John was meant to conduct using a newly revised edition of Vivaldi's text. Determined to carry on because it was planned for television, he went to some of the rehearsals in his wheelchair. Lotfi Mansouri brought in a young conductor, Randall Behr, from Los Angeles Opera, who knew Marilyn Horne, the lead in *Orlando*. Standing behind John, who could barely lift his arm, he would direct the orchestra making it seem as though John was still in control. It was a very delicate situation. Agreeing that his assistant should conduct the first two performances, John did not want to accept that he was dying, that he could not continue. Everybody could see that he was not going to do the performances. The pretence began. The pretence that if he rested he would be able to conduct the next performance – and then the next.

As in his Liverpool days, during his time in San Francisco, John gave 'insides' about the music he was conducting, giving the audience the opportunity to ask questions. He would share the platform with Dr Clifford (Kip) Cranna, the Musical Administrator who had become a good friend. The discussion session about *Orlando Furioso* was given by Cranna alone.

If he was in America it was traditional for John to spend Thanksgiving with Peter Brown and the previous year they had celebrated in the latter's home in Palm Springs. 1989 was no exception. As was customary, the house was packed with friends, one of whom flew from New York just to spend the afternoon with John. Oxygen gave support. Coughing badly throughout the night, he was hardly able to speak but he enjoyed sitting and watching everybody, absorbing everything.

Convincing himself that he was getting better, John returned to San Francisco. It was to be his last week. He was a gentle man, a gentleman and remained so until his death, grateful for every little caring gesture. Barely able to speak, he expressed his thanks with his eyes. Refusing to admit that he would not conduct *Orlando* and never doubting that he would travel to Cologne the following week for Mozart's *La Finta Giardiniera*, this was never cancelled. Another conductor was engaged only when Cologne heard of John's death. When he realised that he was not going to conduct the last performances of *Orlando* which were going to be televised, his reason for conducting that opera, it suddenly became very clear to John that he was not going to conduct again. He stayed in bed all day, not moving. To cheer him, Terry went out and bought videos of *Lost Weekend* and *A Fish Called Wanda* which they enjoyed. The next morning Terry went to his room at 7am. He could not be roused and was breathing strangely. Terry called the nursing service who had been visiting daily. An ambulance took him to the Medical Centre.

Taking tapes of the *Idomeneo*, Lotfi Mansouri together with Sarah Billinghurst from the Opera, went to see John in his private room, to convince him that he should return to London. Making the arrangements for the limousine to the airport, it was like the closing of a door.

Having suffered a slight stroke, as he lay heavily sedated, Terry played the tapes of his beloved *Idomeneo*. Death was registered at 8.15am, 5th December 1989.

In Cologne, when they heard the news of his death, his colleague, Georg Fischer, summed up their feelings: 'Now the world is a poorer place than it was yesterday.'

San Francisco Opera dedicated Strauss' *Die Frau ohne Schatten* on 10th December, the final performance of the season, to him. The following day, Monday, as the coffin left for John's last journey by plane for England, San Francisco Opera held a Memorial Service in Grace Cathedral. Amongst the moving tributes and music, Lotfi Mansouri selected 'The March of the Priests' from *Idomeneo*. When he and John were working together on *Così* at Geneva Grand Theatre, the director, Herbert Graf, died just before the opening night. He and John decided to play that same March and accordingly Lotfi Mansouri chose the piece for John's own Memorial, little knowing this had been requested in his will.

After Mass on 13th December in the Roman Catholic Church in Soho Square, London, John was buried next to Audrey Mildmay Christie in the small graveyard close to Glyndebourne. Tributes and Services of Thanksgiving for his life were given throughout the music world.

At the crowded Memorial Service in London, one was aware of being surrounded by memories that together form the mosaic of life. The faces belonged to an era, to people who had shared in each other's lives and experiences, who had come to give thanks for the life of a man who had touched and influenced their own. Today, on the British music scene, there are many more famous stars but there are great personalities, particular people, who have gone. For many, John does not seem to be missing. He remains with them, a part of them. He's there in the stories, in the moments they shared on and off stage.

The following prayer was found amongst John's papers, written in his own hand and was read at his Memorial Service in London by Tom Redman.

Prayer of St Thomas of Aquinas, before study
O ineffable Creator, who, out of the treasure of Thy wisdom, hast ordained three hierarchies of angels, and placed them in wonderful order above the heavens, and has most wisely distributed the parts of the world; Thou, who art called the true fountain of light and wisdom, and the highest beginning, vouchsafe to prove upon the darkness of my understanding, in which I was born, the double beam of Thy brightness, removing from me all darkness of sin

and ignorance. Thou, who makest eloquent the tongues of the dumb, instruct my tongue, and prove upon my life the grace of Thy blessing. Give me the quickness of understanding, capacity of retaining, subtlety in interpreting, facility in learning, and copious grace of speaking.

Guide my going in, direct my going forward, accomplish my going forth: through Christ our Lord.

Amen.

Appendices

APPENDIX A: *Liverpool*

> PROFESSIONALISM IN MUSIC
> THE POSITION OF OPERA OUTSIDE LONDON
> BEHIND THE BATON

APPENDIX B: *Glyndebourne*

> MEMORANDUM: GLYNDEBOURNE'S FUTURE
> 'CAPRICCIO'
> THE OPERAS OF MOZART
> GLYNDEBOURNE AND ROSSINI:
> THE STYLISTIC APPROACH

APPENDIX C: *Germany*

> CORRESPONDENCE WITH DR HAMPE ON
> *PETER GRIMES*
> MEMORANDUM: THE FINANCIAL SITUATION
> PROPOSALS FOR CONTRACT

APPENDIX D: *Brussels*

> DRAFT PRESS ANNOUNCEMENT

APPENDIX E: **BBC Symphony Orchestra**

> TEMPO

Appendix A
Liverpool

PROFESSIONALISM IN MUSIC

'We all know that the *competition* we shall have to face in the musical jungle just outside will all too soon *weed out* bad or unprofessional habits or attitudes. Yet the more flexible attitudes which are acceptable today make it advisable to try to define the *disciplines* which we can accept as guidelines in our professional careers. These *disciplines* apply to the organisation of our daily work routine to our *relations* with fellow artists, managements and the public.

'I remember that as the son of a violinist in a big symphony orchestra, some of the *essential mystique* of being a *professional* musician in a country of "unbelievers" rubbed off onto my early musical life, so that my piano studies were always conducted under the titillating thought that *one day* it could be decided whether I should "become a professional" like my father. I may say that the overwhelming prejudice in family circles was *against* this suggestion and many hopes were expressed that one might be attracted to banking, insurance or the stock exchange – something *SAFE*! There came a moment when I had to decide whether to "go professional". Of course, in that moment one never questions the *talent* that is available – only the likely "breaks" one can expect from a massively entrenched musical establishment which seems able and willing to get on *without* one.

'So the first brush with the immense concealed iceberg of professionalism occurs. You turn your back on the safe prospects of a job in commerce and take your decision. Now this decision is essentially a decision to be *lonely*. Society is organised with a deceptive willingness to take care of you. Its price is that you

328

will sell your working life, as far as the majority are concerned, to some big corporation, some organisation of Mammon. There is no doubt that Governments think no longer in terms of the individual. Whatever lip service might be paid to the role of artists in the community, there is no doubt that *as soon as* you come out from under the educational umbrella you are on your own.

'Now in this brave solitude at the start of a musical career, we are already close to the heart of the *raison d'être* of professionalism in the arts. Not one of you listening to me has really any doubt about the *rightness* of your decision to become a professional artist. Your doubts, in varying degrees, according to your temperament, are about how fortunate you may be. When at the end of the war I found myself as a young man playing viola as a deputy up north in a professional symphony orchestra, of course I knew my skill was too limited to follow my father's career in the orchestra but my eye was on the conductor. A vague surmise was forming in my mind but, honestly, it was not because it seemed like a rewarding job to conduct an orchestra but because my involvement in the music was such that I felt a growing desire to communicate ideas to people who might follow. But this organisational or teaching wish of the embryo conductor comes from the same source as if you, for example, feel that your voice is above the average in quality. It is not *at first*, that you envisage the public as being better off for hearing you sing. It is more like a flower in bud, you have a natural necessity to unfold and fulfil your nature. The *second* stage is for people to admire the bloom. So here I suggest we have the crux of professionalism. A facile definition of the professional is that it is someone who earns his living wholly by the exercise of a talent which has been trained. But we know that we earn our living by being a singer, producer or conductor but that what makes us a professional is the inescapable urge, irrespective of reward, to do what we have been (in the old-fashioned term) called to do.

'My father used to talk a lot about the fantastic organisation which Sir Henry Wood brought to his professional life. One of the marks of *care* in a conductor is the attention he gives to orchestral parts and my father told me how amused they were in the orchestra when a set of parts heavily marked in blue pencil would be set in front of them, with nothing left to chance, tempi changes marked in 4, in 6, etc. This was all based on the "one rehearsal" concert which was still the order at the time and we realise how much work Henry Wood must have done at home to make sure nothing was wasted in the precious rehearsal.

'Instead of resting in his dressing-room before the start of the concert, Henry Wood kept guard over the entrance to the platform with a large tuning fork mounted on a resonator. Each player was required to tune. Nothing was left to chance – another mark of the *professional*.'

THE POSITION OF OPERA OUTSIDE LONDON

Talk 7th January 1956 to Liverpool Opera Circle prior to visits of Covent Garden Opera and Glyndebourne.

'The other day the Government rejected the idea that too much money was being spent on opera and ballet for London and too small a slice of cake came to the provinces. (I would like, by the way, to welcome the mere *fact* of a Government pronouncement on opera. We are progressing when in this way the very strong feelings of music-lovers all over the country do get a *response* from the Government itself.) But I think this is a very natural feeling for opera and ballet-lovers living outside London: a feeling of slight resentment when they read of an Italian season at Covent Garden employing famous artists from the Continent, which for geographical and financial reasons they cannot derive any benefit from. The trouble is however that even if the grant to Covent Garden were reduced by one-third and that third were allocated to some operatic purpose elsewhere in the country, the result, I am afraid, would merely be that Covent Garden would be hamstrung and no longer provide a fitting opera centre for the capital, *without* any corresponding practical advantage to the provinces because the sum involved would be too small – the jam would have to be spread so thin.

'No. I should like to say that my view is we must all gradually but firmly aim for the day when it will be possible to establish a working opera theatre outside London – logically it would be in the north of course. Mr A K Holland recently pointed out the possibility, I think a most interesting one, of the country regional symphony orchestras presenting short seasons of opera as part of their regular work in the year. In September, here in Liverpool, we shall have an example of the sort of thing he meant – the visit of the Glyndebourne Company will see the Liverpool Philharmonic in the opera pit, I imagine for the first time in its own city.

'I don't feel I am speaking of never-never land when I say that the establishment of a Northern centre for Opera might quite easily come about and probably before as long as ten years have elapsed. Never has there been such a public for opera throughout the country. The Carl Rosa Company is valiantly on the road throughout the year and nearly always has full and enthusiastic houses. In fact I can say that at a time when critics were sniping constantly at the Carl Rosa, belittling its standards and prophesying its total collapse, the constant loyal support of the public in many towns throughout the country kept up the morale of the company. Now we see it established on better lines and with a degree of Arts Council support.

'But the trouble with any touring company is that the shortness of the visit to any one place imposes a burden of rather an artificial kind on the people who love and support opera in that city. When the Covent Garden Company comes here in March there is no doubt at all that for hard reasons of Lsd (pounds, shillings and pence) many people who would by inclination be at the theatre almost every night will be unable to do so more than once or twice: and they will have an agonising time choosing which operas to attend and which to sacrifice. For the rest of the year they must get their opera from gramophone records, the sales of which show that this is precisely what they do. You can be quite sure that whatever authorities eventually give financial backing to the establishment of a Northern Opera House, there will be no enthusiastic subscriptions from the gramophone companies!

'Of course, the expenses of opera are notoriously great. I believe the Opera Circle recently had a visit from Mr Pat Terry, Manager of the Covent Garden Company and he gave you some facts and figures behind the presentation of opera. A Northern Opera Theatre, to get under way at all, would need to count on:

1. The services at stated times of the regional symphony orchestra. It would be quite impossible to find players for a sixty-piece opera orchestra, but it might be possible to increase the size of, for example, the Liverpool Philharmonic *and* the Hallé orchestras so that players on an annual engagement would spend so many weeks of the year playing for the opera.

2. Next I would like to suggest that the Northern Theatre should be self-governing from the region, with its own Board of Management, but with an understanding arrangement with Covent Garden or Sadlers Wells as far as those rare birds, opera singers, are concerned. There are already too few good singers available and although a Northern theatre would give new opportunities to local artists of all kinds, it would have to borrow quite extensively from time to time in order to cast the operas satisfactorily.

'*Audiences*: You will perhaps question whether an audience could be found for opera week-in-week-out in any city, however large, apart from London. Personally I should envisage quite a large amount of touring for a company *based upon* a Northern Centre. Thus the provision of opera, the number of visits to any one place, could tend to be in proportion to the size of the town and its opera-loving public.

'I make no charge for presenting you with all these ideas, as I have no illusions that by this time next year there will have arisen a gleaming new Opera House, bustling with activity, in Church Street, Liverpool or Piccadilly, Manchester. I merely say that all of you who care for opera and want to have opera performed within reach of your homes ought to be clear on the ultimate aim and through your organisations, such as the Opera Circle, keep local interest in these matters alive.

'Well, having attacked the present methods of touring opera in this country, I will now say a word in gleeful anticipation of the visit of the Royal Opera House Company in March. It is a remarkable fact, not to be denied, that during 1956, Liverpool will hear performances of the following operas: *Carmen, Die Walküre, Tannhäuser, Troïlus, Marriage of Figaro, Bartered Bride, Madame Butterfly, Don Giovanni, Cenerentola.*

'This is quite a remarkable list and means that all of you must scarcely smoke a cigarette or drink a Coca-Cola for the next six months, in an all-out effort to save up for tickets and live up to your frightening responsibilities. Above all, you must make sure that Liverpool measures up to this large-scale operatic challenge – and in your own interests because, in the first place, if Covent Garden are not well supported they will tend to omit Liverpool from a future tour and there you'll be out in the desert again and secondly, as regards the Glyndebourne visit, the city council has made a superbly enlightened gesture in sponsoring such an undertaking and they must be shown that the citizens appreciate it.

'Just one thing before I come to the operas being performed, and it's a personal point. I am, as you may know, closely associated with both Covent Garden and Glyndebourne. I will conduct *Figaro* for Covent Garden during their tour and *Don Giovanni* for Glyndebourne, and I would like to say from long knowledge of opera singers and their ways – don't be shy of them, treat them as pets, they're almost human. When one of them you particularly admire sings well, let them know it by your applause. Ignore those stuffy notices in the programme, please don't applaud while the music is playing. You must remember that in all the operas you will hear this year, except *Walküre*, the composer himself indicated the places in which he *expects* applause – he writes a loud orchestral conclusion and then the conductor has to wait a moment before continuing. You have no idea what a difference it makes to everyone when an appreciative applause fills the gap. I'll swear the singers give a better, more confident performance after it.

BEHIND THE BATON

When I go on holiday in Europe I am always happy to find a spot in the more remote villages well away from the big towns in which a musician has to spend his working life. In such places I have noticed a certain amount of wide-eyed surprise on the part of inn-keepers and so on, when they ask for my passport and see my occupation described as 'Orchestral Conductor'.

This wonder of theirs *could* of course mean that they regard the holder of the passport as an obvious impostor, but I suspect it is actually a complete *unfamiliarity* with a certain grade of musical performers who imagine themselves very essential to the world of art. Their attitude does lead me however to think about the meaning of my job and what value it may really have, first of all to fellow musicians and secondly to the public.

It is rather amazing you know to realise how the influence and apparent importance of the conductor has increased during the past 150 years. A very famous English tenor worked with me some time ago at the opera and (as happens sometimes) we would occasionally disagree about his interpretation of a role. When this happened and he had tired of the argument, he would never fail to remind me, in uncompromising north country tones, that a hundred years ago 'the conductor's name wasn't even printed on the so-and-so bill, old boy!' We all know how Verdi and Wagner, on the whole, disliked the breed and accused them of falsifying the composer's ideas and preening themselves before the public. But, thinking aloud to you now, I am more concerned to consider what the good conductor has to contribute to our appreciation and understanding of music. In Wales of course, where there are scores of choral groups to whom their conductor is a respected and valued musical leader, we are not likely to hear the question 'what *use* is the conductor – wouldn't the orchestra do just as well without him?' The trouble is, the conductor's job *looks* easy, glamorous and flatteringly prominent. There's a saying in the profession 'the baton is always in C major' – and it's certainly a fact that if the conductor makes a mistake on the rostrum, usually only his players and singers know – the music goes on under its own momentum and the audience is unaware of the momentary hesitation flashing through the minds of perhaps a hundred people. I wonder if I dare tell you of a recent example where confusion was spread by a moment's loss of concentration on the part of the conductor. It is a *true* story but I am sure that no one listening could possibly identify the central character, a conductor of much experience abroad. One of this gentleman's little vanities is to conduct always by heart and on the occasion I am thinking of he was directing a performance of a major orchestral piece by a French composer. This is a complicated score technically and one in which however familiar the players are with the general sense of the music, there are always moments when the whole orchestra welcome a decisive lead because of the rhythmic complexities. One of these trouble spots occurs when, in the midst of a long spell of quick four-in-a-bar time, perfectly straightforward, there is suddenly a *trick* bar when the conductor must give a clear *five* beats. Needless to say, this passage had given no trouble at rehearsals (when the conductor had the score in front of him), but in performance, somehow – who knows – he became confused or forgetful and in the decisive moment continued to beat a vigorous *four* instead of the stipulated five. Now orchestral players are extremely sensitive to the lead they receive from a conductor and often some at least (bless them) are ready to assume *they* have perhaps made a small mistake rather than the man on the box. So what happened when they saw a new unexpected strong down beat a second sooner than the music in front of them required? I want you to follow me closely. The players who were willing to give the unfortunate conductor the benefit of the doubt obediently jumped a beat and played with great fortitude and strength to influence their colleagues who *hadn't* jumped. These latter, including the more experienced and wily players who realised the conductor's mistake, and were determined to keep the orchestra together in the correct course of the music, played even louder with *strong downward motions of the arms* and feet, so that to the onlooker a section of the orchestra appeared to be afflicted rather painfully with spasmodic jerking. The worst was yet to come. A few bars on from this fatal point in the score there should be a strong fortissimo entry by the three trombones. These players, *isolated somewhat at the back of the orchestra* and *alarmed by the confusion before them*, entered raggedly but with a very desperate conviction, at least a bar too early. At this stentorian sound, any stragglers in the rest of the orchestra who had been unable to decide which of the two warring factions to favour, came down at once on the side of the trombones and thus created a third battalion in the general mêlée.

I'll not harrow you by describing the sufferings of the conductor during all this time, his perspiring brow and wildly flailing arms, but will pass on with a shudder to say that during a momentary calm in the battle, a resourceful oboist gave out an unmistakeable theme occurring *much* later in the music, and the whole orchestra, grasping at this lifeline with intense relief, hauled themselves back into comparative order once again. Need I tell you, as a postscript to this cautionary tale, that the end of the performance was greeted by the public with the most rapturous enthusiasm and prolonged applause?

I hope no one will think that I have told this story with a mocking or malicious intention, least of all at the expense of a colleague. As a conductor, I am only too conscious how on certain occasions a moment's interruption of concentration on my part can put a smooth-running performance in peril.

Now having shown you in rather a severe way the dangers of the conductor's craft, I'd like to take you behind the scenes to demonstrate a little how his job is carried on from day to day. I find that many people, even concert-goers and other music lovers who appreciate the amount of study and practical experience necessary for a conductor's training, nevertheless fail to realise how incessantly he ought to apply himself if he is to satisfy his own standards and therefore the public who hear what he has to offer. A lady recently told me how envious she was because I conducted only two evenings in a particular week at the opera house: 'how nice to have all that time off', she said. As I had been rehearsing every single morning with the orchestra and full company for a following presentation at the opera house and had daily piano rehearsals with the principals as well, I wasn't leading quite such a life of leisure as she supposed.

A very great and real danger for the conductor who begins to get on in his profession is that he will allow himself to become *too* busy, rushing from place to place and even country to country and pointing to the black pages of his engagement book as evidence of his success. It is I suppose easy to be idealistic and the problem always facing a young conductor is that at first he can by no means afford to pick and choose his engagements: I feel however that as soon as he has a sufficient achievement to keep the wolf well off the doorstep, he should begin to be wary of doing too much.

It would be out of place for me to lecture my colleagues on such a point, but I have been rather lucky in the fact that a good deal of hard sense was pushed into my head at a receptive age by my own father, an experienced orchestral violinist, who was by temperament suspicious of conductors and used to scoff at the idea that they could really be taught their job. He used to say 'study the fiddle hard, my boy, and play in an orchestra like me – you'll soon learn enough from watching conductors make fools of themselves!' He thought, in his more mellow moments, that a real conductor's best influence on his men lay in what sort of a man-plus-musician they thought he *was*, much more than in what he had to tell them in rehearsal.

Years and years later a similar idea was expressed by the great German conductor Fritz Busch, who told me 'don't just think your scores contain *all* the meaning and all the beauty – how long is it since you walked around a picture gallery?' I always place a strong personal importance on that remark – it seemed to bring before my eyes an inspiring picture of the conductor as a man whose mission was to breathe in as much beauty as he can find in the arts of the world, so as to assimilate it, work on it and interpret it in the fullest way he can to the audience.

To continue with my description of a day in the life of a conductor, I find there is no such thing as a set procedure, because for example on the Continent a conductor will spend a good deal of his time in the opera house, whereas here most of them are concerned with one or other of the leading orchestras or the manifold activities of the BBC. Apart from the widely different work in these two categories, there is also an important difference of organisation. In the opera there is always a large staff of administrators and managers, who concern themselves with every detail of what happens until the curtain goes up – the conductor's *main* function, in a way, is to take over from that point. But (as I have found in my own work with a regular symphony orchestra such as the (London &) Liverpool Philharmonic(s)) in the concert world the conductor must work hand in hand with the administrators: not a programme can be planned without his approval, the schedule of work and travel for the orchestra affects the success of concerts and therefore the box office, problems of individuals in the orchestra have a vital relation to the morale of the whole team and so on. A regular conductor of a symphony orchestra will usually spend three or four mornings a week on rehearsals for programmes to be played in the next seven days. If he's lucky some time will be spent on difficult works to be given in later concerts. Now this raises an important point – the conductor's own preparation of intricate scores. Modern orchestral players are so efficient (and so busy) that very rarely will they be able to practise at home a new and technically difficult piece of music, unless it contains a notorious solo or something of that kind, which will cause them loss of face if they muff it! Thus the players all come to the first rehearsal of such a piece with no idea what it is about and they will have to concentrate, count hard during bars rest and so on – waiting for the familiarity which repetition during rehearsal will bring. So it is just *then*, at the very first rehearsal, that they need the most patient correction and positive guidance all along the line from their conductor. He for his part must come to that first rehearsal with the kind of inside, complete knowledge of the work which the players have only to achieve at a much later stage!

Before leaving the subject of rehearsals, I would like to urge some of the more musically inclined of you to seek permission, sometime, to attend an orchestral rehearsal when the opportunity offers. Many conductors do not object to a limited number of listeners at rehearsals and it is an extremely interesting experience to hear a symphony take shape under a conductor's hands. When I am asked how I 'learned' conducting I always reply, 'by sitting for hours at the rehearsals of the great conductors, with the score, *hearing* the improvement when they go over and over certain passages, watching how they obtain the effects they want.'

I am quite sure by now you are ready to shed a tear in sympathy with the hard life a conductor leads – and remember I have not detailed to you the extensive work which must go into planning a whole concert season – agonised pondering on what you, the public will pay to hear, how to fill the seats if we play Mr X's new symphony – and even will last season's financial results justify a raise in pay to the first clarinet who otherwise may decamp (terrible thought) to a rival orchestra?

Is it worth it? Well, 'YES'. If the responsibility is great, so is the satisfaction when a performance really 'comes off'. Every conductor cherishes a memory or two of some splendid moment of real exaltation, when all our hopes as artists seem to receive their satisfying fulfilment.

Appendix B

Glyndebourne

MEMORANDUM - GLYNDEBOURNE'S FUTURE.

December 1964.

As a preamble I want to emit a 'mea culpa'. The thoughts to be expressed in this paper have been revolving in one form or another in my mind for months. Yet if I believe in them sincerely there is NO task in however busy a life which should take precedence of 'putting GB to rights', if that rather too sweeping and facile expression be accepted for want of a better. But (and now I welcome my colleagues to join me on the confessional stool) are we not all of us too complacent, lulled into inactivity by our good luck over the years – luck in the circumstances of GB's original founding, its masterly first triumvirate which enabled GB to shine out over Europe when the rest of Britain's opera was merely an annual beanfeast in Wagner etc. with no relation whatever to the hardly awakened national interest.

We all know how great an inheritance of esteem and solid achievement passed into our hands, but in the peculiar climate of European opera at this time [there are] a collection of really troublesome problems which I propose to suggest we are not equipping ourselves to tackle. We are too slow, too divided, too NICE, too late, too choosey, too cliquey and much too diffuse in our system of inter-consultation. Let me speak for myself, I don't do *enough* by merely attending meetings for next season's casting, hearing a few auditions and 'adorning' the rostrum for a good number of Glyndebourne's performances. Although I'm committed emotionally to GB I don't satisfy myself *or the inescapable pressure of events* by what I do at present. This paper will at least help me to be a true Counsellor.

Sir John Pritchard

A. SHORTAGE OF SINGERS

We are all aware of the problems of intense competition from other houses, including the now much better organised Covent Garden and the multiplication of summer Festivals even in England. Before coming onto the obvious question of fees, allow me to remark one thing which I regret. We are less and less able, apparently, to keep the nucleus of a *Glyndebourne Company* at our disposal. Were not our happiest post-war days those in which we could call year after year on Jurinac, Bruscantini, Oncina, Evans, Lewis, Lorengar, Noni, Cadoni and Wallace who *have not been replaced* by any regularly available singers.

Then we have had fleeting visitors of the first class such as Alva, Freni and Sutherland.

Every opera house, be it a Festival or not, depends for its very life on an adequate supply of the following categories: soprano: dramatic, lyric and soubrette; mezzo of the Cherubino type; lyric tenor; dramatic tenor; high baritone and *Figaro*-baritone, Basso. The second part of our difficulty under shortage of singers brings us face to face with the fee problem!

The fees of the English based artists, except the outstanding ones, do not constitute a problem. The real difficulty is that while we all applaud GB's refusal to adopt a 'star system', nevertheless we are up against a real difficulty if it comes to casting a Mozart opera such as *Così*. Fiordiligi need not be a star but we shall be very lucky if we can find one to satisfy our standards who is commanding a fee per evening of less than (minimum) £180 in Germany or Austria, let alone Italy. Now I may hear someone say that the number of performances at GB brings up the total earnings over two months to a respectable figure, even at a top GB figure of £120. But it is the lowered average of earnings caused by a non-paid rehearsal period of three weeks that invalidates this way of looking at it. The type of artist we are speaking of, *if not giving his time to GB*, would earn more elsewhere.

Of course I don't want to underestimate the imponderables which have and will again bring artists to GB, their love of the atmosphere and the care taken of them, all they learn there, but these aspects so enjoyed at the time of the season are apt to loom less large when the singer is back at home and soberly considering alternative offers. Another point is that nearly all the people we want are highly thought of by the opera houses to

340

which they are attached and are apt to be required for interesting premières in their own cities.

In a way I criticise our approach to the whole problem of singers as out-of-date and unrealistic. It's an infernal nuisance I agree but we need them and we haven't so many cards to bargain with as we had. Think of the much lower standard of artist auditioning now for us, both in England and abroad, which seems to show that really the artists we are after are already singing big parts and tend to say 'let them come and hear a performance!'

We have to discover annually sufficient young artists already before the public (GB is no place for beginners in main parts) who can obtain leave from their opera houses and for whom the scale of fees is at the moment no deterrent because of the prestige they gain by a GB appearance. I do not say that our endeavours are without success. But when we strike gold I suggest we shall have to be bolder in our decisions.

Now let me come to my proposals, realising that where financial matters are involved I am not equipped to know what is possible.

1. GB should create a category of 'Special Division Artists' limited, say, to six members (not regular, of course) who would be paid up to £200 per performance for a maximum of ten performances. If word of this got around and caused demands from other singers, they would be refused *whatever the result* to avoid a general inflation. This action would probably produce two enormous advantages (a) one really noted representative of each category of voice in my list of vocal types above, and (b) a change NOTICEABLE TO THE PUBLIC in the number of famous artists appearing at GB.

2. As a corollary to No. 1, my proposal for the type of season given by GB in the future will be based, for the Special Division Artists and all the main roles, on a total span of FIVE weeks from the first musical rehearsal to the end of their engagement on one opera. This proposal will, I fear, bring opposition from quarters anxious to preserve GB's high musical and stage standards which they may feel threatened by any reduction of rehearsal time. But I make no apology in saying that a way MUST be found to do it. It would require

two things – much harder work by the artists on arrival – you will all remember the celebrated start of Rennert's rehearsals when he first came to GB, the locked doors and banned tea-breaks; but in a way it did us all good! The second thing might be a distinct increase in the numbers of repetiteurs and stage assistants, on which I will be guilty of a cynical sounding comment. The cost of these is small indeed compared to the cost of opera singers!

3. As distinct from the creation of a Special Division we should proceed to build up a Glyndebourne Company by instituting, for younger artists in England and abroad, a two year contract system with a built-in option on our side at a slightly higher fee, for a third year. The institution of such a system presupposes a greater confidence in our joint powers of selection than we have previously had and also a longer term view on repertory.

B. REPERTOIRE

It goes beyond my intention here to embark on a general survey of the repertoire, as our normal conversations cover the situation and trends. But what I do think is that we really ought not to wait and see what success a new production has before planning firmly to do it a second year. I expect of course Henze's *Elegy*, as a modern piece, would not be intended for two consecutive years. We thus have a fairly good record which positively should embolden us to plan two seasons ahead. It is not enough that we should sit down next June to discuss EVEN THE OPERAS we shall rehearse in less than twelve months, before we start on the casting! We do enjoy good relationships with certain impresarios on the Continent, and I can think of nothing which would encourage them to help us more than a decision to get ahead now with 1966!

C. PRODUCERS

I feel, as I know you all do, that GB's role as a teaching theatre for younger singers and a refresher course for older ones must be maintained and extended. On musical grounds the organisation is already far-reaching, but probably Dr Rennert will agree that we are in trouble where producers are concerned. It is not so much the shortage of clever young producers but the lack of someone older to take over the revivals and give singers the feeling that they are absorbing the wisdom of someone steeped in stagecraft. All singers seem to need this and if they get it they really profit from the stage rehearsals with piano. I would not mind an elderly director if he had Rennert's confidence and was willing to be present from start to finish of the season. It is one thing to stipulate such a thing, quite another, as we all know, to find the right person.

D. CONDUCTORS

The first thing I should like to reduce is the practice of handing over performances . . . and I know how I have been guilty myself in this respect! From one aspect, it is nice for us to be able to satisfy the aspirations of chorus masters, but in the end it places us in an invidious position. We finish up with a request, sooner or later, for a new production or an entire opera, which we are unable to grant. The guiding principle must be that if we are unable to conclude that anyone will at some time be entrusted with an opera, then he should not be given subsidiary performances. Here I would like to see the reverse situation on the production side, in other words a young conductor who had already made some progress in the opera or concert world given a chance with an opera which Maestro Gui or I did not want to repeat ourselves, but would be at hand to watch over from the standpoint of GB's requirements.

GENERAL COMMENT

A factor very much in my mind in all I have written is the 'public image' of Glyndebourne here and abroad. I do meet a lot of our artists when I am abroad and talk to them . . . and I do not mean just in Vienna where talk is always so amusing but shall I say not necessarily a pure compound of the verities! It saddens one to hear doubts and uncertainties not of Glyndebourne as an admired institution but in a way, of us as its managers and counsellors. Everyone has his own way of saying 'it's not like the old days' and we know it never could have been anyway! All the more reason to cut through a lot of the tethers holding us back and to present, with all the decent Press coverage we can get, a new and exciting picture of our aims and what we want the GB of the '70s to look like. In a way I feel that our public is expecting more from us than just a year by year attempt to prevent standards from sliding – because however well we do that, there will always be someone to say 'Sadlers Wells does it better'; the critics being, as we know, always prone to praise an inexpensive thing to the disadvantage of the higher priced article! I certainly think each year we should have a Press Conference and go into the background of the season's planning and our hopes and aims. The GB Book, which is one of our greatest successes, will each year present a fine opportunity to state our case.

'CAPRICCIO'

In considering the re-orientation of a *Capriccio* set notionally in the 1920s, I suggest the musician has to ask the question 'will the opera speak more directly?' Personally, I felt that understanding and appreciation of the text by the public is so vital, that I even suggested to the Producer we should play the opera in a half-lit theatre, so that the audience could read the synopsis as the musical conversation flowed on. This may not be possible (after all, the theatre must keep its illusions!) but the supreme importance of avoiding just a gentle and remote *acquiescence* as an audience, in a passive acceptance of the sensuously beautiful music, has constantly to be kept in mind.

Strauss himself seems to range in composition freely over the styles of two centuries – I do not mean just in his explicit quotations from Gluck and Rameau, his references to Rossini and Donizetti and the pastiche of Couperin in the ballet of *Capriccio*. How true to eighteenth-century style, for example, can we really consider the music to *Bourgeois Gentilhomme* to be? It is brilliant in sound, witty and sophisticated, but unmistakably Strauss of the twentieth century.

We hope by borrowing a little of the freedom of epoch which Strauss allowed himself, to present his operatic message more acutely and evocatively.

344

Appendix B

THE OPERAS OF MOZART

I should like to speak to you for a while about Mozart's operas, but from the viewpoint of a practical performer who has been much concerned with the presentation of these works in the opera house itself. This will mean that I shall be taking for granted a great deal that has been written and said about Mozart by musicologists and historians: the shelves in the libraries are already heavy with discussions of his life and amazing output, and I suppose of the great composers probably only Beethoven and Wagner have had their works analysed to a greater extent.

Well, generally conductors and musicians are rather neglectful of this wealth of somewhat technical literature: we tend to work so much from the printed score that we build up, by increasing familiarity with a composer's work, our own ideas of his methods, peculiarities and as it were distinguishing marks . . . Then, at a rather later stage, our curiosity is aroused and we seek out from the books any illumination which will deepen our view of the composer, for example the letters he has written, the circumstances and mental climate in which his work was carried on, and so forth.

This sort of approach was certainly the one in which I began my own study of Mozart. Many of you will know the name of Glyndebourne, or will perhaps have visited the lovely little theatre in the Sussex Downs whose Opera Festivals are now so famous, and when I began there in 1947 I often played the piano for stage rehearsals of *Figaro*. Carl Ebert, the producer, would explain and demonstrate his points at great length to the singers, and while I waited alone in the gloomy orchestra pit, I had time to read and learn practically by heart the Italian of da Ponte's libretto of *Figaro*. I enjoyed having the full score in front of me so that I could read all the original stage directions, and also it was enthralling to see the many little touches of orchestration by which Mozart brought out some facet of the stage character he was depicting. I remember my surprise when I realised what an instinct he had for the stage and that he was a highly *practical* opera composer. I realised that when for example the chorus entered or made an exit, the operation took time on the stage and therefore a beautiful introduction or postlude to a choral number was not just a lovely piece of music – it had been accurately timed and judged by Mozart himself for a specific purpose on the stage. I found that often Mozart would introduce a silent pause in the flow of music – a moment which had most likely always delighted me by its sheer musical effectiveness: and I would now realise that the pause had a very definite significance for some essential bit of action on the stage. This all added up to the fact that Mozart was 'operatic' in his bones, in his thinking, not merely a composer who adapted instrumental styles to the task of setting a dramatic libretto.

However, I am going too fast and giving you general conclusions and opinions, which is not quite what I set out to do in these remarks. I should like quite briefly to say something always as a practical performer, about those of the operas which today are to be found in the repertory of theatres throughout the world.

But before I begin my summary of those great operas I must say a little about the performance and rehearsal of Mozart's operas and in what way these are different from other operas in the repertoire. The first thing to point out is that the theatre in which the opera buffa or comedies are played should be of a suitable size. This sounds rather obvious but it is not so much that the *scale* of the operas such as *Figaro* and *Così fan Tutte* is small, but that they deal with universal and very human emotions which can only be appreciated in a framework which permits some degree of subtlety and highly sensitive characterisation. I have many times conducted *Figaro* in the Royal Opera House, Covent Garden, a theatre which ranks in *size* as one of the smaller European establishments, but I cannot feel even with the use of a well-known and amusing English translation, that the whole of the wit and humanity of the opera manages to penetrate to the back row of the gallery. There is no doubt that the small baroque private theatres of the eighteenth-century were ideal for these operas and here of course Glyndebourne stands as the quite exceptional twentieth-century equivalent. There the orchestra is of the right size, about forty players, and the ensembles achieve a blend only secured when singers do not have to force their voices.

The next vital thing is care in *casting*. To find the right singers! A well-known Opera House administrator once said to me: 'There is no Opera House in Europe which cannot put on a decent performance of a Mozart opera at a moment's notice.' I have never heard a statement with which I agreed less. All of us who love Vienna and what its name stands for in music (especially Mozart) have at times, I suppose, suffered bitter disappointment at the kind of cast for *Figaro* and *Don Giovanni* which one is only too liable to find, on any ordinary visit to the State Opera. And that remember is in a city boasting more famous Mozart singers to the square mile than almost anywhere one can go!

No, the trouble is that it is too easy to adopt a slack attitude to these operas which are familiar favourites in the repertory. Of course an atmosphere of routine is *always* unpleasant but I think it is particularly deadly where the fine balance of Mozart's creation is undermined. It is so facile for an opera Intendant to think along lines such as these: 'Ah, now we're going to put on *Così*.' That adds up, rule of thumb, to one popular soubrette type (Despina), one of our lyrical-dramatic sopranos for Fiordiligi, almost any rather colourless mezzo for Dorabella, a tenor and baritone who can deliver some slap-stick humour for the masquerade, and an elderly, reliable, dry baritone for the philosopher Don Alfonso. Six artists, the sets which were the last word in novelty eleven seasons ago, and the magic name of Mozart to bring in a very inexpensive evening for the opera house, and a good result at the box-office.

If only all Mozart performances could be mounted on a Festival level! I spoke rather critically a moment ago of some blasé performances in Vienna – let us listen for a moment to what *can* be done by their most famous artists when the gramophone companies pay the piper and call a tune such as this.

Trio
(No. 10 of the score)
'Soave sia il vento'
Così fan Tutte
Act I

This kind of ensemble can also be achieved in the opera house, but only when the *back-room boys* of the musical staff – in other words the expert coaches on whom the conductor relies for preparation of the artists – only when *they* carry out their work with real care. You know it is just not sufficient for the conductor to call together the singers and work on them to produce an ensemble. What is necessary is for each singer to have a number of hours' work individually before meeting his or her colleagues and proceeding to the difficult problem of vocal blend. And if a singer has performed a Mozart role many times, there will be problems: somehow the coach must instill a fresh outlook, small errors which have crept in by repetition will have to be corrected, and above all the ideas of the particular conductor on phrasing, so important in Mozart, will have to be insinuated into a mind which is probably already made up.

Then when the ensemble rehearsals are held, the trouble really starts. I recently directed at a Glyndebourne Festival a cast of singers made up as follows: three Italians, one Yugoslav, one Austrian, one Scotsman, two English, one Swiss, one Welsh! You can imagine the vocal and language difficulties which presented themselves – and yet the final blend of voices was very fine. With a group like this we always found that the sheer infectious joy of working out and balancing a Mozart concerted piece overcame any feeling of laborious repetition.

I must now come to the first of the great operas of Mozart. It is *Idomeneo*. I always feel ashamed, as a lover of Mozart, that before I assisted Fritz Busch to present this opera in 1951, I had always thought of it as belonging mostly to the history books. I should have paid more attention to Mozart's own opinion of it: to the end of his life he held the music in the highest esteem. I want you to listen now to the great quartet, without any description on my part – just allow if you will the perfect proportion and rather sombre beauty of this writing to fill your mind: and remember it was composed by Mozart at the age of twenty-five.

Quartet
'Andrò Ramingo'
Idomeneo
Act III

In that excerpt conducted by Fritz Busch there are two sopranos and two tenors, an arrangement which Mozart himself later permitted, but in the original performance in 1781 one of the tenors would have been replaced by a male soprano. Mozart at this time had enjoyed a brilliant career as a virtuoso but was now settling down to the drudgery of a cathedral organist at Salzburg. We can imagine the joy with which he suddenly received a commission to write a serious opera for the Elector's court at Munich. He didn't enjoy however collaborating with the librettist, a chaplain called Abbé Varesco, who had no stage sense whatever and regarded his work as a great literary masterpiece, not to be altered! Then Mozart had to cope with a leading tenor for the part of Idomeneo who was sixty-five years old and we can imagine with what insufferable condescension he treated the young composer, demanding alterations to suit the remnants of his voice and so on. The male soprano had never been on the stage before and apparently had no voice training to speak of either. Poor Mozart! Perhaps we are better off two centuries later when we can appreciate, by decent performances, the power and imagination of this early opera. Mozart dared to do things in *Idomeneo* which with widening experience later he didn't attempt, but it is wonderful to see in some of the great choruses of this opera how he transcends the classical demands of the plot and almost overwhelms us with his conception of the drama.

Listen to the exciting chorus at the end of Act II. The people are appealing to the king, Idomeneo, for help in the terrible afflictions which have been imposed by Neptune as a result of Idomeneo's own broken vow – and at this very moment a frightful sea-monster arises and begins a new scourge. The idea is old-fashioned, classically primitive, but the music sends a chill direct to the heart.

Chorus
'Corriamo, fuggiamo'
Idomeneo
Act II Finale

Let us now turn away from opera seria. The perfect comedy opera is, without doubt, *The Marriage of Figaro*. Five years after *Idomeneo*, Mozart met a Jew from Venice called Emanuele da Ponte, very much a man of the world but a clever literary craftsman. He worked to make an operatic version of a play by Beaumarchais and produced one of the best operatic librettos the world has seen. When the opera had its first performance it was such a success that most of the numbers had to be repeated and the opera lasted twice its proper time. As even with some cuts today *Figaro* lasts for $3^{1}/_{2}$ hours, it must have been *quite* an evening . . .

Before everything else, the music of *Figaro* is Italian and civilised. Of course da Ponte had given Mozart something new, no longer the stock characters of the old opera buffa, but a real interplay of intelligent people living in a world of elegance. Mozart for his part wrote music which besides being beautiful presented to the *last second* the timing and development of the intricate plot. It is now a commonplace to point to the second act Finale as a masterpiece, but it will bear repetition to marvel how faultlessly the composer leads us on with the tension ever increasing, to the final ding-dong of opposing forces, the general confusion in which it was right for the second act curtain to fall. You will remember the moment when the Count, infuriated to think that Cherubino is concealed in the Countess' anteroom, shouts out to the *garzon malnato* to emerge. The Countess is terribly agitated and tries to oppose him. Soon we shall come to the marvellous moment when, just at the right climax of tension, the door opens and to the stupefaction of both Count and Countess, *Susanna* minces out. We can hear her pert little steps in the music and soon after there is a *sotto voce* trio when you can sense, as it were, the thoughts of each character adjusting to the new situation.

'Mora, Mora' to Allegro
Le Nozze di Figaro
Act II Finale

My words on the operas of Mozart would be incomplete without a short reference, in conclusion, to the *dramma giocoso* of *Don Giovanni*. This is the opera in which every conductor certainly, and probably every singer as well, aspires to give his finest performance. I wonder just what it is about this mixed and rather contradictory masterpiece which inspires us. It is amazing that even now there can be discussion and disagreement over which aspect of the opera, its drama or its comedy, should remain uppermost in the mind after a performance. Last year in England after the Glyndebourne performances of *Don Giovanni*, letters were written to the *Times* suggesting that the Finale of the opera should be cut short at the descent into flames of Don Giovanni, on the grounds that such incomparable music should conclude the opera on its highest dramatic level. This suggestion obviously came from Mozart lovers, but it is unfortunately years out of date, because this bad practice was followed for some years, shame to say, in Vienna and elsewhere. However there is the much more compelling reason that anyone who looks at the score with the slightest eye to Mozart's intention and with a thought to the mentality of the period, must realise quite plainly that even if the following music were *less* wonderful than it is, the express wish of the composer is to send his audience home, in a typically eighteenth-century fashion, uplifted, scourged, edified but finally with a pleasing recollection of an amusing evening. It is false logic to try to tamper with this great Finale, as though indeed in a Shakespeare comedy one were to cut out the parting words of the clown, as he pats his audience metaphorically on the back and bows low in effect asking for their generous applause.

I would like to finish my bicentenary tribute by playing this music which seems to me to sum up Mozart's intention and in a gay and joyous fugal round tells us the entertainment, for just this evening, is over.

Finale
Don Giovanni
Presto to end

GLYNDEBOURNE AND ROSSINI: THE STYLISTIC APPROACH

The first bar of Rossini's overture to *Il Barbiere di Siviglia* (which, as we all know, was annexed from his *Elisabetta, Regina d'Inghilterra*) begins with a favourite device of the composer: a forceful and imperative attack on the chord of E major, rather resembling a 'rat-tat' on some closed and impressive portal, which must open to reveal various delights. Of course Rossini was following contemporary practice in assuming that a loud summons, or perhaps several, would be necessary if the evening's proceedings were to get under way, with the fashionable Rome audience at last persuaded to abate their conversation and settle into their seats. I often think the realistic composer may have delighted in the implied reproach to that restive audience, evidenced by the springy *pianissimo* which follows the first loud orchestral bang: almost certainly the buzz of talk persisted until a moment later a second emphatic summons assailed the ears, the soft little scurrying figure ensuing – as though Rossini said, 'Why not listen to it the first time?'

Curiously enough, discussion of this 'rat-tat' in the *Barbiere* overture plunges Rossini conductors straight into a practical and stylistic difficulty which, in a small way, encapsules questions of much more far-reaching implication in the performance of his operas. Since every craftsman's professional approach to his job is usually of some interest, a brief consideration of this musical 'motto' is not irrelevant to our subject; because the attitude of Glyndebourne from the very beginning of its Rossini series was in effect to say unequivocally, 'Rossini is *not* Mozart. His music, though perhaps in texture similar, derives from a totally different creative impulse, in which, perhaps for the first time in musical history wit touched with irony is given a very clear form. Thus, the music of Rossini – at Glyndebourne – is to be performed and translated into stage action with emphasis on its intrinsic *wit*, which in turn must imply refinement of treatment.' Of course Glyndebourne would never be didactic enough to express the matter thus, but in effect the ideology behind the entire Rossini series could have been summarised in some such way.

When I was a young conductor, performing in concert the Overture of *Barbiere*, I used to worry about the technique of getting the first 'rat-tat' chords *together*: nervous wavings in the empty air, giving the already apprehensive musicians silent beats, produced (eight times out of ten) a minor rhythmic shambles. The public, expecting to enjoy a trouble-free experience of favourite music, were understandably irritated when the very beginning of the programme displayed the orchestra in disarray, and were inclined to be censorious of the musical inexperience of the conductor, who had, as it were, 'shuffled' his way into the Overture.

Some years later, when I was Vittorio Gui's disciple and assistant in the Glyndebourne 'Rossini team', I of course questioned the Maestro about this vexing little problem arising in so many of the Rossini overtures and throughout the operas themselves. Vittorio, laconic in oracle-like utterance, replied in a sentence which I have never forgotten and which for me resolved the question totally: 'Pa-Pa,' he said, 'is PA-PA!' At once I sensed, more than in the answer to a probably needless question, a whole attitude of practicality and instinctive understanding of Rossini's intentions; for Gui had no objection to shortening Rossini's *written* notes in these instances to fulfil the composer's practical aim – to arrest attention. However, in a somewhat similarly assertive beginning in Mozart's *Magic Flute* Overture

a conductor would never dream of playing anything other than the exact printed rhythm. The reason is that with Mozart we are in a world of musical symbolism, based on the composer's use throughout the opera of the 'Three-Chord' motif associated with Masonry, and no abbreviation here would be appropriate or possible. I have often thought that if one could accept as a definition of *style* 'an informed and *instinctive* interpretation of the composer's intentions in comparison with or contrast to his contemporaries', then Rossini has to be approached with the respect due not merely to a lucky, albeit meteoric, musical inventor, but as a composer bringing unique insight into the realm of opera buffa.

It was this belief in the unique role of Rossini which from his early years had activated Vittorio Gui and was to bring him to a pinnacle as surely the most authoritative interpreter of the operas in this century: Glyndebourne can never congratulate itself enough on the almost haphazard chain of events which brought Gui to the helm for nine successive seasons beginning in 1952, in which he, together with Carl Ebert as stage director and Oliver Messel as designer, established a level of Rossini performance which remains a model – alas, I fear, a model still to be fully studied or emulated elsewhere in the operatic firmament. My own experience around the world in many opera houses (and as Music Director in at least three of them) is that a new production of a Rossini opera, instead of being a mirror of the grace, style and glitter of the music, is too often an excuse for yet another banal romp and exaggerated scenic farce, which it is mistakenly thought the opera requires if it is to 'bring the house down'.

When, with Gui as a kindly but exigent supervisor, we addressed ourselves at Glyndebourne to the preparation of the first Rossini production in the Sussex theatre since the war (*Cenerentola* in 1952), I think the choice of a less familiar opera than *Barbiere* was dictated not only by Gui's love for the work, but also because he rightly thought it would take a little time and experience before the *Barber*, victim of many jolly rollicking performances in England and Europe generally, could be sufficiently laundered and purified to present in an authentic and stylistic staging at Glyndebourne. In fact, we had to wait two years until the Gui-Ebert-Messel trio turned out an impeccable *Barbiere*. This production, for me and a generation to whom this opera was on the whole a joy liberally laced with embarrassment, at last showed the comic masterpiece in its pristine colours. First however in the series we had *Cenerentola*, which the British public were willing to forgive for not *quite* following their own beloved fairy story, and at once were guided by Gui into realising the crucial importance of judicious casting of the main roles – an approach to casting moreover somewhat different from that used for the Mozart operas, in which Glyndebourne was so experienced. Spike Hughes, in one of the Glyndebourne programme articles, has referred to the 'Gui Male Voice Trio' which formed the centrepiece of *Cenerentola, Barbiere* and *Comte Ory*. The redoubtable Juan Oncina, Sesto Bruscantini and Ian Wallace indeed adorned these particular productions with a con-sortium of talents – Oncina, a mellifluous and fluent tenor with the essential high notes employed with a roguish eye, Bruscantini, the master of stage timing, combined with complete vocal flexibility, and Wallace, not born to Italianate utterance, but quick, instinctive and commendably unexaggerated in *buffo* roles. For his female 'protagonista', Gui selected the Spanish mezzo, Marina de Gabarain, and accepted her occasional waywardness of rhythm for the sake of the typically Spanish soft-grained vocal quality, which later Teresa Berganza displayed, of course, to perfection.

It is, looking back, no exaggeration to say that to begin the study of a Rossini opera score was from the very start a re-education in Gui's hands. His belief and acceptance as self-evident that the Italian melodic phrase, perfected in Bellini, stood calm and enduring above the buffets of musical fashion, was endearing and somehow led musicians and singers into tranquil accord, so that an ensemble or big concerted finale presented few surprises or pitfalls. It was not necessary (I realised as I accompanied so many musical rehearsals at the piano) to keep a wary eye on the Maestro to accommodate some quirk of 'interpretation'. With Gui all would be reasonable, satisfying and – to employ a strange word applied to musical performance – 'wholesome': as a young conductor (like all young conductors) I would occasionally think 'Why doesn't he get a move on?' – only to realise in a moment, as Rossini's vocal melisma and cascades of runs ensued, how wise and practical a beginning steady tempo had been set. Only when a lapse of taste occurred, an ungracious high note held too long, a breathy *staccato* instead of a *legato* phrase would Gui intervene; 'No, no, . . . meglio così.' His method was really to find singers he could trust, show them how he wanted the music to be performed, and set the machine in agreeable operation. There were indeed few disagreements in those early musical ensemble rehearsals.

At times the temptation to have a little innocent fun at the expense of this immensely cultured but endlessly loquacious Maestro was irresistible: I remember one day, in the hall of the Christies' house, as Gui was descending the stairs from his room, I slipped Giulini's recording of the *Cenerentola* overture onto the gramophone. Vittorio immediately asked who was conducting and listened calmly: suddenly the strings could be heard playing *pizzicato* instead of with the bow, as Gui considered correct. To him, an error of taste or scholarship perpetrated by a fellow Italian was doubly heinous and I was rewarded with a lengthy discourse on the Rossini manuscripts, Gui's lifelong familiarity with them, and what seemed to me (itching to escape into the sunshine) a verbal town-plan of the city of Pesaro, where Gui had studied the original Rossini scores.

This leads me to a brief mention of the Rossini orchestral material – an important factor in the musical texture of performance, but one which has led many theatres nowadays eagerly to adopt an almost irresistibly scholarly edition prepared by a noted Italian conductor. Vittorio Gui mistrusted any such general solution to the problems of 'urtext' in Rossini: he was a combative scholar himself and dearly loved a scuffle with the Italian Establishment as represented, say, by La Scala, Milan or the most famous music publishers. One must guard against the possibility of a certain injured vanity influencing the situation, in that Gui had not been consulted about the new Edition, which as a revered expert in the field one might have expected. Nevertheless, when it came to *Barbiere*, Gui trusted the edition prepared from the autograph in the Conservatoire at Bologna, while the overture was copied from the autograph in the Rossini Institute at Pesaro, where the composer was born. I must say that in my turn I have relied on this Edition whenever I have conducted *Barbiere* in the USA or Europe and found it a satisfying mirror in every respect of what a Rossinian could *believe* the composer to have penned. When the musicologists have had their exhaustive say (as I have found in another field with the scores of Haydn) there is still a considerable 'grey area' in which the experience and instinct of the performer are called in play to arrive at a decision. Luckily these textural matters, though important to the interpreters themselves, rarely affect the enjoyment of listeners to any great extent (unless, for instance, a conductor persists in employing three modern trombones in the Overture of *Barbiere!*).

In summary, what we learned from over ten years' experience in casting the Rossini comedies was that a gallery of performers with special talents, exemplified by the Male Trio I have mentioned, became a *sine qua non*:

> — a mezzo-soprano with vocal agility and charm (*Barbiere, Cenerentola, Italiana*).
> — a light tenor, with easy access to high notes and with vivid stage personality (*Barbiere, Cenerentola, Ory, Turco*).
> — a *basso buffo* with great agility in fast music and impeccable stage timing (*Barbiere, Cenerentola*).
> — a brilliant baritone, usually in the role of manipulator of the action (*Barbiere, Cenerentola, Ory*).
> — a true *basso cantante* with rich low notes and sense of comedy, an unusual combination (*Barbiere, Italiana, Turco*).

The list, which is incomplete, reveals at a glance the problems facing operatic managements today. It is strange how various countries and regions of Europe, in a changing pattern, have contributed gifted performers to this essential gallery. Thus for a time the especially Latin talents of Supervia, Simionato, de Gabarain, Berganza have facilitated the casting of the leading female roles; Valetti, Alva, Oncina, Benelli, Gedda for the tenors; Stabile, Bruscantini, Corena, Montarsolo, Wallace, Carlos Feller, in a splendid gallery of *bassi buffi*; Gobbi, Panerai, Bruscantini for the brilliant baritones; Baccaloni, Tajo, Siepi, Rossi-Lemeni, Carlo Cava, the *bassi*. The sopranos, for once relegated to last mention on our roster, of course produced Graziella Sciutti, Alda Noni – and (to drop a name) Maria Callas. Practically all of these performers had or have a lively sense of comedy, and most of them came under the kindly discipline of Vittorio Gui, many actually at Glyndebourne or in performance in Italian theatres. It is quite instructive, in 1984, to try to compile a comparable list of currently active 'Rossini artists', and to examine how far the adoption of a purified performance style in the operas has spread beyond the Italian shores (including, for this purpose, Glyndebourne as an Italian protectorate!). We could cite among the mezzo-sopranos Marilyn Horne, Frederica von Stade (from USA), Ann Murray (UK), Alicia Nafé (Spain); considering the tenors produces the name of Araiza (Mexico), followed by an embarrassing pause – with a hopeful look towards promising newcomers such as Rockwell Blake and John Aler (USA); with the *bassi buffi*, one must hasten on, grateful only that the stalwart Carlos Feller (Argentine) and Bruscantini still give object lessons in such roles as Bartolo and Don Magnifico; baritones are a shade easier, with the skills of Hermann Prey, Wolfgang Brendel (West Germany), Berndt Weikl (Austria), Ingmar Wixell (Sweden) and Leo Nucci (Italy); for the basses, apart from a respectful look towards Giorgio Tozzi (USA) and Justino Diaz (Puerto Rico), I must ask for a recess until perhaps the Glyndebourne *Centenary* book in the year 2034 may denote a more optimistic picture? Despite the restrictions implied by this list of the more recurrent names in Rossini revivals, the operas *do* get performed, extensively in the UK and USA and also (I am rather sorry to say) in Germany. My regret about Germany is occasioned by my impression – in which I should be delighted to find myself wrong – that hardly one of the lessons with which this review is concerned has been learned in the course of the last thirty years. In brief, this is because of the permanent addiction of Intendants to the idea that Rossini's place in the German opera repertoire is under the heading 'Spiel-Oper' (or a comedy with music); the artificiality of the plots is then rammed home with translation into German (as though the most fragile fiction needed profound comprehension), and then usually underpinned with ferociously trivial productions, decked out with painful visual gags. It is not too much to say that in only one of Germany's 200-odd opera houses – and that one I am far too modest to name – could an opera-goer be fairly confident from the stylistic viewpoint when visiting a Rossini performance.

However, lest it be thought that I am adopting too high-minded an attitude towards a country which devotes a huge national budget to the performance and maintenance of opera, I am reminded that a few seasons ago, when I conducted a series of *Barbiere* performances at the Metropolitan Opera, it was *quite impossible* to persuade the Italian *basso*, a favourite of the public and knowing it, to learn the vital recitative in which Bartolo persuades Rosina that her 'Lindoro' is a crafty emissary of Count Almaviva and that therefore her infatuation is misplaced. His reason was that after galloping around the stage, his face freely lathered for shaving by Figaro, he was altogether too tired to remain on the scene. This meant, of course, there was a gaping hole in the plot and when Rosina shows her fury on the arrival of Lindoro-Almaviva, her temperamental display is totally inexplicable. It is unfair to point an accusing finger at German distortion of Rossini, when the principal opera house in the United States could, despite all protests, permit such cavalier mistreatment.

In summary, the feeling that opera establishments care little, providing the box office receipts do not fall off, means that conductors and stage directors invited to direct Rossini opera performances must continually be on their guard. On the musical side we have a mainly good Edition available and singers on the whole are as meticulous as their forerunners in accepting guidance on matters of accuracy and phrasing. It is in my opinion in the field of stage production that the menace threatens: and I hope my colleagues, the stage producers and designers, will allow me a final swipe in their direction. I have been deterred only by the specialist interest of the subject from writing to the *Times* demanding a Charter for Opera Conductors, and since some of its clauses apply with particular force to the Rossini productions, I ask indulgence to outline them here.

1. No, ABSOLUTELY NO, stage action or mime or symbolism during the Overture.
2. No scrim or gauze aimed at giving diffused lighting on the stage – it *does* affect the acoustic and singers detest it.
3. No enlargement of the stage apron by erection of supporting structures in the orchestra pit; no steps into the orchestra utilised by the stage performers; no mounting of lighting equipment in the pit; nothing to fall into the orchestra pit!
4. A more positive acceptance of the validity of the great concerted ensemble as an intrinsic (and mainly static) ingredient of opera; perhaps, even, an encouragement to accept these set pieces at face value, and in need of no accompanying distracting stage movement either by swaying, rocking or marching (I have yet to see an audience whose attention is not riveted by the great operatic *concertato*).
5. More realisation of the fact that it is VOCAL excellence which in the last resort draws people into opera performances:

therefore the available budget must be stretched in the direction of providing fine voices, wherever they can be found, rather than in the building of expensive sets and needlessly rich costumes. One producer not long ago in Brussels demanded 2,600 'props' (stage requisites) and when refused went on to Geneva to demand 3,400 in *Traviata*, including fake ash in the ashtrays!

6. The provision in rehearsal plans of *regular* musical ensemble rehearsals, *interrupting* the sequence of staging rehearsals so that the musical levels are maintained. Stage directors must be barred from these rehearsals.

(A stage director friend to whom I showed this Charter was piqued and countered with: 'First and foremost, the conductor shall maintain the *same* tempi in rehearsals and performances and not cover the singers by the loud orchestra.' Childish, I thought.)

Appendix C
Germany

EXTRACTS FROM EDITED CORRESPONDENCE
WITH DR HAMPE ON 'PETER GRIMES'

'I am sorry when you have so many preoccupations with *Hoffmann* to drop a bomb in your lap, but I want to explain to you a decision I am most regretfully having to take. You know of course how we have all wanted to bring *Grimes* into the repertoire and in time to follow it with other Britten operas; this was always planned as my own distinctive contribution to the development and interest of the Spielplan. Then (to remind you) came the long flirtation with Vickers, for many months regarded as indispensable to the project. With some real heart-searching I gave in to the view that his inclusion would be too expensive. This led us on to consider doing the work in German, and I was again troubled at the unusual prospect of a conductor closely associated with this opera all over the world, English himself, and introducing the work in another language. Nevertheless, I went along with that idea too and was persuaded that the impact of the opera might be increased by doing it in the language of the audience. We then proceeded to cast the work provisionally and I was struck by the possibilities we had in the house of filling a number of the important minor parts, with Bill Lewis in mind for the title role. Bill was at this time in upcoming form following Aron and Oedipus. I thought Griffel just right for Ellen, and Victor Braun completed the trio of important characters: there was never any doubt that in Schmitz' hands the chorus would rise to their great challenge.

'The next step was to consider the producer and for a time you could envisage doing the opera yourself. Then we tried repeatedly to interest Peter Hall, eventually without success. We

360

talked of a British producer in any case, as I considered this an essential with a piece so very idiomatic and specialised: I was already fearing the opera would seem to have switched location and bring in a whole series of alien influences, as though The Borough had somehow become a village near to Kiel, let us say. But gradually and, I feel, very regrettably the search roved around the German realistic theatre and all sorts of Kupfer-like names were thrown up for discussion. Meanwhile I was mentioning names like . . . John Copley, who knows the piece perhaps better than anyone and is particularly fitted to work with large choruses.

'Despite some pressure . . . about Copley . . . you did not react: this about a British producer with whom I personally have done about ten successful premières! About this time I began to feel the seeds of disillusionment on the *Grimes* project altogether, and two months ago I wrote you insisting on a decision about the producer and stating very clearly I did not wish to start on the piece with any experimental producer at all, but with someone who would do a realistic interpretation on the lines of the many successful performances around the world, with a designer who would construct a realistic fishing village in which these unique characters could play out the drama.

'It was shortly after this that you made your suggestion, I now feel under the influence of the success he had with a piece of atheistic music theatre. I was rather shocked, as you'll remember the doubts you and I both had after — . . . doubts which personally I still hold and which accounted for my dropping it from my Cologne repertory for an entire season . . . However, still thinking of the German nature of the project, I tried to swallow this pill. I must tell you that shortly after the decision to take him I ran into Donald Mitchell, the official biographer of Britten and a musicologist of repute. I told him about *Grimes* in Cologne and he was *bouleversé* at the news – in fact he would not believe I was serious. After a week he wrote me begging me, for the sake of Britten and my own reputation, to think again.

'I think, despite this long catalogue of disappointments, I would still have persevered if it had not been for yesterday's casting meeting (so-called) to make the final decisions on the smaller parts. I had prepared everyone concerned with a carefully written précis of the background picture of the opera, and a brief sketch of each character to aid in ruling out the more ridiculous suggestions, such as XY for Bob Boles (a fiery religious maniac!) At the meeting, the only result for me was a clear understanding I cannot work with the producer. He showed little pleasure at my two main ideas (Lewis and Griffel), proposed some mezzo quite unknown to me for Mrs Sedley . . . and another unknown from Düsseldorf for Boles. Worse still, I find I was not asked in time. We were quite unable . . . to find a casting for the two Nieces, who would thus have to be Guests (the Two Nieces!).

'After this disappointing session, in which I continually had to pinch myself to make sure I was actually sitting in what is presumably an International Opera House, so heavy was the shadow of the truly provincial over the proceedings, I wrestled with the matter in my thoughts nearly all night . . . You must forgive my saying that it appears that the history of the planning of this opera, so important to me, has been from start to finish one long decline. The cast, still incomplete in vital areas, is just the kind of collection of names one would read, say, passing through Bremen or Essen and instantly deciding to continue one's journey with some haste. And since my successes in Cologne in all the new productions I have done have been in association with star names (with which you have had a lot to do) I simply cannot associate myself with this homespun version of a masterpiece.

'Although you will naturally let me know your reactions to this upsetting news, I do beg you not to spend too much time on trying to make me change my mind: I would not have written at this length if my very deepest instincts were not involved. I'm afraid, and I have just lost all heart for this enterprise which started out so well. You know too well how it is when things "go sour" in an opera house in any direction – it is always better to cut your losses and start again. I can only recommend that we announce a postponement of *Grimes* and plug this gap with an opera, perhaps *Onegin*, in which we could use Lewis, and which also employs the Chorus . . .'

Writing again to Michael Hampe on 4th June 1980 after he had '"let the dust settle" a little on the problems which worried me when we had our conversation (and which of course still worry me). I think the best thing is to sum the matter up this way: it is clear, if I were to be approached by ANY theatre ANYWHERE with the cast as it stood *when we spoke*, and with your proposal for Regisseur, I would unhesitatingly decline the offer! But we have (with my agreement) got ourselves into rather a tangle for which (in view of my responsibilities in Cologne) I am partly answerable. Thus I can only withdraw accompanied by a scandal, and with bad moral repercussions in the house. This would be more particularly upsetting as *Grimes* calls on so many of our regular singers, who would be confused and amazed if I did not conduct! I must say I was a little surprised by your praise of the producer and disappointed by your condemnation of "the English directors" who are uniquely fitted to do this work.

'So I have to agree to carry on, with the following *provisos* from me which I think are only common sense:

1) The producer will state *clearly* his intentions for the set design, with *sketches* available by Sept. 30th, 1980;
2) We complete the cast *satisfactorily* before I depart in middle June;
3) Satisfactory outcome of my forthcoming discussion with the producer when playing the tape of Met (my Metropolitan Opera performance – in other words he will accept my musical view of the opera and intend to work dramatically in the identical direction);
4) *Most important*: A private understanding between you and me that if I am eventually seriously worried by his staging rehearsals or by what I regard as misconceptions, you will intervene on my side and undertake such persuasion as you think necessary to let my views have effect.'

When John began rehearsals the following April, he continued to voice anxiety. In a telex message to Dr Michael Hampe on 13th April 1981, he said how unhappy he was about the supporting cast and felt that the 'scholastic approach causes frustration in singers who are not being taught sweep of the drama. We lack Tate's instinctive understanding in musical preparation. My feeling is this production at low level initially and please understand as foremost Britten interpreter I cannot risk failure in my own theatre. Suggest for Tuesday April 21 full ensemble without single absentee. I will then judge Beresford and all other cast members as they present themselves that day and following that we must make decisions without delay. On short rehearsal last week chorus was excellent.'

Once stage rehearsals commenced John continued to write to the Intendant (20th May) underlining frequently, revealing his stress.

'I think the *most important* influence you could have now on *Peter Grimes* would be to insist on improvement of the *sight lines*. The *only* substantial building, church, Moot Hall etc. will not be seen *at all* by one third of the public! Also I find the *floor-covering* too like *snow*, bad for sound and *delaying the scene changes* because nothing can move on the stage over it! Can you help?

'Firstly he has taken care to give us a blackened scratchy impression of possibly some burned-out Mexican village in which the only civilised feature is a large highly Catholic Christus (Bob Boles would have chopped it down as hideous idolatry in two minutes). Then he has deliberately set this poor ravaged set so that a very considerable section of the public will be simply unaware of any building structure whatever. (This section incidentally will include ALL your guests and mine.) The "building" on the other side, to which Kay Griffel and Victor Braun are confined like prisoners for their expressive arias and the duet, is a ramp which again is invisible to the *other* third of the audience, and is continually hindered by that ridiculous toy "capstan" of a type never to be seen in any part of the English coast.

'With this set, the producer sticks deaf to all entreaties by you or me, in detailed reasoned suggestions aimed at making the production work for the singers. More than that he is not concerned by the obvious ill-design of the Pub scene which prevents Haydn and his team from completing a scene change which has an orchestral interlude of over four minutes! Do you honestly suppose that change is going to succeed today at the Hauptprobe? It was at least sixty seconds behind schedule last evening.

'I could list the production faults on ten sheets of paper, but I shall restrict myself to one which alas is typical: in the third Act there is a charming short scene in which ten "burghers", a little bit the worse for drink perhaps, emerge from Auntie's and say Good Night to the Rector. It is always nicely done and essential is the grave dignity of these worthy men as they put their hats on and slightly unsteady make their way home . . . what does the producer do? He brings the men out in a chain walking backwards and flops them out like dead fish on the ramp, needless to say BEHIND the useless capstan so that they time after time miss their musical entries: meanwhile the Rector is saying goodnight to the empty air. The producer has ruined the Epilogue by not bringing the chorus on until far too late, then too few of them so that a final great orchestral *fortissimo* obliterates any sound whatever from the stage. This negates entirely Britten's design that another day's work is beginning and Grimes' boat is sunk practically unobserved out at sea. I think it was the dismal meandering conclusion last night which brought me the deepest grief: I can picture the Cologne public going home (if they have not left at the interval) and saying "Well . . . so what?"

'Somehow the mistreatment on such a scale of a contemporary work is more dangerous than, for example, with an established classic which has any number of previous productions to give it authority. Here you will have a public seeing *Grimes* for the first time: what do they get? They do *not* get the chosen alternative, a highly intelligent musical performer who is always well prepared. They get instead a man well chosen for Boles but with as yet insufficient experience of this demanding part to be comfortable in it – though I blame him not (the producer did not produce him at all in the final mad scene which is the climax of the opera!). They get a chorus INSUFFICIENTLY prepared and deprived – here I blame myself – of the invaluable direction of Schmitz. In any case I intend to conduct the production NEVER AGAIN here and hereby withdraw from the performance on 9th June in accordance with our agreement on this point. So ingloriously ends our attempt to have a Britten Cycle in Cologne!'

MEMORANDUM – THE FINANCIAL SITUATION

(This Memorandum was written as a reaction to a recent nationwide Chorus strike for more free days. The Union handed the management a note only ten minutes before a performance was due to start, with the result that performances had to be cancelled and the audience sent home. Traditionally an 'SPD' city where the authorities were 'soft' in their attitude towards strikes, Cologne was selected for action. A performance of *Lohengrin* was cancelled and in the increasingly tense atmosphere, Dr Hampe sensed correctly that the next performance of Jean-Pierre Ponnelle's *Turandot*, a chorus opera, would be a victim. Receiving the note of intention ten minutes before 'curtain-up', he asked the conductor, Nello Santi, if he would be prepared to continue without the chorus. Receiving an affirmative, three minutes before the performance, Dr Hampe informed the audience of his intention. With their support, the nationwide strike was broken. *H.C.*)

Although I am not really informed of the exact financial situation of the Oper, I am aware that the city of Cologne is running a deficit. Since the Arts are everywhere regarded as a vaguely pleasant addition to the amenities of life and not as a necessity such as football, it is clear to me as a realist that the days when you and I could hope for 'our million marks back' – which would solve all our troubles – are gone, probably for ever. We shall in fact be lucky not to face ever increasing attrition and reductions of our financial support by indifferent politicians who have already decided, even if they are not ready to publish it, that in the 1980s the Oper represents a MINORITY CULT, excessively expensive and on the whole 'not worth the trouble'.

The anomaly for Pritchard, and increasingly for Hampe, is that both are heavily engaged elsewhere in the artistic world in places where, despite the world economic picture, opera is still respected and even loved for what it brings to the people. Thus PARIS, under a Socialist Government not specially friendly to 'entertainments for the rich', can still announce the building by 1985 of a 'new modern Opera House for the people's needs'. In embattled Britain with three million unemployed, Covent Garden's extension building is nearly finished and one can be certain (in a House with subsidy comparable to Cologne's) to hear month by month Domingo, Pavarotti, Caballé and Sutherland with regularity!

I strongly suggest that it is against the artistic and moral principles of the two of us to submit weakly and obediently to the attacks of ignorance and prejudice which are gaining ground around us. I was very much struck by your report of the inept and uncaring attitude of the city authorities to the situation created by the chorus strike. I am horrified that those high in responsibility did not FIRST consider their duty to the PUBLIC in that situation. And are we to go on, year after year making ends meet, watching either the performances decreasing in numbers, quality or both?

What I do suggest to you is that your reputation and mine will accord very badly with the dismal prospect in Cologne. What we should do now is prepare our strategy with great care, and then go direct to the media with our manifesto. I must confess that my own thinking is at the moment in direct contrast to the principles you and I discussed and agreed when I was first appointed. Then, we agreed to limit the singers on Fest contract to the absolute lower limit. I remember it was then in the low 20s, and our intention was to bring in regular distinguished guests. All my new productions (two per season, often in collaboration with yourself as Director) were to be cast from strength and establish a standard for the House which could hardly be equalled in Germany. I am sure we can take comfort from the fact that we have partially succeeded and in fact have a string of productions which would adorn the Spielplan anywhere. But you more than anyone know the ferocious spasms we must go through to try to repeat those successes in the day to day running of the house. They are too expensive or too technically demanding!

My thoughts therefore are tending towards not a limitation of the 'Company' but an extension of it, engaging for ten, fifteen or twenty evenings some of the up-and-coming singers whom already we like to have working with us. I would be prepared to work out casts for my productions which employ younger talent provided we honestly believed in it. You and I hear around the world quite a sufficient number of talented artists to 'plug the gaps' in an already gifted group of singers loyal to us. I am not saying that in a co-ordinated production we would be unable to show off occasionally with a Domingo or a Ricciarelli in a main role: but the sense of satisfaction would certainly be stronger for me if I felt that the Cologne Spielplan presented a *recognisable line* of opera performance in our time, with much less of the spectacle afforded by an execrable *Trovatore* side by side with a starry *Turandot*.

Like a careful shopkeeper whose supply lines are threatened, we must keep the caviar under lock and key and push the special Pastete [pâté] (Hausgemachte) [homemade] which need cause us no shame.

Sir John Pritchard

PROPOSALS FOR CONTRACT

1. It being clear that an extension of my contract should *not* coincide with the end of Michael Hampe's own contract in 1988, he has said to me that my own prolongation should be from 1985 to 1987, *or* from 1985 to 1989 (i.e. four years or two years). One must consider the changing situation always in the opera world and I would suggest that an excellent compromise suiting *both* sides, would be to make a new contract *to August 1987* with the *option* to make another extension to *August 1989*, this option to be decided upon (let us say) by *1st July 1986*. I have in mind, in suggesting this, that you may wish later to give effect to your original plan to find a GMD for Köln, and the extension of my contract in this way would give you the required flexibility – and I would also be on hand, to give advice *if needed* on the question of a successor.

2. If this idea finds favour with you, there is one *important proviso* of which I must advise you. It is a 'fact of life', regrettably from the point of view of the Oper finances, that my devotion to Köln and its Opera, always faithful, is increasingly under strain because when I came to Köln in 1978 my Honorar was slightly *in advance* of my world fee! Since that date, the small annual percentage increases have totally failed to keep level with the demand for my time and services throughout the world. It is a fact which can be verified in London and Brussels and the USA, that for the *present* Season at the BBC and Théâtre de la Monnaie, my fee is approximately equivalent to DM 13,000+, with in *both* cases *less severe* tax deductions than those now obtaining in Germany.

I really think and hope that this need not be a serious obstacle to our reaching agreement: for example, I think it would be realistic to agree on, in effect, an Abend-Vertrag of *less* evenings per annum than the present contract – perhaps based on *one* new production in the year plus a number of evenings from the repertoire. This would take into account that you would wish to include for Maestro Janowski (or the new Chef of Gürzenich-Orchester) a new production at certain intervals . . . This way the total budget for John Pritchard need not be from your point of view, excessive!

368

Appendix D
Brussels

DRAFT PRESS ANNOUNCEMENT

I would like your opinion of the following 'draft' for a Press announcement:

The TRM announces the resignation of Sir J. P. as Directeur de la Musique of Opéra National. It will be recalled that Sir J. joined M. Gerard Mortier's team at the inauguration of the regime in 1981 and he has conducted many notable premières, including the opening *Don Carlo, Die Meistersinger, Le Comte Ory, Idomeneo* and culminating in *Der Rosenkavalier* for the reopening of la Monnaie in 1986. He has been associated with his colleague M. Sylvain Cambreling in the augmentation and refinement of the Orchestra and Chorus, bringing both to the present enviable standard, and has brought his great experience to support M. Mortier in establishing the Opéra National as a world centre of enlightened opera production.

In 1986 Sir John who holds the positions of Chef Dirigent at the Cologne Opera and Chief Conductor of the BBC Symphony Orchestra, accepted the Musical Directorship of the San Francisco Opera, and his long absences in the USA involved some curtailment of his European activities. However the TRM is pleased to announce he will conduct an opera in the 1988 – 89 season and hopes to continue his happy association in the future with the Opéra National.

Please let us discuss this?

Appendix E
Tempo
(Edited)

Commenting on a performance of *Tristan* he attended in New York, John had been surprised to find the first Act of this great music drama 'had been discharged in sixty-eight minutes', cutting twelve minutes from the usual eighty. Interestingly Wagner who 'rarely indicated metronome speeds but had recourse to some quite flowery word indications in poetic German' had failed to indicate adequately 'the pulse at which the music should go'.

In looking at the 'pulse', John felt it important to look 'at the methods which have been used to indicate speed by mechanism'. Before the metronome, introduced by Mr Mälzel in 1815 'in time for Beethoven to play with it', Joachim Quantz had found a method for measuring pace by means of the human pulse. He estimated eighty pulse beats to the minute and equated this movement with the Italian terms, *allegretto, allegro moderato* or *allegro non troppo*. John supported the Quantz idea of 'eighty' as an *allegretto* pulse. When listening to the *allegretto* movement from Beethoven's 7th Symphony, although the indication in the score for this movement is actually only seventy-six to the minute 'we may feel that fifty years after Quantz had developed his method, Beethoven would have gone along with it as far as his *allegretto* was concerned.' John believed that problems arose through a breakdown of communication between the composer in his tempo indications and the performer in trying to carry them out. 'After a good start in which Beethoven immortalised the metronome by basing the second movement of the Eighth Symphony on its tick-tock sound, the machine rather fell into disrepute, or at least was regarded as useful only as a guide for the *starting* measures of a composition.' (One should remember that John himself used this method for 'marking' the score of a well-known work.) 'When the music publisher

Schott asked Beethoven to "metronomise" the movements of his Ninth Symphony, he obliged, but somehow the copy he marked disappeared in his Vienna apartment. Then the composer bad-temperedly marked up a second copy, whereupon, as always happens, the original promptly came to hand. You can imagine Beethoven's consternation when a comparison showed quite a wide variation of metronome indication for every movement! Beethoven is said to have shouted "No metronome at all! Whoever has the *right feeling*, doesn't need it . . ." In this opinion he was joined by Wagner who was always very critical of his conductors. At a rehearsal of *Tannhäuser* he complained to the conductor about his choice of tempi, and was answered "But what do you want? We are playing exactly the tempi indicated by your own metronomic marks." Experiences like this led Wagner to give up metronome indications altogether. He thought that the *absence* of tempo indications in Bach's music was an indication that the true *musical* speed could be judged by any good musician from the internal evidences – how quick or slow the note values were, and so forth (because obviously a bar containing lots of demisemiquavers would *have* to be limited in speed to some extent). Nevertheless, as an interpreter I can't help wishing that despite the limitations of the metronome, Beethoven and Wagner had both used the numbered metronome indications in *more* of their works. They would always be of value to prevent or at least to censor conductors' more outrageous excesses.

'With modern composers the metronome (which had degenerated into a sort of threatening instrument encountered perched on the upright pianos of music teachers, always ready to be appealed to, to keep young players "in time"), has rather come back into its proper function as a performing guide. Bartók not only gives indications for every section of his works, but even times, in minutes and seconds, every few pages of the score. Also he gives the metronome the ultimate promotion of excluding an Italian word to alter the pace, such as *più* or *meno mosso*, and merely marks up or down the metronome number at the appropriate place. This is pretty definitive, but I wish I had a clearer picture of conductors armed with stopwatches during rehearsals of his "Concerto for Orchestra": somehow we conductors, you see, imagine WE KNOW THE SPEED at which the music should go, and no amount of forethought and precautionary instructions by composers seems able to do more than dent the conductor's self-esteem on this question. You may well wonder, if great composers like Wagner, Berlioz and Verdi – who were never slow to criticise their interpreters – if *they* could not with all their vocal and written admonitions secure the right tempi during their active life times, then how much less can we be sure that Mozart and Haydn are not the constant sport of wayward conductors? Mozart, living happily in ignorance of the doubtful benefits of Mr Mälzel which the future was to bring, was always content with Italian indications, quite basic ones such as *allegro, allegro molto, andante, adagio,* and so on. Another method of indicating the speed was by time signature: he often wrote in 4/4 time but put a line through the common time sign which indicated the movement was not in 4 but in 2 beats to the bar. Most significantly, in the finale of his String Quartet in B flat K458, he threw out his first version which was written in longer note values (4/4, *alla breve,* marked *prestissimo*) and substituted an *allegro assai* in 2/4. The music was exactly the same, but this proves that to Mozart the look of his music written in 4/4 did not betoken a very fast tempo, even with the word *prestissimo* added! Incidentally, in all the great output of Mozart, in symphonies, quartets or piano music, these extreme indications hardly ever occur, not one *largo* and at the moment though I can think of several *prestos, prestissimo* doesn't exist for him.

'I do think that in considering the question of tempo, of all the great composers perhaps it is Mozart who best repays study to see if we can establish any useful guidelines to the speed at which the music should go. As I've said, he had no metronome, he relied on basic Italian terms without much embellishment and he must have thought (in the fairly small and aristocratic musical world of the eighteenth century, where *style* was rather like *dress*, a question of the good taste of gentlemanly people) – he must have agreed with the principle later stated by Wagner, that the inner content of the music is sufficient to establish fairly exactly the pace. But I'm going to give you some examples based on his Symphony no. 40 in G minor to demonstrate that musicians of very great fame and discernment have notably different views of that "inner content". If I may use a personal example to introduce a short study of various approaches to this Symphony, I was recently, after a performance of no. 40 at last year's Promenade Concerts, specifically attacked by a critic (whose name was unknown to me) writing in, I think, a Birmingham evening paper. He criticised my tempo for the first movement, implying it was too slow, and I must confess I would not have reacted especially had he not used this question calculated to bring me down in confusion. He wrote "if the *pop version* of Mozart 40 can get the tempo right, why do Mr Pritchard and the BBC Symphony Orchestra get it wrong?" No half-shades about this, you notice, it's a question of right and wrong, almost of morals. Now this question aroused my curiosity mingled with a certain pique, and when I had time I did a little research with quite amusing results. First, you might like to hear the most famous of the Pop treatments of Mozart's Symphony. Here it is: (Play 50″ of Band 3, Side 1, Waldo de Los Rios, Symphonies for the Seventies).

'Now there are several things to say about that and I'm not intending to be sniffy or high-hat about it. If you concede the principle of squashing Mozart's delicate accompaniment given to the violas with a cheerful, breezy rhythm section, and out of concession to an eighteenth-century piece you throw in a dash of harpsichord tinkle and you don't mind audacious cuts and switches of tonality which Mozart hadn't considered, then it's a good highly extrovert treatment of music which it's almost impossible to destroy. I can't resist reminding you of the "play-out" tacked in this version onto Mozart's final definitive chords, listen to this: (Play last 15″ of same band, above).

'Now I've promised not to be superior about this, and I'm told I mustn't forget how many thousands of youngsters may be introduced to Mozart's 40th Symphony, which they might otherwise never hear, because they like the Pop version, but I *do* doubt this, for one thing because my suspicions about the Birmingham critic had been aroused, *just because* he chose the Pop version as his authority on a question of tempo. I must beware of giving any impression I'm doing some special pleading about something which is hardly of much interest now, but nevertheless when I played a tape of the Promenade Concert performance, and took a metronome reading of my tempo, I found it was 2 beats to the bar at 106. Eagerly I tested the Pop Version, and found it to be 2 beats at 108! This confirmed my suspicions that it was the snap of the rhythm section and the generally cheerful, uncomplicated attitude to the music which gave a quite artificial impression of greater speed. And what the critic found dragging and perhaps dreary in the concert performance was occasioned, I admit it proudly, by my view of this Symphony as an exceptionally serious piece with strong undertones of pain and resignation. Einstein described this Symphony as this "fatalistic piece of chamber music" and descriptive of "the abyss of the soul". Otto Jahn spoke of it as "a piercing cry of anguish".

'With this view of the inner content of the music in mind, let us now hear a few recordings of the opening of this Symphony made by some very great musicians: (I've thought it more diplomatic to choose conductors now dead, but I've an idea a comparison among living conductors might be just as revealing!).

'First we'll hear one of the greatest of Mozartians and a supreme example of what could be called the classical approach, Bruno Walter with the Columbia Symphony Orchestra. (Play 25″ Side 1, Columbia SO, CBS 72138.)

'There is great graciousness and style here. (By the way the metronome reading is only a fraction over 100, and is the slowest of any recording I listened to – apart from one rather amazing oddity which I'll play in a moment. Walter is even more leisurely in the 2nd subject, with metronome 96.) I don't feel that he is overconcerned with storm and stress and anguish, but he is certainly spacious and dignified. Now, what would you expect when I mention the name Wilhelm Furtwängler, the high priest of poetic feeling and lyrical expressiveness? I certainly thought his reading would be highly charged with all the introspective emotion which Mozart has taught us to expect when he uses the key of G minor. Well, here it is: (Play 40″, 1st Movement, Vienna Philharmonic, HMV ALP1498). This is certainly a highly nervous performance. Did you notice that quaver accompaniment of the violas, not really contributing as an emotional factor as one might expect, but just a purely background effect.

'The metronome reading is 126 and is the fastest first movement on any of six recordings I heard.

'Now I promised you an oddity. Many years ago Serge Koussevitzky, the great American-Russian conductor, made some recordings with the London Philharmonic Orchestra. Among them was the Mozart G minor, and when I listened to this 78 recording I was at first stupefied and feverishly adjusting the metronome to try to register the slowest speed ever, about 84 to the minute! But Koussevitzky had a surprise up his sleeve, after 30″ of a tempo which would doubtless give my Birmingham critic an apoplexy: (Play 50″ 1st Movement, Koussevitzky / LPO on 78s).

'One is reminded of the car advertisements which speak of "zero to 60 miles per hour in 4.7 seconds", when one hears *that* tempo change. For the record, Koussevitzky advances from metronome 84 to metronome 120 in 3 bars of music! WHY? Needless to point out that there is not the slightest written indication in the score for the *accelerando*. What about the inner content? I really think that Koussevitzky must have felt so strongly about the languishing, poignant nature of the first theme that he *needed* to load it with expression in a way that necessitated the very slow tempo. Then when he arrived at the emphatic *forte* music, he didn't want to be ponderous, and charged ahead. It's a case, so often occurring with interpreters, of preoccupation with a short section of the music, possibly to the detriment of the architectural line of the whole work.

'Of course, the trouble about finding guidelines on tempo is that essentially any involved movement of a symphony or a quartet or a sonata is by its form and content expressive of varying emotions, and variation of mood is by definition resistant to *rigidity*. I often think that some of the great composers in the past who were also conductors may very possibly have had insufficient stick technique to have been very elastic or pliable as orchestral conductors. Certainly both Brahms *and* Berlioz were dubbed "mere time-beaters" by Wagner, who was particularly caustic about (guess what?) – Berlioz' interpretation of Mozart's Symphony no. 40!

'As a performer I know that when the lights in the opera house lower and I enter the pit, *so much* depends on me for the audience to feel that the music is flowing, that the time changes are fluent and (most important) UNobtrusive, that aversion to dragging is not made an excuse for unfeeling speed and that whatever the length of an Act of the opera, it must have the proportion and sense of form which is the mark of a great symphony. These considerations make the continuing search for the RIGHT TEMPO well worthwhile.' (Toscanini recording RCA 16137.)

Select Bibliography

Busch, Fritz, *Pages from a Musician's Life*, Hogarth Press 1953.

Caplat, Moran, *Dingies to Divas*, Collins 1985.

Haltrecht, Montague, *The Quiet Showman: David Webster and the Royal Opera House*, Collins 1975.

Herbert, David (ed.), *The Operas of Benjamin Britten*, Hamish Hamilton 1979.

Hughes, Spike, *Glyndebourne*, David & Charles 1981.

Kennedy, Michael, *Adrian Boult*, Papermac 1989.

Paris, Alan (ed.), *Dictionnaire des Interprètes*, Bouquins/Robert Laffont 1989.

Piemme, Jean Marie, *Un Théâtre d'Opéra, L'Équipe de Gerard Mortier à la Monnaie*, Duculot 1986.

Discography

The following discography has been extracted from the archives of the recording companies and orchestras with whom John was associated.

As in the text of the biography, all spellings of composers' and artists' names are as they were in the programmes etc. of the time.

Dates included in brackets are, in all cases, dates of issue or re-issue.

Recording Date (date of issue)	Composer	Work	Orchestra & soloist
July/ Sept 1952	Mozart	Arias	Philharmonia
		Don Giovanni, K527	– Elisabeth
July 1		1. Batti, batti	Schwarzhopf
July 2		4. Vedrai, carino	
July 4		★7. Crudele? . . . Non mi dir	
		Le Nozze di Figaro, K492	
July 1		2. Voi che sapete	
July 1		3. Porgi amor	
July 2		5. Non so più cosa son	
July 2		6. Giunse alfin il momento	
Sept 9		9. E Susanna non vien? . . .	
Sept 9		10. Dove sono	
		Die Zauberflöte, K620	
July 5		8. Pamina's Aria:Ach, ich fuhl's	
		Idomeneo, K366	
Sept 10		★11. Zeffiretti lusinghieri	
		Motet	
Sept 15, 16 Kingsway Hall, London (Nov 1952)		12. Exsultate Jubilate, K165	

COLUMBIA: CX 1069 (LP:M) Compilation Nos 1–7, 10, 11; LB 145 (78:M) Compilation Nos 1, 4 (March 1954); SEL 1515 (7″ 45:M) consists of 2 Arias marked ★(Oct 1954); HMV: RLS 763 (LP:M Box) (Nov 1981); EMI: CDC 7479502 (CD:M) Compilation Nos 1, 2, 4–6, 7, 11 (June 1987) (all deleted)

Oct 3 1952 Kingsway Hall, London (Nov 1952)	Gruber	Silent night, holy night (arr. Salter)	Philharmonia – Covent Garden Chorus
		Traditional- The First Noël (arr. Salter)	/Hampstead Parish Church Choir – Elisabeth Schwarzkopf
		O come all ye faithful (unpublished)	

COLUMBIA: LB 131 (78:M); SCD 2112
(7″ 45:M) (Nov 1959) (deleted)

| Jan 28, 29
1953
Vienna
(July 1953) | Mozart

Mozart | Flute Concerto
in G major, K313
Flute Concerto
in D major, K314 | Vienna Symphony
– Hubert
Barwahser |

PHILIPS' PHONOGRAPHISCHE
INDUSTRIE: Continental issue A 00166 L
(LP–M) (deleted):
U.K. issue: ABL 3059 (LP:M) (July 1955)
(deleted);
Continental issue 6530 046 (deleted);
Re-issued as enhanced for stereo: 412 502–4
(MC:S) (June 1984)

| Jan 25–31
1953
Vienna
(Oct 1953) | Mozart | *Bastien und Bastienne*
K50 (complete) | Vienna Symphony
– Ilse Hollweg/
Waldemar Kmentt/
Walter Berry |

PHILIPS' PHONOGRAPHISCHE
INDUSTRIE: Continental issue A 00167 L
(LP:M) (deleted);
U.K issue ABL 3010 (LP:M) (Sept 1954)
(deleted)

| March 17–24
1953
Vienna
(Jan 1954) | Mozart

Mozart | Piano Concerto
in B flat major,
K456
Piano Concerto
in F major, K459 | Vienna Symphony
– Hans Henkemans |

PHILIPS' PHONOGRAPHISCHE
INDUSTRIE: A 00184 L (LP:M) (deleted)

Discography

March 23, 24　Manfredini　Christmas　　　　Vienna Symphony
April 30　　　　　　　　　Symphony for string orch.
1953　　　　　　　　　　& organ in C major
Vienna　　　　Corelli　　Concerto Grosso op. 6
(Oct 1953)　　　　　　　no. 8 in G minor
　　　　　　　Handel　　★Concerto Grosso op. 6
　　　　　　　　　　　　no. 12 in B minor

PHILIPS' PHONOGRAPHISCHE
INDUSTRIE: Continental issue A 00668 R
(10″LP:M) (deleted); ★(Handel:side 2,
S06105 R) (LP:M) (July 1956) (deleted);
U.K issue: ABR 4014 (LP:M) (deleted)

April 11–13　Mozart　　Four Concert-Arias　Vienna Symphony
1953　　　　　　　　　Popoli di Tessaglia,　– Ilse Hollweg
Vienna　　　　　　　　K31
(May 1953)　　　　　　Nehmt Meinen Dänk K383
　　　　　　　　　　　Vorrei Spiegarvi, Oh Dio, K418
　　　　　　　　　　　Voi Avete Un Cor Fedele, K217

PHILIPS' PHONOGRAPHISCHE
INDUSTRIE: Continental issue A 00657 R
(10″LP:M) (deleted);
U.K issue: ABR 4054 (LP:M) (June 1957)
(deleted)

April 28, 29　Beethoven　Symphony no. 1　Vienna Symphony
1953　　　　　　　　　in C major op. 21
Vienna
(Oct 1953)　　　　　　PHILIPS' PHONOGRAPHISCHE
　　　　　　　　　　　INDUSTRIE: Continental issue A 00179 L
　　　　　　　　　　　(LP:M), side 1 (deleted);
　　　　　　　　　　　UK issue GBL 5539 (LP:M) (June 1960)
　　　　　　　　　　　(deleted)

Dec 8, 19　　Hindemith　Viola Concerto,　　Chamber Orchestra
1953　　　　　　　　　'Der Schwanendreher'– William Primrose
Walthamstow
Town Hall,　　　　　　PHILIPS' PHONOGRAPHISCHE
London　　　　　　　INDUSTRIE:
(May 1955)　　　　　　ABL 3045 (LP:M) (deleted)

Jan 6 1954　　Mozart　　Violin Concerto　　Philharmonia
Kingsway　　　　　　no. 5 in A major,　– Yehudi Menuhin
Hall, London　　　　　K219.
(Oct 1955)

HMV: ALP 1281 (LP:M) (deleted)

April 7 1954	Mozart	Piano Concerto in G major, K453	Vienna Symphony – Hans Henkemans
April 8 1954 Vienna (March 1955)	Mozart	Piano Concerto in B Flat major, K595	

PHILIPS' PHONOGRAPHISCHE
INDUSTRIE: A 00239 L (LP:M) (deleted)

April 9–13 1954 Vienna (Feb 1955)	Handel	Concerto Grosso op. 6 no. 1 in G major Concerto Grosso op. 6 no. 7 in B flat major Concerto Grosso op. 6 no. 2 in F major Concerto Grosso op. 6 no. 6 in G minor	Vienna Symphony

PHILIPS' PHONOGRAPHISCHE
INDUSTRIE: Continental issue A 00235 L
(LP:M) (deleted);
U.K issue ABL 3075 (LP:M) (July 1955)
(deleted)

April 9–13 1954 Vienna (April 1955)	Folk Songs *Drink to me only with thine eyes; *The plough boy; *My Lady Greensleeves; *Oh, my love is like a red, red rose; Think on me; *Bonnie Mary of Argyle; An Eriksay Love Lilt; Kishmul's Galley; Land of Heart's Desire; Kitty of Coleraine; *Believe me, if all those endearing young charms; *The Star of the County Down	Murray Dickie – John Pritchard (piano)

PHILIPS' PHONOGRAPHISCHE
INDUSTRIE:
NBR 6016 (LP:M) (deleted
*NBE 11070 (7" 45:M) (1958) (deleted)

Discography

July 17–20　Busoni　　*Arlecchino*　　　Glyndebourne
1954　　　　　　　　　(Complete)　　　Festival Opera:
Abbey Road,　　　　　　　　　　　　Royal Philharmonic
London　　　　　　　　　　　　　　– Ian Wallace/
(April 1955)　　　　　　　　　　　　Sir Geraint Evans/
　　　　　　　　　　　　　　　　　Fritz Ollendorf/
　　　　　　　　　　　　　　　　　Elaine Malbin/
　　　　　　　　　　　　　　　　　Murray Dickie/
　　　　　　　　　　　　　　　　　spoken role,
　　　　　　　　　　　　　　　　　Kurt Gester

HMV: ALP 1223 (LP:M) (deleted)
HTA 14 ($7^{1}/_{2}$ ips tape:M) (deleted)

Aug 13, 14　Fricker　　Symphony no. 2,　Royal Liverpool
1954　　　　　　　　　op. 14　　　　　Philharmonic
Philharmonic
Hall,　　　　　　　　HMV: in association with the British Council
Liverpool　　　　　　DLP 1080 (LP 10″:M);
(Sept 1955)　　　　　HQM 1010 (LP:M) (Feb 1966);
　　　　　　　　　　finale only: CDM7 63370 (CD:M),
　　　　　　　　　　EG7 63370–4 (MC:M) (all deleted)

Dec 6 1954　Mozart　　Violin Concerto　Philharmonia
Kingsway　　　　　　no. 4 in D major　– Yehudi Menuhin
Hall, London　　　　K218
(Oct 1955)

HMV: ALP 1281 (LP:M) (deleted)

Dec 20, 21　Haydn　　Symphony no. 80　Philharmonia
1954　　　　　　　　in D minor
Kingsway　　Mozart　　Serenade no. 6 in D, K239,
Hall, London　　　　'Serenata notturna'
(Feb 1956)　Haydn　　Nocturne no. 5

HMV: CLP 1061 (LP:M) (deleted)

April 12,　　Stravinsky　*L'Histoire du Soldat*　Glyndebourne
13, 28　　　　　　　　(as performed at the　Festival Opera:
May 4, 25　　　　　　Edinburgh Festival　Royal Philharmonic
1955　　　　　　　　1954)　　　　　　　– Robert Helpmann/
Abbey Road,　　　　　　　　　　　　Terence Longdon/
London　　　　　　　　　　　　　　Anthony Nicholls
(Sept 1955)

HMV: ALP 1377 (LP:M) (deleted)
HQM 1008 (LP:M) (Dec 1965) (deleted)
(HMS 109 History of Music and Sound,
contains: L'Histoire du Soldat – Marche
royale. (Feb 1959))

381

| July 6, 7, 30
Aug 4, 6, 8
13, 26, 27
1956
Kingsway
Hall &
Abbey Road,
London
(Oct 1957) | Mozart | *Idomeneo*, K366
(Complete) | Glyndebourne
Festival Opera:
Royal Philharmonic
– Sena Jurinac/
Richard Lewis/
Léopold Simoneau/
Lucille Udovick/
James Milligan/
William McAlpine/
Hervey Alan |

HMV: (recorded in stereo) ALP 1515–17
(3LP's:M) (deleted)
WORLD RECORD CLUB: OC 201–3
(3 LP's:M), SOC 201–3 (3 LP's:S)
(May 1968) (deleted)
EMI: CHS 7636852 (Historic Box)
(2CD's:M) (Nov 1990), (ALP 1731 (LP:M)
Album to celebrate "Glyndebourne –
25 Years" includes an extract) (deleted)

| March 17–19
1957
(June 1958) | Tippett | *A Child of our Time* | Royal Liverpool
Philharmonic
and Choir
– Richard Lewis/
Richard Standen/
Elsie Morison/
Pamela Bowden |

PYE (Recorded in association with the
British Council): CCL 30114/5 (LP:M)
(deleted); acquired,
1. ARGO: DA 19–20 (LP:M) (deleted)
ARGO: ZDA 1920 (LP:S) (deleted)
2. ARGO: DPA 571–2 (2 LP's:S)
(Feb 1977) (deleted)
3. DECCA: 425 158–2 (CD:S) (Aug 1989)
(deleted)

| Sept 8 1957
BBC
broadcast | Donizetti | *Emilia di Liverpool*
(excerpts) | Royal Liverpool
Philharmonic
Joan Sutherland |

VOCE: MCD 915–46 (LP:M) (deleted)

Oct 27, 31 1957 (June 1958)	Tippett	Ritual Dances from *The Midsummer Marriage*	Royal Opera House

PYE (Recorded in association with the British Council): CCL 30114/5 (LPM) (deleted); acquired,
1. ARGO: DA 19–20 (LP:M) (deleted) ARGO: ZDA 1920 (LP:S) (deleted)
2. ARGO: DPA 571–2 (2 LP's:S) (Feb 1977) (deleted)

June 17 1958 Granada Television (ATV b/cast for 'Chelsea at Eight') Kings Road, London	Puccini Rossini	*Tosca*: Vissi d'arte *Il Barbiere di Siviglia*: Una voce po fà	Maria Callas

LEGENDARY RECORDINGS: LR 111 (LP:M) (deleted)

Nov 20 1960 (Remake Dec 16 1960)	Beethoven	Violin Romance no. 1 in G major, op. 40	Philharmonia – Yehudi Menuhin
Nov 20 1960 Abbey Road London (March 1965)	Beethoven	Violin Romance no. 2 in F major, op. 50	

HMV: ASD 618 (LP:S); ALP 2070 (LP:M) (March 1965); SXLP 30249 (LP:S) (Nov 1977); TC2MOM 118 (MC:S) (April 1981); TC2–COS 54252 (MC:S) (June 1982) (all deleted)
EMI: CDM 7643242 (CD:S) (July 1992)

Nov 22	Paganini	I Palpiti: Variations on the aria 'Di Tanti Palpiti' from Rossini's opera *Tancredi*, op. 13	Philharmonia – Yehudi Menuhin

HMV: unpublished

Nov 22 1960 (Remake Dec 16 1960)	Chausson	Poème, op. 25	Philharmonia – Yehudi Menuhin
Nov 27 1960	Wieniawski	Légende, op. 17	
Feb 24 1964 (March 1965)	Berlioz	*Rêverie et Caprice, op. 8	

HMV: ASD 618 (LP:S); ALP 2070 (LP:M)
(March 1965); SXLP 30249 (LP:S)
(Nov 1977); (all deleted)
*EMI: CDM 7635302 (CD:S) (Aug 1990)

July 27 – Aug 7 1961 Accademia di Santa Cecilia, Rome (Nov 1961)	Donizetti	*Lucia di Lammermoor* (complete)	Orchestra e Coro Dell'Accademia di Santa Cecilia, Roma – Joan Sutherland/ Renato Cioni/ Robert Merrill/ Cesare Siepi/ Kenneth MacDonald/ Ana Raquel Satre/ Rinaldo Pelizzoni

DECCA: MET 212/214 (3 LP's:M)
(deleted);
SET 212/214 (3 LP's:S) (deleted);
Highlights issued Nov 1964 LXT 5684
(LP:M);
SXL 2315 (LP:S) (deleted);
411 622–2 DM2 (2 CD's:S)
GOS 663–5 (3 LP's:S) (Nov 1975) (deleted)

Aug 10–12 1961 Abbey Road, London (Feb 1962)	Beethoven	Violin Concerto in D major, op. 61	Royal Philharmonic – Alfredo Campoli

HMV: XLP 20043 (LP:M) (deleted)
SXLP 20043 (LP:S) (deleted)
CLASSICS FOR PLEASURE: CFP 40299
(LP:S) (1978) (deleted)

Dec 8 1961 Walthamstow Town Hall London (Sept 1963)	Schubert	Symphony no. 8 in B minor, D759 'Unfinished'	London Philharmonic

MILLER/PYE: GGL 0212 (LP:M) (deleted);
GSGL 10212 (LP:S) (Sept 1963) (deleted)
MAL 552 (LP:M) (Jan 1965) (deleted)

Discography

Dec 8 1961   J Strauss II   An der schönen   London Philharmonic
Walthamstow   blauen Donau,
Town Hall   op. 314;
London   Kaiserwalzer, op. 437
(June 1962)   Lehar   Gold und Silber, op. 79
              Ivanovici   Waves of the Danube
              Sibelius   Valse Triste, op. 44
              Schubert   Symphony no. 8 in B minor,
                                 D759 'Unfinished'

MILLER/PYE: GGL 0127 (LP:M) (deleted);
GSGL 10127 (LP:S) (June 1962) (deleted)

Jan 29, 30   Rachmaninov   Piano Concerto   Philharmonia
1962   no. 2 in C minor,   – John Ogdon
Abbey Road,   op. 18
London
(July 1962)   HMV: ASD 492 (LP:S); ALP 1928
                             (LP:M) (July 1962);
                             SXLP 30552 (LP:S) (Sept 1982);
                             SLS 5033 (LP:S Box) (Nov 1975);
                             EMI: CDM 7635252 (CD:S) (March 1991)
                             (all deleted)

Nov 7–16   Verdi   *La Traviata*   Maggio Musicale
1962   (complete)   Fiorentino –
Teatro della   Joan Sutherland/
Pergola,   Carlo Bergonzi/
Florence   Robert Merrill/
(August 1963)   Miti Truccato Pace/
                             Dora Carral/
                             Piero De Palma/
                             Paolo Pedani/
                             Silvio Maionica/
                             Giovanni Foiani

DECCA: MET 249/51 (LP:M);
SET 249/51 (LP:S) (deleted);
Highlights issued March 1965:
LXT 6127 (LP:M), SXL 6127 (LP:S)
(deleted);
411 877–2 DM2 (2 CD's:S) (Oct 1988)

Dec 15, 18 20, 21, 1962 Kingsway Hall, London (May 1963)	Mozart	Arias: *Le Nozze di Figaro,* K492 Non so più cosa son; Voi che sapete che cosa è amor *La Clemenza di Tito,* K621 Parto, parto *Così fan Tutte, K588* Come Scoglio; E amore un ladroncello; Per pietà, ben mio Ch'io mi scordi di te? Concert Aria, Non temer amato bene, K505	London Symphony – Maria Teresa Berganza

DECCA: LXT 6045 (LP:M);
SXL 6045 (LP:S) (deleted);
SDD 176 (LP:S) (June 1968) (deleted)
7 arias on compilation 421 899–2 DA
(CD:S) (Dec 1992)
K505 included in: D251D5 (5 LP's:S)
(Feb 1982) (deleted), and in 430 300–2
DM5 (5 CD's:S)

April 1, 2 1963 Kingsway Hall, London	Handel	*Messiah* (excerpts) Reader's Digest:	London Philharmonic – Heather Harper/ Norma Proctor/ John Holmes/ Richard Lewis

April 25–28 1963 Walthamstow Assembly Hall, London	Verdi	*Aida* (Highlights) Ritorna Vincitor!; Fu la sorte dell' armi a tuoi funesta; Qui Radamès verrà; Rivedrai le foreste imbalsamate; La fatal pietra sovra me si chiuse	Royal Opera House – Birgit Nilsson/ Grace Hoffmann/ Louis Quilico/ Luigi Ottolini

DECCA: LXT 6068 (LP:M) (deleted)
SXL 6068 (LP:S) (deleted)

July 1.3, 30, Aug 1, 3, 6 & 8 1963 Abbey Road, London (June 1964)	Monteverdi (arr. Leppard)	*L'Incoronazione di Poppea* (excerpts as continuous performance – including complete arias)	Glyndebourne Festival Opera: Royal Philharmonic – Walter Alberti/ Magda Lazló/ Richard Lewis/ Oralia Dominquez/ Frances Bible/ Soo-Bee Lee/ Carlo Cava/ Duncan Robertson/ Lydia Marimpietri/ Hugues Cuénod/ Dennis Brandt/ Gerald English/ Elizabeth Bainbridge/ John Shirley-Quirk/ Annon Lee Silver/ Dennis Wicks

HMV: AN 126/7 (2 LP's:M Box),
SAN 126/7 (2 LP's:S Box) (deleted),
SLS 5248 (LP:S Box) (June 1982)
(deleted);
TC SLS 5248 (2 MC's:S)

Dec 21, 22 1963 Abbey Road, London	Rachmaninov	Rhapsody on a theme of Paganini, op. 43	Philharmonia – John Ogdon

HMV: unpublished

Dec 22 1963 Abbey Road, London (Nov 1964)	Liszt Liszt-Busoni	*Fantasy on Hungarian Folk Themes, S123 Rapsodie espagnole, S254	Philharmonia – John Ogdon

HMV: ASD 600 (LP:S); ALP 2051
(LP:M) (Nov 1964);
WORLD RECORDS: ST 697 (LP:S)
*SLS 5033 (LP:S Box) (Nov 1975) (all
deleted)

| July 24 1964 Opera House Glyndebourne (live) | Mozart | *Idomeneo*, K366 (Complete) | Glyndebourne Festival Opera: London Philharmonic – Richard Lewis/ Luciano Pavarotti/ Gundula Janowitz/ Enriqueta Tarrès/ Neilson Taylor/ David Hughes/ Dennis Wicks |

BUTTERFLY: BMCD 010 (2 CD's:M)

| Dec 17 1964 Paris, Radio France (Dec 1987) | Mozart | Davidde Penitente, K469: Tra L'oscure ombre funeste; Il sogno di Scipione, K126: Ah! perchè, cercare deggio? | L'Orchestre National de France – Teresa Stich-Randall |

LE CHANT DU MONDE: LDC278 887 (CD:M) K478 887 (MC:M)

| (Nov 1966) | Bartók | Piano Concerto no. 3, Sz119 | The Pro Arte – Bela Siki |
| | Liszt | Piano Concerto no. 2 in A major, S125 | |

PYE-GOLDEN GUINEA: GGC 4054 (LP:M); GSGC 14054 (LP:S) (deleted) (acquired by EMI)

| Jan 11, 13 1966 Watford Town Hall (Nov 1966) | Chopin | Piano Concerto no. 2 in F minor, op. 21 *a*. | Philharmonia – Charles Rosen |
| | Liszt | Piano Concerto no. 1 in E flat, G124 *b*. | |

COLUMBIA: CX 5273 (LP:M), SAX 5273 (LP:S) (deleted); CBS CLASSICS: 61094 (LP:S) (Aug 1969) (deleted); *a*. SONY: SBK 46336 (CD:S), SBT 46336 (MC:S); *b*. SBK 45504 (CD:S), SBT 45504 (MC:S)

Discography

| Jan 13 1966 | Mendelssohn | *A Midsummer Night's* Philharmonia
Dream, op. 64 –
Wedding March
and Nocturne |

CBS CLASSICS: unpublished

June 16, 18 1969 Barking Town Hall (May 1970)	Berlioz	*Les Troyens* – London Philharmonic [The Trojans], Royal Hunt and Storm
	Debussy	*Prélude à l'après-midi d'un* *faune* [Prelude to The Afternoon of a Faun]
	Stravinsky	*The Firebird*, Ballet Suite (1919 version)

PYE VIRTUOSO: TPLS 13032(S)(LP:S)
(deleted);
PYE GOLDEN GUINEA: GSGC
15002(S) (LP:S) (Aug 1975) (deleted);
'Prélude à l'après-midi d'une faune' on
PYE GOLDEN HOUR: GH 670(LP:S)
& ZCGH 670 (MC:S) (deleted)
(acquired by EMI)

| June 16, 18
1969
Barking
Town Hall
(May 1970) | Sibelius | Symphony no. 2 London Philharmonic
in D major, op. 43 |

PYE VIRTUOSO: TPLS 13033(S) (LP:S)
(deleted)
PYE GOLDEN GUINEA: GSGC
15003(S) (LP:S) (Aug 1975) (deleted)
(acquired by EMI)

| Dec 8, 9
1971
Abbey Road,
London
(March 1972) | Dohnányi | Piano Concerto New Philharmonia
no. 1 in E minor, – Balint Vazsonyi
op. 5 (1898) |

PYE VIRTUOSO: TPLS 13052 (LP:S)
(deleted)
PYE GOLDEN GUINEA: GSC 2052
(LP:M)
ZCGC 2052 (MC;M) (deleted)
PRECISION RECORDS AND TAPE:
PVCD 8398 (CD:S) (1986) (deleted)
(acquired by EMI)

April 7, 8 1970 Barking (1970)	Tchaikovsky	*Romeo & Juliet*: Fantasy Overture	London Philharmonic

MUSIC FOR PLEASURE: CFP 106 (LP:S), CFP 40042 (LP:S) (1971); also: CFP 40319 (LP:S), CFP 40307 (LP:S) (May 1979) (all deleted)

April 7, 8 1970 Barking (1970)	Tchaikovsky	Piano Concerto no. 1 in B flat minor, op. 23	London Philharmonic – Peter Katin

MUSIC FOR PLEASURE: CFP 115 (LP:S) (deleted)

June 16, 17 1970 Barking (1970)	Litolff	Scherzo from Concerto Symphonique no. 4 in D minor, op. 102	London Philharmonic – Peter Katin

MUSIC FOR PLEASURE: CFP 115 (LP:S) (deleted)

June 16, 17 1970 Barking (1971)	Grieg	Piano Concerto in A minor, op. 16	London Philharmonic – Peter Katin

MUSIC FOR PLEASURE: CFP 160 (LP:S) (deleted), TCCFP 160 (MC:S) (deleted)

June 19, 22 1970 Barking (1970)	Mussorgsky (orch. Ravel)	Pictures at an Exhibition	London Philharmonic

MUSIC FOR PLEASURE: CFP 106 (LP:S); CFP 40319 (LP:S) (1979); CFP 4554 (LP:S) (1989); CDCFP 4554 (CD:S) (1989); TC 4554 (MC:S) (1989) (all deleted)

Jan 7 1971 Barking (1971)	Grieg	Music from *Peer Gynt*	London Philharmonic

MUSIC FOR PLEASURE: CFP 160 (LP:S), TCCFP 160 (MC:S) (deleted)

Discography

April 4 1971 Barking (1971)	Ravel Chabrier Rimsky- Korsakov	Rapsodie Espagnol España – Rhapsodie Capriccio Espagnole, op. 34	London Philharmonic

MUSIC FOR PLEASURE: CFP 169
(LP:S) (deleted)

July 20, 22 1971 Barking (1971)	Bartók	Concerto for Orchestra, Sz116	London Philharmonic

MUSIC FOR PLEASURE: CFP 176
(LP:S) (deleted)
CFP 4504 (LP:S) (1978), TCCFP 4504
(MC:S) (1978) (deleted)

July 22/24 1972 Glyndebourne Organ Room (Nov 1972)	Mozart	*Die Entführung aus dem Serail*, K364 (excerpts)	Glyndebourne Festival Opera: London Philharmonic – Margaret Price/ Ryland Davies/ Daniele Perriers/ Kimmo Lappalainen/ Noel Mangen

CLASSICS FOR PLEASURE: CFP 40032
(LP:S) (deleted)
(Wills Embassy Master Series Nov 1972)

Feb 10, 11 1973 Watford Town Hall (1973)	Haydn Haydn	Symphony no. 44 in E minor, 'Trauersinfonie' Symphony no. 45 in F sharp minor, 'Farewell'	London Philharmonic

CLASSICS FOR PLEASURE: CFP 40021
(LP:S) (deleted)
(TCFWM 6, previously TCFWM 2909204,
'Papa Haydn's Surprise' – Fun with Music
Series for teaching children, contains
4th Movement. Symphony no. 45
(June 1986))

Feb 21/23   Mozart   Arias: London Philharmonic
1973 (LSO)   *Don Giovanni*, K527   and London
Kingsway   ★Il mio tesoro; *LPO*   Symphony
Hall, London   Dalla sua pace *LPO*   – Stuart Burrows
&   *Die Entführung aus*
June 19, 21   *dem Serail*, K384
(1974) (LPO)   Hier soll ich dich; *LSO*
Kingsway   Wenn der Freude; *LSO*
Hall, London   Constanze; *LSO*
(Oct 1976)   Ich baue ganz *LSO*
                         Die Zauberflöte, K620
                         Dies Bildnis; *LPO*
                         Wie stark ist nicht *LPO*
                         Così fan Tutte, K588
                         Un'aura amorosa; *LSO*
                         Ah lo veggio; *LPO*
                         In qual fiero; *LSO*
                         Idomeneo, K366
                         Fuor del mar *LSO*

                         DECCA/L'OISEAU-LYRE: DSLO 13
                         (LP:S) (1976) (deleted):
                         Re-released (1983) on 'Grandi Voci'
                         410 143–1 (LP:S)
                         ★One aria on 'Jubilee' Golden Opera
                         Vol. 2 414 497–4 (MC:S) & on 'Opera
                         Gala' LP of Mozart Famous Arias

April 13/15   Britten   Violin Concerto in   London Philharmonic
1974   D minor, op. 15   – Rodney Friend
Fairfield
Hall, Croydon   CLASSICS FOR PLEASURE:
(1974)   CFP 40068 (LP:S);
                         CFP 40250 (LP:S) (1976);
                         CFP 4489 (LP:S) (1985);
                         TCCFP 4489 (MC:S) (1985)
                         (all deleted)

Dec 19 1974   Britten   Serenade for Tenor,   London Philharmonic
Fairfield   Horn and Strings,   – Ian Partridge/
Hall, Croydon   op. 31   Nicholas Busch
(1976)
                         CLASSICS FOR PLEASURE: CFP 40250
                         (LP:S) (deleted)

Feb 23, 24 1975 Fairfield Hall, Croydon (1976)	Gershwin Gershwin/ Bennett Copland	*An American in Paris* London Philharmonic *Porgy and Bess* – Suite El Salón México CLASSICS FOR PLEASURE: CFP 40240 (LP:S) CDCFP 4537 (CD:S) (1988); TCCFP 4537 (MC:S) (1988); CDCFP 9019 (CD:S) (1988) (all deleted)
Feb 2–4 1975 Watford Town Hall (Nov 1976)	Schubert Schubert	Symphony no. 5 in London Philharmonic B flat major, D485 Symphony no. 8 in B minor, D759, 'Unfinished' CLASSICS FOR PLEASURE: CFP 40245 (LP:S) (deleted); CFP 40370 (LP:S) (1982) (deleted)
March 3 1975 Watford Town Hall (May 1976)	Schubert	Symphony no. 9 in London Philharmonic C major, D944, 'Great' CLASSICS FOR PLEASURE: CFP 40233 (LP:S) (deleted)
March 25 1975 Kingsway Hall (June 1977)	Rawsthorne	Symphony no. 1, London Philharmonic 1950 LYRITA RECORDED EDITION: SRCS 90 (deleted)
March 25 1975 Kingsway Hall (1979)	Rawsthorne	Street Corner London Philharmonic Overture LYRITA RECORDED EDITION: SRCS 95 (deleted)
Dec 1–3 1975 Barking (1977)	Prokofiev	*Romeo & Juliet* London Philharmonic (Ballet highlights) CLASSICS FOR PLEASURE: CFP 40266 (LP:S) (deleted)

Jan 4, 8 & 10 1976 Henry Wood Hall, London (Aug 1976)		French Operatic Arias	London Philharmonic
	Gounod	*Roméo & Juliette* – Depuis hier je cherche	– Frederica von Stade
	Berlioz	*Béatrice & Bénédict* – Dieu! Que viens-je *Le Damnation de Faust* – D'amour l'ardente flamme	
	Thomas	*Mignon* – Connais-tu le pays?	
	Massenet	*Werther* – Va, laisse couleur les larmes *Cendrillon* – Enfin, je suis ici	
	Offenbach	*La Périchole* – Ah! Quel dîner *La Grande Duchesse de Gérolstein* – Dîtes lui	
	Meyerbeer	*Les Huguenots* – Nobles seigneurs	

CBS CLASSICS: 76522 (CD:S) (deleted);
MK 39315 (CD:S) (deleted)

Jan 11 1976 (June 1977)	Rawsthorne	Symphonic Studies	London Philharmonic

LYRITA RECORDED EDITION:
SRCS 90 (deleted)

Jan 11 1976 (1979)	Francis Chagrin	Overture Helter Skelter	London Philharmonic

LYRITA RECORDED EDITION:
SRCS 95 (deleted)

Feb 8 1976 Henry Wood Hall, London (Jan 1978)	Rachmaninov	Piano Concerto no. 3 in D minor, op. 30	London Philharmonic – Craig Sheppard

CLASSICS FOR PLEASURE: CFP 40257
(LP:S) (deleted)

Discography

Feb 24 Nov 9 & Dec 4 1976 Henry Wood Hall, London (March 1977)	Donizetti Mozart Puccini Verdi	Sings Mozart, Donizetti, Verdi and Puccini: *Don Pasquale* So anch'io la virtù magica *Le Nozze di Figaro*, K496 Giunse alfin il momento – Deh vieni, non tardar *Die Zauberflöte*, K620 Ach, ich fühl's *Die Entführung aus dem Serail*, K384 Ach ich liebte *Turandot* Tu, che di gel sei cinta *La Rondine* Folle amore *La Bohème* Sì, mi chiamano Mimì *Rigoletto* Caro nome *La Forza del Destino* Pace, pace, mio dio	New Philharmonia – Ileana Cotrubas

CBS CLASSICS: 76521 (deleted)

Jan 1977 Abbey Road, London (Nov 1977)	Donizetti	*L'Elisir d'Amore* (Complete)	Royal Opera House Orchestra & Chorus – Ileana Cotrubas/ Placido Domingo/ Sir Geraint Evans/ Ingvar Wixell/ Lillian Watson

CBS CLASSICS: 79210 (2 LP's:S);
79210 (CD:Stereo Box) (Nov 1989);
40 79210 (MC:S);
arias included on 74022 (CD:S) 'Placido
Domingo sings Operatic Arias & Duets'

| 1977
Huddersfield
Town Hall
(Aug 1977) | Handel | Coronation
Anthems
– *Zadok the Priest*;
Let thy hand be
strengthened;
The king shall rejoice;
My heart is inditing | Northern Sinfonia
& Huddersfield
Choral Society |

ENIGMA CLASSICS: K 53542 (LP:S)
(deleted);
re-issued 1982 by
ACADEMY SOUND & VISION:
ACM 2041 (LP:S) (deleted);
ZC ACM 2041 (deleted)

| June/July
1978
Cologne
(Oct 1979) | Humperdinck | *Hänsel und Gretel*
(Complete) | Gürzenich Orchestra
Children's Chorus
of Cologne Opera –
Frederica von Stade/
Ileana Cotrubas/
Kiri Te Kanawa/
Siegmund Nimsgern/
Christa Ludwig/
Elisabeth
Söderström/
Ruth Welting |

CBS CLASSICS: 40–79217 (2 MC's:S)
(deleted); 72217 (2 LP's:S) (deleted);
M2K 79217 (2 CD's:S)

| Aug 3, 4,
7, 9, 1980
Abbey Road,
London | Wolf-Ferrari | *Il Segreto di Susanna*
(Complete) | Philharmonia
– Renata Scotto/
Renato Bruson |

CBS CLASSICS: DC 40134 (2 LP's:S)
(July 1988);
DCT 40134 (2 MC's:S)(July 1988);
MK 36733 (CD:S) (all deleted)

Discography

Sept 17,		Italian Operatic Arias	London Philharmonic
18, 20, 21	Puccini	*Tosca*: Vissi d'Arte	- Kiri Te Kanawa
1981		*Madama Butterfly*:	
Abbey Road,		Un Bel Dì	
London		*La Rondine*:	
(Nov 1983)		Ch'll bel sogno di Doretta	
		Manon Lescaut:	
		In quelle trine morbide	
		La Bohème:	
		Quando me'n vò'	
		Le Villi:	
		Se come voi piccina io fossi	
		Gianni Schicchi:	
		O mio babbino caro	
	Verdi	*La Traviata*:	
		E strano! . . . Ah fors' è lui . . .	
		Sempre libera	
		Don Carlos: Tu che le vanità	
		Il Trovatore:	
		D'amor sull'alli rose	

CBS CLASSICS: 37298 (LP:Digital:S);
CD 37298 (CD:Digital:S);
40 37298 (MC:Digital:S);
Arias included on MK 39208 (CD:Digital:S)
(July 1987) 'A Portrait of Kiri'

June 29–	Ravel	*Shéhérazade*	Brussels Opera
July 2			– Kiri Te Kanawa
1983	Duparc	Seven Songs	
Radio		Phidylé (de Lisle)	
Building,		L'Invitation au Voyage	
Brussels		(Baudelaire)	
(Oct 1984)		La Vie Anterieure	
		(Baudelaire)	
		Le Manoir de Rosemonde	
		(de Bonnieres)	
		Testament (Silvestre)	
		Au pays où se fait	
		la guerre (Gautier)	
		Chanson Triste (Lahor)	

EMI: EL 270135–1 (LP:Digital:S) (deleted);
EL 270135–4 (MC:Digital:S) (deleted);
CDC 747111–2 (CD:Digital:S) (Jan 1985)
(deleted)

June 20–22,   Mozart   *Idomeneo*, K366   Wiener
24, 25   (complete)   Philharmoniker/
Sept 7, 8,   Wiener
10, 12, 15,   Staatsopernchor –
19–23, 1983   Luciano Pavarotti/
Sofiensaal,   Lucia Popp/Agnes
Vienna   Baltsa/Edita
(April 1988)   Gruberova
                                              /Leo Nucci

DECCA/LONDON: 411 805–1DH3 (3
LP's:Digital:S);
411 805–2DH3 (3 CD's:Digital:S);
(Excerpts in Mozart Almanac 1781:
430 120–2 (CD:Digital:S) (Sept 1990))

1984   Scriabin   Symphony no. 3,   BBC Symphony
(Nov 1984)   op. 43 'Divine   Orchestra
                           Poem'

BBC: REGL 520 (LP:S) (deleted)
ZCF 520 (MC:S) (deleted)
CD 520 (CD:S) (deleted)

Nov 12–15   Mozart   Opera Arias   Philharmonia –
1987   *Die Entführung aus* Karita Mattila
Henry Wood   *dem Serail*, K384:
Hall, London   Martern aller Arten
(Aug 1988)   *Zaide*, K344:
                         Ruhe sänft, mein holdes Leben
                         Don Giovanni, K527:
                         In quali eccessi –
                         Mi tradì quell'alma ingrata
                         Die Zauberflöte, K620:
                         Ach, ich fühl's
               Weber   *Der Freichütz*:
                         Wie nahte mir der Schlummer
               Rossini   *Guillaume Tell*:
                         Ils s'éloignent enfin
                         – Sombre fôret
               Gounod   *Faust*:
                         O Dieu! que de bijoux
               Dvořák   *Rusalka*:
                         Mesickŭ na nebi hlubokem

PHILIPS CLASSICS: 422 073–1PH
(LP:Digital:S) (deleted);
422 073–2PH (CD:Digital:S) (deleted)

Dec 9–12 1988 All Saint's Church, Tooting (Aug 1990)	Canteloube	Songs of the Auvergne PICKWICK: PCD 938 (CD:Digital:S), CIMPC 938 (MC:Digital:S)	Philharmonia – Patricia Roszario
March 20 – 22, 1989 Konzerthaus Vienna (May 1991)	Mozart	*Der Schauspieldirektor,* K486 (complete) *Le Nozze di Figaro,* K492: Overture DECCA: 430 207–2DH (CD:Digital:S)	Wiener Philharmoniker – Kiri Te Kanawa/ Edita Gruberova/ Uwe Heilmann/ Manfred Jungwirth Wiener Philharmoniker

BBC SOUND ARCHIVES

Royal Liverpool Philharmonic Orchestra (1957–1963)

	Duration
ELGAR The Dream of Gerontius Richard Lewis, tenor Marjorie Thomas, mezzo-soprano Huddersfield Choral Society	88'43"
HAYDN Symphony no. 95 in C minor	17'39"
BERG Violin Concerto	23'24"
RAVEL Albondada del Gracioso Isaac Stern (violin) Recording Date: 1960 14th Edinburgh Festival	7'34"
BUSONI Comedy Overture	6'40"
BORODIN Jaroslavna's aria (Prince Igor)	9'16"
SCHUBERT/WEBERN German Dances	6'55"
MOZART Porgi amor (Le Nozze di Figaro, K492)	3'33"
MOZART Dove sono (Le Nozze di Figaro, K492)	6'22"
LISZT Piano Concerto no. 1 in E flat Elisabeth Söderström (soprano) John Ogdon (piano) Promenade Concert	18'36"

399

Sir John Pritchard

BERLIOZ Symphonie Fantastique   48′20″

WALTON Symphony no. 2 (World Première)   26′52″
Recording Date: 1960
14th Edinburgh Festival

Opera

ARIADNE AUF NAXOS Richard Strauss   126′43″
Royal Philharmonic Orchestra
Cast includes: David Franklin, Geraint Evans, Sena Jurinac,
Richard Lewis
Recording Date: 16.7.54
Glyndebourne Opera House

ARLECCHINO Busoni (sung in German)   58′50″
Royal Philharmonic Orchestra
Cast includes: Kurt Gester, Ian Wallace, Geraint Evans, Fritz
Ollendorff, Elaine Malbin and Murray Dickie
Recording Date: 16.7.54
Glyndebourne Opera House

COSI FAN TUTTE, K588 Mozart   148′58″
Royal Philharmonic Orchestra
Cast includes: Ilva Ligabue, Gloria Lane, Graziella Sciutti, Juan
Oncina, Sesto Brusantini, Carlos Feller
Recording Date: 17.7.59
Glyndebourne Opera House

LUCIA DI LAMMERMOOR Donizetti   114′25″
Covent Garden Opera Chorus and Orchestra
Cast includes: John Shaw, Joan Sutherland, André Turp, Kenneth
MacDonald, Joseph Rouleau, Margreta Elkins and Edgar Evans
Recording Date: 22.8.61
King's Theatre, Edinburgh

ELEGY FOR YOUNG LOVERS Hans Werner Henze   160′44″
Royal Philharmonic Orchestra
Cast includes: Dorothy Dorow, Kerstin Meyer, Thomas Hemsley,
André Turp, Carlos Alexander, Elisabeth Söderström and John
Kentish (speaker)
Recording Date: 15.7.61
Studio recording

BBC Sound Archives

L'INCORONAZIONE DI POPPEA Monteverdi   141'35"
Glyndebourne Opera Chorus
Royal Philharmonic Orchestra
Arranged by Raymond Leppard
Cast includes:Walter Alberti, Dennis Brandt, Gerald English,
Magda Laszlò, Richard Lewis, Jean Allister, Frances Bible, Soo-
Bee Lee, Carlo Cava, Duncan Robertson, Lydia Marimpietri,
Elizabeth Bainbridge, John Shirley-Quirk, Hugues Cuénod, Annon
Lee Silver and Dennis Wicks.
Recording Date: 29.7.63
Promenade Concert at Royal Albert Hall, London

IDOMENEO, K366 (Act III) Mozart   50'00"
Glyndebourne Opera Chorus
London Philharmonic Orchestra
Cast includes: Luciano Pavarotti, Gundula Janowitz, Enriqueta
Tarrés, Neilson Taylor, David Hughes and Dennis Wicks.
Recording Date: 17.8.64
Promenade Concert at Royal Albert Hall, London

EUGENE ONEGIN Tchaikovsky   99'25"
Glyndebourne Opera Chorus
London Philharmonic Orchestra
Cast includes: Elisabeth Söderström, Nikola Vassilev, Wieslaw
Ochman, Alexanderina Milcheva, Pamela Bowden, Virginia Popova,
Terry Jenkins, Hugues Cuénod, Anthony Williams, Richard van Allan
Recording Date: 11.8.70
Promenade Concert at Royal Albert Hall, London

INTERMEZZO Richard Strauss   150'35"
Glyndebourne Opera Chorus
London Philharmonic Orchestra
Cast includes: Elisabeth Söderström, Marco Bakker, Elizabeth
Gale, Richard Allfrey, Angela Whittingham, Alexander Oliver, Rae
Woodland, Cynthia Buchan, Donald Bell, Dennis Wicks, Anthony
Rolfe Johnson, Brian Donlan and Thomas Lawlor.
Recording Date: 13.7.74
Glyndebourne Opera House

IL MATRIMONIA SEGRETO Cimarosa   140'47"
Scottish Chamber Orchestra
Cast includes: Eric Saeden, Barbara Daniels, Krisztina Laki,
Marta Szirmay, Peter Christoph Runger, David Kuebler.
Recording Date: 25.8.80
King's Theatre, Edinburgh

GUNTRAM Richard Strauss   106'44"
BBC Singers (men's voices)
BBC Symphony Orchestra
Cast includes: William Lewis, Nigel Douglas, Sarah Walker, Sean
Rea, Henry Newman, John Tomlinson, Carole Farley, Patrick
Wheatley, Terence Sharpe, Bernard Dickerson and Laurence Dale.
Recording Date: 19.3.81
Studio Performance

Sir John Pritchard

KING PRIAM (World Première) Michael Tippett   125'00"
Chorus and Orchestra of
the Royal Opera House, Covent Garden
Cast includes: John Dobson, Margreta Elkins, Richard Lewis,
Marie Collier, Joseph Ward, Noreen Berry, David Kelly, Robert
Bowman, John Lanigan and Paula Dean.
Recording Date: 29.5.62
Coventry Cathedral

Promenade Concerts

ROSSINI Overture: La Cenerentola   8'01
EDWARD MACDOWELL Piano Concerto no. 2 in D minor   27'52
PROKOFIEV Peter and the Wolf (Slobodskaya, narrator)
CIMAROSA Il Maestro di Cappella – Intermezzo giocoso   20'38
FRANCK Symphonic Variations for piano & orchestra   15'20
JOHANN STRAUSS II Overture: Waldmeister   9'17
London Philharmonic Orchestra
Clive Lythgoe, piano
Carlos Feller, tenor
Recording Date: 24.8.63

HAYDN Symphony No. 98
RAWSTHORNE Concerto for Two Pianos and Orchestra   18'15
STRAVINSKY Concerto for Two Solo Pianos   21'00
London Philharmonic Orchestra
John Ogdon, piano
Brenda Lucas, piano
Recording Date: 14.8.68

HAYDN Symphony no. 85 in B flat (La Reine)   19'17
MOZART Piano Concerto in E flat, K482   34'04
JOSEF STRAUSS Music of the Spheres – waltz   8'03
LEHAR Giuditta – du bist meine Sonne (Burrows)   3'40
LEHAR The Merry Widow – Vilja (Wilson)   6'18
LEHAR Gold & Silver Waltz   7'20
JOHANN STRAUSS I Explosion Polka   2'44
JOSEF STRAUSS (I & II) Pizzicato Polka   2'32
HEUBERGER Der Opernball – Ins Chambre separee (Wilson & Burrows)   4'30
JOHANN STRAUSS II Emperor Waltz   10'01
JOHANN STRAUSS II Perpetuum Mobile   2'58
BBC Symphony Orchestra
Michael Roll (piano)
Stuart Burrows (tenor)
Catherine Wilson (soprano)
Recording date: 14.8.71

MOZART Masonic Funeral Music, K.477   5'43
BRAHMS Piano Concerto no. 2 in B flat   47'26
New Philharmonia Orchestra
André Watts (piano)
Recording Date: 13.9.72

HAYDN Symphony no. 52 in C minor	23'27
BEETHOVEN Piano Concerto no. 2 in B flat major	30'09
JOHANN STRAUSS II Banditen-Galop – Polka schnell	2'14
JOSEF STRAUSS Mien Lebenslauf ist Lieb' und Lust – Waltz	7'27
JOSEF STRAUSS Feuerfest – Polka	2'52
LEHAR The Merry Widow – Vilja (Wilson)	6'20
JOHANN STRAUSS II Ritter Pasman – Czardas	4'11
JOHANN STRAUSS II Die Fledermaus – Czardas	4'19
MILLOEKER The Dubarry – I give my heart	2'24
JOSEF STRAUSS Plappermaulchen – Polka	3'01
JOHANN STRAUSS II Freikugeln – Polka schnell	2'45
JOHANN STRAUSS II An der Schoenen blauen Donau – Waltz	8'29
JOHANN STRAUSS I Radetsky March	2'26
JOHANN STRAUSS II Perpetuum Mobile	2'44

BBC Symphony Orchestra
Charles Rosen (piano)
Catherine Wilson (soprano)
Recording Date: 12.8.72

ELGAR Overture: In the South	20'00
DELIUS Dance Rhapsody no. 1	11'40
HOLST Hymn to Jesus	22'35
WILLIAMSON Hammarskjöld Portrait (BBC Commission – first performance)	31'10
BRITTEN Young Person's Guide to the Orchestra	17'10

BBC Symphony Orchestra
Elisabeth Söderström (soprano)
Recording Date: 30.7.74

RICHARD STRAUSS Don Juan, op. 20	17'58
BEETHOVEN Symphony no. 6 (Pastoral)	43'37

London Symphony Orchestra
Paul Crossley (piano)
Recording Date: 28.8.75

BRUCKNER Overture in G minor	9'32
RICHARD STRAUSS Don Quixote – Symphonic Poem	41'30
BRITTEN Young Person's Guide to the Orchestra	18'20

BBC Northern Symphony Orchestra
Heinrich Schiff (cello)
Recording Date: 11.8.76

MOZART Symphony no. 40 in G minor, K550	27'57
DELIUS Piano Concerto	25'53
BRAHMS Symphony no. 2 in D	39'39

BBC Symphony Orchestra
Clifford Curzon (piano)
Recording Date: 3.9.81

Sir John Pritchard

Public Concerts

IAIN HAMILTON Circus for two trumpets and orchestra	14'02
BEETHOVEN Triple Concerto in C major	34'53

BBC Symphony Orchestra
Philip Jones (trumpet)
Elgar Howarth(trumpet)
Iona Brown (violin)
Tomas Igloi (cello)
Michael Roll (piano)
Recording Date: 21.1.70
Royal Festival Hall, London

ANTHONY MILNER Symphony (BBC Commission: 1st performance)	29'00"

BBC Symphony Orchestra
Recording Date: 17.1.73
Royal Festival Hall

RICHARD STRAUSS Don Juan, op. 20	16'50
ROGER SESSIONS Concerto for Orchestra	11'45
BRAHMS Piano Concerto no. 1 in D minor	51'45

BBC Symphony Orchestra
Elisabeth Leonskaja (piano)
Recording Date: 17.12.82
Royal Festival Hall

SCHUBERT Symphony no. 3 in D major, D.200	22'56"
MOZART Piano concerto in C major, K467	28'58"
MOZART Symphony no. 39 in E flat major, K543	

BBC Symphony Orchestra
Walter Klien (piano)
Recording Date: 17.1.83

SCHUBERT Symphony no. 4 in C minor, D417 (The Tragic)	26'59"
MOZART Piano Concerto in A major, K488	26'40"
MOZART Symphony no. 40 in G minor, K550	24'15"

BBC Symphony Orchestra
Walter Klien (piano)
Recording Date: 20.1.83

SCHUBERT Symphony no. 5 in B flat major, D.485   25'09"
MOZART Piano Concerto in C minor, K491   30'34"
MOZART Symphony no. 41 in C, K551 (Jupiter)   32'38"
BBC Symphony Orchestra
Walter Klien (piano)
Recording Date: 22.1.83

Miscellaneous Studio Recordings

EDMUND RUBBRA Festival Te Deum   9'30
Royal Philharmonic Orchestra
Elsie Morrison (soprano)
BBC Chorus
Recording Date: 10.9.52

STOCKHAUSEN Setz die Segel zur Sonne (performed without
  conductor)   23'45
STOCKHAUSEN Telemusik for magnetic tape (Original Tape directed
  by the composer)   17'25
STOCKHAUSEN Punkte   27'05"
BBC Symphony Orchestra
Recording Date: 14.1.70

RICHARD STRAUSS Four Last Songs   22'10
BBC Symphony Orchestra
Kiri Te Kanawa (soprano)
Recording Date: 3.2.72

MOZART Serenade in G major, K525 (Eine Kleine Nachtmusik)   17'25
BRITTEN Symphony for cello and orchestra   36'33
RICHARD STRAUSS Tod und Verklarung, op.24   24'20
BBC Symphony Orchestra
Julian Lloyd Webber (cello)
Recording Date: 10.1.80

HARRISON BIRTWISTLE The Triumph of Time   27'04
BBC Symphony Orchestra
Date: 19.4.82

SZYMANOWSKI Harnasie   34'40
BBC Symphony Orchestra
Rodney Friend (violin)
BBC Singers
BBC Syphony Chorus
Recording Date: 17.3.87

Sir John Pritchard

Festival Performances

1961 Edinburgh Festival

MOZART Symphony no. 31 in D major, K.297	18'00
TCHAIKOVSKY Romeo & Juliet: Duet for soprano, tenor	
& orchestra	11'40
NONO Cantata: Sul ponte di Hiroshima	19'20
DEBUSSY Nocturnes for Orchestra	23'00

London Symphony Orchestra
Marie Collier (soprano)
Richard Lewis (tenor)
June Holden
Dorothy Dorrow
Edinburgh Royal Choral Union
Usher Hall, Edinburgh

1973 Cheltenham Festival

LENNOX BERKELEY Symphony no. 3	12'39
STRAVINSKY Violin Concerto	22'11
DEBUSSY Images for orchestra: Iberia	19'47

BBC Symphony Orchestra
Wolfgang Marschner (violin)
Recording Date: 6.7.73
The Town Hall, Cheltenham

BBC SOUND TAPE LIBRARY
Complete works & excerpts

Recording Date (first transcription)	Composer	Work	Duration
Sept 3 1981 (Sept 3 1981)	Mozart	Symphony no. 40 in G minor, K550	27.22
	Delius	Piano Concerto in C minor	25.03
	Brahms	Symphony no. 2 in D major, op. 73	38.52
Dec 1 1981 (Aug 13 1982)	Strauss, R	Ein Heldenleben, op. 40	46.30
Apl 19 1982 (Feb 17 1983)	Birtwistle	The Triumph of Time	27.04

Aug 20 1982	Mozart	Symphony no. 38 in D major, K504	25.50
(Aug 20 1982)	Swayne	Orlando's music for orchestra	21.50
	Strauss, R	Don Quixote, op. 35 (Yo Yo Ma)	45.25
Oct 5 1982	Cowie	Clarinet Concerto no. 2, op. 5	24.24
(Mar 30 1983)	Vaughan-		
	Williams	Symphony no. 4 in F minor	32.15
Oct 7 1982	Copland	El Salón Mexico	11.55
(Mar 15 1983)	Ives	Symphony no. 1	36.56
Nov 19 1982	Haydn	Symphony no. 95 in C minor	21.00
(Nov 19 1982)	Rachmaninov	Three Symphonic Dances, op. 45	34.59
Dec 14 1982	Vaughan		
(Dec 28 1982)	Williams	Symphony no. 2, 'A London Symphony'	46.26
	Brahms	Symphony no. 2 in D major, op. 73	39.24
Jan 14 1983	Stravinsky	Fireworks, op. 4	3.43
(June 12 1983)	Prokofiev	Violin Concerto no. 1	23.34
	Rachmaninov	Three Symphonic Dances, op. 45	35.16
Jan 15 1983	Rachmaninov	Three Symphonic Dances, op. 45	35.49
(July 3 1983)	Britten	Sinfonia da requiem, op. 20	20.58
Jan 26 1983	Prokofiev	Piano concerto no. 2, op. 16	31.22
(Mar 13 1986)	Scriabin	Symphony no. 3 in C major, op. 43	43.19
Jan 28 1983	Beethoven	Piano Concerto no. 3 in C minor	36.05
(Jan 28 1993)	Bruckner	Symphony no. 5 in B flat major	69.40
Jan 30 1983	Schubert	Symphony no. 3 in D major, D.200	23.12
(Jan 30 1983)	Mozart	Violin Concerto no. 4 in D major, K218	26.45
	Dvořák	Symphony no. 8 in G major, op. 88	38.00
Feb 7 1983	Bartók	Cantata profana	21.38
(Feb 7 1983)	Beethoven	Symphony no. 9 in D minor, op. 125	68.58
Mar 9 1983	Bliss	Music for strings	27.36
(May 4 1983)	Gipps	Symphony no. 4, op. 61	33.51
Mar 22 1983	Brahms	Academic Festival Overture, op. 80	10.30
(Apl 10 1983)	Schumann	Concertstuck for 4 horns	
		and orchestra, op. 86	17.25
		Elgar Symphony no. 1 in A flat major,	
		op. 55	50.26
Mar 24 1983	Bliss	Music for strings	27.33
(Dec 28 1983)	Bartók	Concerto for orchestra, Sz.116	39.19
Mar 25 1983	Bliss	Music for strings	27.21
(Mar 25 1983)	Ravel	Piano Concerto in G major	23.22
	Bartók	Concerto for orchestra, Sz.116	38.38

Sir John Pritchard

May 19 1983	Brahms	Tragic Overture, op. 81	14.48
(Oct 17 1983)	Elgar	Symphony no. 1 in A flat major, op. 55	53.30
May 22 1983	Berkeley	Symphony no. 3, op. 74	12.38
(May 18 1984)	Rawsthorne	Piano Concerto no. 2	28.42
	Searle	Labyrinth, op. 56	19.55
May 24 1983	Strauss, R	Symphonia domestica, op. 53	46.26
(Oct 24 1983)			
July 22 1983	Beethoven	Mass in C major, op. 86 (Cotrubas,	
		Kuhlmann, Tear, Howell)	49.50
	Wagner	Trauermusik [on motifs from	
		Weber's Euryanthe]	8.00
	Berlioz	Symphonie Funèbre et Triomphale	33.17
July 25 1983	Brahms	Tragic Overture, op. 81	13.20
(July 25 1983)	Goehr	Babylon the great is fallen	52.21
	Beethoven	Symphony no. 5 in C minor, op. 67	32.11
Aug 13 1983	Schubert	Symphony no. 5 in B flat major D.485	30.55
(Aug 13 1983)	Mahler	Das Lied von der Erde	66.55
Aug 16 1983	Walton	Crown Imperial	6.40
(Aug 16 1983)	Walton	Violin Concerto in B minor	30.40
	Elgar	Symphony no. 1 in A flat major, op. 55	49.55
	Walton	Henry V – suite	
		(adapted by Muir Mathieson)	3.08
Dec 9 1983	Mahler	Das Lied von der Erde	64.45
(Dec 9 1983)	Parry	Blest Pair of Sirens	10.05
	Elgar	Variations on an original theme – 'Enigma'	29.55
Jan 5 1984	Strauss, R	Eine Alpensinfonie, op. 64	48.30
(July 6 1984)			
Jan 14 1984	Haydn	Symphony no. 104 in D major – 'London'	27.12
(Jan 14 1984)	Schumann	Cello Concerto, op. 129	24.50
	Schumann	Symphony no. 4 in D minor, op. 120	29.00
Jan 19 1984	Henze	Los Caprichos – fantasia	17.45
(Oct 5 1984)	Henze	Symphony no. 6 for 2 chamber orchestras	41.27
Jan 22 1984	Tchaikovsky	Francesca da Rimini	23.00
(Mar 5 1984)	Kalinnikov	Symphony no. 1 in G minor	30.30
	Rimsky-		
	Korsakov	Sheherazade	42.00
Feb 10 1984	Stravinsky	Symphony of psalms	19.45
(Feb 10 1984)	Brahms	Ein Deutsches Requiem, op. 45	68.00

1Feb 11 1984	Milner	Variations for orchestra, op. 14	
	Milner	Symphony no. 1, op. 28	
Apl 3 1984	Haydn	Symphony no. 83 in G minor – 'The Hen'	21.21
(June 3 1984)	Mahler	Lieder eines fahrenden Gesellen	18.55
	Brahms	Symphony no. 1 in C minor, op. 68	43.02
Apl 5 1984	Mozart	Symphony no. 34 in C major, K338	21.57
(June 30 1984)	Brahms	Symphony no. 1 in C minor, op. 68	42.25
Apl 9 1984	Elgar	Variations on an original theme – 'Enigma'	29.50
(Sept 27 1984)	Strauss, R	Symphonia domestica, op. 53	43.17
Apl 10 1984	Berlioz	Le Carnaval romain – overture, op. 9	8.30
(May 7 1984)	Chopin	Piano Concerto no. 1, op. 11	39.10
	Strauss, R	Symphonia domestica, op. 53	44.20
Apl 13 1984	Elgar	Violin Concerto in B, op. 61	49.51
(Apl 13 1984)	Tippett	Symphony no. 4	29.38
	Britten	An American overture	9.30
Apl 14 1984	Scriabin	Symphony no. 3 in C major, op. 43	48.34
(Oct 5 1984)			
Apl 17 1984	Delius	Paris – the song of a great city	23.45
(May 30 1985)	Britten	Nocturne	26.57
Apl 18 1984	Delius	Paris – the song of a great city	23.20
(Apl 18 1984)	Mahler	Lieder eines fahrenden Gesellen	16.30
	Strauss, R	Eine Alpensinfonie, op. 64	47.40
	Delius	Summer night on the river	6.45
May 8 1984	Mozart	Symphony no. 38 in D major, K504	25.27
(June 9 1984)	Delius	Paris – the song of a great city	22.26
	Bartók	Concerto for orchestra, Sz. 116	38.33
May 14 1984	Mozart	Symphony no. 38 in D major, K504	29.10
(May 14 1984)	Britten	Nocturne	26.50
	Bartók	Concerto for orchestra, Sz. 116	38.15
May 26 1984	Mozart	Symphony no. 38 in D major, K504	29.08
(Aug 17 1984)	Bartók	Concerto for orchestra, Sz. 116	37.43
	Britten	Nocturne	25.50
July 17 1984	Stravinsky	Symphonies of wind instruments	8.54
(Aug 19 1954)	Saxton, R	Concerto for orchestra	18.17
July 20 1984	Vaughan		
(July 20 1984)	Williams	Symphony no. 2, 'A London Symphony'	46.35
	Elgar	Sea pictures, op. 37	23.15
	Walton	Belshazzar's feast	35.30

Aug 13 1984	Strauss, R	Till Eulenspiegel, op. 28	15.20
(Aug 13 1984)	Rachmaninov	Three Symphonic Dances, op. 45	34.35
	Saxton, R	Concerto for orchestra	17.20
	Strauss, R	4 Letzte Lieder	22.25
Aug 23 1984	Bruckner	Symphony no. 5 in B flat major	70.09
(Setp 16 1984)	Liszt	Piano concerto no. 2, S. 125	22.09
Aug 25 1984	Bruckner	Symphony no. 5 in B flat major	70.00
(Aug 25 1984)			
Oct 27 1984	Mahler	Symphony no. 9 in D	80.48
(Nov 3 1984)	Britten	Phaedra	15.29
Oct 28 1984	Mozart	Symphony no. 34 in C major, K338	21.48
(Dec 6 1984)	Mahler	Symphony no. 9 in D	80.14
Nov 1 1984	Bainbridge	Fantasia for double orchestra	19.45
(Oct 13 1985)			
Nov 2 1984	Tippett	Praeludium for brass, bells and percussion	6.27
(Nov 2 1984)	Bainbridge	Fantasia for double orchestra	19.05
	Tippett	The Shires suite	18.40
	Britten	Les Illuminations	23.28
Nov 28 1984	Britten	Les Illuminations	23.24
(Dec 23 1984)	Bruckner	Symphony no. 7 in E major	61.32
Nov 30 1984	Mozart	Vesperae solennes de Confessore, K339	27.35
(Nov 30 1984)	Bruckner	Symphony no. 7 in E major	62.20
Dec 5 1984	Delius	A Mass of Life	105.52
(Dec 5 1984)			
Dec 8 1984	Schmidt	Symphony no. 4 in C major	48.30
(Dec 8 1984)	Schmidt	Notre Dame	
Dec 14 1984	Stravinsky	Symphonies of wind instruments	8.19
(Dec 14 1984)	Mozart	Concerto for two pianos	25.25
	Strauss, R	Ein Heldenleben, op. 40	45.00
Dec 20 1984	Berlioz	L'Enfance du Christ, op. 25	100.07
(Jan 13 1985)			
Jan 19 1985	Beethoven	Symphony no. 8 in F major, op. 93	26.49
(Feb 7 1985)	Strauss, R	Ein Heldenleben, op. 40	45.13
Jan 21 1985	Shostakovich	Symphony no. 11 in G minor, op. 103	66.06
(Oct 2 1985)			
Jan 25 1985	Beethoven	Symphony no. 8 in F major, op. 93	26.24
(Jan 25 1985)	Tippett	A Child of our Time	65.34

Jan 27 1985	Strauss, R	Ein Heldenleben, op. 40	45.16
(Feb 28 1985)	Brahms	Piano Concerto no. 1 in D minor, op. 15	45.58
Apl 12 1985	Rachmaninov	Piano Concerto no. 1 in F sharp minor, op. 1	27.30
(Apl 12 1985)	Shostakovich	Symphony no. 11 in G minor, op. 103	62.17
Apl 22 1985	Chabrier	Joyeuse marche	3.40
(June 8 1985)	Beethoven	Symphony no. 8 in F major, op. 93	27.08
	Shostakovich	Symphony no. 11 in G minor, op. 103	61.45
Apl 23 1985	Strauss, R	Don Juan, op. 20	17.50
(June 15 1985)	Gerhard	Concerto for orchestra	22.00
	Brahms	Symphony no. 4 in E minor, op. 98	40.40
Apl 25 1985	Strauss, R	Don Juan, op. 20	17.55
(July 12 1985)	Gerhard	Concerto for orchestra	21.00
	Brahms	Symphony no. 4 in E minor, op. 98	42.15
Apl 28 1985	Mozart	Symphony no. 33 in B flat major, K319	21.35
(May 2 1985)	Britten	Violin Concerto, op. 15	29.30
	Brahms	Symphony no. 4 in E minor, op. 98	39.30
July 19 1985	Mozart	[Handel] Der Messias, K572, arr.	145.26
(19 July 1985)			
July 22 1985	Sessions	When lilacs last in the dooryard bloom'd	46.10
(22 July 1985)	Mahler	Symphony no. 1 in D major	54.45
July 25 1985	Holst	The Planets – suite, op. 32	48.30
(July 25 1985)	Ives	Symphony no. 4	33.45
Oct 4 1985	Beethoven	Leonore – Overture no. 1, op. 138	9.55
(July 24 1986)	Beethoven	Symphony no. 7 in A major, op. 92	42.05
Oct 6 1985	Beethoven	Leonore – Overture no. 1, op. 138	9.30
(Oct 6 1985)	Bruckner	Mass no. 3 in F minor	58.34
	Beethoven	Fantasia in C minor, op. 80 for piano, orchestra and chorus	20.45
Oct 9 1985	Liszt	[Schubert] Fantasy in C major, S. 366	24.24
(Nov 5 1988)			
Oct 14 1985	Wagner	Die Meistersinger von Nurnberg	
(Oct 14 1985)	Schubert	Rondo for violin and string orchestra, D.438	13.27
	Beethoven	Piano Concerto no. 1 in C, op. 15	37.30
	Mahler	Des Knaben Wunderhorn	
	Brahms	Three Hungarian dances [nos. 1, 3, 10]	7.07

Oct 16 1985	Janáček	The Ballad of Blanik Hill [Balada Blanicka]	8.34
(16 Oct 1985)	Shostakovich	Violin Concerto no. 1, op. 77	36.20
	Scriabin	Symphony no. 3 in C major, op. 43	46.20
Oct 20 1985	Bliss	Colour Symphony, T. 24	31.08
Oct 21 1985	Hamilton	Circus for 2 trumpets & orchestra	15.57
(Apl 5 1986)	Barber	Violin Concerto, op. 14	24.30
	Bliss	Colour Symphony, T. 24	32.50
Feb 5 1986	Brahms	Symphony no. 1 in C minor, op. 68	43.20
(Feb 10 1986)	Brahms	Symphony no. 2 in D major, op. 73	39.00
Feb 7 1986	Brahms	Symphony no. 3 in F major, op. 90	38.00
(Feb 13 1986)	Brahms	Symphony no. 4 in E minor, op. 98	40.55
Feb 16 1986	Mahler	Symphony no. 2 in C minor –	
(Feb 18 1986)		'Resurrection'	83.34
Apl 12 1986	Mozart	Die Zauberflöte, K620	
(June 29 1986)	Brahms	Violin Concerto, op. 77	41.38
	Beethoven	Symphony no. 5 in C minor, op. 67	33.21
	Fauré	Pavane	5.20
Apl 20 1986	Haydn	Symphony no. 98 in B flat major	26.30
(Apl 22 1986)	Rossini	Stabat mater	60.17
July 12 1986	Beethoven	Piano Concerto no. 3 in C minor, op. 37	39.11
(Sept 19 1986)	Bruckner	Symphony no. 4 in E flat major –	
		'Romantic'	63.05
July 30 1986	Elgar	Violin Concerto in B, op. 61	48.20
(July 30 1986)	Bruckner	Symphony no. 4 in E flat major –	
		'Romantic'	62.50
Aug 3 1986	Berlioz	Grande messe des morts, op. 5	87.48
(Aug 3 1986)			
Aug 9 1986	Strauss, R	Eine Alpensinfonie, op. 64	50.35
(Dec 24 1986)			
Aug 11 1986	Beethoven	Piano concerto no. 5 in E flat,	
(Sept 13 1986)		op. 73 – 'Emperor'	
	Strauss, R	Eine Alpensinfonie, op. 64	48.58
Aug 13 1986	Strauss, R	Eine Alpensinfonie, op. 64	48.00
(Aug 13 1986)	Schumann	Piano Concerto in A, op. 54	33.35
Sept 28 1986	Britten	War requiem, op. 66	84.35
(Sept 28 1986)			

Oct 8 1986 (Jan 2 1990)	Tippett	Symphony no. 3	52.45
Oct 12 1986 (Oct 12 1986)	Tippett Britten Britten	Symphony no. 3 Our hunting fathers – symphonic cycle Sinfonia da requiem, op. 20	52.50 26.50 18.25
Oct 22 1986 (Oct 22 1986)	Wagner Tchaikovsky	Wesendonk Lieder, arr. Henze Manfred Symphony, op. 58	23.11 61.25
Dec 3 1986 (Dec 3 1986)	Prokofiev Shostakovich	Piano Concerto no. 2, op. 16 Symphony no. 11 in G minor, op. 103	34.08 63.22
Dec 7 1986 (Jan 17 1988)	Maw Matthews Sibelius	Spring music for orchestra, revised version Symphony no. 3 Violin Concerto in D, op. 47	15.32 20.04 32.20
Jan 10 1987 (Feb 12 1987)	Strauss, R Matthews Tchaikovsky	Till Eulenspiegel, op. 28 Symphony no. 3 Violin Concerto in D major, op. 35	15.08 20.47 35.52
Jan 11 1987 (Mar 2 1987)	Maw Sibelius Beethoven Glinka	Spring music for orchestra, revised version Violin Concerto in D, op. 47 Symphony no.6 in F major, op. 68 Ruslan i Lyudmila	14.35 32.00 35.56
Jan 16 1987 (Apl 12 1987)	Walton Tchaikovsky Elgar Glinka	Portsmouth Point – Overture Violin Concerto in D major, op. 35 Symphony no. 1 in A flat major, op. 55 Ruslan i Lyudmila	5.37 36.00 50.00 5.13
Jan 17 1987 (Mar 21 1987)	Maw Shostakovich Tchaikovsky	Spring music for orchestra, revised version Symphony no. 11 in G minor, op. 103 Violin Concerto in D major, op. 35	14.27 63.30 36.00
Jan 18 1987 (Jan 18 1987)	Walton Shostakovich Tchaikovsky Berlioz	Portsmouth Point – overture Symphony no. 11 in G minor, op. 103 Violin Concerto in D major, op. 35 La Damnation de Faust	
Feb 21 1987 (Mar 12 1987)	Elgar Beethoven	Symphony no. 1 in A flat major, op. 55 Piano Concerto no. 3 in C minor, op. 37	50.44 36.50
Feb 27 1987	Vaughan Williams	Job – a masque for dancing	
Mar 3 1987 (Jan 2 1989)	Henze Scriabin	Symphony no. 4 La Poème de l'extase, op. 54	23.41 17.38
Mar 4 1987 (Mar 9 1987)	Brahms Henze Scriabin	Piano Concerto no. 2 in B flat, op. 83 Symphony no. 4 La Poème de l'extase, op. 54	50.30 22.39 19.00

Mar 6 1987 (Oct 3 1987)	Goehr	Behold the sun – opera	177.24
Mar 11 1987	Goehr	Behold the sun – concert aria	
Mar 17 1987 (Apl 2 1989)	Szymanowski	Harnasie – ballet pantomime, op. 55	34.37
Mar 18 1987 (Mar 18 1987)	Dvořák Sibelius Szymanowski	Te Deum Symphony no. 4 in A minor, op. 63 Harnasie – ballet pantomime, op. 55	20.22 35.32 32.48
Mar 22 1987 (Mar 22 1987)	Knussen Elgar Scriabin Wagner Mozart	Symphony no. 3, op. 18 Cello Concerto in E, op. 85 Symphony no. 3 in C major, op. 43 Lohengrin Le Nozze di Figaro, K492	14.18 28.48 47.04 4.05 3.45
Mar 26 1987 (June 14 1987)	Knussen Elgar Scriabin Wagner Mozart	Symphony no. 3, op. 18 Cello concerto in E, op. 85 Symphony no. 3 in C major, op. 43 Lohengrin Le Nozze di Figaro, K492	14.09 29.56 46.05 3.17 4.06
July 14 1987 (Aug 30 1987)	Janáček Elgar Britten	Sinfonietta Symphony no. 2 in E flat major, op. 63 Phaedra	24.05 41.12 36.15
July 17 1987 (July 17 1987)	Janáček Tippett	Sinfonietta A Child of our time	22.44 66.30
July 20 1987 (July 20 1987)	Vaughan Williams Britten Falla	 Job – a masque for dancing Violin Concerto, op. 15 El Amor brujo	 44.25 30.25 25.05
Aug 22 1987 (Aug 22 1987)	Rimsky- Korsakov Milhaud Ravel Lambert Berlioz	 Sheherazade Le Boeuf sur le toit – pantomime-ballet La Valse The Rio Grande La Damnation de Faust	 45.30 18.18 12.05 15.15 2.35
Nov 18 1987 (Nov 18 1987)	Bantock Gounod Walton	The National anthem orch. Bantock Messe solennelle de Sainte Cécile Belshazzar's feast	3.35 43.45 34.03
Feb 8 1988 (Apl 27 1990)	Powers	Stone, water, stars	

Feb 10 1988	Powers	Stone, water, stars	22.04
(Feb 10 1988)	Walton	Cello Concerto	30.45
	Strauss, R	Ein Heldenleben, op. 40	46.30
Mar 29 1988	Shostakovich	Cello Concerto no. 1, op. 107	28.45
(Nov 16 1989)			
Mar 30 1988	Prokofiev	Symphony no. 4 in C major, op. 112	36.36
(Nov 16 1989)			
Apl 3 1988	Mahler	Symphony no. 2 in C minor –	
(Apl 3 1988)		'Resurrection'	83.50
Apl 21 1988	Walton	Symphony no. 2	27.04
(May 8 1988)	Liszt	Piano Concerto no. 2, S. 125	22.15
	Schumann	Symphony no. 3 in E flat major, op. 97	32.55
Apl 25 1988	Donizetti	Lucia di Lammermoor	123.58
(Apl 25 1988)			
May 5 1988	Bennett	Symphony no. 3	
May 9 1988	Strauss, R	Macbeth, op. 23	18.27
(May 29 1988)	Prokofiev	Violin Concerto, no. 2	28.44
	Schumann	Symphony no. 3 in E flat major, op. 97	34.00
May 11 1988	Strauss, R	Macbeth, op. 23	18.22
(June 19 1988)	Brahms	Violin Concerto in D, op. 77	41.20
	Schumann	Symphony no. 3 in E flat major, op. 97	33.17
May 18 1988	Tchaikovsky	Hamlet – fantasy overture, op. 67	17.14
(June 12 1988)	Krommer	Concerto for oboe and orchestra no. 2,	
		op. 52	20.24
	Beethoven	Symphony no. 3 in E flat major, op. 55	49.27
May 22 1988	Wagner	Götterdämmerung – [Der Ring	
(June 26 1988)		des Nibelungen]	18.11
	Bruckner	Symphony no. 0 in D minor – 'Die Nullte'	44.20
	Bennett	Symphony no. 3	34.00
May 23 1988	Wagner	Rienzi, der Letzte der Tribunen (overture)	11.18
(July 3 1988)	Britten	Piano Concerto, op. 13	34.00
	Prokofiev	Symphony no. 6 in E flat minor, op 111	38.04
May 26 1988	Bruckner	Symphony no. 0 in D minor – 'Die Nullte'	45.40
(July 10 1988)	Wagner	Götterdämmerung – [Der Ring	
		des Nibelungen]	
	Bennett	Symphony no. 3	32.07
July 8 1988	Beethoven	Symphony no. 1 in C major, op. 21	25.20
(July 12 1988)	Hummel	Concerto for trumpet and orchestra	17.50
	Brahms	Symphony no. 1 in C minor, op. 68	43.39

July 9 1988 (Sept 11 1988)	Wagner	Götterdämmerung – [Der Ring des Nibelungen]	
	Hindemith	Nobilissima visione – suite from the ballet	20.52
	Brahms	Symphony no. 1 in C minor, op. 68	42.04
July 22 1988 (July 22 1988)	Verdi	Requiem	84.52
July 26 1988 (July 26 1988)	Debussy	Le Martyre de St Sébastien	24.45
	Britten	Symphony for cello and orchestra, op. 68	37.04
	Lloyd	Symphony no. 4	30.26
	Ravel	Daphnis et Chloe – suite no. 2	15.56
Aug 21 1988 (Aug 21 1988)	Bellini	I Capuleti ed i Montecchi	124.05
Oct 5 1988 (Oct 5 1988)	Schoenberg	Moses und Aron	95.00
Jan 25 1989 (Jan 25 1989)	Strauss, R	Festliches Praludium, op. 61	12.30
	Mozart	Symphony no. 38 in D major, K504	26.09
	Strauss, R	Don Quixote, op. 35	41.29
	Strauss, R	Taillefer for soprano, tenor, baritone	18.15
Feb 1 1989 (Feb 1 1989)	Strauss, R	Metamorphosen for 23 solo strings, AV. 142	25.55
	Strauss, R	4 Letzte Lieder	20.19
	Mozart	Symphony no. 40 in G minor, K550	23.00
	Strauss, R	Symphonic fantasy from Die Frau ohne Schatten	19.55
Feb 4 1989 (Feb 5 1989)	Mozart	Serenade in B flat major, K361	42.04
	Strauss, R	Die Gottin im Putzzimmer, AV.120	5.05
	Strauss, R	An den Baum Daphné for unaccompanied chorus	17.00
	Strauss, R	Sonata no. 1 for 16 wind instruments, AV.135	33.30
Feb 9 1989 (Feb 12 1989)	Strauss, R	Macbeth, op. 23	18.07
	Strauss, R	Daphné, op. 82 [1936–37]	
	Strauss, R	Tod und Verklarung, op. 24	23.52
	Mozart	Symphony no. 39 in E flat major, K543	29.30
Feb 12 1989 (Feb 19 1989)	Mozart	Symphony no. 41 in C major, K551	31.10
	Strauss, R	2 Songs for chorus, op. 34 [1897]	31.49
	Strauss, R	Concerto no. 2 for horn and orchestra, AV.132	19.55
	Strauss, R	Deutsche Motette for chorus, op. 62	20.40
Feb 14 1989 (Feb 14 1989)	Strauss, R	Eine Alpensinfonie, op. 64	49.25
	Strauss, R	Capriccio, op. 85 [1940–41]	32.11

May 25 1989	Bax	Tintagel	14.35
(June 18 1989)	Elgar	Variations on an original theme – 'Enigma'	30.41
	Vaughan Williams	Job – a masque for dancing	43.12
May 27 1989	Hamilton	Aurora	10.30
(Apl 14 1991)	Hamilton	La Mort de Phèdre	20.03
Sept 16 1989	Berlioz	Le Corsaire – overture, op. 21	8.31
(Sept 16 1989)	Saint-Saëns	Violin Concerto no. 3 (Ida Haendel)	28.55
	Bizet	Carmen suite	
	Coates	London every day – Knightsbridge suite	
	Saint-Saëns	Samson et Dalila – aria 'Softly awaits my heart' (Sarah Walker)	
	Delius	Summer night on the river	6.00
	Elgar	Pomp and circumstance march no. 1 – 'Land of hope and glory'	1.50
	Wood	Fantasia on British sea songs	8.05
	Arne, T	Rule, Britannia! (Sarah Walker)	
	Parry	Jerusalem, arr. Elgar	2.50

Index

Index

Index

425

Index

427

Index

Index

Index